A Student's Guide to Developmental Psychology

This major new undergraduate textbook provides students with everything they need when studying developmental psychology.

Guiding students through the key topics, this book provides both an overview of traditional research and theory as well as an insight into the latest research findings and techniques. Taking a chronological approach, the key milestones from birth to adolescence are highlighted and clear links between changes in behaviour and developments in brain activity are made. Each chapter also highlights both typical and atypical developments, as well as discussing and contrasting the effects of genetic and environmental factors.

The book contains a wealth of pedagogical features to help students engage with the material, including:

- learning objectives for every chapter
- key term definitions
- over 100 colour illustrations
- chapter summaries
- further reading
- suggested essay questions.

A Student's Guide to Developmental Psychology is supported by a companion website, featuring a range of helpful supplementary resources including exclusive video clips to illustrate key developmental concepts.

This book is essential reading for all undergraduate students of developmental psychology. It will also be of interest to those in education, healthcare and other subjects requiring an up-to-date and accessible overview of child development.

Margaret Harris is Professor and Head of the Department of Psychology, Social Work and Public Health at Oxford Brookes University.

Gert Westermann is Professor of Psychology at Lancaster University.

For Karl, Elise and Francesca, who have taught us a great deal about children's development

A Student's Guide to Developmental Psychology

Margaret Harris and
Gert Westermann

Psychology Press
Taylor & Francis Group

LONDON AND NEW YORK

First published 2015
by Psychology Press
27 Church Road, Hove, East Sussex BN3 2FA

and by Psychology Press
711 Third Avenue, New York, NY 10017

Psychology Press is an imprint of the Taylor & Francis Group, an informa business

British Library Cataloguing in Publication Data
A catalogue record for this book is available from the British Library

Library of Congress Cataloging-in-Publication Data
Harris, Margaret, 1951–
   A students' guide to developmental psychology/Margaret Harris &
   Gert Westermann.
   pages cm
   Includes bibliographical references and index.
   ISBN 978-1-84872-017-6 (softcover : alk. paper) – SBN 978-1-
   84872-016-9 (hb : alk. paper) – ISBN 978-1-315-86721-2 (ebk)
   1. Developmental psychology. 2. Developmental psychology –
   Textbooks. I. Westermann, Gert, 1966– II. Title.
   BF713.H3667 2015
   155–dc23
   2014008976

ISBN: 978-1-84872-016-9 (hbk)
ISBN: 978-1-84872-017-6 (pbk)
ISBN: 978-1-31586-721-2 (ebk)

Typeset in Times New Roman and Franklin Gothic
by Florence Production Ltd, Stoodleigh, Devon, UK

Printed by Bell and Bain Ltd, Glasgow

Contents

About the authors

Margaret Harris first lectured at Birkbeck College, moving to Royal Holloway University of London in 1989 as Senior Lecturer and then Reader and Professor. She moved to Oxford Brookes University in 2006. Much of her recent research has focused on the language development of deaf children. She is the author of six books and many articles. She is an Associate Editor of the *Journal of Deaf Studies and Deaf Education* and *Mind & Language* and was Editor-in-Chief of the *British Journal of Developmental Psychology* (2008–13).

Gert Westermann received his PhD in Cognitive Science from the University of Edinburgh. He worked in research positions at Sony Computer Science Lab in Paris and at Birkbeck, University of London, before taking up a lectureship at Oxford Brookes University. In 2011 he joined Lancaster University as Professor of Psychology. His work focuses on infant cognitive development as well as language processing. The writing of this book was supported by a Lichtenberg Fellowship to Gert Westermann from the University of Göttingen, Germany, which he held January–July, 2013.

Photo credits

Chapter 10
p. 174 © Pavel L Photo and Video/Shutterstock.com; p. 180 © Andrey Stratilatov/ Shutterstock.com; p. 181 photo reproduced with permission from S. Einav.

Chapter 11
p. 186 © absolute-india/Shutterstock.com; p. 187 (t) © Fotokostic/Shutterstock.com; p. 187 (m) © Dmitriy Shironosov/Alamy; p. 188 David M. Phillips/Science Photo Library.

Chapter 12
p. 212 (A) Reproduced from Isaacs et al. (2001) with permission from Oxford University Press. (B) From Rotzer et al. (2008), © 2008, with permission from Elsevier. © From Rykhlevskaia et al. (2009).

Chapter 13
p. 226 © Tania Kolinko/Shutterstock.com; p. 230 © Anthony Hatley/Alamy.

Chapter 14
p. 236 © Junial Enterprises/Shutterstock.com.

Chapter 15
p. 251 PR Michel Zanca, ISM/Science Photo Library; p. 253 From Wang et al. (2008), reproduced with permission from Wiley-Blackwell.

Chapter 16
p. 268 Massimo Brega, The Lighthouse/Science Photo Library.

Chapter 17
p. 275 © Galina Barskaya/Shutterstock.com; p. 276 © Kirn Vintage Stock/Corbis; p. 283 (t) © wavebreakmedia/Shutterstock.com; p. 283 (b) © Blend Images/Alamy.

CHAPTER 1

CONTENTS

Framework and methods

1

After reading this chapter you will be able to

- formulate several of the big questions that we can ask about child development
- discuss the main aspects of the nature–nurture debate
- understand the concept of critical periods
- describe the main behavioural and neurophysiological methods used in developmental studies.

1.1 THE BIG QUESTIONS IN DEVELOPMENTAL PSYCHOLOGY

Studying the development of children can address many of the big questions that we ask about ourselves. If we want to understand why we as adults are what we are, we must understand how we get there. How do we learn and gain knowledge of the world? How is our character shaped, our abilities, our social skills? How much are we subject to the genetic endowment passed down from our parents, and to what extent are we affected by our experiences? Where does it all start – what abilities do babies bring to the world?

Studying children can, of course, also help us better understand their needs and what makes them thrive and flourish. How can we improve our children's lives? How can we provide them with an environment in which they feel safe and happy? Is their view of the world different from that of adults? How can we educate our children to become good people and good citizens, encouraging them to become adults who themselves care about the generations following them? Should we punish our children for transgressions, or should we focus on encouraging their good behaviour? How can we help children with learning disabilities such as developmental dyslexia, and developmental disorders such as autism?

Finally, in studying development we can try to answer questions about the developmental process itself: Why do children develop? What drives developmental change? How does a child move from not being able to do something to being able to do it? Do children take an active role in their development or are they merely the recipient of environmental stimulation, or subject to the genetically-determined maturation of abilities? Is the development of children's ability continuous or can we see stages in development, i.e. abrupt changes between phases of relative stability? If we observe such abrupt changes, does this mean that something inside the child is changing rapidly, or can a gradual change in underlying processes lead to sudden changes in behaviour and abilities? Are there specific ages at which abilities, such as speaking a language, can be learned and, if so, why?

It should be obvious that many of these questions are very important from a variety of viewpoints – helping children to thrive and be happy, helping society to create a positive environment and helping science to understand more about human development. The answers to these questions also have many practical implications, ranging from political decisions about the provision and quality of childcare, the right age to enter school, the structure of schooling and assessment, to giving parents the knowledge to judge the merits of educational toys, CDs and DVDs. No wonder that, through history, many of these questions have been debated with great passion and conviction – albeit sometimes not with the basis of factual evidence that one would wish for with questions of such importance. It is the task of developmental psychology as a sub-discipline of the science of psychology, to collect and evaluate evidence, to formulate hypotheses and to understand how development unfolds in the child.

We will now consider two of the main questions that have been asked about developmental change: the question of nature vs. nurture, and the question of critical periods for learning.

The nature–nurture debate

Why are we the way we are? Is it because of our biological predispositions – our genes – or because of the environment in which we have grown up, the experiences we have had? This question of whether children are predetermined by nature or shaped through nurture has been one of the most long-standing debates in psychology and, before that, philosophy. This is partly because, depending on the viewpoint one takes in this debate, one's view of how a society should be organised can be very different. If you believe in a predominantly biological basis for people's abilities and behaviour, you will see little benefit in trying to change them. There would be no use in trying to help weaker pupils in school through extra tuition and coaching – one is born with one's abilities, and that's that. Likewise, putting people who have committed a crime into prison would mainly serve two purposes: to punish them by taking away their freedom, and to protect society from them by locking them up.

Taking the view that people are the product of their experiences would, however, lead to very different conclusions. If it is the environment that makes us what we are, then by adapting this environment anything can be achieved. Anyone could be a genius, given the right environment! Or at least, one would put great emphasis on providing support for disadvantaged children because their weaker performance in school would be explained with not having had the same rich experiences and opportunities as their peers. As for prisons, one would put an emphasis on rehabilitating offenders so that the time spent in prison is a productive means to re-integrate people into society.

Given these wide-ranging implications it should come as no surprise that the nature–nurture debate has provoked controversy and that many different viewpoints have been articulated. Although the ancient Greek philosophers already had their views on this question, the debate was first labelled the 'nature-nurture problem' by Francis Galton (1822–1911), a polymath cousin of Charles Darwin, who was impressed by the tendency of genius to run in families (including his own). Galton speculated that there must be a strong inherited, biological basis for intellectual ability, and he argued for this view in his book, *Hereditary Genius* (1869).

Historically, most views have acknowledged that some parts of people's behaviours and abilities have a stronger biological component and others are more prone to be affected by the environment. A strong position about the importance of 'nurture' was articulated by the English philosopher John Locke (1632–1704). Locke believed that children were born as a '**tabula rasa**', a blank slate, and that all of their experiences would shape them into their final self. He wrote that we can imagine 'the mind to be, as we say, white paper, void of all characters without any ideas; how comes it to be furnished? [. . .] Whence has it all the materials of reason and knowledge? To this I answer, in one word, from experience: in that all our knowledge is founded, and from that it ultimately derives itself' (Locke, 1690, vol. 1, book 2, section 2).

Locke's strong environmentalist argument was partly a reaction to the widespread belief of his time that many ideas, such as the belief in God or some mathematical truths, were innate. According to his views (and we will return to them in some more detail in the next chapter), innate factors do not make important contributions to psychological development.

In contrast to Locke, Jean-Jacques Rousseau (1712–1778), a Swiss philosopher, took a more 'natural' view of human development. He believed that children grow according to nature's plan, best guided by nature alone, and that education by others was not a good way of forming a good human being. He believed that children are innately 'good' and that education, moral guidance and constraint would corrupt more than benefit them. His was the view of a '**noble savage**' unspoilt by society and contrasting with the corrupted product of education. This viewpoint emphasises the child's natural predispositions and minimises the role of education in forming the child. We will also return to Rousseau's ideas in the next chapter.

The nature–nurture debate has continued ever since these early philosophical arguments. Historically, there was little empirical evidence either way, but one source of evidence concerned so-called **feral children**: children who had grown up in the wild and were brought back to civilisation. There have been many reports of such children, with one famous case that of Victor, the Wildboy. Victor was captured in 1799 when he was 11 or 12 years old, wandering naked in the forests near Aveyron in southern France. Around a year later he was taken to Paris to great public interest. People wanted to see first hand the 'wild and noble savage' described by Rousseau. Instead they saw a disturbed child, incapable of speech, unable to maintain attention, spending his time rocking backwards and forwards. Victor was placed in the care of the physician Dr Jean-Marc-Gaspard Itard. Itard believed that Victor's deficits stemmed from a lack of socialisation and he set out to educate Victor over a period of five years. He attempted to teach Victor to speak but eventually had to acknowledge failure. By the time Victor died at age 40, he was able to speak only three words.

With Victor, as with other feral children, it was not clear whether their atypical behaviour was due to their unusual experiences – lack of parents and of social contact with other humans, potential traumatic experiences and so on – or whether they had a marked disability such as severe learning disability or autism. It may well have been that Victor was abandoned by his parents because he was abnormal in some

Der Wilde von Aveyron.

A picture of Victor, the Wildboy, from Itard's book.

Twin studies are used by researchers to investigate the relative contributions of genetic predisposition and the environment to human behaviour and the interaction between genetic and environmental factors.

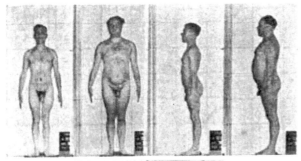

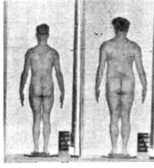

Identical twins reared in different circumstances apart from each other. (From Gottlieb, 1998 with permission from Harvard University Press.)

way. For this reason, although none of the feral children that were found ever resembled Rousseau's 'noble savage', it was recognised that the evidence they provided for the nature–nurture debate was questionable.

The advent of experimental psychology brought a new way to study the relative contribution of genetic predispositions on one hand and the environment on the other to human behaviour: this is the study of twins. **Monozygotic** (i.e. identical) twins are genetically identical, and therefore they come to the world with the same biological endowment. Any differences in the appearance, character and abilities of identical twins must therefore be due to the environment, that is, to nurture. Of course most twins grow up together and therefore they also share a large amount of environmental experiences. By contrast, **dizygotic** (non-identical) twins are genetically only as closely related as regular siblings (note that according to current estimates (Levy *et al.*, 2007) all humans share 99.5 per cent of their genes anyway by virtue of being human). Nevertheless, even dizygotic twins usually share many of their experiences.

In comparing large groups of identical and fraternal twins and observing the similarities and differences between twin pairs, scientists have estimated the contribution of genetic predispositions, the contribution of the environment shared by both twins and also the environment unique to each twin, to a large number of traits. For example, if identical twins are more similar in height than fraternal twins one would conclude that height has a relatively strong genetic basis, because both types of twins have a shared environment, but identical twins additionally have more shared genes.

However, twin studies have been criticised because their results might not be generalisable to the wider population. First, being a twin is different from being a single born child in a number of respects. Twins begin by sharing the womb and then, after birth, they share their parents' attention. They grow up with an identical-aged peer always around. Another criticism is that, although twin studies rely on the assumption that shared environments are the same for identical and fraternal twins, the shared environment of identical twins is different in many ways from that of fraternal twins. For example, identical twins spend more time with each other and they have more common friends than fraternal twins. Therefore, traits in which identical twins are more similar than fraternal twins might not be due to shared genes but to their greater shared environment. The debate on the value and validity of twin studies has not yet been resolved (Freese & Powell, 2003; Horwitz, Videon, Schmitz & Davis, 2003a, 2003b).

Many scientists now agree that thinking of nature–nurture as a dichotomy is not useful and that the question of which aspects of people's behaviour and abilities are due to genes and which to the environment is too simplistic. The reason for this emerging consensus is that it is becoming clear that nature and nurture are very closely tied together. Whereas the traditional view of genes was as a blueprint for development, we now know that the way in which genes function can be regulated by the environment (Gottlieb, 1998). Whether a specific gene becomes *expressed* (active) depends on signals it receives from other genes or hormones, and these signals can be affected by nutritional cues, physical contact, environmental stress, learning and other environmental factors. You can see a striking illustration of the impact of the environment on gene expression in the photo (page 4), which shows a pair of monozygotic twins who were reared apart in different circumstances. Despite identical DNA the twins differ very much even in traits such as height, which one might expect to be immune to experience. You can read more about the effects of experience on gene expression in Box 1.1 where we discuss epigenetics.

BOX 1.1: EPIGENETICS

The field of **epigenetics** studies how genes can be turned on and off by experiences. Each of your cells contains identical DNA, and yet there are vast differences, for example, between a skin cell and a neuron in your brain. Why is this? During the development of the foetus, genes in individual cells are switched on and off by *epigenetic tags* so that only genes relevant to the final role of the cell remain active. More recently it has been discovered that such epigenetic tags work throughout life so that genes can be switched on and off due to experiences. There are several striking examples of this process and it has become clear that, not only can maternal behaviour affect the genetic tags of a baby in the womb, but also that we can pass on some of our own tags to our offspring.

An example of the effects of maternal experiences on the epigenetic makeup of the unborn child comes from a group of people born in the Netherlands during the Second World War. In the German-occupied Netherlands, food supplies had been cut off to the densely populated western cities, resulting in a great famine called the Dutch Hunger Winter that lasted from November 1944 to the late spring of 1945. Many people died and others survived on as little as 25 per cent of the normal food intake (Roseboom, de Rooij, & Painter, 2006). After the war ended, epidemiologists followed up on the long-term effects on the survivors of this severe malnutrition. Of particular interest were children who had been in the womb during the famine. Unsurprisingly, babies whose mothers were undernourished during the last three months of pregnancy were born small. In contrast, babies conceived during the famine but whose mothers ate normally for the final three months of

Lamarck theorised that acquired characteristics (such as a long neck, developed from reaching to eat leaves high up in a tree) could be passed on to offspring. Although Larmarck's idea was wrong in its specifics we now know that, to an extent, epigenetic information can be inherited.

pregnancy (after the famine had ended) had a normal birth weight.

But the long-term effects for these babies also differed. Those babies who had been born underweight stayed small throughout their lives and had below-average weight and below average obesity rates. However, the normal birthweight babies later, as adults, showed higher than average obesity rates than the general population. Although at birth they seemed perfectly healthy and normal, their mothers' malnutrition during the early stages of pregnancy had changed them in a way that made them more susceptible to obesity later in life. The way in which this effect from early foetal development to adult life was transmitted was found to be through atypical epigenetic markers on genes associated with growth hormones, cholesterol transport and ageing (Heijmans *et al.*, 2008).

There are many other examples of epigenetic effects, both in animals and humans (Carey, 2012). Epigenetics can explain why, in two people with the same genetic predisposition for a certain illness (e.g. diabetes, breast cancer), one of them might actually develop the illness while the other will not. This is because genetic predisposition and environmental effects (perhaps through smoking, over-eating, lack of exercise) act together to switch the relevant genes on and off.

Epigenetic research has even cast doubt on the long-held belief that acquired traits cannot be passed down to offspring. The idea that parents can pass on acquired traits was first advanced by the French naturalist, Jean-Baptiste Lamarck (1744–1829). One example he gave for his idea was that a giraffe, straining its neck to reach the leaves high in a tree, would gradually develop a longer neck. This acquired long neck would then be passed on to that giraffe's offspring who would be born with a longer neck than the parent giraffe had at birth. Lamarck's theory of evolution preceded that of Darwin's view of natural selection and, after the general acceptance of Darwin's far more plausible theory, it fell out of favour and was dismissed, and even ridiculed. However, while Lamarck's idea was wrong in its specifics – and his example may have been unfortunate – we now know that, to an extent, epigenetic information can be transmitted to offspring. While the traditional view was that all epigenetic information is erased in sperm and egg cells, it now appears that some of this information survives. The mechanisms by which this happens are currently a field of very active research. What is clear already is that the newly emerging understanding of epigenetics – the switching on and off of genes on the basis of experiences without changing the DNA – shows that nature and nurture cannot be separated.

Critical periods

A second big question in developmental psychology is whether there are time windows in development during which the learning of certain skills is possible or, at least, better than at other times. If you have learned a foreign language in school then you probably have an accent. If you learn to play the piano as an adult, the chances are that you will not be able to become a concert pianist. Why is this?

Scientists have, for a long time, recognised that the timing of development matters. Not every ability can be learned equally well at any age. The period of time during which a particular ability can be learned has been termed the **critical period**. One of the most striking examples of a critical period came from the biologist Konrad Lorenz (1903–1989). Lorenz carried out detailed observation on a number of species, including geese. When a gosling is newly hatched it forms a life-long attachment to the first moving object it sees and follows it around. This process is called **imprinting**: a biological predisposition for a behaviour that is triggered by, and linked to, a specific environmental stimulus. Normally the object on which the gosling imprints would be the mother goose, but Lorenz showed that goslings could imprint on a large variety of objects such as rolling balls or Lorenz's boots. Whatever the goslings imprinted on could not be reversed. According to Lorenz, a critical period is therefore characterised by the ability to learn only during a short, sharply defined period of life, and by the irreversibility of this learning later in life. You can read more about imprinting in Chapter 2.

Since Lorenz published his observations, it has become clear that the timing and duration of critical periods can be affected by experience. For example, the imprinting of domestic geese and chicks can be delayed if no suitable object for imprinting is present. For this reason, the term **sensitive period** is often used to refer to a time of heightened ability to learn. In human development critical/sensitive periods have been postulated for a large range of learned abilities, from the acquisition of language (with different critical sub-periods for different aspects of language such as phonology, syntax and so on), second language learning, for binocular vision, the ability to learn about solid food and the forming of attachments.

The main questions that researchers have asked about critical and sensitive periods are whether, and under what circumstances, they are flexible in onset and duration, whether what is learned during such a period can be reversed and what the origins of such periods are. These questions are important both for ensuring that children receive relevant experiences during development and for understanding what the consequences might be of not receiving the right kind of experience at the right point in development, and how this might be remediated. For example, the deprivation from a caregiver during the first years of life results in problems with emotional development and attachment, and a focus of research has been how these negative outcomes can be reversed or mediated by subsequent therapeutic interventions.

Lorenz hatched some goslings and arranged it so that he would be the first thing they saw. From then on they followed him everywhere and showed no recognition of their actual mother. The goslings formed a picture (imprint) of the object they were to follow.

There are different possible explanations for why sensitive periods occur (Thomas & Johnson, 2008). One is maturation: at a certain point in development the neurochemistry of the brain might change so that plasticity – the ability of the brain to learn – becomes greatly reduced. If we imagine that the brain's flexibility in learning is based on many connections between neurons, the closure of a sensitive period for a particular ability could come about with the pruning of all those connections that have not been used. For example, initially the motor neurons in the brain might have many interconnections that would enable children to develop the finger dexterity necessary to play the violin. If a child actually learns to play the violin, these connections would be strengthened and stabilised. However, if this skill is not learned the necessary connections would be pruned and, once gone, it would be impossible to develop the same ability to play the violin that existed when all the original connections were in place.

A second possible explanation is that sensitive periods are a by-product of learning itself. Learning involves specialisation and, once specialisation has taken place, it is difficult to reverse this process and learn something new. In terms of the brain this could mean that a brain region might initially be responsive to a wide range of inputs. Through development, in interaction with other brain areas, this region would become more specialised. For example a brain region might become especially responsive to faces but less responsive to other visual stimuli. It would then be difficult to re-organise the brain so that this region again responds to a wide range of visual stimuli.

Finally, sensitive periods might just appear to end because the learning system has become stable as there is little more to be learned. For example, when growing up in a language environment, the brain adapts to the specific sounds and structures of that language. As long as the language environment is not disrupted there would then appear to be little change in abilities, but a complete change of this environment could de-stabilise this system and learning might again take place.

There are many disparate strands of research into critical and sensory periods, in different domains and with humans and animals. Much of the received wisdom of sharply defined, unalterable critical periods has been modified, and more scientists now question whether behaviours that have been observed in animals, such as imprinting, are relevant to understanding aspects of human learning and development, such as attachment. Research has been carried out on the neural mechanisms underlying plasticity in learning, and more is underway. We can say with certainty that there is certainly much more to find out about this topic.

1.2 COLLECTING AND INTERPRETING PSYCHOLOGICAL DATA

In conducting psychological research we plan and design studies, collect experimental data, analyse these data statistically and interpret our results. You will see many examples of this process described in this book. You will also see some examples where data have been collected but there are conflicting interpretations of the results. Because interpretations of the same data can be so different it is important to understand how the data were collected and what the link is between the data and the conclusions drawn from them. In this part of the chapter we will therefore explain some of the most common methods of collecting data in developmental psychology.

Longitudinal and cross-sectional designs

The topic of developmental psychology is the nature of change in children. We can examine this change in two principal ways. In longitudinal designs researchers follow a group of children over time, testing them at different ages. The main advantage of this method is that one can see how individual children change over time. There are fewer problems with individual differences between children: a child tested at different ages is still the same child. However, longitudinal studies are challenging for a number of reasons. First, they take a long time to carry out. For example, if you are interested in the effects of vocabulary size at age two on writing ability at age eight, it will take six years before you have an answer. Second, in longitudinal studies, there usually is a high drop-out rate: during the study many children will move away, or lose interest in participating. Therefore, a high number of participants have to be recruited at the beginning of the study to compensate for potential loss. Third, there might be a systematic difference between those participants staying in the study and those dropping out, and this could create a biased sample. For example, children who struggle with reading might be less likely to participate at age eight than those who excel at reading, and this non-representative sample could then lead the researcher to under- or overestimate the effect of early vocabulary size on reading ability.

In a cross-sectional design, different children at different ages are tested at the same time and are compared. For example, when studying the development of vocabulary between one and three years of age, one could test different groups of 12-, 15-, 18-, 24- and 36-month-olds and count the words that the children in each of the age groups can understand or produce. With this method it is not possible to study, for example, how predictive vocabulary at 15 months is for vocabulary at 36 months, since different children are tested at these ages, but one can measure how quickly vocabulary develops on average and find out whether it grows linearly or exponentially during that age range. Cross-sectional studies are faster and easier to do than longitudinal studies, but they also have their downsides. First, there will be greater individual differences among children in different age groups than in longitudinal studies, making it necessary to test more participants. Second, there could be systematic differences between the age groups, so-called *cohort effects*. For example, if the provision of early nursery education was increased, and the 18-month-olds had benefitted from this but the 36-month-olds had not, then it would be difficult to draw firm conclusions from a comparison of the vocabulary scores of these two age groups. Nevertheless, cross-sectional designs are by far the more common method used in developmental psychology mainly because they take considerably less time and money to carry out.

Observational studies

Many developmental studies involve the observation of children's naturalistic behaviour. Such observation studies can make use of diaries where parents regularly record their child's behaviours or utterances. In recent years, however, it has become more common to use videotaping. This can be done, for example, by setting up cameras in the child's home or nursery, or by setting up recording sessions in a specially equipped lab (see the photo overleaf). Observation labs usually contain several cameras that can record the child from different perspectives. After the end

A child observation laboratory. One-way mirrors can be used to observe what is going on in the playroom.

of the session it is then possible to analyse the recordings in great detail. For example, by using slow motion one can analyse subtle behaviours that would be impossible to record from live observation. These settings are also valuable for studying the interactions between children or between children and their parents in an *ecologically valid* setting, that is, a setting that is similar to what children experience in their everyday life.

A drawback of using video recording is that it is very onerous to transcribe and analyse such recordings. In studies that analyse the language spoken by children it typically takes 20 hours or more to transcribe and code one hour of recording (Kirjavainen & Theakston, 2012). Therefore, most such studies involve at most one or two sessions per week. In a particularly rich study, one child (Brian) was recorded interacting with his mother during meal times and play sessions for a total of 330 hours from two years to nearly four years of age (Maslen, Theakston, Lieven & Tomasello, 2004). This involved a one-hour recording five days a week for 14 months and then four or five sessions per month for eight more months. The researchers estimated that the recordings captured around 8–10 per cent of Brian's utterances. Using such rich data led to some interesting insights. For example, the scientists found a difference between the frequencies of errors for past tenses (such as 'yesterday I eated ice-cream') and noun plurals (such as 'three blind mouses') that had not been found in earlier, less rich studies.

In an ideal world we would be able to record every waking moment of a child over a lengthy period of time, but naturally such an undertaking would pose formidable challenges as well as obvious ethical considerations. The first challenge is how to do the recordings. Asking the parents to carry a camera at all times is not an option, and even if the recordings were made, how could a researcher analyse at least ten hours of video and audio recordings per day, seven days per week? On the other hand this large amount of data could be very useful because we would get a very fine-grained record of the specific experiences of the child (such as face-to-face interactions with a parent, or the amount and type of language to which the child is exposed) and of the child's changing abilities.

In nature/nurture debates the precise nature of children's experiences is often a contentious issue. This is because children's knowledge in the absence of experience has been counted as a strong argument for the innate nature of that knowledge. For example, if a child expects that a ball that is hit by another ball will roll away without having experienced such an event before, it could be claimed that knowledge of cause and effect is part of our innate endowment (Leslie, 1995). By having a full account of a child's experiences we could check if this knowledge could have been learned. Likewise, in characterising developmental change as slow and gradual (continuous) or abrupt and rapidly changing (discontinuous) it is important to have fine-grained observations that will either confirm or disconfirm rapid changes in an ability. In short: to understand the causes and mechanisms of development we need at least a good understanding of the child's experiences and behaviours.

In other areas of science (e.g. genetics, physics) an approach called 'big data' is becoming popular. The idea here is to collect as much data as possible and then develop automated, computer-based ways to analyse this data. In psychology as well this approach is taking a foothold (Ivry, 2013) and in developmental research some scientists now aim to record most of a child's first few years of life (see Box 1.2). One way in which a large data set has been used is to automatically differentiate early utterances from children with typical speech from those with language delay or autism (Oller *et al.*, 2010), showing that in early speech such differences already exist (see 5.2). Undoubtedly, this big data approach will become ever more important in psychological research in the future.

Related to observational studies are **clinical interviews** in which the researcher asks the child questions but tries to keep the conversation as open as possible. Depending on the child's response the interview can take different directions but the researcher can direct the conversation to find out more about the issue in question.

BOX 1.2: 'BIG DATA' STUDIES

In one example of a big data study (Roy *et al.*, 2006), a researcher installed cameras in the ceiling of every room in his family home and recorded his son's first three years almost in their entirety. These were 90,000 hours of video and 140,000 hours of audio recordings (Roy, 2009). This amount of data could not be transcribed and coded by hand, and the focus of work in this project was therefore to develop computerised methods of speech and video analysis. A similar large-scale project has used small sound recorders attached to a pocket in the clothing of young infants between 10 and 48 months of age to record them for whole-day sessions several times a month (Zimmerman *et al.*, 2009). This project resulted in 1,486 all-day recordings from 232 children and here, as well, software was developed to automatically identify and analyse the children's utterances.

Looking time and eye movement measures

The most common method of data collection in developmental psychology (and indeed, psychology as a whole) is to carry out an experiment and collect appropriate measures of children's behaviours. The advantage of this method is that many aspects of the environment and other key variables can be closely controlled. This allows for a more precise testing of hypotheses than observational studies.

Older children can be studied in similar ways to adults. We can ask them questions about their experiences, opinions and memories, and they can listen to and follow instructions to provide responses in experiments. You will find many examples of such studies in the chapters where we describe the development of children during the preschool period and beyond. Studies with very young children face particular challenges because they require different kinds of methods. Depending on their age, young children may not understand verbal instructions and may be unable to give verbal responses. Complex non-verbal responses such as choosing between alternatives may also be difficult. Finally, young children have shorter attention spans and they may not be willing or able to sit still for long enough to complete a study. For these reasons, researchers have had to develop alternative methods to examine the knowledge and abilities of young children and, especially, infants.

The measurement of looking time has become established as the main method for investigating infant cognition. The basis of this measure is the finding that infants usually prefer to look at something novel and unfamiliar compared with something old and familiar. One widely used technique that employs this finding is the **habituation** paradigm, which can, for example, be used to find out whether infants can discriminate between different stimuli. Infants are first shown one stimulus, for example a triangle, repeatedly on a computer screen and the time they spend looking at each presentation is measured. You can imagine that on being shown the same item again and again, looking times will gradually decrease as infants become less interested. When looking time has decreased by a certain amount (for example, by 50 per cent) we assume that an infant has habituated to this stimulus. Then, a novel stimulus, for example a square, is shown. If infants now look longer at the square than at the last triangles we can conclude that they can distinguish between the triangle and the square.

An important feature of this method is that it is *infant-controlled*: whether or not we proceed to the test phase (here: the square) depends on the infants' own looking behaviour. A related, non-infant-controlled method is the *familiarisation-preferential-looking* paradigm, which is also very popular (see the photo on page 13). Here, the familiarisation stimuli are shown for a fixed number of times (e.g. ten). A decrease in looking time across these presentations is assumed to show that the infants have become familiarised to the stimuli and have actively processed them. The familiarisation phase is followed by a test phase in which two objects are shown side-by-side: one is from the familiarised objects and one is a new object. If the infants look longer at the new object, as in the habituation paradigm, we assume that they can distinguish between the two objects.

In the *intermodal preferential looking* paradigm (IPL) looking behaviour in response to an auditory stimulus is assessed. This measure is useful, for example, in assessing infants' and young toddlers' understanding of words. For instance, infants could be presented with two pictures on a screen side-by-side, e.g. a cat and a ball. Two seconds into this presentation the word 'ball' is then played through

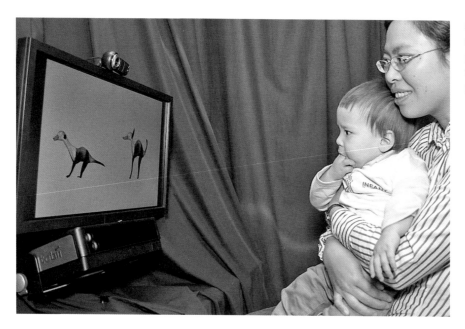

An infant participating in a familiarisation/novelty preference study. An eye tracker is positioned below the screen.

loudspeakers. If the infant then increases looking towards the ball we can assume that she understands the meaning of this word.

Another useful application of eye tracking is to see if children can predict the outcome of an event, for example the re-appearance of an object that is moving behind a wall, or the goal of an action. In a study to investigate action goal understanding (Falck-Ytter, Gredebäck & Von Hofsten, 2006), six- and 12-month-old infants as well as adults watched movie clips where an actor was moving a ball into a bucket. Eye-tracking of the participants showed that the 12-month-olds and the adults anticipated the outcome of the action and looked at the bucket before the actor's hand had reached it. In contrast, the six-month-old infants just tracked the ball in the actor's hand.

BOX 1.3: MEASURING LOOKING TIME

When looking time techniques were first developed, the looking times of infants were often coded online, by an experimenter pressing one button when the baby looked to the left and another one when she looked to the right. Another, more accurate way of coding was offline. This involved recording the infants' eyes with cameras placed above the screen where the stimuli are shown. After the study has finished the video recording can be analysed frame by frame to determine where the infant is looking at each time point. Although several researchers have written specific software for this purpose the scoring is nevertheless a laborious task and takes far longer than a testing session (around 15 minutes for one minute of video).

More recently, an increasing number of infancy researchers are using eye tracking to automate the scoring process. An eye tracker,

Left: the way in which an individual infant has scanned a face.
Right: A heat map of the areas of the face that were fixated by infants in a face processing study.

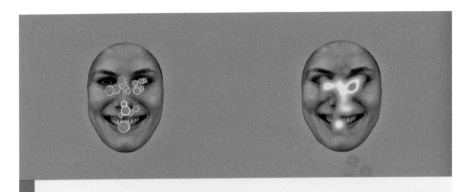

which is usually attached to the bottom or top of a computer screen, works by shining an invisible infrared light at the eyes of a participant and using an infrared camera to measure the reflection from the pupil and iris of the eye. Using complex computations the eye tracker can then determine where on the computer screen (or in a real scene) the participant is looking. Older eye trackers were sensitive to head movements and they were therefore either attached to the head, or participants had to place their head on a chin rest to minimise movement. Newer models can now compensate for a certain amount of head movement automatically, making them ideal for studies with infants and children. By using eye trackers the amount of time that the child spends looking at the displayed stimuli is measured online and is usually quite accurate. In addition, because the spatial resolution of eye tracking is high, rather than just distinguishing looks to the left or right side of the screen, eye tracking offers the possibility to examine more closely at which parts of an image (e.g. the head, tail or legs of an animal) the child looks, and in what order.

Eye trackers not only record the position of where someone is looking, but also the size of the pupil. It has been known for a long time that people's pupils dilate (become larger) when they are aroused, attentive or under high cognitive load (such as when solving a difficult maths problem). More recently scientists have begun to use pupil size in developmental contexts as well, where it is used to complement looking time measures to give a more fine-grained temporal picture of processing (Laeng, Sirois & Gredeback, 2012). Some researchers have argued that changes in pupil dilation can give a better measure of cognitive processing than looking times.

Imaging

In the past 20 years, methods have been developed that enable researchers to visualise children's brain activity while seeing objects or hearing sounds. Measuring brain activity directly has several advantages. First, it is not necessary for the child to show an overt response (such as looking longer at an object, showing surprise, or giving a spoken answer), and therefore brain measures can potentially pick up more subtle effects. Second, some of these measures (e.g. ERP, described below) are very time sensitive and this allows for the analysis of the timing of mental processes. Third, in being able to localise where in the brain certain processes occur, it is possible to compare brain function in children and adults and thus to gain further insights into how the brain changes across development and how these changes in the brain relate to changes in cognition. The ability to link brain and behavioural development has given rise to an entire new research field called Developmental Cognitive Neuro-science (Johnson & de Haan, 2011). In the following section we briefly describe the most common neuroscientific methods used with children.

Some of the established methods that are commonly used with adult participants are usually not suitable for use with children. For example, **functional Magnetic Resonance Imaging (fMRI)**, which measures regional blood flow in the brain that correlates with neural activity, requires participants to lie completely still in a narrow tube, often for long sessions, while wearing noise-protecting headphones. Children from around five years onward can be trained to lie still, but younger children move too much. Sometimes fMRI scans are done with infants but most of the few existing studies were done while the infants were asleep and did not move. Necessarily, the questions that can be addressed with sleeping children are limited. For example, one study using fMRI in three- to seven-month-old sleeping infants asked whether the infant brain processes emotional vocalisations (laughter, crying) differently from environmental sounds (Blasi *et al.*, 2011). The researchers found that, like in adults, the brain regions for processing these types of sounds differed considerably.

EEG and ERP

Far more common methods of measuring children's brain activity are **electro-encephalography (EEG)** and **event-related potentials (ERP)**. In recording an electroencephalogram using EEG, a number of sensors (electrodes) are placed on the head and they pick up the tiny changes in electrical activity generated by neural activity in the brain. These small signals are then amplified and can be analysed.

KEY TERMS

functional Magnetic Resonance Imaging (fMRI)
A technique that measures regional blood flow in the brain that correlates with neural activity.

Electroencephalo-graphy (EEG)
A technique that uses sensors placed on the head to measure changes in electrical activity generated by neural activity in the brain.

Event-related potentials (ERP)
Specific waveforms of neural electrical activity that are derived from the EEG.

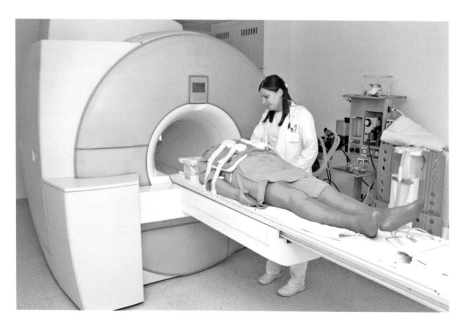

An fMRI scanner.

Using EEG it is, for example, possible to measure the synchronised firing of large groups of neurons at specific frequencies. Special interest in the developmental literature has focused on gamma-band activity: here, groups of neurons in the brain synchronise their firing at around 40 Hz (that is, the neurons fire 40 times per second). In infants, this synchronised activity has been linked to object processing. For example, when six-month-old infants watched an object on a screen that then disappeared behind an occluder, they showed a burst of such gamma-band activity in the temporal lobes, indicating that the infants were continuing to represent the object after it had disappeared (Kaufman, Csibra & Johnson, 2003).

Event-related potentials (ERPs) are specific waveforms of neural electrical activity that are derived from the EEG. For example, a researcher interested in the question of whether upright faces are processed in a special way might want to compare brain responses to seeing upright faces compared with inverted (upside-down) faces. The EEG signal is very noisy because it reflects all measured brain activity and not just that linked to looking at faces. The idea in ERP is that by using a large number of waveforms recorded when seeing faces, the non-face related parts of the EEG will average out and what remains is the response that is specific to faces. Therefore, in a typical ERP study participants view a large number of stimuli. For example, in a study that examined face processing in 12-month-old infants (Halit, de Haan & Johnson, 2003), the infants viewed up to 80 upright and 80 inverted faces. Averaging the brainwave responses to the upright faces and those to the inverted faces showed a characteristic response profile that differed between the two types of faces, suggesting that at this age infants, like adults, process upright and inverted faces differently. You can see the pattern of responses in Figure 1.1.

One of the main advantages of EEG and ERP measures is that they have a very high temporal resolution. This makes it possible to observe changes in neural activity on a scale of milliseconds and to observe the temporal unfolding of the processing of information. Despite this advantage, these methods also have a number of draw-backs. First, because electrical activity is measured by the sensors at the scalp it is not straightforward to infer from which parts of the brain the measured activity has originated, and it is therefore difficult to say precisely which parts of the brain are involved in processing a specific type of information. Second, the recorded neural activity is much smaller than the electrical activity generated by muscle movements. Therefore, if children move their eyes, head or jaw this creates so much electrical noise that the neural activity cannot be measured. As a consequence, in studies with infants many participants have to be tested. For example, in the study on face processing described earlier, 85 infants were tested but 58 of them moved around so

Figure 1.1

Pattern of responses. Reproduced from from Halit, de Haan, and Johnson (2003). Copyright © 2003, with permission from Elsevier.

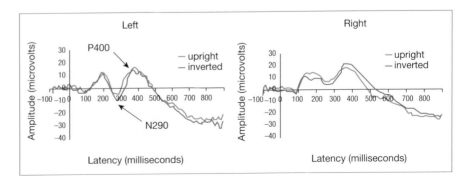

much that their data could not be used. Nevertheless, ERP is currently the most widely-used neuroimaging method for children.

NIRS

A recent technique to visualise even young infants' brain activation is **Near Infra Red Spectroscopy (NIRS)** (Gervain *et al.*, 2011). This method is based on the observation that increased neural activity in a brain region is associated with changes in the oxygenation of blood in this region. Children wear a custom-made cap that contains LEDs emitting near infrared light of specific wavelengths, and light sensors that register the emitted light. The light travels through the skull and, depending on the amount of oxygen in the blood, is absorbed and scattered. The light sensors measure the amount of light reflected from the surface of the cortex and this can be used to calculate the level of blood oxygen that is linked to neural activity. NIRS has several advantages over other imaging methods: because the sensors are attached directly to the child's head it is not necessary to keep the head completely still as in fMRI and ERP. Furthermore, unlike fMRI but like ERP, NIRS is completely silent. The temporal resolution of NIRS is around five seconds, similar to fMRI, with a spatial resolution (i.e. to pinpoint where on the brain increased neural activity occurs) of around four centimetres (Shalinsky, Kovelman, Berens & Petitto, 2009). Finally, NIRS systems are relatively cheap, although at present there are only a few fully functioning out-of-the-box systems for developmental research. A drawback of NIRS is that, because light does not enter very deeply into the head, it can only probe the surface layers of the cortex and not deeper brain structures.

One well-known NIRS study investigated how newborns process language (Pena *et al.*, 2003). As you will see later (and may already know), in most adults language function is lateralised in the left hemisphere of the brain. In the NIRS study the researchers wanted to see if this lateralisation is already present at birth or if it develops gradually. To answer this question, newborn infants (two to five days old, asleep) were played three types of auditory stimuli: one was normal infant-directed speech, one was speech played backwards (which is usually not processed as speech) and one was silence. The researchers found that the infants showed increased activation in the left temporal area when listening to forward speech, but not to backward speech or silence. It therefore appears that left-hemisphere lateralisation of the native language is already present at birth.

Computational modelling

The methods we have described so far all allow us to describe and measure children's behaviour or their brain activity. What they cannot do, however, is to explain these behaviours and patterns of brain activity, and they also cannot explain changes in behaviours and abilities across age. Computational modelling is a way to do this: to link observation with explanation.

This baby is wearing an EEG 'hair net'. Sensors placed on the head record the changes in electrical activity produced by neural activity in the brain.

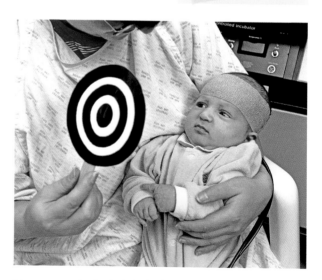

Measurement of a baby's brain activity using NIRS.

KEY TERMS

Connectionist models
Models of learning implemented on a computer in which there are many interconnected nodes.

A computational model is in essence a computer program that mimics human behaviour. Importantly, it does so in a way that is based on our theory of how humans generate this behaviour. This approach differentiates computational modelling from Artificial Intelligence – there, scientists try to program computers so they display 'intelligent' behaviour but they are less concerned with whether the computer uses the same processing principles as humans. For example, chess computers can play chess very well and even beat the human world champion (Hsu, 2002), but everyone agrees that the way in which they play is very different from humans. A chess computer therefore is not a good computational model of human chess playing.

In a psychological computational model the aim is to accurately mimic people's behaviour, even the errors they make when they learn a task. When a new model has been developed, it can be exposed to an experimental situation that is similar to one in a psychological study. For example, when modelling a familiarisation/novelty-preference study we can develop a model of looking times. We can then show the model, like the infant, a certain set of objects, and examine if the modelled looking times are similar to those obtained from children. If they are then we can use the model as an explanation of the infants' behaviour and learning process: we know why the model performs the way it does (since we developed it), and an assumption can then be that the infants' behaviour is based on the same principles as those used in the model.

In developmental psychology in particular, a specific type of computational models called *artificial neural networks* or **connectionist models** have become popular. Connectionist models (Figure 1.2) are loosely inspired by the way that neurons function in the brain. As you perhaps know, a neuron generates electric impulses in its cell body, and these impulses travel along the neural axon to its synapses. At the synapse, which is a connection between two neurons, the electrical signal leads to the release of neurotransmitters, which are taken up by the other neuron where they are re-converted into electricity. This electric charge travels through the neural dendrites to the cell body. If this incoming electric signal is high enough the neuron itself fires an electric impulse.

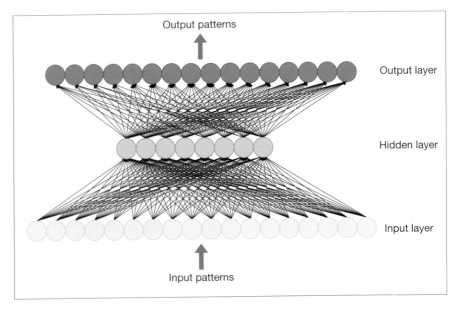

Figure 1.2
A simple neural network.

Neural processing – and thus, thinking, sensing, acting – can be described as originating from the exchange of electric impulses across biological neural networks. Each single neuron thereby performs a simple function: it integrates (adds up) the activation received through its dendrites, and if this activation is high enough, it generates an electric impulse (spike) which then travels along its own axon and synapse to other neurons. A neuron does not 'know' if it is processing visual, auditory, motor or any other kind of information; the principle of summing up incoming activation and sending activation to other neurons is common to all neurons. Learning happens by changing the strength of a synapse so that the amount of neurotransmitter that is released and taken up varies over time (learning can also involve generating new synapses or pruning existing synapses).

Artificial neural networks are meant to capture these (necessarily brief and oversimplified) basic operating principles of biological neural networks. The units in a network sum up the activation they receive through their incoming connections. This incoming activation is then transformed into activation of the neuron, which is sent through its outgoing connections to other neurons. What makes connectionist models attractive for modelling developmental phenomena is that they can learn from experience, by increasing or decreasing the strengths of the connections between the units. You can find out more about how this happens in Box 1.4.

From a psychological perspective the learning that takes place in computational models is interesting because we can observe how learning actually proceeds. For example, in a model that learns the names for objects (see Box 1.4), we can find out which names are learned first (perhaps those for more frequently seen objects, or those for objects with highly characteristic features), which names are hard (perhaps cases in which two very similar objects have different names, such as birds and bats) and whether the learning of names is linear or non-linear (that is, if there is a sudden spurt in which the model learns many names in a short time after being initially very slow at learning). We can then compare our findings of how the model learns names for objects with what we know about how children learn them. If we find that the model learns in similar ways to children – that is, it finds the same names easy and hard to learn, and it shows the same overall learning profile – then we can say that the model provides a good explanation of children's learning. But what does this mean? We know that the model learns names for objects simply by associating the visual appearance of objects with their name, and the characteristics of learning performance come out of this simple association process. So if the model's behaviour corresponds to that of children, this is the same claim we could make about children's word learning.

The explanation of human processing that is provided by a computational model can be further evaluated by considering the *predictions* such a model can make. In our example, after the model has learned all the names for the objects we have presented, we could 'damage' it by removing some of the connections between units. This damage would most likely make the performance of the model worse and it would lose the ability to name all objects it had learned. We can then study precisely which names get affected the most by damage and which others are more robust to damage, and we could make the prediction that adults who have had a stroke or who are suffering from dementia might show a comparable profile of breakdown in their ability to name objects. If this prediction turns out to be accurate this would be additional evidence for the validity of the model.

BOX 1.4: HOW CONNECTIONIST MODELS LEARN

Many connectionist models are organised like the one in Figure 1.2 (although some are considerably more complicated). Units are arranged in three layers. The input layer receives information from the environment, which means that some of the input units will become activated. This activation then flows through the connections to the intermediate hidden layer (which is called 'hidden' because it is not connected to the external world). There, based on the incoming activation, the hidden units will become active to different degrees and send on their activations through the connections to the output layer.

In this type of network the model typically learns a task that is given by a teacher. For example, the model might be used to learn the names for different objects. The input to such a model could then be a representation of the visual appearance of an object, and the output the phonological representation of the name of the object. Initially, before the network has learned anything, the strengths of the connections are set to random values. This means that when the model is presented with an object and activation flows through the hidden to the output units, the output will not be meaningful. The model, however, can learn to produce the correct name for the object, and this learning is achieved by changing the strengths of the connections. This works as follows: when the model is producing an output, this output is compared with what the model should produce (i.e. the correct name for the object, also called the target). Some of the output units of the model will be more activated than they should be, and some less. In essence then, the connection strengths (also called weights) are changed so that those that feed into units that are too active are reduced and those feeding into under-active units are increased. In this way, the activation pattern that the network produces gradually becomes more like the (correct) target pattern. The most popular method for computing the weight changes is called the **backpropagation algorithm**.

1.3 SUMMARY

In this chapter we have considered the questions that can be asked and answered within the framework of developmental psychology, and we have gone into some detail for two of these questions: the nature–nurture debate, and the question of critical or sensitive periods in development. Then we described methods by which we can study the development of children. While older children can be tested like adults, specific methods used with younger children are based on looking time analyses. We discussed a number of methods to study how the developing brain processes information, mainly EEG/ERP and NIRS. Finally, we discussed computational modelling with artificial neural networks as a way to develop and test theories of development and developmental change. At the end of this chapter you should now be equipped with knowledge of the questions we ask in developmental psychology, and the ways in which we set out to answer them.

FURTHER READING

Carey, N. (2012). *The epigenetics revolution: How modern biology is rewriting our understanding of genetics, disease, and inheritance.* New York: Columbia University Press.

Elman, J. L., Bates, E. A., Johnson, M. H., Karmiloff-Smith, A., Parisi, D., & Plunkett, K. (1996). *Rethinking innateness. A connectionist perspective on development.* Cambridge, MA: MIT Press.

Harris M. (2008). *Exploring child development: Understanding theory and methods.* London: Sage Publications.

Lewkowicz, D. J. (2011). The biological implausibility of the nature-nurture dichotomy and what it means for the study of infancy. *Infancy, 16*(4), 331–367.

ESSAY QUESTIONS

1. Critically discuss the nature–nurture debate.
2. 'Genes make us who we are.' Discuss.
3. Are there critical periods in development?
4. Give examples of the use of imaging methods in infant research and discuss their benefits and drawbacks.

CHAPTER 2

CONTENTS

Theories and approaches

2

After reading this chapter you will be able to

- describe the early developmental theories of John Locke and Jean-Jacques Rousseau and relate them to more recent theories of development
- explain the main aspects of Jean Piaget's view of development and contrast it with that of Lev Vygotsky
- describe attachment theory and its origin in ethology
- discuss dynamic systems and neuroconstructivist views of development
- explain how developmental disorders such as Williams syndrome can be understood within a neuroconstructivist framework.

In Chapter 1 we discussed some of the big questions that have been asked in developmental psychology. Since the times of the Greek philosophers, and probably before, people have asked how development happens, where it begins and how it is shaped. In this chapter we will discuss several of the main views on these questions that have been framed in theories of development.

2.1 EARLY VIEWS

It seems that for a long time in history children were not seen as different in important ways from adults. As a consequence the concept of childhood as a separate and important stage in life did not exist. Although young children received care and protection, from age six or seven years they often left home to learn a trade in a different village (Crain, 2005). There they interacted with children and adults of different ages and were not treated much differently. People were not sensitive to the fundamental differences between children and adults and in medieval paintings children were often portrayed as 'little adults' instead of with child-like proportions.

Madonna with Child by the Italian artist Berlinghiero (c.1236). The child Jesus has the proportion of an adult instead of typical baby-like proportions.

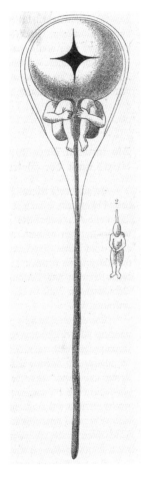

A fully pre-formed human in the sperm (From Nicolaus Hartsoeker, *Essai de diotropique*, 1694).

The view of children as little adults was also confirmed in ideas of human development. In the **preformationist theories** that were prevalent for a long time it was believed that developmental change is illusory because the essential characteristics of an individual are fully specified at the outset of development. This view is illustrated in the photo (left): for many the view was that a fully formed, tiny human is contained in the human sperm and that development is thus growth without transformation.

The early notion of children as adults changed with the advent of the printing press in the 1500s and the rise of the cities and commerce (Crain, 2005). The ensuing need for a better education that involved training in reading, writing and maths led to the opening of more schools so that, for the first time, many children now received a school education instead of going off to learn a trade. This more extensive schooling led to a greater separation between adults and children and highlighted the differences between them. Furthermore, it became important to consider how best to educate children.

Two philosophers of the seventeenth and eighteenth centuries developed the foundations for what became developmental psychology: John Locke and Jean-

Jacques Rousseau. Their philosophy and views of child rearing influenced many subsequent theories and in this way both are still influential today. We have already encountered Locke and Rousseau in Chapter 1 because of their strong and opposing views in the nature–nurture debate, but their influence goes far beyond their views on this particular issue.

2.2 JOHN LOCKE

John Locke (1632–1704) was born in Somerset in England. He was a student at Oxford University and then became a tutor there for Greek and moral philosophy. He was torn between a career as a priest and a physician and finally decided on the latter, learning much about natural sciences. Locke became one of the great thinkers of his time and wrote a number of very influential books: *Some Thoughts Concerning Education* (1693) laid out his ideas on how best to educate children, *An Essay Concerning Human Understanding* (1690) developed his empiricist philosophical ideas and his views on human learning, and *Two Treatises on Government* (1689) outlined his vision for a civilised society based on natural rights and became a core work in the development of the US constitution.

As we saw in Chapter 1, Locke did not believe in the existence of innate ideas. Instead he argued that people are shaped by their environment, especially through education, describing the newborn child as a 'blank slate' (*tabula rasa*) on which all experiences would be imprinted to shape her into her final self. This view naturally places a great emphasis on education: Locke asked how children could be shaped through education to become good citizens and how the education practices at the time should be improved. In Locke's view, the shaping of the developing mind proceeded through *association* (linking together two things that are experienced together so that one cannot have one thought without thinking the other), *repetition* (doing something again and again and thus helping to develop it into a natural habit), *imitation* (copying behaviours observed in others, especially adults), *reward* and *punishment*.

John Locke (1632–1704).

These are the principles of Locke's educational philosophy (Crain, 2005): educating children is the way to ensure their development of a good character, and instilling self-control is one of the main goals of education. When children are able to overcome instant gratification and impulse-driven behaviour, and when they learn to deny themselves the pursuit of every whim and desire, then they can form a good character.

A healthy body is needed to achieve this self-control, and thus, physical exercise is important. Children should therefore play outdoors year round. While firm discipline is needed to avoid the forming of bad habits that will be hard to break later on, care has to be taken in how to reward and punish children. Locke thought that rewards should not tempt children's self-control (e.g. giving them ice cream or sweets), but instead positive behaviours should be praised so that they are reinforced. He argued that punishment should not be physical because it would create undesirable associations. For example, if a child is hit for not eating his vegetables then he will develop an association between vegetables and being hit, and this will not increase his willingness to eat them next time. Instead, punishment should be through showing disapproval and, wherever possible, positive behaviours should be encouraged through praise.

Locke thought that, in general, education should not be through rules and punishment, but through leading by example. In other words, he thought that children need role models. He also emphasised that children are different from adults both in their ability to comprehend rules and in their temperament. Therefore education of children's behaviour should be matched to their developmental state. Children show a natural curiosity and we can take advantage of this by designing educational games that they will enjoy and through which they learn, and by listening to their questions and answering to them.

It is clear that Locke's ideas were very enlightened and progressive: they could be taken straight from a modern parenting guidebook (although contemporary accounts put less emphasis on self-denial and the experience of hardship). Locke takes both the character of childhood and the behaviour of adults as important aspects of the socialisation process that is education. His view emphasises the need for adults to understand how children function and the need to monitor and adapt their own behaviours in order to bring out the best in children, allowing them to develop into people with good character and an educated mind.

2.3 JEAN-JACQUES ROUSSEAU

Where Locke outlined in detail the ways in which educators can make children become good adults, Rousseau had a very different view: he argued that children do not need the ideas of adults to be impressed on them in order to flourish but, instead, they should be protected from society and be allowed to develop on their own terms.

Jean-Jacques Rousseau (1712–1778) was born in Geneva. His mother died at his birth (Crain, 2005) and he was raised by his father (who always reminded him that he had caused his mother's death) and his aunt (who forbid him to play outside, making him turn to books). Jean-Jacques was a shy and introverted boy who did not get along with his masters. By the age of 16 he began to lead an itinerant life, travelling and trying to earn money, living on the favours of older women. When he moved to Paris at age 29 he came into contact with some of the great minds of the age, including Voltaire, but despite moving in these circles he always felt an outsider, being too shy, and developing different views from those of the other Enlightenment thinkers (Crain, 2005). When he was 33, Rousseau got together with an illiterate servant girl and stayed with her for the rest of his life, fathering five children, all of whom he gave away to a foundling home because he felt he did not have the means to provide them with a good upbringing.

Rousseau is recognised as one of the great thinkers of the Enlightenment. His most famous book is *The Social Contract* (1762). This was a political work in which he set out a theory of how to organise a political community in which the people were sovereign. The book was highly influential in the French Revolution. He also wrote *Confessions* (1782), the first modern autobiography, and *Emile* (1672), in which he developed his principles of education, using a fictitious character, a boy who was educated by Rousseau's alter ego, Jean-Jacques. It is this latter book that was important for developmental psychology.

Rousseau was wary of the role of society in trying to shape a child because this type of education would make the child too dependent on others' approval – unfree and enslaved by social forces. You may note that Locke's principles of rewarding by praise and punishing by disapproval place great emphasis on the child becoming dependent on the judgement of another person. Instead of this approach, Rousseau argued that education should limit itself to keeping children out of danger and to nurturing the natural predispositions of each child so as to produce a strong, complete and independent person.

Like Locke, Rousseau thought that it was essential to understand the child and his capacities, and to understand that children are fundamentally different from adults. Rousseau described four main stages of development through which, he believed, nature would guide each child. Stage 1, infancy (*Age of Nature*) ranges from birth to around two years of age. At this stage the child experiences the world through his senses, actively seeking to learn by exploring through vision, touch and the other senses. The role of the educator at this stage is to satisfy the child's physical needs. Stage 2, childhood (*Age of Strength*), ranges from three to 12 years, and involves children's increasing ability to explore the world and gain independence. Children now learn by imitation and through their own explorations. Their thinking is concrete and they have difficulty dealing with abstractions. The educator should guide the child to make his own discoveries and experiences and to learn himself by trial and error. Stage 3, late childhood (*Age of Reason*), from 12 to 15 years, shows the arising of reason and rationality and the need for instruction of knowledge. This instruction should take the form of awakening the child's interests and to teach him 'learning to learn'. Finally, in Stage 4, adolescence (*The Age of Insight*), from 15 to 20 years, the child, with the onset of puberty, becomes a social being who now becomes dependent on others and whose awakening passions threaten to overwhelm him. The educator's role is to ensure that the adolescent will be able to feel emotion while also remaining self-sufficient. Passions can be channelled into activities such as hunting and sport, and empathy should be nurtured. The study of history and literature should provide insight into the nature of man.

Jean-Jacques Rousseau (1712–1778).

In striving to understand the nature of childhood at its various stages Rousseau laid the foundation for developmental psychology and he exerted a strong influence on more recent theorists such as Jean Piaget. Unlike Locke, Rousseau saw the child not shaped by external forces but developing according to an inner biological timetable that resulted in distinct developmental stages. The idea that children at different ages should be educated in an age-appropriate manner with specific games and questions was a revolutionary insight for educational theory. In effect, it was the birth of a child-centred approach to education. However, Rousseau was too pessimistic about the social abilities of children. He places the onset of the child as social being at the beginning of puberty but, as we will see in the section on Bowlby, even young infants form a strong bond with their mothers, and more recent research in the new field of Developmental Social Cognition has revealed many social abilities even in very young children (Striano & Reid, 2006).

Nevertheless, Rousseau's influence both on psychology and education was immense. In education, Rousseau's most influential follower was Johann Pestalozzi (1746–1827) whose views had a worldwide impact on educational practice. Pestalozzi argued that teaching methods should be adapted to the natural development of the child, and in 1805 he opened a school where he was able to test his ideas. His school was attended by pupils from all over Europe and Friedrich Froebel (1782–1852), who founded kindergarten education, was a teacher there for four years and was greatly inspired by Pestalozzi's ideas.

2.4 JEAN PIAGET'S CONSTRUCTIVISM

Jean Piaget
(1896–1980).

Jean Piaget was undoubtedly the most important developmental psychologist of the twentieth century, and his influence looms large even more than 30 years after his death. His productive life spanned many of the important developments in his field that he shaped like no other scientist.

Piaget was born in Neufchatel in French Switzerland in 1896. He was interested in biology from his childhood, particularly in the collection of shells from Lake Geneva. Precociously he published his first scientific paper, on the albino sparrow, at the age of ten, followed by a series of papers on molluscs that established him as an international expert in the field by age 15 (he used to hide his age in order to be taken seriously). After his doctorate in Natural Sciences at age 21 Piaget's interest turned towards the origins of knowledge in the developing minds of children. He took a job in the lab of Alfred Binet, who developed the first intelligence test, where his task was to design an intelligence test for use with children. Ultimately he found this work unsatisfying because he saw that children's answers should not be merely scored as correct or wrong. Instead he became intrigued with the errors that children made, which seemed to show an internal consistency to their thinking. Therefore, it seemed that children's thinking was not a 'faulty' version of adult thinking, but that it was entirely different from it. Piaget believed that the errors made by children might be informative of the organisation of their system of thinking.

These insights – that children's thinking is qualitatively different from that of adults, and that errors can reveal the nature of this thinking – became the foundations of Piaget's theory of cognitive development. He began to study individual children in great depth, using the clinical interview method to find out in detail how the children were reasoning, and he also closely observed children's natural behaviours. With the birth of the first of his three children in 1925 he began to focus on his own offspring, studying them in great detail from infancy to childhood. In 1921 Piaget moved to Geneva where he stayed for the rest of his life. During his long and productive life he investigated first children's dreams and morality, then the developing scientific thinking and mathematical concepts and social thinking. In his later life he tried to develop a formal characterisation of his theory, but this endeavour was ultimately unsuccessful.

Piaget published many papers and books. His most influential books were *The Origins of Intelligence in the Child* (1923/1926) in which he describes how intelligence progressively arises in the infant's repetitive activities, *The Construction of Reality in the Child* (1937/1954), which described how elementary concepts of space, time, causes and physical objects arise in development and *Play Dreams and Imitation in Childhood* (1945/1962), which describes the beginning of fantasy and symbolism in infancy.

Piaget's main assumption about development was that knowledge has a biological basis: the precursors of thinking and language lie in the infant's elementary actions (reflexes), perceptions and imitations. On the basis of these basic building blocks the child actively *constructs* systems of thinking and knowledge. The child is therefore active in his or her development. Knowledge is not merely absorbed or imprinted on the child, but actively built into a coherent system of thinking. Across development, this system changes repeatedly, so that development proceeds in qualitatively different *stages* where each stage is characterised by a different system of thinking.

KEY TERMS

Schemas
Structured organisation of knowledge and actions.

Assimiliation
When dealing with new information that is consistent with an existing schema the information is assimilated into this schema.

Accommodation
When a new experience is inconsistent with existing schemas the system must be adapted to accommodate the new information.

How are new experiences integrated into the child's system of knowledge? According to Piaget, previous experience is represented in a series of **schemas** – structured organisation of knowledge and actions. When new information is encountered that is consistent with an existing schema it is **assimilated** into this schema. However, when this new experience is inconsistent with existing schemas the system must be adapted to **accommodate** the new information. This adaptation process ensures that there is an equilibrium between the external world and the internal organisation of knowledge in the child.

Development therefore happens through a process of **equilibration**: the re-balancing between the external and internal world when they are inconsistent with each other.

According to Piaget, development proceeds along a series of **stages** that are characterised by *qualitatively different* systems of thinking and action. This means that going from one stage to the next does not merely mean that the child can do more of something, but that she does things differently. For example, babies usually move around first by crawling (or bottom shuffling) and only later by walking. These are qualitatively different types of locomotion: walking is not an improved version of crawling but is something different altogether.

Similarly to Rousseau, Piaget identified four distinct stages of development from birth to adolescence. Although the ages by which a child moved from one stage to the other could vary between individuals, the order of the stages is invariant: they always occur in the same sequence. In the **sensorimotor period** that spans the time from birth to around two years of age, cognition is based on the infant's physical interactions with the world. In this stage, infants co-ordinate their sensory perceptions and motor abilities to acquire knowledge of the world. The **preoperational stage**, lasting from two to around seven years of age, sees the onset of language and with it, symbolic and representational thought, and involves the child's understanding of the properties of concrete objects as well as the relations between these objects. At this stage, however, children are not yet able to mentally manipulate information, and they are unable to take another person's perspective. These abilities arise in the **concrete operational stage** (lasting from seven to 12 years of age) when children become able to use logic in their reasoning. The final stage in Piaget's theory is the **formal operational stage**, which is reached at around 12 years of age, although Piaget noted that not everybody reaches this stage. Here, children become able to think about abstract concepts and to reason about entirely hypothetical situations.

Despite its influence Piaget's view of development has received a good deal of criticism and some aspects of his theory have turned out not to be correct. One example was Piaget's belief that transitions from one stage to the next – characterised by a new way of thinking – occurred simultaneously across all domains. This view was challenged by work showing that children can show one way of thinking in one domain (for example, when reasoning about weight) but a different way characteristic of a more advanced stage, in another domain (for example when reasoning about number). It therefore appears that stage transitions are not general but specific to different domains.

A second criticism, and one that has perhaps the most profound impact on the development of the field post-Piaget, was that Piaget underestimated the ability of children, especially in infancy. Piaget assessed children by asking them questions or by observing their actions. When children cannot do something in these tasks it could be that they do not have the mental representations to do the task, but it could also

KEY TERMS

Equilibration
Using the processes of accommodation and assimilation to produce a state of equilibrium between existing schemas and new experiences.

Stages
Piaget's theory says that development proceeds along a series of stages that are characterised by qualitatively different systems of thinking and action.

Sensorimotor period
Piaget's first stage in the process of adaptation, from birth to about two years, in which infants co-ordinate sensory perceptions and motor abilities to acquire knowledge of the world.

Pre-operational stage
Piaget's second stage of cognitive development involving internalisation of forms of actions that the infant has already mastered. The key feature of this stage, which lasts from the age of two to six or seven years, is that the child is able to focus only on one salient feature of a problem at a time and is dominated by the immediate appearance of things.

KEY TERMS

Concrete operational stage
Piaget's third developmental stage in which children begin to use logical rules to solve problems. They can deal with more than one salient feature of a problem at a time and are no longer dominated by appearance. However, they are not yet able to deal with abstract problems. This stage lasts from the ages of six or seven to 11 or 12.

Formal operational stage
The final stage in Piaget's theory from 11 or 12 years onwards, in which the child becomes able to consider all possible combinations in relation to the whole problem and to reason about an entirely hypothetical situation.

be the case that the response required to show it is too complex. One example is the case of object permanence: Piaget believed that infants up to nine months of age are unable to maintain a mental representation of an object that is hidden from view. According to Piaget, children do not understand that objects continue to exist when they move behind an occluder. Piaget found evidence for this theory by observing that infants younger than nine months of age do not reach for a toy that is placed under a cloth in full view of the infant. However, the reaching action itself is complex and it requires that the infant has integrated the knowledge of the location of the hidden object with the motor commands to initiate the reaching movement to that location. More recent research, using more subtle measures such as looking patterns and ERP (see Chapter 1), has provided evidence that infants as young as three months are able to maintain representations of hidden objects.

This criticism of Piaget's methods has led to a rise in alternative theories that deny the core aspects of Piagetian development by ascribing sophisticated knowledge to even very young infants. These views reject the view of a gradual construction of knowledge in favour of innate core knowledge about, for example, objects, agents, numerosity and geometry (Spelke & Kinzler, 2007), theory of mind (Leslie, 1992) and face processing (McKone, Kanwisher, & Duchaine, 2007). Other scientists have taken on the main ideas of Piaget's view of knowledge construction from simple beginnings and have developed it further by linking it to brain development and by using computational modelling to understand how complex knowledge can arise from general learning mechanisms (Elman et al., 1996; Johnson & de Haan, 2011; Mareschal et al., 2007; Newcombe, 2011). There is a lively debate in the field at the moment as to which of these approaches can better explain the development of children.

2.5 LEV VYGOTSKY'S SOCIOCULTURAL THEORY

Both Piaget and Vygotsky were born in the same year (1896) and both their theories have had a profound impact on the field of psychology; yet, their theories are as different as were their lives. Whereas Piaget lived until 1980 and found wide recognition and even fame during his lifetime, Vygotsky fell victim to tuberculosis in 1934 and his works were not known in the West until 1962, when his major book, *Thought and Language*, was first translated into English.

Lev Vygotsky studied literature and cultural history at Moscow University and graduated in 1917, the year that saw the Russian Revolution in which the autocratic tsarist government was overthrown and replaced with communist rule. From 1917 on Vygotsky taught literature and psychology at the teacher training college in Gomel, a port city in western Russia. In line with the prevailing Marxist theories of the time, Vygotsky saw culture and social organisation, and the historical forces that shape society, as having an important influence on the development of the child's mind. Nevertheless, Vygotsky's work fell foul of Stalin and his writings were suppressed in Russia. As a consequence of this suppression and his early death, Vygotsky's work was known only to a small circle of students and colleagues until the translation of *Thought and Language* (1934/1962).

We saw that Piaget's theory is focused on the 'child as a scientist', actively constructing knowledge about the world by assimilating and accommodating observations of this world into her schemas, but ultimately in isolation, independent from social interaction. Piaget's focus was therefore on a theory of the origins of knowledge and the characterisation of cognitive stages, but not on the factors affecting child development. Vygotsky's theory is the opposite: for him, development is based on social interactions where children learn from adults and from peers and become socialised in this way (Vygotsky, 1980). According to Vygotsky knowledge comes out of social activity, and language takes an important role in the learning process. Cognitive development can therefore be understood as arising from and being shaped by cultural context, social interactions and language, and learning from more experienced teachers or peers. In contrast with Piaget's theory, Vygotsky did not believe that cognitive development proceeded from within the child in a fixed timetable but, rather, that it was driven by social interactions.

KEY TERMS

Zone of Proximal Development
The gap between what a learner can do without help and what she cannot do even with help. Therefore, it describes the problems that the learner can solve with someone's help.

Language takes a central role in Vygotsky's theory. He believed that language served to organise higher psychological function and that it mediated cognition. This was not to deny that pre-linguistic infants have cognitive abilities, but, for Vygotsky, the most important moment in cognitive development was when speech and practical activity were integrated (Crain, 2005). Following this integration the child would use private or egocentric speech. This 'talking to oneself' would serve to organise the child's cognitive activities and allow her to plan and guide her actions, and it would gradually become internalised as inner speech.

Apart from language, Vygotsky also identified a number of other sociocultural tools that can aid in cognitive development. These were drawing, writing and reading, using numbers, maps and diagrams. Like language these tools can organise and enhance cognitive behaviour. For example, memory capacity could be extended by using drawing or writing to externalise it and thereby in turn shape the memories. Cognitive development thus extends beyond the child but is based on the interactions between the child and these tools.

Another important concept of Vygotsky's theory is the **Zone of Proximal Development** (ZPD). The ZPD defines the difference between what the child can do unaided in a particular situation, and what she can achieve with the help of an adult, older child or even another child of similar age. The ZPD therefore describes how much further a child can go with the help of a teacher. Importantly, two children who show the same abilities can still have different ZPDs. Vygotsky gave an example of two ten-year-old children who both scored like eight-year-olds on standardised tasks assessing cognitive abilities, so that both children have a mental age of eight years. Imagine that then the experimenter showed them how to solve several of the problems in these standardised tasks. Now, one child could solve tasks up to the 12-year level and the other child up to the nine-year level. Clearly these children differ in their ZPD.

The concept of the ZPD has had a profound impact on education. In order to enable children to learn effectively it is not enough to teach to their current developmental stage. Instead, teaching should be to the ZPD of each child because the learning of skills that go slightly beyond the child's current abilities is what drives cognitive development. The adult teacher should begin by modelling and explaining the behaviour to be learned and then gradually withdraw support as the child first imitates and then gradually internalises the new knowledge. See Box 2.1 for an example of the ZPD in operation.

Long after his death, Vygotsky's theory of sociocultural development remains very influential, particularly in the field of education. For example, his influence is

Lev Vygotsky (1896–1934).

BOX 2.1: MORE ON THE ZONE OF PROXIMAL DEVELOPMENT

The functioning of the ZPD was illustrated in a study by Linnell and Fluck (2001), who investigated the counting skills of preschool children. Children of this age usually find it difficult to count but they often carry out this activity with a more experienced partner. Linnell and Fluck compared children's counting in two conditions: one, on their own; and the other, with assistance from their mothers. They found that the children were more accurate both when counting out objects and when selecting the correct number of objects when they were guided through the task by their mothers. The following extract illustrates the important role of the mother's guidance in the task of counting out three toys and placing them in a basket for a clown doll called Billie to play with. The child in this example is 32 months old.

Mother: *'Right shall you give Billy some? You have to count them as you put them in. You've got to give him three pieces'*

Child: *'Yeah' (taking one item from the basket)*

Mother: *'Now you count them'*

Child: *'One' (takes out another and holds one in each hand) 'Two'*

Mother: *'That's it'*

Child: *'Put them in there?' (holding them over Billie's basket)*

Mother: *'Yeah' (child drops toys into the basket) 'And Billie would like one more. One, two, . . .' (does not point to the objects)*

Child: *'Three. And this one' (saying the word three before taking another toy out of the basket)*

Mother: *'Go on then. Give it to Billie'*

Child: *(picks up another toy so again he has one toy in each hand)*

Mother: *'He only wants three'*

Child: *(drops both toys into Billie's basket)*

Mother: *'That's four'*

clear in the work of the American developmental psychologist Jerome S. Bruner (b. 1915), who played an important role in introducing Vygotsky to Western scholars. Bruner offered a synthesis of many aspects of Piaget's and Vygotsky's theories. He described three forms of knowing: enactive representation (i.e. knowledge based in action or knowing how to do things), iconic knowledge based on representing knowledge through visual imagery, and symbolic knowledge that is based on language and is transmitted through culture. These forms of knowledge only partially overlap. For example, when learning how to ski, enactive representations are particularly important and merely reading books on how to ski will not guarantee success. On the other hand, once an expert skier one might improve performance by visualising the downhill course and through being given verbal feedback on performance.

2.6 JOHN BOWLBY'S ATTACHMENT THEORY

Piaget's and Vygotsky's theories are concerned mainly with the cognitive development of children. In contrast, the theory of John Bowlby is focused on emotional development.

John Bowlby (1907–1990).

John Bowlby (1907–1990) was born in London as the fourth of six children of a distinguished family. After completing a first-class degree in preclinical sciences and psychology at Cambridge he worked in a school for maladjusted children. There he became convinced that some of the problem behaviours he saw in the disturbed and antisocial young people were the result of a faulty relationship between parents and children. He was especially interested in disturbed adolescents, who seemed incapable of giving or receiving affection, a deficiency he thought was the consequence of prolonged lack of affection in early childhood. Specifically he believed that children reared in orphanages could not form lasting relationships later in life because they had not had the chance to form a solid attachment early in life.

Bowlby subsequently trained as a psychoanalyst and qualified in medicine and psychiatry at the University of London in the early 1930s. In his work as a child psychoanalyst Bowlby developed a unique synthesis of methods and theories drawn from the tradition of Freudian psychoanalysis, from observation and recording of natural history, from field studies of behaviour in the natural environment (especially the work of Konrad Lorenz in ethology, see Box 2.2), from comparative studies of attachment in non-human primates, and from cognitive developmental psychology.

The basis of Bowlby's theory was the attempt to explain the formation of the earliest attachment bonds between infant and mother along ethological principles that he reformulated in human terms. As animals of different species imprint on their mothers to form early and lasting social bonds, so he believed that human children are guided by a similar evolutionary mechanism to bond with their mothers (or other caretakers).

A key aspect of the social bond between infant and mother is the mother's provision of a secure base to which the infant can periodically return while exploring the world. The emotional attachment of the baby to the mother provides the baby with a sense of safety and security. As in animals, the evolutionary function of this attachment is the protection of the infant from predators and, in the longer term, to provide the model on which all other relationships are based. A secure attachment in infancy will pave the way for secure and successful attachments in adulthood.

Bowlby suggested that the child's attachment proceeds in four phases (Crain, 2005). In phase 1, from birth to three months, infants are interested in humans (faces and voices) but respond to all people in the same way. When they begin social smiling at around six weeks of age they smile at all faces. Bowlby believed that this smiling served the purpose of maintaining the proximity of the caretaker because it promoted loving and caring behaviour. In phase 2, from three to six months, the infant's smile becomes restricted to only two or three familiar people and she simply stares at strangers. One of the familiar people, usually the mother, becomes preferred, which is indicated by readily smiling and babbling when this person is near. In phase 3, from six months to three years of age, attachment becomes increasingly intense with the infant greeting the mother when she returns after a brief time by smiling and reaching to be picked up. At the same time, between seven and eight months, the infant exhibits a fear of strangers that often results in crying at the mere sight of

In phase 3 of Bowlby's attachment theory, children use their parents as a secure base for exploring their environment.

a stranger. Once the baby starts crawling (at around eight months of age) she also begins to follow a departing parent. When more mobile, infants then begin to use their parents as a secure base for exploring their environment (such as a playground). They will venture off but periodically look back to exchange smiles, and sometimes return to the mother. During this period the child also builds a working model of the behaviour of the parent and comes to understand the accessibility and responsiveness of the parent. In phase 4, which ranges from three years to the end of childhood, the child develops an understanding of the needs of the caretaker, for example, to briefly leave, without wanting to come along. This phase therefore sees the development of a more partnership-like relationship with the caretaker.

Bowlby argued that secure attachment to a caretaker – where the child can rely on the caretaker as being there when needed and providing safety and comfort – leads the child into a range of psychologically healthy developmental pathways. In contrast, insecure forms of attachment – either through malformed or disrupted attachments – contribute to the formation of neurotic personality because they take the child down unhealthy psychological pathways. This work was continued by Mary Ainsworth, who worked with Bowlby for 40 years and closely studied the different patterns of attachment in babies by observing their reactions to being left with a stranger or alone for brief periods of time.

Bowlby's theory had important impacts in different areas. One notable impact was on the management of children's visits to hospital. Nowadays, when young children go to hospital their parents are allowed to stay with them. This was not the case in the first half of the twentieth century. A major factor in bringing about this change was a film made by Bowlby's co-worker James Robertson, in 1952, about the eight-day hospitalisation of a two-year-old girl. Visiting times for parents were very restricted, and the film clearly showed the resulting suffering for the child. This film had a major impact and led to swift changes in the visiting arrangements for parents. (You can read more about this film in Chapter 6.)

Bowlby's theory has also been important for considering the effects of children growing up in institutions, such as orphanages, where often staff were not able to provide enough one-on-one care to enable the children to form strong attachments. Modern residential care tries to provide children with similar levels of care to that provided by parents. Finally, attachment theory can inform the debate on when to send infants to day care and how to organise day care settings.

BOX 2.2: KONRAD LORENZ AND ETHOLOGY

Ethology is the scientific study of animal behaviours under natural conditions (as opposed to laboratory studies). Ethology as a scientific subject emerged in the 1930s with the work of the Austrian biologist Konrad Lorenz and the Dutch biologist Niko Tinbergen.

Konrad Lorenz (1903–89), who we introduced in Chapter 1, is the founder of modern ethology. His father was a prominent physician in Vienna and Konrad studied medicine but also had a keen interest in the study of nature and wildlife. On his family estate he had many opportunities to closely observe animals of different species, and he became convinced that the innate behavioural patterns (instincts) of animals had evolved in the same way as their physical characteristics.

Lorenz was particularly interested in instincts that are triggered by an environmental stimulus. One of the most striking of these instincts is **imprinting** (see also 'Critical periods' in Chapter 1). When a young bird is newly hatched it will orient to its mother and form a life-long attachment to her. Lorenz found, however, that young birds do not necessarily imprint on the mother but on the first moving object they see (under normal circumstances this would be the mother). He also found that imprinting needed to occur during a critical period: an attachment would only be formed to an object when the chick was exposed to it during this critical period, not before or after. As we saw in Chapter 1, however, the concept of critical period has been replaced by the notion of a sensitive period because it is less fixed than previously believed.

Although goslings and ducklings may imprint on something other than their mother, Lorenz found that the range of objects on which animals will imprint is species specific. While greylag goslings would imprint on almost any moving object, mallard ducklings were more specific and imprinted on Lorenz only when he bent down to them and made quacking sounds. Lorenz also found that early imprinting shaped the birds' adult social behaviour: for example, a jackdaw that had imprinted on humans as an adult courted Lorenz by trying to insert crushed worms into his mouth (Crain, 2005).

Imprinting as a mechanism for forming strong early social attachments also occurs in other species such as deer, sheep and buffalo. Young chimpanzees only form a marked preference for their mother over other chimpanzees after three or four months of age, when they become wary of other adults (Crain, 2005). After that they

Goslings that have imprinted on Konrad Lorenz follow him around in the characteristic single file.

stay close to their mother and return to her regularly. This behaviour is similar to that found in human children, as described by Bowlby.

For their work on the organisation and elicitation of individual and social patterns in animals, Konrad Lorenz, Niko Tinbergen and Karl von Frisch shared the 1973 Nobel Prize in Physiology or Medicine.

2.7 CONNECTIONISM

In the previous chapter you saw that computational modelling is a research method that can be used to develop and test theories of development. We chose artificial neural networks as the most popular example for computational models. Above and beyond allowing researchers to implement and test their theories, however, computational models also provide their own theoretical framework. Here we will briefly describe the developmental view suggested in the connectionist framework and then turn to a related framework, dynamic systems.

Remember that connectionist models learn by gradually adapting their connection weights in response to experience with the environment. In a typical model learning occurs by associating an input with a certain output. In this way, learning in a connectionist system occurs by gradually internalising environmental structure through adapting the strengths of the connections between the units. Furthermore, higher-level behaviour (such as naming an object, forming the past tense of a verb and so on) **emerge** on the basis of interacting low-level processes. This concept of emergence is central to the connectionist approach: as described in the previous chapter, each unit in a model merely sums up incoming activation and, depending on this activation, becomes active itself. Nevertheless, these low-level interactions give rise to complex cognitive behaviours.

The connectionist view of development – which is based on learning as statistical extraction from the environment and emergent behaviour has provided new answers to a range of the most fundamental questions in developmental psychology. One is about the origin of non-linear changes in development. As we have seen, development does not usually proceed in a linear way with children's ability at a given skill improving at a constant rate. Instead, development proceeds non-linearly (see Box 2.3). Connectionist models have shown how such non-linear change can occur on the basis of gradual learning in a constant learning mechanism. Imagine, as an analogy, the transition of the state of water as the temperature is gradually increased from –20 to 120 degrees at a constant rate. For a large range of temperatures, the water is solid ice; but as the temperature reaches 0 degrees, there is a sudden transformation from the solid into the liquid state. For the next 100 degrees of change the water is liquid, and above 100 degrees it is transformed into steam (gas).

Connectionist models have been used to examine how such non-linear developmental trajectories can arise from continuous learning. For example, one model that was used to account for the vocabulary spurt is depicted in Figure 2.1. This model received images of objects and their names as input and it had the task to reproduce both image and name on the output side. This model learned to name objects by being shown an object at input and generating the label at output, and to recognise named

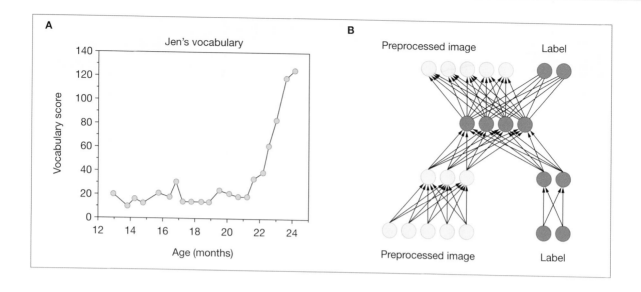

objects by being shown a label at input and producing the object at output. Despite small continuous weight changes in the model the ability to correctly name objects showed the non-linear profile of the vocabulary spurt in children. Whereas most other explanations of the vocabulary spurt argued that it occurs as a consequence of changes in the way in which a child learns new words (for example, by suddenly discovering that words refer to objects in a systematic way), in this model the vocabulary spurt emerged out of a constant learning mechanism. This and other connectionist models have highlighted that to explain a non-linear change in behaviour it is not necessary to assume qualitative changes in the learning system.

2.8 DYNAMIC SYSTEMS

Dynamic systems theory describes how systems that are open to the effects of the environment changing over time. They are focused on the real-time interactions of separate parts of the developing system and ask how these interactions generate change in the system as a whole. In this view there is no central driver of development. Instead, developmental change emerges from these lower-level interactions. In dynamic systems theory it is crucial to view the nervous system as situated in the body and the body in the environment. This is because interactions are considered in this brain-body-environment loop.

An important concept in dynamic systems is **self-organisation**. Self-organisation means that a system can arrange itself in an orderly state without an external agent or plan. Using another example from chemistry, the atoms in a crystal arrange themselves in an orderly grid merely through their local interactions. Similarly, people in an elevator often arrange themselves to maximise the distance between each other (and thus shuffle around when another person enters). Dynamic systems views of development likewise argue that coherence in the developing system is achieved through the real-time interactions between different parts of the system and its environment. This emerging coherence can lead to relative stability in some cases but also to rapid changes in others.

Figure 2.1
On the left is the typical development in vocabulary size. On the right is the connectionist model that was used to successfully model this non-linear developmental trend.
Reproduced from Plunkett (1997). Copyright © 1997, with permission from Elsevier.

KEY TERMS

U-shaped development

A type of non-linear development where performance is initially high but then temporarily decreases before recovering again.

BOX 2.3: NON-LINEAR DEVELOPMENT

Development can show different types of non-linearities. For example, change can be slow initially, then increase rapidly and eventually level off again (Figure 2.2). This *sigmoid* ('shaped like an S') profile is, for example, found in children's vocabulary development where, after a slow start in which only a few words are learned per week, there is a sudden increase around 18–24 months of age when children learn several words per day. As vocabulary increases when children get older the rate of learning new words slows again. Another non-linear change is *step-wise change*. As you saw, developmental stages in which children's behaviour is relatively constant and then rapidly changes to a higher level, is characteristic of Piaget's theory of development. A third non-linearity is found in **U-shaped development**. Here, performance is initially high but then temporarily decreases before recovering again. The best-known example of this developmental course is past tense inflection of irregular verbs such as *ate, came, swam, went*: initially children produce only a few of these past tense forms, but do so correctly. Between two and a half and three years of age, as children learn more past tense forms, they can suddenly produce wrong forms such as *comed, eated, swimmed* and *goed* before finally learning all correct past tense forms (Berko, 1958). There are also inverted U-shaped developmental trajectories that are encountered, for example, in brain development: an initial increase in grey matter (mainly neuronal cell bodies and dendrites) is followed by a decline, at different stages of development in different parts of the brain. For example, grey matter density peaks in children between 11 and 12 years of age, followed by a gradual decline (Giedd, 2004).

Figure 2.2
Developmental functions showing change with age. (Note: all 4 are non-linear)

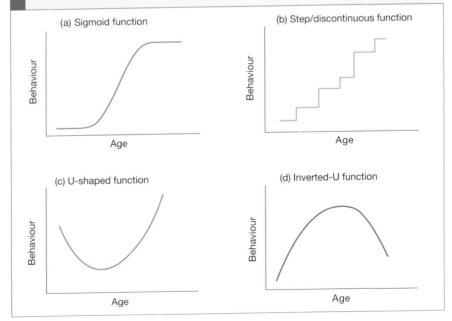

(a) Sigmoid function

(b) Step/discontinuous function

(c) U-shaped function

(d) Inverted-U function

As in connectionist models, the aim of dynamic systems is to explain how qualitative changes in a developing system can arise out of small-scale quantitative changes. In these systems there is also a focus on explaining non-linear changes such as those described in Box 2.3. It is perhaps useful to return to the question of the vocabulary spurt and to ask how dynamic systems theory explains this non-linearity. One example (van Geert, 1991) begins by identifying a number of variables that are relevant to describing vocabulary development. In van Geert's model these are the growth rate (a measure of how quickly vocabulary size is increasing) and a 'feedback delay'. In simple terms, feedback delay is the effect of already knowing a number of words on learning new words. Both

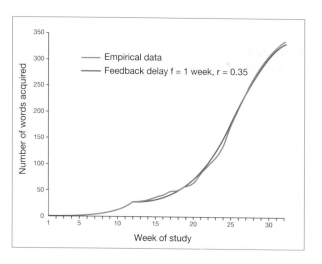

growth rate and feedback delay can be independently changed in the model. Van Geert aimed to model the vocabulary development of a specific child, and he found that for this child a growth rate of 0.35 and a feedback delay of one week provided a very close fit between the model and the observed data (Figure 2.3).

Figure 2.3
A well-fitting curve develops if the empirical curve is considered as a two-step process. The first step seems to be an initial growth period that stabilises at about 25 words in week 12. Then there is a secondary growth period that starts at about 350 words. Adapted from van Geert (1991).

Knowledge – often the basis of action – in dynamic systems is emergent in the moment. It is an outcome of the intrinsic dynamics and the state of the system at a particular moment, and the immediate input. This view is quite different from classic views of knowledge where concepts, non-changing symbols and logical propositions form the basis of explanations (Smith, 2005).

One example might help to illustrate the difference in thinking between 'classic' and dynamic approaches to cognition. Imagine that you are trying to catch a ball that your friend is throwing at you from some distance away. In a traditional view of cognition your attempt at catching it might be explained by judging how far your friend is from you, estimating the speed of the ball and the angle at which your friend has thrown it, implicitly computing the equation that predicts where the ball will land and moving there. A dynamic systems explanation of the same task would focus on the moment-by-moment interactions between yourself and the ball. You would move at any moment so that the ball is coming directly at you, adjusting your position as the curve of the ball begins to decline. Through these real-time adaptations you would be at the location where the ball lands without the need for complex off-line computations of its trajectory.

2.9 NEUROCONSTRUCTIVISM

The theory of neuroconstructivism makes a close link between brain development and cognitive development. Mental representations – the basis of thought – are characterised as patterns of activation of the neural network of the brain. Therefore, to understand the changes of these representations across development it is necessary to consider how the brain itself changes. Specifically, in the past decade or so we have learned much about how the developing brain adapts to the child's experiences at various levels, and the neuroconstructivist view is focused on how these adaptations come about.

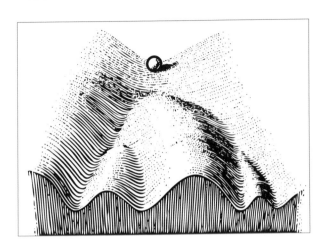

Figure 2.4

Waddington's epigenetic
landscape (from
Waddington, 1957).

Development in neuroconstructivism is viewed as a trajectory that is shaped by multiple interacting constraints at different levels that affect brain development. The idea of development as a trajectory is inspired by the *epigenetic landscape* of Conrad Waddington (Waddington, 1957) (Figure 2.4). In this landscape, development is likened to a marble rolling down a hill with different valleys that become progressively deeper. While Waddington used this metaphor to describe how cells in the body become specialised for different functions, we can use the same image to describe cognitive development. As the marble rolls down the hillside its path is determined by where it is at a certain moment, what forces push it in either direction, and how the landscape is shaped.

What are the constraints that shape the developing brain, and with it, the developing mind? Neuroconstructivism considers such constraints at different interacting levels. At the lowest level is the biological action of genes. We saw in Chapter 1 that the view of genetics as providing a blueprint for development has been modified in recent years to recognise that the function of genes can be switched on and off through external factors that relate to the experience of an individual (epigenetics). Genes therefore shape the developmental trajectory, but gene expression is likewise shaped by developmental experiences.

A second constraint has been termed 'encellment', the fact that the development of neurons is constrained by their cellular environment and interactions with neighbouring neurons. The way in which developing neurons form connections with each other is regulated by chemical interactions that can be guided by genetic actions or be subject to neural activity. That is, experiences that lead to neural activity can take an active role in forming the neural networks that are used to process these experiences (Quartz & Sejnowski, 1997). In this way, a progressively more complex neural network becomes able to process progressively more complex experiences: there is an interactive loop between the 'software' (experiences) that changes the 'hardware' (the brain), resulting in more complex 'software' to change the 'hardware' further and so on. This view makes it clear that one cannot understand the changes in mental representations and abilities without considering the changes that occur in the brain at the same time.

One level up is the constraint of 'embrainment' – the interactions of different brain areas in the development of the overall structure of the brain. Different parts of the brain can send information to each other and these neural activity patterns will have an effect on how the functional specialisations of brain areas emerge. For example, in people who are blind from birth the 'visual cortex' becomes activated by Braille reading (Sadato *et al.*, 1996). It seems, therefore, that the functional specialisation of cortical areas is shaped by experiences, and in the absence of visual input different sensory modalities come to utilise what would be the visual cortex in sighted people.

It is important to remember that the brain is embedded in a body, and the constraint of '**embodiment**' stresses that the body allows the developing child to generate his or her own experiences with increasing sophistication. For example, the ability to grasp objects and bring them to the mouth will greatly enrich the sensory experiences a baby has with objects, as will the developing ability to move around by crawling or walking. These developments on the one hand allow for an enriched experience of the world, and on the other hand they enable the infant to manipulate the environment to gain specific new experiences. In this way, the developing body will enable the child to take a proactive role in her development by creating her own experiences, which in turn lead to changed neural network structures that support the processing of these new experiences.

The individual exists in a network of people – parents, siblings and others – and these social interactions are captured in the constraint termed 'ensocialment'. For example, the pattern of mother–child interaction will have profound effects on the development of the child (see Bowlby's attachment theory). In the neuroconstructivist view social experiences lead to specific experiences that again shape the neural networks that are processing these experiences.

Although the described constraints act at different levels they nevertheless interact (Figure 2.5). For example, a congenitally blind person will have an altered experienced environment, and these specific experiences will lead to a flexible adaptation of the developing brain structures through interactions between different brain areas (for example, the shrinkage of areas processing visual input and the expansion of areas responsive to tactile processing). These altered patterns of neural

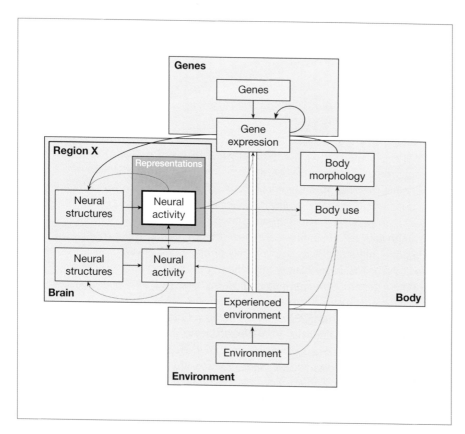

Figure 2.5

The interacting constraints in the neuroconstructivist framework. The link between brain and cognitive development is made in 'Region X' where mental representations are instantiated as patterns of neural activity. These patterns are constrained by (solid lines) and affect (dotted lines) all other parts of the gene-brain-body-environment system. Reproduced from Westermann et al. (2007) with permission from Wiley-Blackwell.

activity could lead to epigenetic effects on gene expression, which in turn could further shape neural development. At the same time, the absence of visual input will also affect the way in which a child uses her body, for example by enhancing tactile exploration, leading to further changes in experiences and thus, neural adaptations. In this way, interactions between these constraints drive development forward along a trajectory unique to the developing individual.

An attractive property of the neuroconstructivist view is that it provides an integrated view of typical development and developmental disorders. Development is always a trajectory shaped by interacting constraints. What is different in developmental disorders is that the constraints are different (see Box 2.4). For example, in a genetic disorder such as Williams syndrome the typical developmental trajectory will be pushed off-track already at conception, and early deviations will lead to a cascade of later effects that manifest themselves across a range of domains. This view of developmental disorder is very different from other views that sometimes argue that a specific disorder leads to the failure of one or several specific modules to develop while the rest of the cognitive system is unaffected.

An important implication of the neuroconstructivist view is that adult cognition can only be fully understood when considering how the developmental process has given rise to the adult system. In fact, adult cognition is a point (or rather, a region) on the developmental trajectory. Traditional cognitive psychology views the adult cognitive system as relatively uniform and static, but a developmental view can give rise to new insight into the mechanisms underlying adult cognitive abilities (Westermann & Ruh, 2012).

BOX 2.4: WILLIAMS SYNDROME FROM A NEUROCONSTRUCTIVIST PERSPECTIVE

Williams syndrome (WS) is a developmental disorder that affects approximately one in 10,000 babies. It is caused by a deletion of genetic material from chromosome 7. WS affects the growth, physical appearance and the cognitive abilities of children suffering from it. Children with WS have characteristic facial features such as a wide mouth with full lips and widely spaced teeth. Because the missing genetic material affects the flexibility of blood vessels WS children often suffer from heart problems. In terms of mental function, WS children show a general developmental delay, but language and face processing abilities are relatively preserved.

Annette Karmiloff-Smith and colleagues have conducted detailed research on WS and they have characterised this developmental disorder within the neuroconstructivist framework. They have also used WS as an example to critically discuss *modular* views of cognitive development. According to the modular view, the brain/mind is organised in a set of independent functional parts (modules), and developmental disorders can manifest themselves in the inability of one or several modules to develop. According to this view developmental disorders should lead to highly specific deficits in one domain and the sparing of abilities in other domains. For the case of WS, one proponent of this modular view (Piattelli-Palmarini, 2001) states: 'children with WS have a barely measurable general intelligence and require constant parental care, yet they have an exquisite mastery of syntax and vocabulary. They are, however, unable to understand even the most immediate implications of their admirably constructed sentences' (p. 887).

A child with Williams syndrome. Photo courtesy of the Williams Syndrome Foundation.

This description of WS very much emphasises (and exaggerates) the distinction between spared and impaired abilities. For example, a closer look at face processing abilities (which are also said to be selectively spared in WS) shows that, although WS children perform within the normal range on tasks measuring face-processing ability, they tend to perform near the bottom of this normal range. Some more specific aspects of face processing (such as a difference between recognising upright and upside down faces that is observed in typically developing children) also appear to be atypical in WS (Karmiloff-Smith *et al.*, 2004). The developmental trajectory of the brain systems supporting face processing is also atypical in WS: whereas in typically developing children the brain areas responsible for processing faces become gradually localised and specialised, in individuals with WS this specialisation does not appear even in adults (Karmiloff-Smith *et al.*, 2004). Thus, even though the face processing abilities of typically developing children and those with WS appear similar – both pass the face recognition tests – in WS children this ability seems to be achieved using very different underlying processes. Scores in the normal range can therefore still be achieved on the basis of atypical developmental trajectories.

Instead of a set of damaged modules with spared language and face processing modules, from a neuroconstructivist perspective WS is therefore better characterised as early, general deficits pushing the developmental trajectory off course and leading to cascading, more specific deficits later on in development. On the other hand, the interactive nature of brain development can also lead to compensatory strategies using different brain areas.

2.10 SUMMARY

In this chapter we have traced the changing views of how children develop and the explanations that have been given for developmental change. We saw that the notion of children as different from adults is no more than 400 years old and that early views imagined a fully formed human to be present at conception. In the seventeenth century John Locke, the great English philosopher, developed very enlightened ideas of how to educate children, assuming that they come to the world as blank slates and it is the responsibility of the educator to shape them into good adults. Rousseau, the great Swiss philosopher of the eighteenth century, realised that children are fundamentally different from adults and he laid the foundations for developmental psychology by describing different developmental stages through which all children pass. He rejected the notion of a blank slate in favour of natural predispositions that unfold according to 'nature's plan'.

Jumping ahead by 200 years, John Bowlby synthesised research and theorising from a range of fields to develop his theory of attachment, stressing the importance of the social bonding between children and their caregivers (usually their mothers), and he argued that this bonding behaviour had evolved and was comparable to imprinting in animals. Jean Piaget, in Rousseau's tradition, developed his constructivist theory of cognitive development and through his detailed studies of children's behaviours and errors at different ages became the most influential developmental psychologist of the twentieth century. Lev Vygotsky, whose life was cut short by illness, nevertheless developed highly influential theories of education and his notion of the Zone of Proximal Development has had a strong influence on educational practice. More recent theories of cognitive development, such as connectionism, dynamic systems and neuroconstructivism, have moved beyond considering only the development of the mind and have begun to try to integrate the brain and other aspects of the developing child into the picture. Development of these newer theories has been aided by significant advances in methodology over the past 30 years, including computational modelling, brain imaging and epigenetic studies.

It will be evident that none of the theories provide an all-encompassing explanation of every aspect of development – some focus on education, others on the cognitive development of the mind, and others again on the real-time dynamics and brain mechanisms underlying development. This is good, because they all have their strengths in the domain they consider, and there is truth in all of them. It also follows that these different theories are not incompatible. All of them recognise that development is non-linear, and Rousseau, Bowlby and Piaget described explicit stage models of development. Dynamic systems and connectionism then are concerned with how stages can arise out of continuous learning and, together with neuroconstructivism, they ask how developmental change arises out of the interactions between different parts of the developing system. We will encounter these theories again in subsequent chapters when we discuss how they have been used to account for different aspects of psychological development.

FURTHER READING

Crain, W. (2005). *Theories of development: Concepts and applications* (5th edition). London: Pearson Education. This book provides a very readable and deep introduction into many different theories of development.

Newcombe, N. S. (2013). Cognitive development: Changing views of cognitive change. *Wiley Interdisciplinary Reviews: Cognitive Science, 4*(5), 479–491.

ESSAY QUESTIONS

1. Compare and contrast Locke's and Rousseau's view of child development.
2. Compare and contrast Piaget's and Vygotsky's view of child development.
3. Why do you think so many different theories of development have developed?
4. How is neuroconstructivism related to Piaget's constructivism?

CHAPTER 3

CONTENTS

Introduction to infancy

3

After reading this chapter you will be able to

- understand how prenatal development is affected by environmental factors, including maternal diet and stress.
- explain some of the long-term cognitive effects of premature birth
- explain how IQ is calculated
- describe how early motor abilities develop and explain how development is affected by babies' experience
- understand what babies can see, hear and taste in the first weeks of life.

3.1 PRENATAL DEVELOPMENT

We saw in Chapter 1 that development is the result of a complex interplay between genes and environment. During the prenatal period, genes and the uterine environment interact to shape the development of the foetus. An understanding of how this complex process takes place has begun to emerge in the last two decades although there is still much to discover. However, it is already clear that genes do not exert their influence in a fixed and inflexible way. Two recent overviews (deRegnier & Desai, 2010; Fox, Levitt, & Nelson, 2010) argue that genes should be thought of as providing a rough draft or framework for development. From this framework, a more defined structure will evolve, which gradually becomes more and more differentiated as the distinctive areas of the foetal brain develop.

In the prenatal period, babies share their immediate environment with their mother; and so in order to understand development from conception to birth we have to consider the many ways in which mothers can exert an influence on their babies' development. Some of the effects – such as those produced by drugs, alcohol and tobacco – are relatively well understood. Others – such as the effects of stress and depression – are just beginning to emerge as highly significant factors.

Effects of maternal nutrition, alcohol and drugs

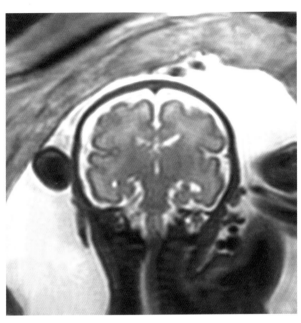

A magnetic resonance imaging (MRI) scan of a section through the brain of a 25-week-old foetus in its mother's womb. At 25 weeks the connections within the foetus' brain are developing, especially in the areas responsible for emotions, perception and conscious thought. The foetus is also able to hear at this stage.

The foetal brain grows more rapidly than any other organ and, in a resting newborn, it uses up 87 per cent of the available energy resources (i.e. total resting metabolic rate). This rate is higher than the rate for older children or adults or for any other species (deRegnier & Desai, 2010). During prenatal development, the foetal brain demands a rich supply of nutrients, including protein, fats, iron, zinc, copper, iodine, selenium, folate and vitamin A. All of these are supplied through the mother's diet so it is not surprising to find that poor maternal nutrition can have serious consequences for a developing baby.

A stark illustration of the impact of poor maternal nutrition on foetal development came from a long-term follow up of babies born during a severe famine in Holland during the latter stages of the Second World War (1944–45). Dutch ports were blockaded and there was such a shortage of food that people were reduced to eating tulip bulbs. Dutch women who did not receive sufficient food during the second and third trimesters of pregnancy gave birth to babies with unusually small head circumferences, indicating poor brain growth. Lack of specific nutrients, even when general nutrition is good, can also affect foetal brain development. Where the deficiencies are severe, there can be marked effects on intellectual ability, memory and behaviour (deRegnier & Desai, 2010).

A wide variety of drugs and toxins have been shown to adversely affect foetal development. Often the effects are complex because there are both direct and indirect effects. Mothers who have a heavy alcohol intake or make use of physically addictive drugs often experience mental health and/or social problems that may affect the care they take of themselves during pregnancy. For example, they may have poor nutrition and they may not have regular medical support, both of which may have an impact on the prenatal development of their baby.

The direct effects of alcohol consumption are well documented although it has been difficult to determine whether very low levels of alcohol consumption pose a risk. Recent medical advice is to abstain from alcohol during pregnancy. As you might expect, the most serious risks are posed by heavy drinking, which brings with it the possibility that a baby will be born with **Foetal Alcohol Syndrome** (FAS). Just over one baby in every 1,000 is born with FAS. The main indicators are distinctive facial deformity, retarded growth and intellectual disability. None of these features is reversible although successful early intervention can reduce some of the long-term risks. The effects of alcohol during pregnancy interact with other features of the inter-uterine environment so that the effects will be more severe when the mother has poor nutrition or a poorly functioning liver (which is common in cases of alcoholism) (Karp, 2010).

The use of illegal drugs also poses a serious risk for a foetus. As with alcohol, there are both direct and indirect effects since pregnant women who are addicted to drugs are less likely to have a healthy lifestyle. They may, for example, smoke, use other illegal drugs or eat poorly. The direct effect of cocaine is that it causes narrowing of the blood vessels to the placenta, thereby reducing the blood supply to the foetus. This, in turn, affects the level of oxygen and nutrients that the foetus receives and leads to poor growth. Cocaine can also raise the mother's blood pressure, resulting in premature birth.

Newborn babies whose mothers have used cocaine shortly before they are born may show signs of cocaine intoxication such as an unstable heart rate, abnormal muscle tone, high-pitched crying and excessive crying. It is not clear whether these symptoms are caused by cocaine or by the effects of withdrawal but the good news is that the effects disappear after a few days (deRegnier & Desai, 2010).

The effects of withdrawal are particularly marked in infants born to mothers who are addicted to heroin or methadone. Uncontrolled withdrawal can prove fatal for a newborn baby and such cases have to be carefully managed by placing the baby in a dark, quiet environment and administering a gradually-reducing dose of methadone over a period of weeks or sometimes months. If the withdrawal is managed successfully, there appear to be minimal direct effects of foetal exposure. However, there remain strong social risks to the baby if the mother remains addicted.

Effects of maternal stress

Maternal stress during pregnancy may have long-lasting effects on development. There are two sources of information about the potential effects of stress. One is the study of babies born soon after natural disasters and the other is the measurement of cortisol levels in pregnant women. **Cortisol** levels rise when someone is feeling stressed so they are a good marker of stress levels.

One natural disaster that has been studied was a severe ice storm in Quebec that took place in 1998. Three million people lost electrical power for up to 40 days and many had to leave their homes and temporarily live in a shelter. Women who were pregnant during the time of the ice storm were interviewed retrospectively about their subjective and objective experiences of distress and the verbal and nonverbal intelligence scores of their children were assessed at five and a half years of age (Laplante *et al.*, 2008). IQ scores proved to be related to the level of objective stress that the mothers had experienced although not to subjective levels.

Field and colleagues measured the cortisol levels of pregnant women and found that those with higher levels were more likely to be depressed (Field *et al.*, 2006). The babies born to these mothers were more likely to be premature and to have a lower birth weight.

Effects of prematurity

For humans, the period of prenatal development lasts for approximately 266 days (38 weeks), just a few days short of nine months. This is the normal interval between conception and birth. The length of a gestation period is largely determined by birth weight. A longer period is required to enable a higher birth weight so very small animals require only a short gestation period to reach a viable level of maturity. For example, the gestation period for a mouse is only 20 days, for a cat or dog it is 60 days and for a rhesus monkey it is 64 days. The gestation period for an elephant is

Prematurity
Babies born before 37
weeks of pregnancy are
classed as premature.

645 days. Humans have very similar gestation periods to other primates such as gorillas (257 days) and chimpanzees (227 days).

Babies who are born at 38 weeks weigh, on average, about 3,150 grams (seven pounds) and they are about 53 centimetres (21 inches) from head to toe. Not all babies reach full term and some are born a number of weeks early. Babies who weigh less than 2,500 grams are classed as low birth weight but babies who are born very early will be considerably below this weight. Being born extremely prematurely (before 25 weeks of gestation) puts the infant at considerable risk of subsequent learning difficulties.

A longitudinal study (Wolke & Meyer, 1999) followed a group of very preterm children over the first years of life to see what effects **prematurity** had had on their cognitive development. The children were compared with a matched group of children, born at the same time and in the same place but at more than 36 weeks (counted as full term). The aim of the study was to determine both the extent and severity of cognitive impairments and so the study focused on a range of language and intellectual abilities. Wolke and Meyer predicted that the children who had been born before 25 weeks would show general delays in comparison to full-term peers.

There were 264 children in each of the two groups so the Wolke and Meyer findings give a reliable indication of the effects of prematurity. The difference in birth weight of the two groups was very large as you might expect with the control children weighing, on average, 3,407 grams and the very preterm children weighing only 1,288 grams. In nearly one quarter of cases the very preterm babies were twins or triplets reflecting the fact that a multiple pregnancy is a risk factor for prematurity. On average the very preterm babies spent 12 weeks in hospital following their birth.

When the children were followed up at the age of six years there were some striking differences between the very preterm and full-term groups. On a developmental measure of intelligence, which included a wide range of different tests, the mean score for the full-term group was just over 100. This is what you would expect for a sample of typically developing children. The mean score for the very preterm group was significantly lower, at just under 85. In terms of learning disability, just over 10 per cent of the full-term sample met the criterion for mild difficulty and under 2 per cent met the criterion for severe difficulty. The corresponding figures for the very preterm group were 25 per cent and 23.55 per cent. You can see that the very pre-term babies were at a much greater risk of having a mild or severe learning disability. (See Box 3.1 to find out more about the way that psychologists measure children's intelligence and how different degrees of learning disability are defined.)

Very preterm babies are
usually kept in hospital for
some time after birth,
often in an incubator,
which maintains suitable
environmental conditions.

Children in the very preterm group also had significantly poorer language skills and had particular problems both with the grammar and meaning of sentences. They also tended to have more problems in articulating words than their peers, especially finding difficulties with 'sch' sounds that require sophisticated articulatory control. On the pre-reading tasks, which included the ability to judge whether two words rhymed and to match sounds to words, there were also marked differences. These kind of sound-based skills are very important for children who are learning to read so

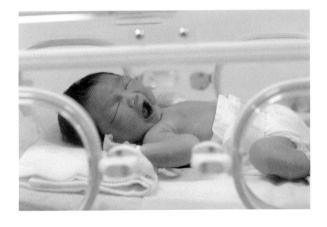

if these skills are poor children are likely to have problems in learning to read. You can find out more about how children learn to read in Chapter 13.

More detailed analysis revealed that a core problem for many of the children in the very preterm group was that they had difficulty in the simultaneous processing of information. This was measured by such tasks as arranging a complex pattern from several pieces where it was necessary to think about several different pieces at the same time in order to assemble the pattern. When this ability was factored out, most of the differences between the two groups disappeared, showing that it was this ability that underpinned the general differences in language and cognition.

What this latter finding suggests is that many cognitive skills are closely related to one another. For example, the speed at which information can be processed is a factor in many cognitive tasks as is the ability to process several different kinds of information at the same time. You will find out more about some of the common factors in cognitive skills as you learn about cognitive development.

BOX 3.1: MEASURING CHILDREN'S INTELLIGENCE

The idea of measuring intelligence in a standardised way was first introduced by the German psychologist and philosopher William Stern (1871–1938), who coined the term Intelligence-Quotient, commonly abbreviated to IQ. The first intelligence test was developed by the French psychologist, Alfred Binet (1857–1911), who was working on experimental studies of thinking in young children. Binet had been critical of diagnoses of mental deficiency made by medical practitioners responsible for placing mentally retarded (learning disabled) children in special schools in Paris. Binet argued that there was no simple way to identify children with learning difficulties and he pointed out that the same child might receive a different diagnosis, depending on which physician had made it.

The need for a valid and reliable test of intelligence led Binet to construct the Binet–Simon scale, published in 1905. Initially the test was used to provide guidelines on the relative intellectual abilities and educational potential of children with learning disability but his work was soon to find much wider application in education and training. Binet and Simon developed tests that were based on norms of performance for a given age and this soon led to the idea of measuring children's **mental age** and comparing it with their **chronological age**. The idea behind mental age is that it gives an indication of a child's level of cognitive function in years and months. You can think of it as the average level of performance at a given age. This may or may not be the same as chronological age, which is the child's actual age in years and months.

The idea is that, if a child has a mental age that is the same as chronological age, they are performing at an age-appropriate level. Such a child would have an IQ of 100. Children whose mental age

KEY TERMS

IQ
The ratio of mental age, defined by an intelligence test, to chronological age, with a score of 100 representing 'average IQ'.

Mental age
This gives an indication of a child's level of cognitive function in years and months. This be or may not be the same as chronological age, which is the child's actual age in years and months.

Chronological age
The child's actual age in years and months.

KEY TERMS

Learning disability
Children who have a low
IQ score are considered
to have a learning
disability. This can be
profound, severe,
moderate or mild,
depending on the IQ
score.

exceeds their chronological age have an IQ greater than 100 and those whose mental age is below their chronological age have an IQ of below 100.

The formula for calculating the intelligence quotient (IQ) defines intelligence relative to age:

$$1Q = \frac{\text{Mental Age}}{\text{Chronological Age}} \times 100$$

For example, an eight-year-old with a mental age of ten years would be credited with an IQ of: 10/8 × 100 = 125, whereas for a child of the same chronological age but a mental age of only six years, the IQ would be: 6/8 × 100 = 75.

Intelligence is assumed to have normal distribution with the majority of people having scores around the mean of 100. Children who have a low IQ score are considered to have a **learning disability**. Learning disabilities are divided into four categories according to the level of IQ. Children and adults with an IQ of less than 20 are considered to have a profound disability. Those within the 20–35 range are classed as having a severe disability, those in the 35–50 range as having a moderate difficulty and those with an IQ between 50 and 70 as having a mild difficulty. In the Wolke and Meyer (1999) study, nearly half of the children in the very preterm group had IQ scores in the mild to severe range (i.e. below 70), which is very considerably higher than in the population of typically developing children where over 90 per cent of children would be expected to have an IQ somewhere between 70 and 130.

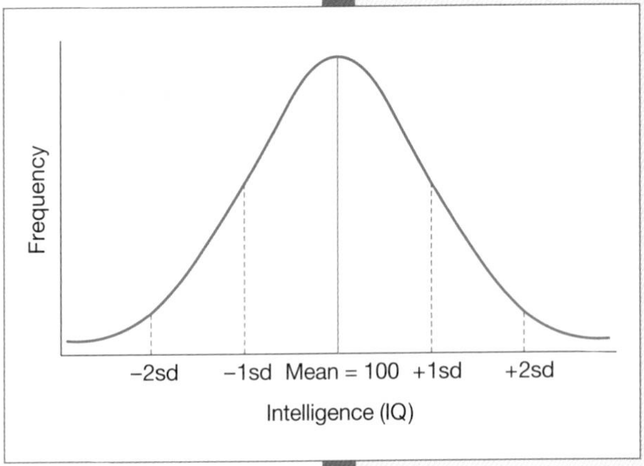

Figure 3.1
Intelligence is assumed to have a normal distribution.

3.2 NEWBORN INFANTS

At first sight newborn babies can appear very helpless. Their inability to move independently or manipulate their environment stands in sharp contrast to the young of many animal species who, within a few minutes of birth, are able to stand and shortly afterwards take their first steps. Wildlife films have recorded the birth of many animal and bird species with remarkable early abilities.

Human infants have a long period in which they are very dependent on an adult to look after them. It is many months before they can move around independently and even longer before they can walk. Full physical and mental maturity takes many more years.

We have to assume that there is an evolutionary advantage to such a long period of immaturity and dependence on other family members since modern humans are

a very successful species. So what might the advantage be? The answer is that a long period of immaturity provides for a long period of learning and development and this, in turn, makes human beings very flexible indeed. Babies and young children can hone their skills so that they are optimal for the environment in which they are growing up. Children who are growing up in a traditional farming or hunting community can learn the skills they need to become expert farmers or hunters; children growing up in a community dominated by technology can learn to master computers, smart phones and the internet.

Newborn babies appear helpless compared to the young of some animal species, that can walk soon after birth.

There are two other, more specific, reasons why human infants have such poorly developed motor skills, even in comparison to other primates. One is that infants are born with disproportionately large heads, with the head taking up about 25 per cent of the total body length. The average weight of the brain in a newborn baby is around 450 grams and it is about 75 per cent of the size of an adult chimpanzee brain. The head of a newborn baby is so proportionately large that it needs to be supported when the baby is held – one of the first, important lessons for a new parent. The other reason why babies take a long time to become fully mobile is because of the complexities of human locomotion. Learning to walk on two legs requires a high degree of balance, co-ordination and muscle strength.

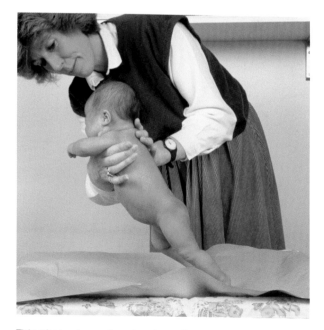

Clearly there are evolutionary advantages to having a large brain and walking on two legs but the price to pay is the long period of time over which early motor skills develop. However, some physical abilities are so essential for survival that they are present right from birth. The most important is the sucking reflex, which is essential for feeding. Newborn babies also have a grip reflex and will close their finger tightly over an object placed against their palm. This is thought to be the vestige of a reflex that is essential for primates who have to cling to the fur of their mothers as they are carried around. Another interesting reflex is stepping.

This photo shows the stepping reflex, elicited when a baby is supported in a standing position and the feet are brought into contact with a surface.

The **stepping reflex** is elicited when a baby' is supported in a standing position and the feet are brought into contact with a surface, such as a table or the floor. The baby responds by making stepping movements, as though walking.

3.3 SITTING, STANDING AND WALKING

In the weeks and months after birth babies progressively gain control over movement. You can think of this control as beginning with the head and gradually spreading down through the body. The major milestones in motor development were first described over 60 years ago (McGraw, 1943). Babies first lift their head, then they become able to raise head and chest, then to lift their head and upper body by raising themselves on arms and hands and, eventually, on all four limbs. By nine months babies can usually crawl although some move around by bottom shuffling. Soon they will pull themselves to stand upright and, by about 12 months, most babies take their first steps in walking.

Data collected by the World Health Organization shows that there is very considerable variation in the age at which infants reach these major milestones. Some infants walk independently well before the end of their first year whereas others may not do so until they are 18 months old. Also, not every infant passes every milestone in a set order. Some infants spend very little time crawling and may go straight from bottom shuffling to pulling to standing.

Although motor development is strongly driven by maturational factors in the first two year of life, child-rearing practices can also have an effect. An early study (Dennis & Dennis, 1940) looked at the Hopi Indians of New Mexico among whom it was traditional to strap the infant securely to a cradle that the mother carried on her back. Use of a cradle enabled the mother of a young infant to move around and work while keeping her baby close at hand but it limited the baby's opportunity for motor activity. Surprisingly, the traditionally-reared Hopi babies learned to walk at

Figure 3.2
Windows of achievement for six gross motor milestones. From WHO Multicenter Growth Reference Study Group. Copyright © 2006 Taylor & Francis.

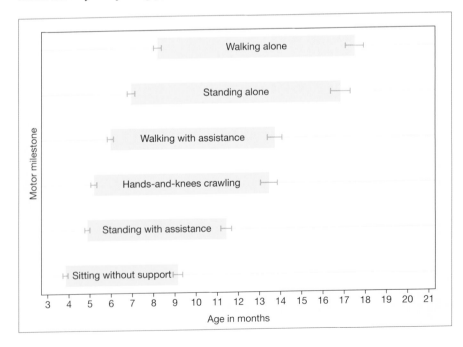

the same age as the babies of Hopi mothers who had adopted Western practices and no longer made use of a traditional cradle. However, a crucial factor was that babies were only in the cradle for a few hours per day and during the rest of the time their movements were unrestricted.

Severe restriction of opportunities to practise movements can have very serious consequences. A study of infants in an orphanage in Teheran found that children as old as two years were unable to sit securely or stand. The authors of the study (Dennis & Najarian, 1957) attributed the delay to the almost total lack of social stimulation in the orphanage. Infants were left alone in their cots for much of the time and were not encouraged to explore their environment or to interact with other people. For most infants, there are adults and older children on hand to help them as they begin to develop their motor skills. For example, a baby who is not yet stable enough to sit unsupported will be supported either by a person or by a suitable object such as a cushion; and an infant who is beginning to take first steps will be given a helping hand.

Specific interventions can directly affect motor development. Zelaso and colleagues (Zelaso, Zelaso, Cohen, & Zelaso, 1993) carried out training of either sitting or stepping in infants over the first ten weeks of life. To train sitting, an adult supported an infant's back and then briefly removed the support, leading the infant to briefly attempt to straighten the back. To train stepping, babies were given an opportunity to place their feet on the floor, which prompted them to produce the stepping reflex. Babies who were trained in sitting improved in the control of sitting but not stepping; and, babies who were trained on stepping improved in stepping but not sitting. Control babies who were observed weekly, but not trained on either sitting or stepping, did not show a comparable improvement in either sitting or stepping in the first ten weeks of life.

The most recent evidence for effects of early child-rearing practices on motor development comes from a change in the advised sleeping position for young babies. In many countries, concerns about cot death led to a well-publicised campaign to place babies on their back or side, rather than their stomach, for sleep. This change produced a gratifying reduction in the incidence of cot death but this change in early sleeping position also

Native American Indian cradle that restricts the infant's movement.

Dennis and Najarian (1957) found that some two-year-old children in an orphanage were unable to sit securely or stand. They attributed this to the lack of opportunities to explore their environment or to interact with other people.

KEY TERMS

Power grip
A grip in which the fingers wrap around the objects.

delayed the age at which babies pushed up with their arms when placed on their stomachs (Davis, Moon, Sachs, & Ottolini, 1998). Babies who are placed on their stomachs to sleep have plenty of opportunity to push their arms against the mattress and so raise their heads. However, babies placed on their backs have much less opportunity to practice this manoeuvre. It should be noted, however, that the babies who were placed to sleep on their backs or sides still had a pattern of development that was within normal range.

3.4 DEVELOPMENT OF HAND CONTROL

Another important aspect of motor development during infancy involves the hands. Humans have hands that have evolved to pick up and manipulate objects and a comparison between a human hand and that of a chimpanzee pinpoints some very distinctive anatomical features. These enable humans to grasp objects in very special ways. From a developmental perspective, it is these special types of grip that take several months to appear in an infant's repertoire.

The hands of chimpanzee are primarily designed for swinging through the trees and for climbing. For these activities chimpanzees use a 'hook grip' involving four flexed fingers (Marzke, 1992). When they pick up objects, such as a stick to push down into a termite mound, they also use a **power grip** in which the fingers wrap around the objects. Chimpanzees have a relatively short thumb and, by comparison with a human thumb, it can exert very little pressure. This means that a chimpanzee cannot press the thumb against the fingers and so cannot use a precision grip to pick

The hand print of an adult male chimp (left) compared to that of a three-year-old female child (right).

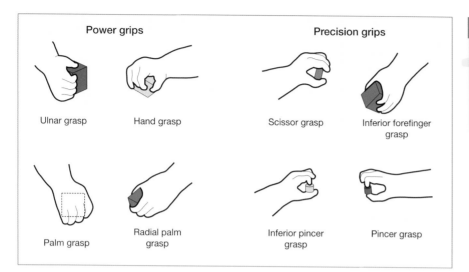

Figure 3.3
Range of power and precision grips in the first year of life.

up and finely manipulate objects. If you try to pick up a small object using only your fingers and not your thumb you will see that it is very difficult.

Contrast the performance of chimpanzees with the achievements of human infants. Like chimpanzees, babies first grasp by wrapping all the fingers against the object in the palm of their hand. These palm grips give way to more precise finger grips, so that by the end of the first year, babies are able to pick up small objects in a 'pincer grip' in which the very end of the index finger almost touches the extreme tip of the thumb. This **precision grip** is only found in humans and it involves full opposition of the fingers and thumb.

Between 6 and 12 months infants gradually use power grips less often and precision grips more often. By the end of the first year, precision grips – which provide considerably more control than power grips – predominate. One common grip is the pincer grip. The other is the inferior forefinger grip, which involves the placement of the thumb against the side of the knuckle joint of the index finger. Of these two grips, the pincer grip gives the greatest degree of control for fine movements.

A direct comparison of the grips used by human babies and chimpanzees highlights the difference in ability (Butterworth & Itakura, 1998). Chimpanzees of various ages were given a graded series of cubes of apple to pick up. Across the age range tested, the chimpanzees showed a transition from a pre-dominance of power grips to more precise grips involving index finger and thumb similar to that shown by infants. However, there were two important differences. First, precision grips were not evident until the chimpanzees were about eight years old, and approaching maturity. These same grips are used by human infants before the end of the first year. Second, chimpanzees never became as precise as human infants in picking up the smallest cubes between thumb tip and index finger. When presented with a small cube of apple, chimpanzees very much preferred to use an inferior forefinger grip rather than a pincer grip.

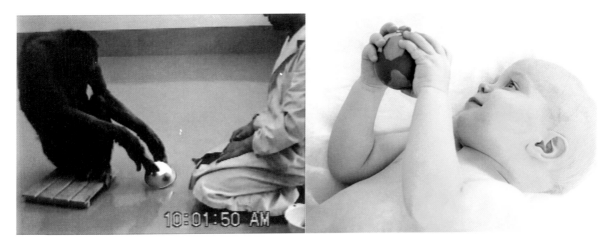

Infants soon become skilled in picking up and holding objects with the right grip. The grip repertoire of chimpanzees in more limited.

KEY TERMS

Pre-reaching

Movements of the arm and hand made by newborns towards an attractive object.

Goal-directed reaching

The ability to successfully attain a desired object. This ability emerges at around three or four months and gradually becomes more precise over the first year of life.

In order to pick up objects and manipulate them infants also have to develop the ability to reach out to an object of interest and to co-ordinate their two hands. These abilities also develop over the first year of life.

Newborns will attempt to make gross 'swiping' movements of the hand and arm in the vicinity of an attractive object that is suspended within reach. If the weight of their head and trunk is supported, newborns will extend a hand and arm towards an interesting object (Amiel-Tison & Grenier, 1985). This early movement of the arm and hand towards an object is known as **pre-reaching**.

Goal-directed reaching, which is the ability to successfully attain a desired object, emerges at around three or four months and gradually becomes more precise over the first year of life. By 12 months infants begin to extend their reaching distance by using an object such as a spoon and, by 15 months, they are capable of precision reaching.

In the first year of life infants will often reach out towards an object with both hands. Towards the end of the first year they begin to use each hand separately. This is an important development because many activities require the hands to carry out different actions. For example, one hand may be used to hold an object and the other to perform some action on the object. A good example of this is taking an object out

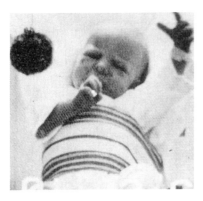
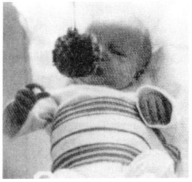

A two-month-old infant showing pre-reaching to an object.

of a container while holding up the lid. The ability to co-ordinate the two hands to perform a bimanual task emerges at around 11–12 months. As with the ability to use precision grips, the ability to use the two hands to perform complementary functions gives human infants an impressive ability to manipulate the objects in their environment.

3.5 HEARING, SMELL, TASTE AND VISION

More than 100 years ago William James published his seminal book, *The Principles of Psychology* (1890), in which he famously described the newborn baby's initial impression of the world 'as one great blooming, buzzing confusion' (p. 462). James' comment captured the view, which held sway until comparatively recently, that the new infant was confronted with an unfamiliar and confusing world. It is easy to see why such a view was popular. At first sight a newborn seems capable of very little apart from sucking. Experimental studies of early infant abilities have, however, shown that the world of the newborn infant is far from being a place of noise and confusion, with some features of the world already familiar.

Visual acuity continues to develop after birth (see below). By contrast, the auditory system is fully functioning at birth and it is one of the first systems to develop

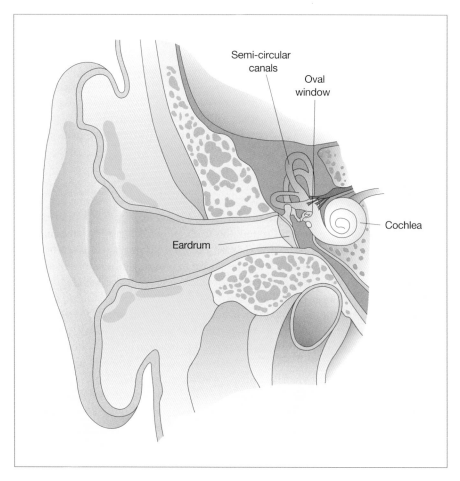

Figure 3.4

A diagram of the ear showing the key parts.

in the foetus (Burnham & Mattock, 2010). The ear develops from the inside out so that the first part to develop is the inner ear, which contains the **cochlea**. This is a spiral shaped organ containing hair cells that are crucial for hearing. By ten weeks the cochlea is already close to its final adult form and it has grown to its adult size by the twentieth gestational week. The hair cells are mature by about 22 weeks with the hair cells closest to the middle of the cochlea maturing first and those on the outside maturing last. The middle ear is near adult size and shape by 15 weeks and the outer ear is close to adult form by 18 weeks, although both the pinna and auditory canal will continue to grow after birth.

Studies looking at the way foetuses respond to sounds suggest that they are able to hear at around the twenty-fourth gestational week. The evidence for this has come from experiments in which a buzzer is sounded close to the mother's abdomen and the baby's response is monitored through ultrasound. Once babies are born, they will blink if they hear a loud sound. The same is true of babies before birth. Using ultrasound, researchers were able to show eye blinks in response to the sound of the buzzer for most babies from the twenty-fourth to the twenty-fifth gestational week (Birnholtz & Benacerraf, 1983).

Given that babies are able to hear well before they are born it is natural to ask what they might be listening to. Until fairly recently, it was thought that the main thing that babies could hear before birth were the strong sounds of the mother's heartbeat and other internal organs that served to mask most external sounds. However, it is now well established that external speech sounds, including the mother's voice, can be heard clearly inside the womb since the internal sounds are not loud enough to mask external sounds (Burnham & Mattock, 2010). Furthermore, in the late stages of pregnancy babies are actually learning to recognise familiar sounds. This astonishing discovery first emerged from a study showing that babies could recognise a story that their mother had read to them before they were born. You can find out more about this study, carried out by DeCasper and Spence (1986), in Chapter 5 (see 5.1).

Smell

Smell is very important for newborn infants. They can use their ability to discriminate smells to recognise their mother through the smell of her breast milk. In one study (MacFarlane, 1975) six-day-old infants were tested by placing a pad worn by their mother to catch seeping breast milk on one side of their head and a pad from another breast-feeding mother on the other. Babies turned their heads toward the side of their mother's pad, preferring the familiar smell.

Interestingly, smell is also important in adult recognition of infants. Mothers learn the smell of their own infants very rapidly and can correctly identify clothing that had been worn by their baby when asked to pick this out from identical clothing worn by two other newborns. This ability to use smell to identify an infant appears to be rather more general than previously thought. In an ingenious study (Kaitz & Eidelman, 1992), women who had not had children were asked to hold a newborn infant for 45 minutes. In order to make this seem a natural request, participants were told that the purpose of the study was to see how newborns reacted to being held by someone other than their mother. Shortly afterwards the non-mothers were tested to see if they could pick out the vest (undershirt) worn by the infant they had held. Their responses were compared to those of mothers. As in previous studies, mothers were very good at recognising the smell of their own baby and were 82 per cent correct. The non-mothers, who had only held 'their' baby for less than an hour, made a correct identification in 10 cases out of 13 (77 per cent).

Taste

Newborns have a preference for sweet tastes and they show aversion to a sour taste just like adults, puckering up their lips and showing a 'disgusted' expression. When sucking sweet liquids they show a contented expression (Steiner, 1979). They will suck more to obtain sweetened water than plain water and suck less when the water is salty (Crook, 1978). Tolerance for salt develops in the months after birth and the preference for plain water rather than salty water has begun to disappear by four months (Beauchamp, Cowart, Mennella, & Marsh, 1994). As breast milk is slightly sweet this preference for sweet tastes has important survival value.

Babies show an aversion to sour tastes by puckering up their lips in a 'disgusted' expression.

Vision

Relative to adults, newborns are not able to perceive fine detail. They can discriminate between a uniform grey surface and stationary black and white stripes three millimetres wide. Visual acuity develops steadily over the next few months and, by the age of three months, infants can perceive stripes that are less than half a millimetre wide.

Although neonates cannot see fine detail at birth, this does not mean that their vision is inadequate for daily life. The ability to perceive fine spatial detail is essential for a task such as reading or sewing but these will only become important several years later. The infant's level of acuity is perfectly adequate for the large social objects, such as faces, that they will frequently encounter.

At birth, the lens of the eye, which brings the visual image to a sharp focus at the retina by a series of muscles that change its shape, is not yet fully functional. This means that the eyes of the neonate have a fixed distance for optimal sharpness. Only objects that are 21 centimetres from the eyes of the newborn will be perceived in sharp focus. This is because, until the infant is about three months old, the lens does not accommodate by changing the curvature of its surface in order to bring objects at different distances into focus.

It is almost certainly no accident that this distance of 21 centimetres coincides with the average distance between an adult's face and the baby's when the baby is being held. So, even though distant objects will be blurred, important social objects can be seen in sharp focus right from birth.

3.6 SUMMARY

In this chapter we have seen that development in the months leading up to birth can be affected by many external factors. The physical and mental wellbeing of the mother are vital for optimal development of the foetus. Babies who are born preterm are at serious risk of cognitive delays and learning disability.

In the first weeks and months of life, babies begin to develop their motor skills. They gain gradual control over their bodies and become capable of sitting, standing and walking. They also develop fine control over their hands and become capable of sophisticated manipulation of objects. During the first months of life visual acuity develops so that babies are able to see increasingly fine detail. Taste also develops but both hearing and smell are fully developed at birth. The different senses allows babies to begin learning very rapidly about the world they have been born into.

It is not only sensory and motor skills that develop over the first years of life. It is also social and cognitive skills. We will see in the next chapters that babies are born with many important abilities that enable them to develop social and cognitive skills. In the past, these skills were often underestimated because the physical helplessness of a newborn baby belies some very sophisticated abilities to perceive and learn from key aspects of the environment. It is these skills that we turn to in the next chapter.

FURTHER READING

Karp, R. J. (2010). Health. In J. G. Bremner & T. D. Wachs (Eds), *The Wiley-Blackwell handbook of infant development* (Vol. 2, pp. 62–86). Chichester: Wiley-Blackwell.

Wolke, D., & Meyer, R. (1999). Cognitive status, language attainment, and pre-reading skills of 6-year-old very preterm children and their peers: The Bavarian longitudinal study. *Developmental Medicine and Child Neurology, 41*, 94–109.

ESSAY QUESTIONS

1. How does maternal health affect the development of the foetus?
2. What might be the evolutionary advantage of a long period of immaturity?
3. How do the motor skills of infants develop over the first year of life?
4. Compare the development of hearing and vision over the first months of life.

CHAPTER 4

CONTENTS

Cognitive development in infancy

4

After reading this chapter you will be able to

- characterise the main aspects of infant cognitive development
- describe the A-not-B task and discuss different explanations for infants' behaviour in this task
- explain the development of object categorisation in infants
- discuss the controversy in early cognitive development
- critically evaluate different interpretations of looking time data obtained with infants.

The period from birth to 24 months sees dramatic changes in the infant. The relatively helpless newborn with very little voluntary motor control has, by 24 months, developed into a confident toddler who runs around, climbs on chairs and playground slides, enjoys looking at picture books and computers, sings and dances, has an opinion on what music to listen to, what food to eat and what clothes to wear, and often has a vocabulary of over 200 words. This period of such profound change and development has become of great interest to psychologists, particularly since the methods described in Chapter 1 have been developed to study children's knowledge and abilities during this early period.

Traditionally the term 'cognitive' has been used to refer to such abilities as reasoning and problem solving and to the acquisition and representation of knowledge. This use of the term came from the idea that mental life can be separated into sensing, thinking and acting: information from the world is perceived, these perceptions are processed, and an action is performed. Cognition was focused on the processing stage – thinking. While many researchers still take this view others have come to the conclusion that it can be very hard to separate perception and action from cognition, and that cognition is firmly grounded in both sensing and acting (Smith & Sheya, 2010). For example, when considering how we recognise the face of a friend the boundaries between perceiving this face and recognising it (comparing it with all the faces we know in memory) becomes decidedly blurred.

In the previous chapter we discussed motor development during infancy. As infants gains more fine-grained motor control – learning first to sit and then to move around – these new abilities offer a vastly increased array of experiences that have important effects on cognitive processing. The dynamic systems view of development, as well as neuroconstructivism, explicitly integrate the close link between action, perception and cognition into their theoretical framework. You will notice that this integrated view is close to Piaget's constructivist ideas since Piaget was concerned with how knowledge could be constructed on the basis of simple sensori-motor primitives.

In this chapter we will provide an overview of several of the main areas that have concerned infancy researchers: the development of categorisation, knowledge about objects in the world and number knowledge. You will learn more about perceptual development in Chapter 6.

4.1 THE DEVELOPMENT OF CATEGORISATION

One of the most fundamental cognitive abilities is grouping objects into categories. Categorisation is here defined as treating a set of discriminable objects as equivalent. For example, when you look at different dogs you can discriminate one dog from another, and yet you consider them all to belong to the single category 'dog'. This is an important ability indeed: imagine that you could not form categories and you encountered a new dog. You would not know anything about this new animal apart from what you directly experienced. This would put a great burden on your memory as you would have to remember all the specific details about this one animal – that it has four legs, a tail and fur, that it barks and likes to chase balls. Perhaps even more importantly, you would know nothing about what to expect from this animal: what does it mean when it wags its tail? What does it like to eat? What is this growling sound?

The ability to form categories enables us to reduce memory load by storing common representations for all members of a category (if you know that the animal is a dog you don't have to remember how many legs it has and if it has a tail), and it allows us to form expectations and make predictions about properties that we have not yet observed (if it wags its tail it may well come and lick our hand next). The ability to categorise is so fundamental that it has been said that it forms the basis for all our thinking and cognitive processing. Given its importance it comes as little surprise that researchers have been very interested in how this ability develops in young infants.

Perceptual categorisation

Most of the work on infant categorisation has used the **familiarisation-novelty preference method** described in Chapter 1. Remember that this procedure uses the fact that infants tend to spend more time looking at new and unusual stimuli than at old and familiar stimuli. In a typical categorisation study infants are presented with a series of pictures from one category (for example, cats). Looking time to each stimulus is measured, and it is expected that as more objects are shown looking time will decrease. If this happens we assume that the infant has become familiarised to the objects from that category. This familiarisation phase is then followed by a test phase in which two objects are presented side-by-side: a new object from the familiarised category (e.g. a new cat), and a new object that is from a different category (e.g. a dog). If infants have formed a category for cats they should find the dog more interesting than the new cat, despite not having seen either of the test pictures before. Therefore, if the infant looks at the dog more than 50 per cent of the total looking time we assume she has formed a category for cats that includes the new cat but excludes the dog.

By using the familiarisation-novelty preference method it has been shown that young infants who are a few months old can form categories of different objects and animals. At its most simple, Slater (1989) described a study in which newborns, three- and five-month-old infants were shown categories of different shapes (circles, squares, triangles and crosses). The examples used for each category differed in the thickness, pattern and exact shape of the lines. Infants were habituated on these shapes and then presented with a shape from the trained category and also with a new shape that they had not seen during training. The three- and five-month-old infants showed a preference for the novel shape (implying that they had formed a shape category) but newborns did not. Other studies have shown that three- and four-month-old infants can form categories of many animals and real world objects. For example, using realistic colour photographs of different animal species it has been shown that infants can form a category for cats and distinguish it from dogs, birds, horses and tigers (Eimas & Quinn, 1994; Quinn, Eimas, & Rosenkrantz, 1993). Other infants were familiarised with horses and formed a horse category that included new horses but not giraffes, zebras and cats (Eimas & Quinn, 1994).

An intriguing result was found by Quinn, Eimas and Rosenkrantz (1993): when they familiarised four-month-old infants on cats and then showed them a novel cat and a dog, the infants preferred to look at the dog, indicating that they had formed a category for cats that excluded the dog. However, when another group of infants was familiarised on dogs and then shown a novel dog and a cat, they had no preference for either animal. This result can only be interpreted by assuming that the infants in the second group formed a category for dogs, but considered the novel dog as well as the cat as members of this category. How can this be?

A possible explanation is that different breeds of dog can look quite different from each other (think of a Chihuahua and a Great Dane) but different breeds of cat are generally far more similar to each other. So when infants are familiarised on cats and then see a dog, the dog is likely to be different from the cats they have seen and they look longer at the dog. However, when they are familiarised on a range of different looking dogs and then see a cat there is a good chance that, to them, the cat might pass off as just another variety of dog.

This explanation has a number of interesting implications. First, it suggests that infants are very good at extracting regularities from their environment: they must be very sensitive to the commonalities between different dogs and different cats and effectively form a category representation based on these commonalities. Second, in this type of experiment infants form their categories rapidly and based only on what they have seen in the lab. The structure of their categories depends on the precise nature of the stimuli they see during the study. Third, these early categories are perceptually based: objects are grouped together when they look similar to each other, and a looking preference to an animal in the test phase is entirely driven by these similarities. Finally, infant categories can be different from adult categories and through development they are shaped to correspond to the adult categories.

What information do infants use to decide which animals belong to the same category? Quinn and Eimas (1996) investigated this question by familiarising infants

Figure 4.1

Examples of the stimuli used by Quinn and Eimas (1996).
Reproduced from Quinn and Eimas (1996), Copyright © 1996, with permission from Elsevier.

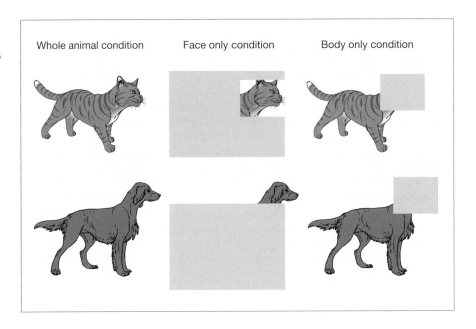

on cats and testing them on dogs. However, whereas one group of infants saw the whole of each animal (as before), for a second group the body of the animal was occluded and only the face was visible and, for a third group the head (i.e. face) was occluded and only the body was visible (Figure 4.1). When tested on a cat and a dog, infants who had seen the whole animal or only the head preferred to look at the dog, whereas infants who had seen only the body looked equally at the novel cat and the dog and showed no preference. It therefore seems that infants use the face of an animal as a main clue to categorising it.

It could be that the infants already know that faces are very important and therefore preferentially look at the face of all animals they see. Another possibility is that, while looking at a number of cats, the infants learn that the head is the most diagnostic feature and therefore look at it more as the study progresses. This question is interesting because, as we will see in Chapter 6, even newborns preferentially look at human face-like stimuli and this has been taken as evidence for innate face-orienting mechanisms.

Quinn, Doran, Reiss and Hoffman (2010) wanted to find out whether animal faces are special for infants as well. To do so they again familiarised six- to seven-month-old infants on cats or dogs. Now they used eye-tracking to measure which part of the animal the infants were scanning the most. What they found was a clear demonstration of a head bias that existed right from the start of the experiment: around 45 per cent of infants' fixations were to the head of the animals despite the head taking up only 17 per cent of the total area; and this was the case even for the first few animals that were shown. It therefore seems that animal faces were special to infants even before they took part in the experiment.

Can we measure neural correlates of infants' category formation? Quinn, Westerlund and Nelson (2006) used an ERP study (see Chapter 1) to answer this question. Using again cats and dogs, they familiarised six-month-old infants on 36 cat images and then tested the infants on 20 new cat pictures interspersed with 20 pictures of dogs. They measured the neural activation patterns corresponding to

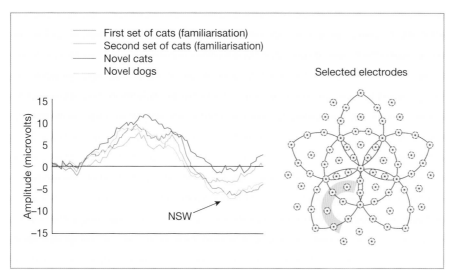

Figure 4.2
Waveform plots from Quinn, Westerlund and Nelson (2006) depicting event-related potentials (ERPs) in response to the first set of cats presented during familiarisation (blue), the second set of cats presented during familiarisation (red), novel cats (orange), and novel dogs (green). To the right of the plot is a two-dimensional electrode layout of the Geodesic Sensor Net with the selected electrodes from which the plotted signals were recorded.
Reproduced with permission from Quinn, Westerlund and Nelson (2006) © Association for Psychological Science.

presentation of the animals at different locations of the scalp for four different conditions: cats 1–18, cats 19–36, novel cats and novel dogs. The idea was that a neural signal of category learning should be the same for cats 1–18 and for the dogs, because both sets represent new experience with a class of stimuli. In contrast, cats 19–36 and the test cats should lead to different neural activation patterns because they are for familiar stimuli. This is exactly what they found: for cats 1–18 and the dogs, a negative slow wave (NSW) was found over left occipital parietal scalp areas (Figure 4.2). This activation pattern had previously been linked to detection of novelty. For cats 19–36 and the test cats, a slow wave that returned to baseline was found. This component had previously been associated with recognition of familiarity. These ERP patterns therefore provided a neural marker of a key characteristic of categorisation, responding to something new as if it is familiar: a new cat is recognised as a cat.

We have seen that young infants can form categories on the basis of object features. In the real world, however, different features tend to occur together. For example, many animals with four legs also have a tail and fur, whereas animals with wings have two legs if they are relatively big (that is, birds) or six legs when they are very small (insects). In order to make use of these *feature correlations* to learn about the world, infants must first be able to detect them. But at what age do infants develop the ability to detect feature correlations?

Younger and Cohen (1986) investigated this question in a looking time study. They familiarised infants on two animal drawings, each with their characteristic body shape, leg shape and tail. At test they presented infants with three animals (Figure 4.3). One was one of the two animals used during familiarisation and one was a completely novel animal with a different body, legs and tail. The third animal was a combination of the two training animals, for example, with the body of animal 1 and the tail of animal 2. The idea here was that if infants only paid attention to features in isolation they should not find this third animal interesting because they had seen all of the features before. However, if they were sensitive to the co-occurrence between features they should find it interesting because they had never seen an animal

Figure 4.3
Examples of the stimuli used by Younger and Cohen. From Cohen (2001).

with this combination of features before. The result of this study was that four-month-old infants did not find this animal interesting: they looked at it as much as at the previously seen test animal and much less than at the completely novel animal. However, ten-month-old infants looked at the 'novel-combination' animal as long as at the completely novel animal: for them, old features in new combinations were as interesting as an animal with completely novel features! This study therefore suggested that the ability to process feature combinations develops between four and ten months of age.

The Younger and Cohen study, and many other studies, show that infants can form categories based on the perceptual properties of objects from very early in life, and that the ability to process the visual characteristics becomes more sophisticated over the first year of life. But at some point categories must go beyond what something looks like. As adults we know that visual features are not the whole story: birds and bats look similar to each other but they do not belong to the same category. Mice and whales look very different from each other but they are both mammals. During development, additional information becomes relevant that allows children to go beyond visual characteristics in forming categories. Language is the key in going from early perceptual categories from more sophisticated, deeper concepts. The role of language in category formation has therefore also become a very active field of research.

Higher-level categorisation

In studies that investigate the role of language in categorisation, infants are familiarised on objects just as before, but while an object is presented it is also labelled. For example, Fulkerson and Waxman (2007) familiarised six- and 12-month-old infants on line drawings of dinosaurs, and each time a dinosaur was shown the phrase 'Look at the toma! Do you see the toma?' was played through loudspeakers. You won't recognise the word 'toma' because it is a made-up or novel word. Researchers often use novel words in infant learning experiments because they do not want the infants' response to be influenced by anything they have learned outside the experiment. In order to see the effects of presenting the novel label there was a control condition in which instead of a name for the object, a tone was played. The test phase of the study was exactly the same as in other categorisation studies: a novel dinosaur and a different animal (a fish) were shown side by side.

The result of this study was that infants formed a category when the animals were labelled, but not when a tone was played. This and many similar studies have been taken as evidence that language facilitates categorisation. The idea is that, when different objects share the same name, commonalities between these objects become highlighted so that infants learn which parts of the animal or object are relevant to its identity. So, for example, when animals of different colours and shapes in an aquarium are all called 'fish', we realise that shapes and colours are less important than the fact that they all have scales and fins and that they swim under water.

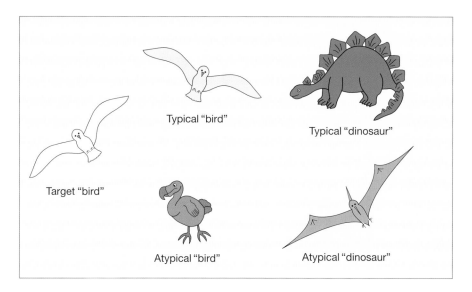

Figure 4.4
Examples of the stimuli used to test the 'bird' category by Gelman and Coley (1990).
© American Psychological Association. Reprinted by permission.

It should be noted that many of the studies claiming this role of language in category formation have come under a great deal of criticism. This is mainly because it can be hard to assess what language offers over and above just showing the objects in silence. As we have seen, three-month-old infants are perfectly capable of forming categories even when they are not accompanied by labels, so what precisely is added by labelling them? This remains an active field of research, but it now seems clear that labels can have an effect on category formation by the age of ten months.

Can language help overcome perceptual similarities, such as enabling children to learn that birds and bats are different animals despite looking so similar? This question has been investigated in a series of studies by Gelman and colleagues.

In one study, Gelman and Coley (1990) showed two-year-old children drawings of birds and dinosaurs and asked them questions about these animals (Figure 4.4). Some of the animals were typical members of their category (e.g. a bluebird and a stegosaurus) but others were atypical and looked more like members of the other category (dinosaur-like birds such as dodos and bird-like dinosaurs, pterodactyls). The children were asked questions about each animal, for example, 'Does it live in a nest?' and 'Does it have big teeth?' The idea was that if children relied on the visual appearance of the animals they should get the answers for the atypical category members wrong and say that, for example, the bird-like dinosaurs also live in nests (they don't) and the dinosaur-like birds also have big teeth (they don't). But if the children were sensitive to the deeper properties of the animals they should be able to disregard the visual appearance and answer the questions correctly. Gelman and Coley found that two-year-old children were indeed driven by the visual appearance of the animals and they only answered 42 per cent of the questions for the atypical category members correctly, compared to 76 per cent for the typical category members. However, these results changed when the children were given labels for

BOX 4.1: A DEBATE ON HOW CATEGORIES DEVELOP

In the large literature on infant categorisation a debate has emerged about how infants move from the early, perceptually-based categories to more mature concepts. One view holds that there is continuity in this process: as infants gain more experience with the world, they gradually enrich their early categories with more sophisticated knowledge (Quinn & Eimas, 2000). For example, the early 'dog' category can become enriched with knowledge about how dogs move and smell, the sounds they make, what they like to eat and where they live. Some of this added knowledge can come from having more direct experience with dogs, but much can be learned from what other people tell us especially about properties that cannot be directly observed. For example, more detailed knowledge of the properties of dogs might include such diverse information as how dogs evolved, what their status was in Ancient Egypt and the fact that not all dogs have hairy coats. Language is therefore an important means to enrich early categories in order to develop deeper concepts.

A contrasting view is that infants possess two separate cognitive systems for categorisation (Mandler, 2000): a perceptual system is functional from birth and is used to learn the early perceptually based categories. A second, conceptual system is responsible for deeper analysis and conceptual knowledge, and this system becomes operational only after six months of age. The conceptual system provides deeper knowledge about observed categories. For example, by analyzing the movement patterns of different objects infants can learn the general distinction between animate and inanimate objects. Based on this conceptual distinction infants then form expectations such as that animate beings have limbs. According to this view, therefore, there is a qualitative distinction between early categories and later concepts.

A considerable amount of research has been done to distinguish between these two competing theories. The current evidence is probably more in line with the first view, that of a gradual enrichment of theories to become deeper concepts. If anything, this is the simpler view because it postulates one rather than two separate mechanisms. One principle in science to choose between two theories that both explain the same results is to choose the simpler one (this principle is called Occam's Razor).

the animals (such as 'This is a bird. Does it live in a nest?'). In this case they answered 69 per cent of the questions correctly for atypical category members as well. Therefore, by providing labels to the children they were able to override perceptual similarity and base their answers on the category membership of an animal irrespective of its appearance. This study and other similar ones provide compelling evidence that language can act to shape concept formation and to enable infants to go beyond perceptual similarity. See Box 4.1 for a discussion of how infants move on from perceptually-based categories.

4.2 OBJECT PROCESSING

Jean Piaget argued that infants have to learn every aspect of the world through experience, constructing their knowledge on the basis of a small number of biological reflexes. One of the best known aspects of this claim was that young infants do not appreciate that objects that are moving out of vision continue to exist and therefore do not have, as it is called, **object permanence**. Piaget demonstrated his theory in ingenious ways. First, he found that infants younger than eight months of age do not search for an object that is occluded (by covering it with a cloth) even though this is done in full view of the infant. At this age infants reach for and retrieve the object only when it is partially covered, and it takes around another month before a fully occluded object is retrieved. Up to the age of 12 months infants commit the so-called A-not-B error (Figure 4.5): when an object is repeatedly hidden in one location (A), infants between 9 and 12 months old can retrieve it. But, when again in full view of the infant, the object is hidden in a different location (B), the infant continues to search in location A. It is almost as if the location where the object was first hidden, and the reaching response to that location, has become for the infant a part of the object's identity; and this is what Piaget believed. According to his view, it is only at 12 months that infants are capable of having an object representation that is detached from their sensory and motor actions.

While the experimental results of Piaget's studies are robust and indisputable, we will see in this section that subsequent research has cast doubt both on the age by which infants have object permanence, and on Piaget's explanation for this phenomenon. As with other studies by Piaget a main criticism of the object permanence and A-not-B results has been that the infants' knowledge was assessed through a reaching response and active retrieval of the hidden object. Since reaching is quite a complex activity it is possible that the demands of the response led to an underestimation of the knowledge of infants. By using paradigms that do not require a complex response it might be possible to find quite different results. This is what happened in a famous experiment by Baillargeon, Spelke and Wasserman (1985).

In their 'drawbridge' experiment, Baillargeon *et al.* (1985) used a **violation-of-expectation** looking time paradigm to see if they could find evidence for object permanence already existing in five-and-a-half-month-old infants. In this study the infants were first familiarised on an event in which a solid screen rotated back and forth by 180 degrees like a drawbridge (Figure 4.6). The test phase consisted of two new events: in the *possible* event, a colourful wooden block was placed in the path of the drawbridge and the drawbridge now rotated 120 degrees, until it made contact with the block. In the *impossible* test event, the block was placed in the path of the drawbridge but the drawbridge nevertheless completed the full 180 degrees rotation,

KEY TERMS

Object permanence
The understanding that objects have substance, maintain their identities when they change location, and ordinarily continue to exist when out of sight.

Violation-of-expectation method
A way of using infants' looking times to infer their knowledge. The assumption is that infants look longer at something unexpected. So, for example, if they look longer at a physically impossible than at a possible event one can infer that they understand the physical impossibility.

Figure 4.5
The sequence of events in the A-not-B error. The experimenter hides an object at location A (1), and the infant reaches successfully (2). The object is then hidden at location B (3), whereupon the infant again searches at A (4). From Bremner (1988). Reproduced with permission from Wiley-Blackwell.

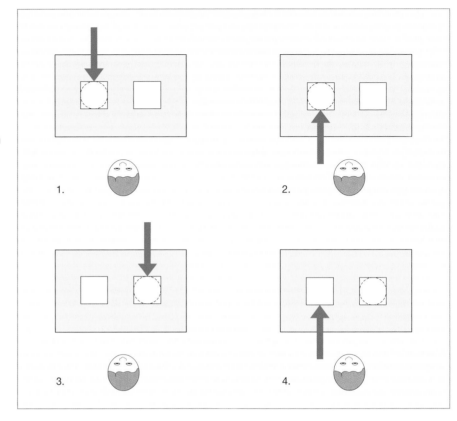

Figure 4.6
Baillargeon's drawbridge study. Adapted from Baillargeon, Spelke, and Wasserman (1985).

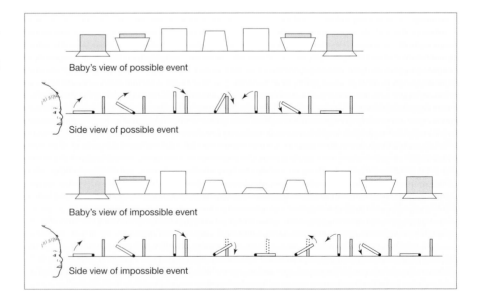

thus apparently passing through the block. The result of the study was that infants looked longer at the impossible event than at the possible event. This was despite the impossible event – the 180 degree rotation – being exactly what they had seen during familiarisation, so perceptually it should have been less interesting than the 120 degree rotation that infants were seeing for the first time at test. Longer looking at the impossible event was therefore interpreted as showing that the infants knew that the block continued to exist even when occluded by the drawbridge, reasoning that two solid objects cannot occupy the same space at the same time. Similar results were obtained in a follow-up study for four-and-a-half-month-olds and even some three-and-a-half-month-olds (Baillargeon, 1987).

In many subsequent studies using the violation-of-expectation method, Baillargeon and others found results indicating that the knowledge of infants develops an impressive level of sophistication between 3½ and 12 months of age (Mareschal & Kaufman, 2012): infants learn to represent the height, location and solidity of hidden objects, they learn the support relations between objects placed next to each other or on top of each other, they represent the trajectories of objects and they can do basic maths (we will describe this study below).

The claims that infants have such sophisticated early abilities have not gone unchallenged. Is it possible that the looking behaviour of infants in violation-of-expectation studies has a simpler explanation that is based on perceptual aspects of the scene so that the assumption of rich knowledge is unwarranted? (See Box 4.2.) Several researchers have suggested such 'simpler' explanations for the drawbridge study. But why would infants look longer at the full 180 degree rotation, which they

BOX 4.2: RICH VERSUS LEAN INTERPRETATIONS

One of the major challenges for researchers who investigate infant cognition is to arrive at the correct interpretation of a particular pattern of performance in an experiment. Often results can be interpreted either as evidence of a sophisticated – albeit unconscious – analysis of events by the infant or as a less sophisticated, perceptually-driven response.

In a discussion paper, Haith (1998) gives an example of how specific results from an infancy test could be interpreted under the rich and the perceptual accounts. Three-month-old infants were seated in front of a video screen and were shown small attractive pictures, alternately on the left and the right side of the screen. Each picture was shown for 700 ms with a 1,000 ms interval between them. The researchers found that within one minute of training on this sequence the infants moved their eyes to anticipate the appearance of the next object on the screen either on the left or on the right side. In a follow-up study, the researchers showed that infants responded in the same way with a more complex sequence such as two pictures on the left followed by one picture on the right. In another study the infants' looking behaviour was disrupted when changing from a left-right to a left-left-right sequence.

Haith describes what a 'rich' interpretation of these results might look like, that is, one that attributes sophisticated cognitive abilities to the infants. The explanation would be that infants anticipate the next location of an object during the break between stimuli and must therefore have *represented* both the objects and the rule that governs the side of appearance (left-right or left-left-right) in their mind. Furthermore, in the left-left-right sequence they must have *counted* how many times the object occurred on the left (once or twice), implying that they have *symbolic representation*. Disruption of looking when the sequence was changed indicates *surprise* because the infants had *inferred* that the next object would always appear on the opposite side of the previous object, *reasoning* on the basis of the learned sequence and forming the *belief* that the sequence would continue. These skills appear to be *innate*, showing up so early in life, and could be explained with *adaptive evolution* to be able to predict future spatial locations, an advantage when escaping predators or when catching prey.

Haith criticises this rich interpretation because it is based on a limited set of data and on the assumption that the cognitive organisation of infants corresponds to that of adults. He argues, in contrast, that the looking data could merely show that a pattern of locations was detected, that expectations were formed, and that looking was disrupted when the learned pattern was changed. This disruption could be explained by the infant programming a looking action with an expected outcome that is not achieved – without needing to make recourse to concepts such as reasoning, inference, belief and surprise. Using terminology for infants that has a clear meaning in adult cognition suggests a similarity between infants and adults that might not be there. Furthermore, a rich explanation like that above does not provide any explanation for how the abilities to reason, infer etc. develop and change. Finally, postulating that these skills are innate and arise from evolutionary adaptation does not add anything to our understanding of how they function. At the same time such claims are very hard to disprove. Haith argues that the core questions to be asked about early abilities are how they unfold and how they depend on experience with the environment.

have seen during familiarisation, if this looking behaviour does not reflect surprise at a physically impossible event?

One possibility is that infants prefer the 180 degree rotation simply because it lasts longer than the 120 degree rotation, and infants like to look at things that are moving. Rivera, Wakeley and Langer (1999) tested this hypothesis by repeating the drawbridge study but without placing a block in the path of the drawbridge at test. This meant that, in their study, both the 120 degree rotation and the 180 degree rotation were possible events. They found that the infants still preferred to look at the 180 degree movement, just as in the original Baillargeon study. They concluded that infants' preference for this event could therefore not be taken as evidence of surprise at a physically impossible event but, rather, a simple preference for an event where the movement lasted longer. As such, the pattern of response in the original drawbridge study could not be taken as evidence for object permanence in these young infants.

Another criticism of the original drawbridge study was put forward by Bogartz, Shinskey and Schilling (2000). We saw in Chapter 1 that infants generally prefer to look at novel objects or scenes, and this is the basis for all of the looking time studies described in this chapter. However, under certain circumstances infants prefer to look at what is familiar to them instead of what is novel to them. This familiarity preference can occur during the first trials of a study when infants have not been fully familiarised with the stimuli, especially when these are perceptually rich and complex. Bogartz *et al.* argued that, in the drawbridge study, infants preferred the 180 degree rotation because they had not seen enough familiarisation trials and were therefore showing a familiarity preference.

These criticisms of the original account have, in turn, been criticised (see Mareschal & Kaufman, 2012), and it has become clear that looking time measures alone cannot answer the important question of by what age infants show object permanence. Researchers have therefore begun to use EEG (see Chapter 1) to study the neural processes underlying object permanence (Kaufman *et al.*, 2003).

The basis of these EEG studies is that adults show characteristic neural activation patterns in temporal cortex when keeping an image of a hidden object in mind. The questions asked by these researchers were: first, do infants also show specific brain activity associated with keeping an object in mind when it is no longer visible; and second, does this brain activity depend on whether the object continues to exist while hidden, as opposed to ceasing to exist?

Kaufman *et al.* tried to answer these questions by showing six-month-old infants either pictures of a ball that became gradually hidden by an occluder sliding in front of it or pictures of a ball that gradually disintegrated. In the former case, the object would be assumed to continue to exist behind the occluder, whereas in the latter case it ceases to exist. Kaufman *et al.* found that infants displayed the temporal cortical activation patterns that are characteristic of maintaining an object representation, but only in the occlusion condition and not in the disintegration condition. They concluded that infants at six months of age therefore maintained a representation of an object that was hidden from sight but continued to exist.

The A-not-B error revisited

We have seen that object permanence is present in infants much earlier than believed by Piaget. But why do infants not retrieve a hidden object if they are aware of its continued existence? Work on the A-not-B error can provide an answer to this question. Remember that this error describes the result that when an object is repeatedly hidden at a location A and then, in full view of the infant, is hidden at another location B, infants between 9 and 12 months of age continue to search for it in location A. Piaget argued that the infant has to learn that the object exists independently of the infant's own action towards this object and that a central aspect of cognitive development is to separate the self from the environment.

Further work on the A-not-B error has served to exclude some possible explanations. In order to see whether the fact that infants repeatedly reach to a location is important, infants just watched an object being hidden and retrieved at location

KEY TERMS

Executive functions
The system that controls
cognitive functions such
as planning and
executing actions. It is
linked to the prefrontal
areas of the brain.

A without reaching for it themselves. However, when the object was hidden at location B, infants still reached for A. This result rules out the explanation that infants merely persevere at a practised movement, and it also rules out Piaget's explanation that the reaching movement to A had become part of the object's identity.

Another possible explanation concerns infants' memory for the location. However, strikingly, Piaget already noted that infants still reach for location A when the object in location B is not covered at all! This happens as long as there is a cover at location A (Bremner & Knowles, 1984). Therefore, the error cannot be due to infants' memory limitations where they forget that the object is now hidden in location B.

An explanation that is based on brain development has been suggested by Diamond (1988). The frontal cortex is involved in planning and guiding actions (so-called **executive functions**). This part of the brain matures very slowly and is not fully developed until adolescence. Diamond argued that it is the immaturity of the frontal cortex that leads to the A-not-B error. According to her view, frontal cortex is responsible both for the maintenance of object representations and for the inhibition of incorrect responses. In order to succeed at the A-not-B task it is necessary to do both. In the immature cortex of infants these functions are not fully developed and, although the infants can do one or the other, they are incapable of doing them both together. They therefore cannot use their memory of the hidden object to suppress their search response at location A. This explanation is an advance on other theories in that it combines memory and perseveration accounts and bases them in what is known about infant brain development. However, as we have seen, infants also reach for B when they only watched the object at A without reaching for it, and Diamond's account cannot explain this result. This is because her account also relies on infants' inability to inhibit a previously learned response.

A more convincing explanation of the A-not-B error has been provided by Smith and Thelen (2003). They used the dynamic systems framework to explain how the real-time interactions between external factors and the internal state of the infants lead to the search error. According to their theory, the two hiding locations stand in competition with each other. When the experimenter repeatedly hides the object at location A this location becomes more highlighted because the visual cue is strengthened by the infant's memory of reaching there. The more A-trials there are the stronger this preference becomes. When then the object is hidden in location B the new visual cue competes with the previously established memory cue. Importantly, whereas the visual cue (hiding the object at location B) decays once the object is hidden, the memory cue retains its strength and eventually wins out – the infant reaches to location A.

This theory predicts that if infants are allowed to search without a delay, immediately after the object is hidden at location B, they should correctly search at B because the strong visual cue dominates the memory cue. This is exactly what happens (Wellman, Cross, Bartsch, & Harris, 1986). The theory also predicts that the error depends on the interaction of several aspects of the task, for example the attention-grabbing properties of the covers under which the object is hidden and of the hiding event, the delay between hiding and searching, and the number of trials where the object is hidden at location A. These predictions appear to be borne out by many experiments (Smith & Thelen, 2003). Another prediction is that infants should search correctly if searching at A is made different from searching at B, because the memory of the A event then exerts less influence over the new B event.

In one study (Smith, Thelen, Titzer, & McLin, 1999), infants were sitting during the A trials and were then stood up for the B trial (see the photo, right). In this case, even eight- and ten-month-olds searched correctly at B, performing as if they were four months older. Similar results were found when infants wore weighted wrist bands either for the A or the B trials: making the bodily experience of reaching different with light vs. heavy arms made the A and B trials sufficiently different that ten-month-olds searched at the correct B location.

An infant in Smith *et al.*'s (1999) study, sitting for an A trial (left) and standing for a B trial (right). This change in posture causes younger infants to search as 12-month-old infants do.

It is clear that this dynamic systems view is fundamentally different from Piaget's explanation of the infant not representing the object as separate from the action towards it. In the dynamic systems view the action of the infant is the outcome of a combination of the perceptual cues (what the covers look like, how the hiding action was performed), the past actions of the infant, the similarity of past to present bodily experience and the delay between hiding the object and reaching for it. Developmental change in this view emerges from a re-weighting of the importance of cues: 12-month-old infants may be better able to sustain the perceptual cue of the object being hidden at location B so that the previous embodied memories for location A do not over-ride them as easily. Again, this ability depends on the cues in the scene. When the A-not-B task is done in a sandbox where no lids for the two hiding locations are visible, even two-year-olds still make the error (Butler, Berthier, & Clifton, 2002).

It appears that a dynamic systems view of the A-not-B error not only explains its origins, but also successfully predicts how infants' successes and failures in this task can be manipulated by changing one or several of many interacting factors in the environment and in the infant's prior experience.

4.3 UNDERSTANDING NUMEROSITY

Since Baillargeon's drawbridge study many violation-of-expectation studies have explored young infants' relatively sophisticated knowledge of objects and events. Another well-known study investigated infants' ability to represent small numbers precisely and to add and subtract.

In this study (Wynn, 1992) infants first saw an empty stage; then a hand appeared and placed a Mickey Mouse doll on the stage. Next, a screen rotated up to hide the doll. The hand then appeared again and placed a second doll behind the screen. When the screen then dropped it revealed either one or two Mickey Mouse dolls (Figure 4.7). Wynn found that the infants looked significantly longer at the impossible event (one doll). In a similar 'subtraction' condition, two dolls were placed on the stage before the screen came up, a hand removed one of the dolls, and the lowered screen then revealed either one or two dolls. Here, infants as well looked significantly longer at the impossible event (two dolls). Wynn concluded from her results that five-month-old infants could compute simple arithmetic operations such as $1+1 = 2$ and $2-1 = 1$.

To exclude the possibility that infants' number sense is only approximate and distinguished between small and large numbers, she conducted a follow-up study in

Figure 4.7
The addition and subtraction events used in Wynn's (1992) study. Reproduced with permission from Wynn (1992). Copyright © 1992 Nature Publishing.

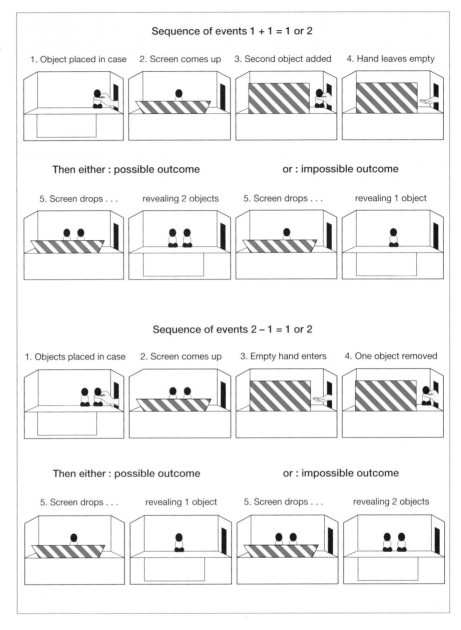

which four-month-old infants who saw the 1+1 event then saw two or three dolls in the test phase. Wynn found that the infants looked longer at the display with three dolls, and she concluded that number representations are indeed precise and infants expect 1+1 to be precisely two and not three.

As with the drawbridge study, this 'maths' study has led to much discussion on the interpretation of the results: the main question again is whether there is a purely perceptual explanation for these results that makes it unnecessary to postulate

BOX 4.3: REPLICATION

When researchers report their work in scientific publications, an important part of this report is an accurate description of how the study was done – the number, age and other relevant details of the participants, the stimuli used, the procedure of the experiment. This description is meant to allow other researchers to do the same study again to see if they find the same results. Such replication is an important part in the verification of scientific findings.

mathematical knowledge in these young infants. Some authors have argued that two dolls have together a larger surface area and more contour lines than one doll, and it could be these perceptual changes that drive looking behaviour. Indeed, when such visual differences are controlled for in addition and subtraction studies, infants' looking behaviour did not show sensitivity to number (Clearfield & Mix, 2001; Feigenson, Carey, & Spelke, 2002). In these cases six-month-old infants can discriminate 8 from 16 and 16 from 32, but not 1 from 2 or even 8 from 12 (Xu & Spelke, 2000; Xu, Spelke, & Goddard, 2005). Evidence for other factors being responsible come also from failures to replicate the original Wynn study (Wakeley, Rivera, & Langer, 2000).

4.4 CORE KNOWLEDGE

These results suggesting that even very young children have sophisticated knowledge of the world have led some researchers to argue that some aspects of knowledge are innate in the form of **core knowledge** (Spelke & Kinzler, 2007). Core knowledge describes evolved task-specific cognitive systems for certain domains of knowledge that are largely unique to humans. The domains that have been argued to encompass core knowledge are the physical properties of objects, actions, number and space. This core knowledge is assumed to form the basis of more advanced learning in each of these domains, before eventually the acquisition of language serves to integrate knowledge across domains (Spelke, 2003). Development of knowledge, in this view, is linked more to maturation than to experience and is relatively independent from the environment (Spelke, 1998).

This view of innate early knowledge is, of course, diametrically opposed to the views of Piaget who believed that all knowledge is constructed on the basis of simple reflexes. And indeed there has been much criticism of this approach. One criticism arises from the debate discussed above: it may not be warranted to interpret looking time experiments as showing that infants possess sophisticated knowledge and the ability to reason (Haith, 1998). Another criticism addresses the claim that environmental input is not important for cognitive development (Newcombe, 2002). The neuroconstructivist and dynamic systems approaches that we discussed in Chapter 2 make this point forcefully, and there is a lot of experimental evidence supporting these positions (Newcombe, 2002). In fact, as we have seen in Chapter 2, the brain itself is shaped by specific experiences with the environment, and these changes in the brain enable cognitive development to proceed.

KEY TERMS

Core knowledge
The idea that certain aspects of knowledge are innate.

4.5 SUMMARY

We have seen that research on infant cognitive development is a very active field, helped by the development of different new methodologies such as looking time measures, eye tracking and EEG. We have also seen that Piaget's legacy looms large over the study of cognitive development, more than three decades after his death. This legacy manifests itself in two distinct ways: on the one hand the findings that infants have certain abilities much earlier than he thought, and that some of infants' early abilities appear rather sophisticated, have led some researchers to reject his theories and adopt a stance that lies at the opposite extreme from his: instead of believing that all knowledge is constructed on the basis of simple reflexes, these researchers argue that sophisticated knowledge in a range of domains is innate in the form of core knowledge. On the other hand, other researchers have built upon Piaget's work by elaborating on his basic assumptions and improving the theoretical framework upon which they are built in the form of neo-constructivist and dynamic systems views (see Newcombe, 2011). This work has attempted to characterise more precisely how different environmental and internal factors interact in the gradual constructions of knowledge.

One might think that this division in the field of early cognitive development is disheartening – how can it be that many decades of research on infant cognitive development have not led to a consensus about how development proceeds and from where it starts? However, we think that far from being downbeat about this state of affairs it is instead cause for optimism for at least two reasons. First, theoretical debate serves far better to advance science than a broad consensus. If different theories about development make different predictions about what infants know and how they change, then this is a strong reason to go and find out. In this way, research and our knowledge of infants are propelled forward far more than if everyone agreed on their knowledge and abilities. Second, these debates are invaluable in refining scientific method: it has become very clear that there is a big difference between the data obtained in an experiment and the interpretation of these data. While two researchers with different theoretical views will likely agree that the data obtained in a specific study are valid, they will nevertheless disagree strongly on what these data mean. We saw this clearly in Haith's (1998) distinction between 'rich' and 'perceptual' interpretations and in the vigorous debate surrounding the 'drawbridge' studies. There is a big difference between saying 'five-month-old infants who have been familiarised on a drawbridge rotating 180 degrees then look longer at the bridge rotating 180 degrees than 120 degrees when a block has been placed in its path' and saying 'five-month-old infants can reason about hidden objects and they know that two objects cannot occupy the same space, and they are surprised if this expectation is violated'. While both may be true, the latter statement does not follow directly from the former; instead more studies, both replications and variations, and ideally others with different methodologies (such as EEG), are needed to exclude alternative explanations and to provide converging evidence for the theoretical claim.

While this chapter has reviewed what we know about infant categorisation, object knowledge and knowledge of numbers, we hope that we have also made clear these more general points about how to study infants and what insights to draw from the data obtained in these studies.

FURTHER READING

Gelman, S. A., & Meyer, M. (2010). Child categorization. *Wiley Interdisciplinary Reviews: Cognitive Science, 2*(1), 95–105.

Newcombe, N. S. (2002). The nativist-empiricist controversy in the context of recent research on spatial and quantitative development. *Psychological Science, 13*(5), 395–401.

Quinn, P. C. (2011). Born to categorize. In U. Goswami (Ed.), *Wiley-Blackwell handbook of childhood cognitive development,* 2nd edition (pp. 129–152). Oxford: Wiley-Blackwell.

ESSAY QUESTIONS

1. What is the role of language in the formation of categories by infants and toddlers?
2. Critically discuss the use of looking time measures to assess young infants' cognitive abilities.
3. What is the A-not-B-error and why does it occur in infant development?
4. Discuss the evidence for and against early mathematical abilities in infants.

CHAPTER 5

CONTENTS

Early language development

5

After reading this chapter you will be able to

- explain why language development begins even before babies are born
- describe how infants learn to discriminate the phonemes of their language community
- describe the main stages of infant babbling and understand why infants do not sound like adults
- explain what is meant by the social context of early language development and why this context is important for learning the meaning of first words
- describe how infants learn to pick out words from the speech stream
- explain how the growth of infant's vocabulary can be measured
- explain what experimental studies have revealed about infant's ability to learn new vocabulary.

As we saw in Chapter 3 infants are able to hear before they are born and they are already beginning to learn about familiar sounds. This ability was first demonstrated in a pioneering study carried out by DeCasper and Spence (DeCasper & Spence, 1986).

5.1 DEVELOPMENT OF SPEECH PERCEPTION

In the DeCasper and Spence study, 12 pregnant women were asked to read a particular passage from a number of different stories, the most well known of which was *The Cat in the Hat*. All of the chosen stories had a strong rhythmic structure and mothers were asked to read them twice a day for the last six weeks before their babies were due. Two or three days after birth, the babies were tested with a special dummy that was wired up to record the intensity of their sucking. The babies sucked for two minutes so that the researchers could get a baseline for each baby – since babies vary in the amount that they suck – and then they were played either the passage from *The Cat in the Hat* or another passage that they had not heard before. Changes in the rate of sucking turned a tape recorder on and off so the more babies sucked the more they heard a particular passage. The babies who were presented with the familiar passage increased their rate of sucking whereas babies who heard an unfamiliar passage did not. It is important to note that this difference in response to the two passages occurred even when babies heard the passage being read by another woman, rather than their mother. This means that the babies were recognising something about the passage itself rather than something about their mother's voice.

Having shown that newborn babies could recognise a spoken passage that they had heard before birth, the next step was to test babies before they were born. This was what happened in an ingenious study of French-speaking women who were in the thirty-fifth week of their pregnancy (DeCasper, Lecanuet, Busnel, Granier-Deferre, & Maugeais, 1994). They were asked to recite a rhyme three times every day for four weeks. Half the mothers recited a rhyme called *La Poulette* (The Chick) while the other half recited a rhyme called *Le Petit Crapaud* (The Little Toad). After four weeks the two rhymes – spoken by another woman – were played to the foetus using a speaker placed 20 centimetres above the mother's abdomen and level with the foetus' head. Since the mother's own reaction to the two rhymes might have influenced her baby, she listened to music through headphones while the testing was carried out.

Foetal reaction to the two passages was measured by monitoring heartbeat. For each baby, heart rate while a rhyme was being played was compared to their baseline heart rate. The idea was that if a baby responded to a rhyme there would be a change in heart rate. There was a clear difference between the familiar and unfamiliar rhymes, with the familiar rhyme producing a significantly greater change in heart rate: there was no significant change in heart rate when the unfamiliar rhyme was played but there was a significant decrease in heart rate to the familiar rhyme. This finding confirmed the view that babies were learning to recognise aspects of spoken language before birth.

Learning about prosodic patterns

Once babies are born they rapidly begin to learn much more about the language that people are speaking around them. It has been known for some time that newborn babies prefer the human voice to other sounds and, at a few days old, will suck on an artificial nipple to hear a recorded human voice but will not to hear music or a rhythmic non-speech sound (DeCasper & Fifer, 1980). More recently it has become clear that babies rapidly develop a specific preference for the language (or languages) being spoken around them. For example, four-day-old French infants can discriminate between French and Russian and showed a preference for French (Mehler, Jusczyk, Dehaene-Lambertz, Dupoux, & Nazzi, 1994).

In the early weeks, babies are tuning into the prosodic (i.e. rhythmical) properties of a particular language and this is the basis on which they are able to distinguish one language from another (Christophe & Morton, 1998). French and Russian have rather different **prosodic patterns** as do English and Japanese. We have seen that babies can distinguish French from Russian. Christophe and Morton showed that at two months English babies could distinguish between English and Japanese. Critically, however, at the same age babies could not distinguish between English and Dutch where the prosodic pattern is very similar. The characteristic prosodic patterns of a particular language continue to be an important aspect of speech perception as babies become increasingly familiar with the patterns that characterise their mother tongue. Nine-month-old English infants prefer to listen to words that follow the stress pattern occurring most frequently in English (Jusczyk, Cutler, & Redanz, 1993).

Phoneme discrimination

Another key aspect of speech perception is the ability to discriminate speech sounds or phonemes. Different languages contain different phonemes so it is important that babies soon learn the phonemes used in their language community. In a pioneering study, using the sucking paradigm described earlier, Eimas and his colleagues (Eimas, Siqueland, Jusczyk, & Vogorito, 1971) presented babies aged from one to four months with a single sound /pa/. When they first heard /pa/ babies increased their rate of sucking in order to hear this new sound. Then, as it became familiar, their sucking rate decreased. Once the babies were familiar with /pa/, a new but similar sound was played. For half the babies the new sound was a different English phoneme, /ba/. The other babies heard a sound that differed acoustically from the original by an equal amount but did not cross the phoneme boundary. (In other words it would still be heard as /pa/ by an English-speaking adult.) The babies in the first group, who heard /ba/, started to suck rapidly again in order to hear the new sound but the second group did not increase their rate of sucking suggesting that, just like an adult, they heard the 'new' sound as similar to the original one.

Many subsequent studies have gone on to show that infants of one month or less are able to discriminate phonemes on the basis of many different kinds of phonetic contrast including place of articulation (/p/, /t/, /k/), manner of articulation (/d//n/, /l/ and between vowel pairs such as /a/ and /i/ or /i/ and /u/). In fact, newborn babies have the potential to make any phonemic discrimination. This potential is clearly important because it means that an infant will be able to learn about the phonemes in any language being spoken in the local community.

The process of learning about the phonemes in a particular language takes place over the first few months of life. Ironically the effect of this learning process is that babies gradually lose the ability to discriminate phonemes that do not appear in the language or languages spoken in the local community. Babies remain excellent at discriminating phonemes in their native language (or languages) but they are often unable to hear phonemic distinctions that occur in other languages. This is especially true if a phoneme boundary in a new language is incompatible with that of a phoneme boundary in the mother tongue. For example, in English, /r/ and /l/ are two different phonemes, but in Japanese both sounds are variants of a single phoneme. This is why Japanese people who learn English as adults often have great difficulty in hearing the difference between these two sounds.

The reason why speakers of a particular language are not aware of phonetic contrasts that occur within a particular phoneme boundary is that, for a very good reason, the brain tends to group similar speech sounds together. This is because there is very wide acoustic variation in the way in which different speakers pronounce particular phonemes and also variation within an individual speaker from one utterance to another. So, in order to identify a phoneme correctly, infants have to learn to group together all variants of a single phoneme and to disregard variations

KEY TERMS

Phonemes
The smallest sound categories in speech in any given language that serve to distinguish one word from another.

in speech sounds that are not phonemically significant in the language of their speech community. In other words, they have to engage in a process of 'learning by forgetting' (Mehler & Dupoux, 1994).

Selective sensitivity to the particular phonemes present in a language – and loss of sensitivity to contrasts that do not distinguish phonemes – develops over the first year of life. In a seminal study phoneme discrimination in groups of babies from three different monolingual speech communities were compared (Werker & Tees, 1984). The languages spoken in the three communities were English, Hindi (Indian) and Salish (North American Indian). Werker and Tees found that at six months babies who had heard only English could distinguish equally well between phoneme pairs in all three languages. However, at eight months infants showed less ability to discriminate phonemic contrasts that occurred either in Hindi or Salish. At one year of age, babies who had heard only English remained completely accurate at distinguishing between English phoneme pairs but were only at chance level in discriminating phonemes that were specific to the other two languages. By contrast, babies who had heard only Salish remained completely accurate with Salish phonemes and babies who had heard only Hindi remained completely accurate with Hindi phonemes.

This pattern of results was replicated in a longitudinal study with monolingual English babies where the ability of babies to discriminate non-English phonemes had declined to adult level by 12 months of age (Werker, Gilbert, Humphreys, & Tees, 1981). Interestingly, babies and adults retain the ability to distinguish contrasts that do not overlap with those of their mother tongue. For example the 'clicks' in Zulu do not involve the same phonetic contrasts as English and so there is no possible source of interference between the perception of clicks and the perception of English phonemic boundaries. Thus they continue to be discriminated by monolingual English speakers of all ages (Best, McRoberts, & Sithole, 1988).

5.2 DEVELOPMENT OF BABBLING

Although infants rapidly become familiar with the phonemes of their language community, it takes several years before they can accurately produce all these different phonemes. Over the first year of life important developments take place as babies gain increasing control over the sounds that they are able to produce.

The development of infant vocal productions – babbling – is usually divided into stages (Oller, 1980). Stage 1 covers the period from zero to two months and is known as reflexive vocalisation. At this very early stage the infant makes sounds to express discomfort and distress as well as vegetative sounds that relate to physical activity or essential bodily functions. By Stage 2 (two to four months), babies begin to use sounds for more directly communicative purposes. They coo and laugh when people are talking to them or smiling. These cooing and laughing sounds are initially produced singly but may then appear in sequence. Sustained laughter emerges around four months. As babies progress through this second stage, the primitive vegetative sounds gradually disappear and the frequency of crying falls. Vowel sounds become more varied.

Even at this early stage babies are capable of imitating aspects of adult vocalisations (Papousek & Papousek, 1989). Between the ages of two and five months the proportion of infant vocalisations that matched immediately preceding maternal vocalisations increased across the age range from 27 per cent at two months to 43 per cent at five months. The most common basis for matching was pitch but babies also became increasingly likely to match falling or rising-falling patterns (pitch contours) in mothers' vocalisations.

Vocal play begins in stage 3, covering the period from four to seven months. During this time babies begin to gain increasing control of the articulation of the larynx and the mouth. They experiment with both the loudness and pitch of their vocalisations and the position of their tongue. This gradually allows the production of adult-like vowels and some of the features of adult-like consonants.

In order to understand why babies' vocalisations sound distinctively different from those of an adult, we need to look at differences between the vocal tract of infants and that of adults. The baby's vocal tract is not simply a miniature version of the adult tract. Indeed, up the age of three months, the infant vocal tract resembles the vocal tract of a primate more closely than that of an adult human (see Figure 5.1). The larynx (voice box) is high up so that the epiglottis nearly touches the soft palate at the back of the mouth. The baby's tongue is relatively large, nearly filling the oral cavity, while the pharyngeal cavity is very short compared to that of an adult, allowing little room for the back portion of the tongue to be manipulated. This allows the newborn infant to make the strong piston-like movements essential for sucking rather than the range of complex tongue movements required for speech.

From the age of four months, the anatomy of the vocal tract gradually changes towards the adult form. At the same time important neural maturation occurs in the brain between three and nine months that allows the baby to develop increasing control over the fine motor movements that are essential to produce the full range of speech sounds. This is evident in the increasing range of sounds that are produced from the age of four months when vocal play first begins.

KEY TERMS

Larynx
Part of the vocal tract, it is involved in breathing and sound production. Commonly known as the 'voice box'.

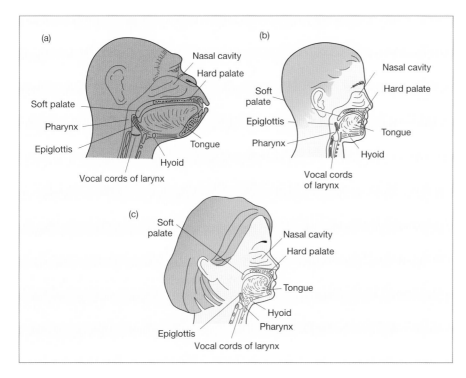

Figure 5.1
Cross section of the heads of (a) an adult chimpanzee, (b) an infant, and (c) an adult human.
From Liebermann (1992), reproduced with permission from Cambridge University Press.

KEY TERMS

Canonical babbling
Babbling that begins at around six months, and consists of recognisable syllables composed of a consonant sound and a vowel.

Reduplicated babbling
Babbling that begins at around eight months, and consists of repetitions of the same sound.

Stage 4 begins at around six months when babies first begin to produce recognisable syllables, composed of a consonant sound and a vowel. Very early sounds include /da/ and /ba/. Oller (1980) describes this stage as **canonical babbling** and it appears quite suddenly. A little later, at around eight months, babies begin to produce **reduplicated babbling** in which the same sound is repeated as in 'da-da' and 'ba-ba'. Around 11 months there is another change as babies become capable of what Oller calls variegated babbling. As this name suggests, at this final stage of babbling, babies begin to follow one sound with another sound that differs from it in some way. For example, babies may produce such combinations as 'ba-da' or 'da-de'.

One question that is often asked about babies' early speech sounds is whether they correspond to the speech sounds that the baby hears in particular language communities. We have already seen that, over the first year of life, babies develop increasing sensitivity to the phonemes present in their language community. Therefore we might expect infants' production of speech sounds to be affected by the language or languages they have been listening to. A study of the types of syllables produced by children in the later babbling period, who were growing up in different language communities (Vihman, 1992), found that the six most frequently occurring syllables (in order of frequency) were 'da', 'ba', 'wa', 'de', 'ha' and 'he'. These syllables were largely independent of the phonology of the language spoken by the parents. For example, French babies produced the /ha/ syllable even though French does not contain the /h/ phoneme. This points to a strong biological influence on phonological development.

However, children's experience also plays a role in shaping the sounds that are produced during babbling. A study of infants in Canada (Rvachew, Abdulsalam, Mattock, & Polka, 2008) compared the emergence of particular vowels among infants aged between 8 and 18 months who were growing up in either an English-speaking or French-speaking community. Vowels such as [a], [i] and [u] are pronounced rather differently in French and English, which is why non-native speakers of English often find it difficult to emulate the pronunciation of a native speaker of French and vice versa. The acoustic parameters of the infants' production of key vowels was analysed and native adult speakers also made judgements about the sounds. Two findings are of note. First, over the age range of the infants studied, there were notable changes in the quality of the sounds produced with vowels becoming more vowel-like with age. Second, there were differences in the characteristics of the vowels produced by infants according to the language they heard at home. In other words, infants growing up in a French-speaking community produced vowels that were typically French whereas infants growing up in an English-speaking community produced more typically English vowels. Interestingly, some differences were evident even in the youngest infants.

Abnormal patterns in early babbling can indicate specific problems. Children who are born with profound hearing loss do not develop canonical babbling within the first year of life; and the appearance of canonical babbling after ten months in child with normal hearing is a strong predictor of later language difficulties (Oller & Eilers, 1988).

5.3 THE SOCIAL CONTEXT OF EARLY LANGUAGE DEVELOPMENT

The social context in which children hear people talking has an important role to play in the way that young children first begin to understand and use language. Infants regularly play games such as 'peek-a-boo' and 'give-and-take' with their caretakers and they take part in a regular pattern of caretaking routines such as eating, bath time or nappy changing. Identical actions are repeated many times over and the words and phrases used by the adult become a consistent part of these games and routines.

Over 30 years ago Jerome Bruner first highlighted the importance of games and routines for early language development (Bruner, 1975). He pointed out that babies encounter language in a highly familiar social context because people talk to them about familiar events and objects. Infants' growing social competence allows them to remember and predict the familiar social events or routines – nappy changing, bath time, meal times, games of peek-a-boo – that occur day after day. According to Bruner, this developing knowledge of the social repertoire supports infants in building up insights into the meaning of the language that adults use as part of these routines.

This view is very widely accepted now in psychology but at the time Bruner's proposal was seen as running counter to the prevailing view that acquiring language was a unique ability, underpinned by innate abilities. This latter view of language acquisition – **linguistic nativism** – was the one advocated by the highly influential linguist Noam Chomsky. In a series of important books and articles, Chomsky set out the view that children's capacity to language was largely driven by internal factors. We say more about the debate between linguistic nativism and other theories in Chapter 9 (see 9.1).

The strong influence of the prevailing view of linguistic nativism can be seen in the way that Bruner developed his theory since there are two, rather different, versions of Bruner's theory. In the earlier version (Bruner 1975), he proposed a very close link indeed between the form of social routines and the form of language. However, in a later version (Bruner, 1983), he argued that there was *not* a direct correspondence between the structure of language and that of social routines. The reason for this change in Bruner's theory was the recognition that there is an important distinction between two aspects of language development. Social routines are important because they provide young children with a context for learning the meaning of words. However, they do not provide a context for learning the morphology and syntax of language since these aspects are not mirrored in social routines.

Morphology is the part of language concerned with the modification of individual words. For example, morphological rules determine how singular nouns are made plural (e.g. ship – ships; man – men) and how the tense of verbs is modified (e.g. I run, I am running, I ran). Syntax is concerned with the way in which individual words are combined into phrases and clauses. Bruner was correct in arguing that the way syntactic and morphological rules operate in language is not at all related to the structure of social interaction or other non-linguistic information. For example, there is nothing about the *meaning* of a noun that determines whether it will have regular plural (shoe – shoes) or an irregular plural (mouse – mice). So, looking for non-linguistic regularities in the world will not help the child at all in learning how to

KEY TERMS

Linguistic nativism
The view that children's capacity for language is largely driven by internal factors.

Morphology
The form and structure of words in a language, especially the consistent patterns that may be observed and classified.

BOX 5.1: AN EXAMPLE OF THE IMPORTANCE OF SOCIAL KNOWLEDGE IN EARLY LANGUAGE LEARNING

This example of the way that a baby's familiarity with a social routine can pave the way for the very beginning of language understanding comes from the following diary extract (Harris, 1996).

Francesca always lay on a changing-table in her bedroom while her nappy was changed. From about three months of age, when Francesca had her new nappy on and her clothes re-fastened, her mother would take her by the hands and ask 'Are you ready?' Then she would gently pull Francesca up into a sitting position. When Francesca was four months old, her mother noticed that she would start to lift her head from the changing-table when her mother asked 'Are you ready?' What was striking was that Francesca did not try to lift her head as soon as her mother took hold of her hands but actually waited for the crucial question. At first, Francesca would try to lift her head only when her mother asked the question in the specific context of nappy changing. However, one month later, Francesca's understanding had increased so that she responded both when her father asked the question and in other situations. Indeed the whole routine had developed into a game in which Francesca lay on her back while her mother or father held her hands. She would look intently up at her parent's face and then attempt to pull herself up as soon as she heard 'Are you ready?' This game was repeated several times on each occasion to the mutual delight of Francesca and her parents.

It is clear from this example that Francesca's understanding of 'Are you ready?' grew directly out of the routine that took place with her mother at the end of a nappy changing session. By the time that Francesca was four months old she had become sufficiently familiar with the routine to be able to predict what came next. She was then able to associate the question 'Are you ready?' with being raised into a sitting position and so to anticipate this event by raising her own head from the changing-table when she heard her mother ask the familiar question.

form noun plurals correctly. However, there is strong evidence about the importance of social knowledge in early language learning, especially as children begin to discover the meaning of words. You see an example in Box 5.1

Development of joint attention

One key aspect of social interaction that supports early language development is **joint attention**. In the earliest months of life, visual attention between infant and parent occurs mainly in face-to-face dyadic interactions. At around six months, however, face-to-face interactions begin to decrease as the infant becomes increasingly interested in objects or events in the environment. This marks the beginning of triadic interaction involving parent, child and the environment and this, in turn, affords an opportunity for joint attention to the external world. Butterworth saw this development of joint attention as 'a precondition for the acquisition and use of language' (Butterworth, 2001).

The ability to co-ordinate visual attention between the environment and a communicative partner may take a child many months to master. It is not until 18 months of age that the great majority of hearing children show evidence of such co-ordinated joint attention (Bakeman & Adamson, 1984). Joint attention is often achieved with younger children but this primarily occurs because adults follow the child's focus of attention (Bakeman & Adamson, 1984; Harris, 1992).

Joint attention enables parent and child to focus on the same objects and activities and this supports the learning of new words.

Conversations with young children who are in the early stages of learning to talk tend to revolve around the focus of joint attention. Much research has shown that that when mothers are interacting with their young child they often label the focus of the child's interest, thus ensuring that the 'label' has a salient nonverbal context for the child. Such 'contingent naming' presents the child with an opportunity to make a link between an object and its label (Baldwin & Markman, 1989; Harris, Jones, Brookes, & Grant, 1986).

Pointing provides a gestural way of sharing joint attention and it appears to be an important marker of the development of shared understanding. A longitudinal study followed both the emergence of pointing and the early understanding of words in a group of children (Harris, Barlow-Brown, & Chasin, 1995). The age at which children first pointed was highly correlated with the age at which they first showed signs of understanding the names of objects. For example, the first object name that Francesca understood was 'nose'. She began by touching the nose on a toy koala when asked and then, the following day, she was asked 'Where's mummy's nose?' and 'Where's daddy's nose?' Francesca reached out and touched her parents' noses. This first occurred when she was just over nine months old. The same day she pointed at a plant in the conservatory. This was the first time that she pointed. This suggests that referring to objects in the world by pointing at them and understanding that they have names are very closely interlinked processes that may well have a common origin.

Francesca pointing.

What adults point at also seems to be important. Children as young as ten months of age spend significantly longer looking at novel objects when they are pointed at than when they are merely presented to the child without pointing. When an object is labelled, as well as being pointed to, the amount of looking is even greater, suggesting that the young child is predisposed to look at objects that are singled out both through pointing and through the use of an accompanying verbal label (Baldwin & Markman, 1989).

5.4 EARLY VOCABULARY: UNDERSTANDING WORDS

Identifying word boundaries

Although parents often pay great attention to the point at which their child first starts to say words the process of learning about words begins some months before as children begin to understand something about the meaning of words. The first signs of understanding usually occurs at around seven or eight months and the first words to be understood are typically the child's own name and the name of other family members – notably 'mummy' and 'daddy' and often the family pet – and familiar objects such as 'clock', 'drink' and 'teddy' (Harris, Yeeles, Chasin, & Oakley, 1995).

In order for children to begin to learn about words there are a number of skills they need. As we saw in the previous section, one important skill is the ability to recognise speech sounds. Equally important for word learning are the ability to recognise the boundaries of words, the ability to integrate information across modalities and the development of social understanding.

Detecting word boundaries

As competent language users it is all too easy to forget that when people talk one word is not neatly separated from the next. Instead people produce a stream of sounds where the boundaries of words are not immediately obvious. If you hear someone speaking an unfamiliar language this problem becomes immediately apparent. What you hear is a long stream of sounds with no obvious breaks between them.

The first researcher to investigate how young infants might learn to segment the speech stream and so detect the boundaries of words was Jusczyk. His studies made use of a head-turning procedure (Jusczyk & Aslin, 1995) in which infant responses to auditory stimuli were assessed by recording the amount of time they turn their head towards the source of a sound. In this first study the sound was a word. Four different words were used, 'feet', 'bike', 'cup' and 'dog'. Half the infants heard the first two and the other half heard the second two. Jusczyk and Aslin initially tested seven-and-a-half-month-old infants and, in the familiarisation phase of the study, they presented each of the two words by presenting them alternately until they had

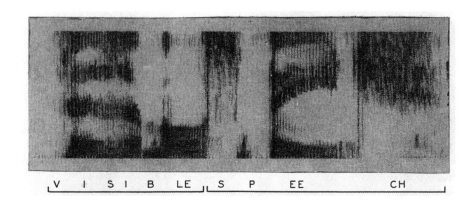

A spectrogram of the words 'visible speech' being spoken.

become familiar. (Familiarity was measured using a variation of the habituation technique described in Chapter 1.) Then, in the test phase, four short passages were played. These had all been recorded by the same female speaker to ensure that were as similar as possible. Each passage contained several mentions of one of the target words. For example, the 'cup' passage was as follows:

> The cup was bright and shiny
> A clown drank from the red cup
> The other one picked up the big cup
> His cup was filled with milk
> Meg put her cup back on the table
> Some milk from your cup spilled on the table

Since each infant heard all four passages but had only heard two target words in the familiarisation phase, two of these passages contained a familiar word and two did not. The prediction was that infants would listen longer to the passages containing the familiar word and this proved to be the case, thus demonstrating that the infants had been able to recognise the target words in the passages.

In a second experiment Jusczyk and Aslin used an identical procedure and stimulus set to test the abilities of six-month-olds. They did this because they wanted to find out whether slightly younger infants would show the same ability to recognise a familiar word in a passage. Interestingly they found that the younger infants did not listen significantly more to the passages containing the target words, showing that this important skill had developed between the ages of six and seven and a half months. It turns out that this age is also significant when we look at the evidence about when infants first begin to understand their first words.

Subsequent research by Jusczyk (Johnson & Jusczyk, 2001) went on to show what kind of information children used in picking out word boundaries. This study focused on two particular cues, syllable stress and transitional probabilities. In English the stress pattern within words is variable. Compare, for example, 'cushion' and 'belong'. You say **cu**shion (with stress on the first syllable) but be**long** (with stress on the second syllable). It turns out that stress patterns are quite a good guide to word boundaries because in conversational English around 90 per cent of content words (i.e. nouns, adjectives, verbs and adverbs) have stress on the first syllable, like cushion. We saw in 5.2 that babies are very sensitive to stress patterns in a particular language and that they can tell one language from another on the basis of its rhythmical structure. We might therefore expect that some of the same information might be useful for picking out words from the speech stream.

The other cue, transitional probability, relies on infants being able to detect regularly occurring patterns. This kind of learning is often called **statistical learning**. The Johnson and Jusczyk study used invented words and a two-phase design (as in Jusczyk and Aslin, 1995). The invented words were made up from 12 syllables that were combined into four sequences to give *pakibu, tibodu, golatu* and *daropi*. In the familiarisation phase, eight-month-old infants listened to the 'words' repeated over and over in random order for three minutes, with no pauses between them. Because the order of the 'words' was randomised infants heard many different syllable sequences. However, the three-syllable sequences that made up a word were heard more often than any other. For example, bu-go-la, would be heard only when *pakibu* came immediately before *golatu*.

KEY TERMS

Statistical learning
The ability to detect regularly occurring patterns in the environment.

In the test phase, the babies were presented with all the words that they had heard and also with part-words – like *bugalo* – formed by recombining syllables from two different words. The only difference between the words and part words was that the syllable sequence of the words had occurred much more frequently. If babies had been able to engage in statistical learning they should have responded differently to the words and part words. This proved to be the case. However, this time babies spent longer listening to the part-words with which they were less familiar.

In a second experiment, Johnson and Jusczyk (2001) compared babies' sensitivity to transitional probabilities with their sensitivity to stress patterns. You can think of sensitivity to stress patterns as another case of statistical learning. Given that infants are clearly capable of such learning it seemed likely that they would respond to stress patterns as well as transitional probabilities.

The methodology of the second study was identical to the first except that whenever a part-word was presented there was stress on the first syllable. The addition of stress in the part-words brought about a significant change in the infants' behaviour. During the test phase they now listened longer to words than to part-words – the opposite of the pattern found in the first study. Remember that infants listened more to unfamiliar stimuli: this suggests that they now perceived the part-words as more familiar. Johnson and Jusczyk concluded that prosodic speech cues such as stress are more important than transitional probabilities in the detection of word boundaries.

Developing understanding

As we have already noted, most children begin to develop their understanding of words some month before they say their first words. Charting the development of vocabulary understanding can be problematic because finding out which words a child knows something about is much more difficult than recording what they say.

There are two rather different sources of information about how children begin to develop an understanding of words. Historically the first line of evidence about developments in the number of words that children can understand came from parental reports. These continue to be an important source of information for researchers but, more recently, experimental studies have become increasingly important for discovering more about the way in which children learn about words.

Parental reports of early vocabulary development

Not surprisingly, parents vary considerably in the accuracy with which they observe and report their children's growing vocabulary knowledge. The reliability of parental reports can be considerably improved through use of a structured questionnaire containing a checklist of the words that a young child might understand. Two widely used checklists make up *The MacArthur Communicative Development Inventories* (Fenson *et al.*, 1990) or CDI as it is more commonly known. The checklists have been used extensively to gather data about early language development from 8 months to 28 months initially in English and now in many other languages.

The CDI has two scales. The Infant Scale covers the period from 8 to 16 months. The Toddler Scale goes from 16 to 28 months. The norms for the CDI were derived from a sample of over 1,700 children living in three different places in the United States and so they provide good evidence about normal language development. Figure 5.2 shows the average number of words understood by boys and girls between 8 and 16 months. The number of words shown as being understood between eight and ten months may well be an over estimate since it is often difficult to decide whether a young child really understands a word or expression or is merely responding to a whole situation. However, two patterns in the development of early comprehension vocabulary are clear. First, girls were generally ahead of boys in the number of words they could understand and they showed a small but statistically significant advantage over boys. Second, both boys and girls showed a similar pattern of development with the number of words understood growing fairly slowly up to about 12 months, at which point there was a sudden increase in vocabulary size. This increase in vocabulary size has been noted in many other studies and a similar increase in the rate of development appears in production vocabulary as well. The increase is often described as a 'vocabulary spurt'.

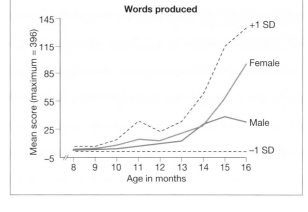

Figure 5.2

The purple and blue lines mark the mean number of words on the infant form reported to be comprehended by females and males at each month. The dotted lines indicate the range at each month for ±1 SD for the sexes combined. From Fenson et al (1994), © The Society for Research in Child Development Inc, reproduced with permission from Wiley-Blackwell.

Experimental studies

We have already seen how researchers such as Juscsyk explored the cues that infants use to segment words to form the speech stream through carefully controlled experiments. Similar experimental techniques have also been applied to exploring infants' comprehension of early words and these have considerably enriched understanding of some of processes involved in learning what words mean.

A major theoretical challenge for child language researchers has been to explain how children recognise the appropriate pairing between a word and all its possible referents. This problem was originally articulated by the philosopher Quine, in a highly influential book called *Word and Object*, published in 1960. Quine posed the problem of how it was that someone hearing a new word, 'gavagai', and seeing a rabbit running around in the countryside would know precisely what it was that the new word referred to. It might be the rabbit, some key feature of the rabbit such as its ears or tail, or some other aspect of the scene.

We have already seen that children can use their familiarity with social situations and with the conventions of pointing to help them link a new word to the correct meaning. Experimental studies have provided further evidence. For example, a recent study explored infants' ability to extract the commonality across a number of different pairings of a new word and a context (Smith & Yu, 2008). The study used made up words so that the infants' experience with each word could be carefully controlled. The words (e.g. gasser, colat) were consistent with the structure of English words so they would seem similar to other real words with which infants, aged 12 and 14 months, were already familiar.

The experiment Smith and Yu carried out was complex but the idea behind it was very simple. They argued that if someone hears the unfamiliar words, BAT and BALL, and at the same time sees a bat and ball, the person will not know which

Preferential looking paradigm

In a preferential looking experiment, an infant is familiarised, over a series of training trials, to a novel stimulus. The infant is then presented with a second, different, stimulus. If the infant looks longer at the second stimulus, this suggests that the infant can discriminate between the stimuli.

word corresponds to which object. However, if on another occasion the same person hears BALL but this time sees a dog chasing a ball it will be obvious what is in common across the two experiences. This will be a good cue to the likely meaning of BALL. The aim of the experiment was to present infants with a similar opportunity to map an unfamiliar word to its meaning by extracting the commonality across a number of contexts associated with that word.

The experiment used a **preferential looking paradigm**. The study began with a series of 30 training trials. On each trial, infants saw two novel objects (see Figure 5.3) and they heard two of the made up words. Each correct word–object pair was presented ten times but there were many other, less frequent, pairings of words and objects. In order to keep the infants' attention during the trials, pictures of Sesame Street characters were interspersed. Once the training trials had been presented, there was a series of 12 test trials. In each test trial, one of the words was repeated four times while pictures of two of the objects were presented. The whole experiment took just under four minutes.

If the infants had managed to learn the association between a word and an object on the basis that that pairing had occurred more frequently than other, accidental, pairings they should look more at the picture of the correct referent when they heard a word. Overall, both 12- and 14-month-old infants looked longer at the correct referent with the older infants showing a greater preference for the correct object than the younger infants. This shows that infants are able to accumulate evidence over time that can help them to correctly identify the meaning of a new word. This is another example of statistical learning.

Another issue that has been investigated in early experimental studies of word learning is the extent to which infants can learn to generalise word meanings. Learning what words mean requires infants to go beyond the formation of links between a word and the consistent appearance of an object or action to generalisation of that word to new instances. Such generalisations had already been noted in observational studies of early word comprehension so it should be possible to observe similar effects experimentally. In one study (Shafer, 2005), infants of between eight and nine months carried out a range of regular activities revolving around picture books and picture cards depicting key words. There were two sets of words, all of which were likely to appear in early vocabulary (e.g. apple, ball, bird, car), and half

Figure 5.3
The novel objects used by Smith and Yu (2008). Copyright © 2008, with permission from Elsevier.

the infants were exposed to Set A and half to Set B. The activities with the picture books and cards involved infants and their parents over a three-month period and involved adults naming the pictures, telling stories involving the pictures, sorting the pictures into categories and finding one picture among others. At the end of the three months, infants took part in a preferential looking experiment in which their understanding of the words was tested by showing a pair of pictures and saying the name of one of them. The idea was that if an infant understood what a word meant they would reliably look at the correct picture. A key aspect of the study was that the pictures the infants saw were all novel. So the experiment did not test whether they could, for example,

correctly link BALL with a picture of a ball they had previously seen but whether they could link BALL with a new picture (novel exemplar).

Schafer found that infants looked reliably longer at the named picture for words on which they had received training. So, infants trained on Set A words at home reliably looked at the correct picture for these words but not for Set B words; and the reverse was true for infants who had been trained with Set B words. Interestingly, all the words the infants heard were spoken by an unfamiliar voice so they were not only able to generalise their word learning to novel items but also to a novel speaker.

5.5 LEARNING TO SAY WORDS

The sounds that children produce towards the end of the first year, such as 'ba' and 'da', feature in their first spoken words. Inevitably, young children's early attempts at words are phonetic simplifications of adult forms since, when children first start to talk, they are only able to produce a very limited number of phonemes. Processes of simplification continue right through the preschool years and, even by the age of five, many children will still have difficulty with some phonemes and especially with certain phoneme combinations.

The most frequent kinds of phonetic simplification include substitution of stop consonants for fricatives (as in 'ti' for see), voicing of initial voiceless stop consonants (as in 'doe' for toe), reduction of consonant clusters to a single consonant (as in 'soo' for shoe or 'sip' for ship), deletion of initial 'h' and deletion of initial and middle unstressed syllables (as in 'na' or 'nana' for banana). Another process of simplification is called consonant harmony. Here the child will alter the production of one sound so that it is produced in a way that is more similar to another sound in the same word. Examples of consonant harmony are 'gock' for sock – in which the 's' is replaced by 'g' which is produced in a similar part of the mouth to the 'ck' ending – and 'means' for beans – where the 'b' is replaced by 'm' which is a nasal sound like the final 'ns'.

Parental reports

Figure 5.4 shows how production vocabulary develops up to 16 months as reported from use of the CDI. Parents can usually provide very reliable information about the new words that their children are producing, providing that they are given clear instructions about what counts as a word. For example, as we saw earlier, children often simplify and shorten long words (e.g. saying 'nana' for banana). The CDI data show that most children say their first word at around ten months and gradually say more words over the next few months. Again there tends to be a sudden increase in the rate of learning new words around 13 months. As for comprehension, girls are significantly ahead of boys in the number of words they are able to produce although the difference is fairly small.

A comparison of the graphs for comprehension and production shows that, on average, the number of words produced tends to be smaller than the number comprehended. Although comprehension tends to follow behind production fairly consistently for the majority of children, the CDI data showed there is a clearly identifiable sub-group with a comprehension vocabulary of more than 150 words but a productive vocabulary of very few words. There also seems to be a third, less

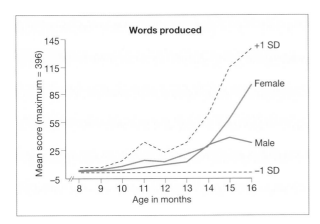

Figure 5.4

The purple and blue lines mark the mean number of words on the infant form reported to be produced by females and males at each month. The dotted lines indicate the range at each month for ±1 SD for the sexes combined.
From Fenson et al. (1994), © The Society for Research in Child Development Inc, reproduced with permission from Wiley-Blackwell.

frequent, pattern. In a longitudinal study of six children, Harris *et al.* (1995) found two children who understood only one or two words before they said their first word. They also showed a lag of less than one month from the time when they first understood a word to the time that they first said one. This compares to a more usual lag of around three months.

Observational studies

One final point to make about the first words that children produce is that they are very closely related to children's early language experience. A study of the first ten words children produced showed that these very closely mirrored their experience of hearing these same words being used by their mothers (Harris, Barrett, Jones, & Brookes, 1988). In the 40 words studied, there were only three where the was no apparent relationship between a child's use and the mother's use of that word in the preceding month; and in 33 of the cases studied, the child's use was identical to the mother's most frequent use. For example, the first word used by James was 'mummy' but, rather puzzlingly, he restricted its use to situations where he was holding out a toy for his mother to take. This unusual use was explained when an inspection of his mother's speech revealed that she most commonly used this word when holding out her hand to take a toy, saying 'Is that for mummy?'

5.6 SUMMARY

In this chapter we have seen how babies begin the process of learning about language even before they are born. Recognition of the characteristic prosodic pattern of a particular language means that newborn infants can tell languages apart, and recognise the language they have been listening to in the womb, providing that the languages they are presented with have different prosodic patterns.

Over the first few months of life infants are developing more detailed knowledge of the language being used in their speech community. As they develop their knowledge of the phonemes in this language they gradually lose the ability to perceive phonemes that do not occur in the local language. By the end of the first year of life, infants have reached adult levels of phoneme perception. At the same time, they are gradually developing an ability to produce phonemes and they progress from cooing and gurgling at two months to being able to produce an impressive range of speech sounds towards the end of the first year of life. These sounds gradually become words although, for most infants, the ability to understand words considerably outstrips the ability to produce words.

Early language development is a very social-engaged process and much early vocabulary grows out of the daily and oft-repeated interactions that young infants have with their caretakers. Joint attention is a key skill for learning language as is the understanding and use of pointing. Other skills, such as the ability to detect the boundaries of words, are more specific to language although they can be seen as examples of statistical learning.

Infants show considerable variation in the rate at which they learn to understand and produce words. A variety of different methods have been used to study infant word learning, including parental reports and experimental studies using preferential looking. As we saw in Chapter 4, infants' developing knowledge of language has an impact on the way that they categorise the world and so delays in the development of language are likely to have wider implications for cognitive development.

FURTHER READING

Harris, M. (2004). First words. In J. Oates & A. Grayson (eds.), *Cognitive and language development in children* (pp. 61–112). Milton Keynes: The Open University/Blackwell Publishing.

Johnson, E. K., & Jusczyk, P. W. (2001). Word segmentation by 8-month-olds: When speech cues count for more than statistics. *Journal of Memory and Language, 44,* 548–567.

Saxton, M. (2010). *Child language: Acquisition and development.* London: Sage.

Shafer, G. (2005). Infants can learn decontextualised words before their first birthday. *Child Development, 76*(1), 87–96.

ESSAY QUESTIONS

1. 'Language learning begins before birth.' Discuss.
2. Explain how children learn to discriminate the phonemes present in the language of their language community.
3. Why do the early words that children produce sound different from the adult form?
4. Why is the social context important in early word learning?

CHAPTER 6

CONTENTS

Social and emotional development in infancy

6

After reading this chapter you will be able to

- understand how infants recognise faces and why this ability is important for development
- explain the role of imitation in early development
- explain the importance of John's Bowlby's work on attachment and its relation to the work of Harry Harlow
- describe the strange situation paradigm and explain what it can reveal about infant attachment
- understand how infancy researchers have assessed infant self-recognition
- explain the significance of 'social referencing' for infants.

So far in this book we have mainly focused on the physical and intellectual changes that take place during infancy. However, it is very important to remember that infancy is also a key period for the development of relationships with other people. Human beings are social creatures and the development of strong bonds with others is essential for good social and emotional development, as well as providing an important context for cognitive and linguistic development. As we will see, what happens in infancy can affect what happens throughout an individual's life.

6.1 RECOGNISING OTHER PEOPLE

A question that many new parents ask is 'What can my baby see?' Often, what they are really asking is whether their baby can recognise them. In fact, as we see in a moment, the ability of babies to recognise faces develops over time but, at birth, babies already have highly developed abilities to recognise familiar voices and smells. Both voice and smell are important in the early recognition of familiar people, usually the baby's mother and other members of the family. So, in real life, babies normally have information from all their senses to help in identifying important people in their lives. However, one important way that infants learn to recognise people is through their faces.

Recognising faces

Human faces vary along many different parameters and being able to recognise people when you see their face is an important human skill. Psychologists have been exploring how well babies can recognise faces for many years. The very first study was carried out by Fantz using a visual preference technique in which he recorded the time that babies spent looking at different kinds of stimuli, including face-like stimuli (Fantz, 1965). Fantz's early work and many, more sophisticated, studies that followed including those of Simion and her colleagues (Valenza, Simion, Macchi Cassia, & Umiltà, 2002) and Johnson and Morton (Johnson & Morton, 1991), initially led researchers to think that babies were born with a very specific preference for faces. Interestingly the stimuli that were used in these experiments were not real faces but very simple schematic faces (see Figure 6.1). This raised the possibility that what babies preferred was something with very general face-like properties rather than faces themselves.

The most recent research has supported this view, showing that newborn babies have a more general preference for certain kinds of visual stimuli. In particular, newborns prefer stimuli that have up-down asymmetry (Simion, Valenza, Macchi Cassia, Turati, & Umiltà, 2002; Turati, 2004) and congruency. Up-down asymmetry means that a stimulus has more patterning in the upper part than the lower part. Faces have this asymmetry because there are more key features in the upper half of the face – eyes, eyebrows, bridge of the nose – than in the lower half. Faces also have congruency. If you think about the shape of a face, it is wider at the top than at the bottom; and there are more features in the wider part and fewer in the narrower part. This is congruency.

In the studies reported by Turati (2004), newborn babies preferred to look at stimuli with more elements in the top half than the bottom half. They also preferred stimuli that were congruent rather than non-congruent. However, these preferences held equally for face-shaped stimuli and for stimuli consisting of squares. You can see some examples of these stimuli in Figure 6.2.

Even though newborn infants may not have a specific preference for faces, it remains the case that they are attracted to faces because of their properties. This means that they spend a lot of time looking at and learning about the faces of the people they see. Learning about specific faces is remarkably rapid and within the first few days of life infants prefer their mother's face to other faces (Bushnell, 2003).

Experience gradually shapes infants' abilities to recognise new faces. As adults, we tend to be much better at being able to tell apart different human faces than animal faces; and we are better at recognising faces from familiar racial groups (including our own) than from unfamiliar racial groups. These effects of experience soon begin to show themselves in infants. At six months, infants are as good at discriminating one human face from another as they are at discriminating one Macaque monkey face from another. By nine months infants have lost their ability to discriminate the faces of Macaque monkeys and they perform like adults in

Figure 6.1

The schematic configuration (face-like stimulus on the left, non-face-like stimulus on the right) used in studies on newborns' face preference.
From Turati (2004), © Association for Psychological Science, reproduced with permission from SAGE.

only being able to reliably discriminate human faces (Pascalis, de Haan, & Nelson, 2002). The trade-off is that over this period infants have learned to make even finer discriminations among human faces.

Effects of racial group on face perception show a similar developmental change. At three months, Caucasian infants were able to discriminate between faces within their own racial group but also within other racial groups – in this case, African, Middle Eastern and Chinese. However, by nine months, this ability was only evident for same-race faces (Kelly *et al.*, 2007).

Linking faces and voices

Another early ability that is important in learning to recognise other people is the linking of faces to voices. This is one example of cross-modal integration i.e. the linking together of information from two or more modalities. In one of the first studies to show auditory visual co-ordination in infancy (Kuhl & Meltzoff, 1982), four-month-old babies were presented with two video-recorded faces of strangers to left and right of the midline. One face was shown repeating the vowel 'i' while the other repeated the vowel 'a'. At the same time babies heard one of these vowels being pronounced repeatedly. As you might have guessed, babies preferred to look at the face that corresponded with the sound track, showing that they had detected a correspondence between the auditory and visual information for the vowel sound.

The fact that infants can link sounds and voices – and prefer the two to be co-ordinated – makes the talking human face a particularly attractive stimulus and it explains why young babies spend a lot of time looking at the faces of their caretakers. However, they are not just looking – they are also learning about the way that their responses and those of their caretakers are linked. See Box 6.1 for some more evidence of this developing ability.

Figure 6.2
Examples of stimuli used by Turati (2004). From Turati (2004), © Association for Psychological Science, reproduced with permission from SAGE.

6.2 IMITATING OTHER PEOPLE

One very important kind of early learning involves imitation, that is, copying what someone else is doing. There has been considerable debate about the extent to which young infants are capable of imitation. In part this is because observing and recording imitation in tiny infants is difficult and it is all too easy to confuse imitation with some random juxtaposition of events. In other words a parent might produce an action and an infant might produce a very similar action but these may not be causally connected.

What was needed to clarify the role of imitation in infant learning was a series of rigorously controlled experiments. One of the leading exponents of the existence and significance of imitation is Meltzoff. His research is summarised in a recent chapter (Meltzoff & Williamson, 2010) entitled, 'The importance of imitation for

KEY TERMS

Still-face procedure
This involves mothers
and their infants and it
is divided into three
periods of interaction.
1. Mothers are
instructed to interact
normally with their
infant. 2. They are
instructed not to
respond as normal and
to adopt a still face with
a neutral expression.
3. Mothers resume their
normal pattern of
responsive interaction.

BOX 6.1: INFANTS ARE DISTRESSED BY A 'STILL' FACE

Analysis of interaction between young infants and their caregivers shows that the adult is typically very responsive to the infant, reacting with smiles, laughs and appropriate comments to the infant's vocalisations and behaviours. Interactions often also involve touch and physical contact. Researchers in the later 1970s (Tronick, Als, Adamson, Wise, & Brazelton, 1978) developed the **still-face procedure** to show just how finely-tuned caregiver responses to infants are and how infants react when the adult response changes.

The standard still-face procedure involves mothers and their infants and it is divided into three brief periods of interaction, each lasting around 90–120 seconds. In the first period mothers are instructed to interact normally with their infant. Then, in the next period, they are instructed not to respond as normal and to adopt a still face with a neutral expression. Finally, in period 3, mothers resume their normal pattern of responsive interaction.

The effect on the infant of the period of non-responsiveness is dramatic. Infants typically decrease the amount of gazing to the mother and smiling while increasing their vocalisation. They rapidly return to their normal pattern of looking and smiling as soon as mothers cease their still face.

The effects of the still face can be ameliorated if mothers continue to touch their infants during the still-face period (Stack & Muir, 1990). When mothers were allowed to touch their infants (aged between three and nine months), but not allowed to change their facial expression or use their voice, the infants continued to smile and look at their mothers. This highlights the important role that touch and physical contact play in caregiver interactions in the early months of infancy (Stack, 2010).

theories of social-cognitive development'. Meltzoff argues that the infant's ability to imitate underpins social–communicative development, cognitive development and serves as a foundation for understanding other minds. This is a bold claim since it puts imitation at the heart of much early development.

What is the evidence for early imitation and why might an ability to imitate be important? In a pioneering study, imitation of tongue protrusion, lip pursing and mouth opening was studied in 12–21-day-old infants (Meltzoff & Moore, 1977). Infants could imitate these actions, sticking out their own tongue, pursing their lips, and opening and closing their mouth in response to the adult. Subsequent studies have shown imitation in infants who were less than an hour old (Meltzoff & Moore, 1989); and they have also demonstrated that infant imitation is very specific. For example, infants distinguish between two types of lip movement (mouth opening and lip pursing) and between straight tongue protrusion and protrusion to the side (Meltzoff & Williamson, 2010).

Infants can reproduce an imitated action independently of the adult model. This aspect of imitation is often overlooked, even though it was present in the original study by Meltzoff and Moore (1977). In their study, infants sucked on a dummy while the adult produced the target actions and later produced the behaviour when looking at a passive face. In more recent studies the delay between the infant's observation of the target behaviour and the imitation has typically been one day (Meltzoff & Williamson, 2010).

A number of researchers have argued that one important function of infant imitation is to socially engage other people (Carpenter, 2006; Meltzoff, Kuhl, Movellan, & Sejnowski, 2009). One clear piece of evidence in support of this view comes from another study (Meltzoff & Moore, 1992) that explored the link between imitation and the identification of individuals. In the study, there were two adult models. One systematically showed tongue protrusion while the other showed mouth opening and closing. Six-week-old infants responded to the two models differentially, producing tongue protrusions when they saw the first adult and mouth opening when they saw the second. However, if one adult exchanged places with the other without the infant seeing, infants produced a surprising error – having stared at the 'new' adult, infants imitated the action associated with the previously-seen adult. Meltzoff argues that this behaviour served to test out the identity of the adult. Infants could see that this was a different person but, as they had not seen one person leave and a new person enter, they had two sources of conflicting information about who this person was.

Why would producing an action associated with a particular person be useful in establishing identity? In order to understand this we have to recognise the other side to infant imitation. When an infant produces an action, an adult is very likely to imitate it. In this way, we can see imitation as a two-way process that enables infants and adults to develop complex sequences of mutual imitation. As we saw in the previous chapter the development of social routines sets the scene for infants to learn about language. Infants also respond to being imitated.

In a series of studies (Meltzoff & Decety, 2003), Meltzoff tested whether infants recognise when another person acts 'like me'. In one experiment 14-month-old infants interacted with two adults. One of the adults imitated everything the baby did while the other imitated what the previous baby had done. Each set of adult actions was therefore 'babylike', the only difference being that one set of imitations was specific to the infant. You would not expect the range of actions to be very different but each baby has a unique combination and sequence of actions. The key question was

Three infants imitating a large tongue-protrusion-to-the-side gesture.

whether infants could distinguish between the adult who was acting 'just like the me' and the adult who was acting like another baby.

The answer was that babies could tell the difference. They looked longer at the adult who was imitating them and they smiled more. Significantly, they also tested out the 'like me' adult. Testing out involves performing sudden and unexpected movements to check if the adult is following what an infant is doing. This kind of deliberate disruption of an expected sequence has also been observed by Reddy, who describes how infants like to 'tease' adults by varying a familiar routine.

Reddy has identified a number of behaviours that appear around six months of age, when an infant and a familiar adult are interacting (Reddy, 2003). These are: showing-off (i.e. the performance of exaggerated or unusual actions to gain attention when it is absent or to retain it when the centre of attention); clever actions (repeating acts to re-elicit praise, or checking on others' attention with pleasure after the completion of difficult actions); clowning (the repetition of odd actions that have previously led to laughter to re-elicit laughter) and teasing (deliberate provocation through the performance of actions contrary to existing expectations or routines). The increasing complexity of the infant's role in these real-life interchanges observed by Reddy in real life is echoed in Meltzoff's finding that the ability to vary an imitative sequence develops over the first year of life. Young infants tend to increase the frequency with which they make a gesture that is being imitated but they do not switch to mismatching gestures to see if they will be copied. Older infants treat the interaction as a matching game that is being shared (Meltzoff & Decety, 2003).

From about three months, smiling is truly social and reciprocal in that the baby's smile is now synchronised with the smiles of familiar adults.

6.3 SMILING AND SOCIAL RECOGNITION

We have already seen that smiling is an important component in a shared social interaction between infant and adult. Very early smiling appears to be internally generated, that is, it does not occur in response to external stimuli. Such smiles are typically fleeting. At about six weeks of age, the first social smiling appears. At this age babies begin to smile at familiar social stimuli, most notably familiar people. Smiles are not restricted to visual stimuli. By six weeks, babies smile to voices, particularly their mother's familiar voice. Congenitally blind babies will smile at the sound of their mother's voice or when touched, although they are often delayed in the development of smiling (Fraiberg, 1974). The sight of the face becomes a particularly strong stimulus for smiling. We saw earlier in this chapter that infants have a general preference for face-like stimuli. It is not surprising to find that babies will also smile at face-like stimuli as well as faces, as a very early study showed (Ahrens, 1954). Ahrens found that babies would smile at a pair of red dots on a white oval background.

From about three months, smiling is truly social and reciprocal in that the baby's smile is now synchronised with the smiles of familiar adults. The baby discriminates between familiar and unfamiliar people, smiling more readily to the former but, at this age, there is no fear of strangers. Smiling, like imitation, is a very strong social signal for adults and both play a key role in ensuring the development of sustained periods of social interaction between infant and adult.

6.4 DEVELOPMENT OF ATTACHMENT

So far in this chapter we have considered the development of a number of important abilities that underpin the emergence of social relationships in infancy. We now turn to a very important topic that brings together many of the ideas we have already considered – **attachment**.

Outside the domain of psychology, the term 'attachment' is widely used to describe a range of different kinds of relationships. In developmental psychology it has a very specific meaning as the term first coined by John Bowlby (1958) to describe the special relationship that exists between a mother and her child. At the time Bowlby was writing, the predominant tradition in Western society was for mothers to take the major responsibility for looking after their children with many mothers staying at home to act as full-time carers. Fathers very often had little to do with the everyday care of their children, especially when the children were young. Changing patterns of childcare have raised questions about the kind of attachment relationships children form as a result of their experiences and we consider some of these issues later in this chapter and elsewhere (see 17.2).

The other key figure in the development of ideas about attachment was Mary Ainsworth. She carried out some key experimental studies of attachment. Her views were strongly influenced by her experiences of observing cultural differences in the quality of mother–child attachments in Uganda and Baltimore. Attachment theory can be seen as a joint product of Bowlby's attempt to explain the psychological impact on the infant or young child of separation from the mother and Ainsworth's concern with individual differences in attachment (Posada & Kaloustian, 2010).

Someone else who made an important contribution to the development of attachment theory was Harry Harlow. We begin with a brief account of his research.

Harry Harlow

Harlow carried out his main studies of the origins and long-term consequences of attachment in the 1960s (Harlow, McGaugh, & Thompson, 1971). Interestingly, like Bowlby, Harlow was influenced by Freud's theory, especially the view that that the mother–child relationship has an important role in the development of personality. Freud had argued that the attachment relationship develops out of the satisfaction by the mother of the infant's bodily needs, especially hunger. However, Harlow argued that hunger may not be the primary driver of attachment and he set out to demonstrate this in a series of now-famous experiments with rhesus monkeys (Harlow *et al.*, 1971). Harlow chose to study monkeys because, like human infants, infant monkeys spend a considerable time with their mother in their early years. At the time Harlow and his colleagues conducted these experiments there was little consideration of the ethics of animal studies and in many countries such experiments would probably no longer be allowed.

Contact comfort in the rhesus monkey.

In what is now his most famous study, Harlow separated baby rhesus monkeys from their mothers and then gave them the choice of clinging to an uncomfortable wire support that dispensed milk or to a comfortable cloth-covered support that did not dispense food. The idea was that, if the satisfaction of hunger underpinned attachment, the baby monkeys would become attached to the wire support. What Harlow found was that the monkeys would feed on the wire support but immediately returned to cling to the preferred cloth-covered support. This suggested that contact comfort was more important for the development of attachment than simply being provided with food.

In further tests Harlow showed that, given the choice of a comfortable cloth-covered support that dispensed milk and an identical one that did not, the monkeys preferred the support that dispensed milk. However, during the first 20 days the infant monkeys actually preferred a heated wire support to a comfortable but cold cloth support, suggesting that warmth was also a factor. These results led Harlow to argue that the Freudian 'cupboard love' theory of attachment was inadequate. Instead, Harlow argued that a multifactorial theory of attachment in rhesus monkeys was required, which includes such species-specific factors as the desire in monkeys to cling, as well as the more general factors of contact comfort and motherly warmth.

John Bowlby

Bowlby applied some of Harlow's ideas to human development. He argued that the first attachment relationship is based on unlearned, species-specific behaviours. To feel attached, in Bowlby's theory, is to feel safe and secure in the particular relationship. Insecure attachment involves mixed feelings – feelings of dependency and a fear of rejection.

In monkeys, clinging and following are early developing response systems by which the infant keeps the mother close at hand. In humans, where motor development is considerably less advanced than in other primates, crying and smiling are particularly important in eliciting caretaking behaviour from the mother. It is from these early interactions, many focusing around caretaking and close physical contact, that the emotional attachment between mother and baby develops.

A key idea in Bowlby's theory – and one that was very similar to Harlow's argument about rhesus monkeys – is that the mother provides a secure base from which the developing infant can explore the world and periodically return in safety. The emotional attachment of the baby to the mother normally provides the infant with a sense of safety and security. The evolutionary function of such attachment behaviour is thought to be that, in the short term, it protects the child from predators and, in the longer term, it provides the model on which all other relationships are based. Thus a secure attachment in infancy will pave the way for secure and

BOX 6.2: BOWLBY'S STUDY OF CHILDREN IN HOSPITAL

Bowlby's work gained wide recognition when he collaborated with James Robertson in the production of the film, *A Two-Year-Old Goes to the Hospital* (1952). The film is about a two-and-a-half-year-old girl, Laura, who is admitted to hospital for an eight-day period. During this period Laura is separated from her parents. The film vividly documented the impact of maternal deprivation on children when separated from their primary carers. In the most moving part of the film, a traumatised Laura is filmed on a hospital ward without her parents. Filming took place through a window, so you cannot hear the sound of the child's screams, but distress is evident. This film was instrumental in a campaign to alter hospital restrictions on visiting by parents. It is now the norm for parents to stay in hospital with their children and this can be directly linked back to Bowlby's work on attachment.

successful attachments in adulthood that will contribute to the reproductive success of the species in the long term.

Where Bowlby differed from Harlow was in separating attachment from the satisfaction of needs and also in arguing for the biological necessity of attachment for psychologically healthy development. Bowlby argued that insecure patterns of attachment contribute to the formation of a neurotic personality because they take the child down psychologically unhealthy developmental pathways, giving rise to personality problems and mental ill health.

Bowlby developed his account of attachment in three volumes, entitled 'Attachment', 'Separation' and 'Loss', the first of which was published in 1969 (Bowlby, 1969). These set out in considerable detail Bowlby's view about the psychological necessity for the infant to form an attachment to the mother and of the damaging psychological consequences of an infant's attachment relationship being disrupted by separation from the mother for an extended period or, in the worst case, forever. Bowlby's books contain many of his observations of the consequences of loss of an attachment figure. For example, he describes infants who were separated from their mothers by a stay in hospital (see Box 6.2).

Subsequent research has confirmed Bowlby's view that permanent separation from an attachment figure had serious long-term consequences. Girls whose mothers die before their twelfth birthday have a greatly increased risk of severe depression in adulthood (Brown & Harris, 1980). It is important to note, however, that such an outcome of disrupted attachment is not inevitable. Large-scale epidemiological studies, exploring the role of family experiences as antecedents of depression and anxiety disorders in later life, show that many factors can ameliorate the long-term effects even of the severe disruption caused by the death of a parent. These include

Staying in hospital can be traumatic for children; thanks to Bowlby's work in the 1950s, it is now the norm for parents to stay with their children when they are in hospital.

good relationships with the surviving parent and other family members, friendships with peers, success in school, making a good supportive marriage and being of resilient personality (Holmes, 1993).

Mary Ainsworth

Mary Ainsworth, who worked with Bowlby in London for a three-year period early in her career, further developed the idea of attachment. In an interview Ainsworth spells out the different influences on her and explains how her own views on attachment and those of Bowlby were influenced by research into animal behaviour that was being carried out at the time (Ainsworth & Marvin, 1994).

There are three key indications of attachment in infancy and they become evident once the infant is capable of independent movement and can crawl or walk unaided. The first of these is *proximity seeking*. If someone is attached to another person they will seek out and spend time with that person. This applies throughout life but it is particularly evident in infants and young children who like to have their attachment figure close at hand. Second, the attachment figure provides a *secure base* from which the child can explore the world. The toddler seems tied to the mother as if by an invisible string that allows exploration only within a particular distance from the mother. The final feature of attachment is *separation protest*, such as crying and screaming following separation from the attachment figure.

These three key aspects of attachment were first studied experimentally by Ainsworth (Ainsworth & Bell, 1970). The paradigm Ainsworth and Bell devised, known as the **strange situation**, proved to be so successful at eliciting attachment behaviours in infants that it is still in use today although some of the original details of the procedure were slightly modified (Ainsworth & Wittig, 1969). You can find out more about the strange situation in Box 6.3.

Around the age of eight months infants typically develop stranger anxiety and will show signs of distress in the presence of a stranger unless the familiar figure of the mother (or other attachment figure) is also there. By the age of 12 months, when the strange situation paradigm is most commonly employed, as soon as the mother leaves her baby alone with a stranger this is likely to provoke a strong reaction. In their original study, Ainsworth and Bell observed three major patterns of behaviour. The majority of infants (66 per cent) were classified as having *secure attachment* (type B). They showed a very consistent set of behaviours during the strange situation. They settled quickly into the testing room and acted as normal, playing and exploring the room. They were distressed by the separation – often crying – but when their mother returned they greeted her, had a cuddle and happily returned to play.

The remaining one-third of babies showed various insecure patterns of attachment. Twenty per cent of babies were classified as *anxious-avoidant* (type A). These babies gave few overt signs of distress on separation and ignored the mother on her return. The smallest group (12 per cent) were classified as *anxious-resistant* (type C). They were highly distressed by the separation but, unlike securely attached babies, they were not easily pacified when the mother returned. They sought contact but then resisted and showed anger.

More recently a fourth – infrequent – pattern of response has been identified, type D. These babies show confused behaviour including freezing or stereotyped movements on reunion with the mother. Such behaviour has been described as *disorganised-disoriented* (Main & Solomon, 1986).

BOX 6.3:
THE STRANGE SITUATION
PARADIGM

The strange situation procedure involves a standardised session carried out in a laboratory, lasting about 22 minutes. The behaviour of the mother and infant is observed through a one-way mirror. Having settled into the observation room and had time to play, the infant is left alone with a stranger as the mother leaves the room. The mother returns and infant and mother are reunited. The behaviour of the child at each stage is observed. The strange situation has been used successfully with infants aged between 12 and 18 months and their behaviour during each stage of the procedure, especially at separation from the mother and when infant and mother are reunited, provides an insight into the relationship between child and mother. Most infants find separation from the mother very stressful and so the procedure can be cut short if the baby cannot be comforted or becomes too upset.

Top: The infant plays happily with the researcher while the mother looks on. Middle: The mother leaves the room and the infant continues to play with the researcher. Bottom: The mother re-enters the observation room and her infant returns to play.

The main stages in the standard procedure are as follows:

- Researcher brings mother and infant into observation room.
- *2–3 minutes*: Researcher leaves. Infant can explore room and interact with mother.
- *3 minutes*: Stranger walks in, talks to mother and interacts with infant.
- *3 minutes (maximum)*: Mother leaves room while stranger remains. (This part of the procedure will be cut short if the infant cannot be soothed by the stranger.)
- *3 minutes*: Mother returns and greets the infant. The stranger leaves unobtrusively.
- *3 minutes (maximum)*: Mother leaves. (This part of the procedure will be cut short if the infant becomes too upset.)
- *3 minutes*: Stranger returns. (If the stranger cannot soothe the infant, this session is cut short and the mother returns.)
- *3 minutes*: Mother returns and greets the infant. The stranger leaves unobtrusively.

Both Bowlby and Ainsworth argued that the way the mother interacted with her infant had an important role to play in the kind of attachment relationship that her child developed. Evidence from Ainsworth's longitudinal study of mothers and their babies in Baltimore (Ainsworth, 1969) led the way in characterising individual differences in style of maternal interaction. She studied 23 mother–infant dyads over the first year of life, making the first observation in a home visit three weeks after birth and making subsequent observations every three weeks. Each observation went on for four hours so that at the end of the study an enormous amount of information about each mother–child dyad had been collected. At the end of the study all the mothers and infants took part in the strange situation.

Ainsworth collected detailed information about the mother's behaviour on a number of dimensions including responsiveness to infant crying, close bodily contact, face-to-face interactions and frequency of use of physical intervention to induce obedience. Using these dimensions, mothers were rated along four dimensions: sensitivity–insensitivity, co-operation–interference, acceptance–rejection, accessibility–ignoring. Each dimension proved to be significantly related to the organisation of attachment behaviour in the strange situation. Ainsworth's general conclusions were that mothers of securely attached one-year-olds tend to be responsive and attentive to their babies at three months and, most importantly, sensitive in their responses. Sensitive mothers alter their rhythm of activity to suit the infant, matching the infant's actions and engaging in mutual attention with the infant. Mothers of insecurely attached one-year-olds tend to be inconsistent in their responses and less attuned to the infant at three months. These key findings have been replicated in many subsequent studies as revealed in a meta-analysis of 24 studies (de Wolff & van Ijzendoorn, 1997).

Cultural differences in attachment behaviour

The observations of Ainsworth and Bell (1970) were carried out in the USA. More recent research has shown that the way babies respond to separation from their mothers depends, in part, on their experiences. These vary from culture to culture. A key study (Miyake, Chen, & Campos, 1985) found that babies in Japan were disproportionately classified as insecure compared with the classification of babies in the USA. This can be explained by the fact that, in Japan, mothers seldom leave their babies alone and hence the strange situation produces a huge effect of separation. In contrast, German babies are disproportionately classified as secure, relative to babies in the USA. This can be explained by the fact that, in Germany, the norm is to socialise infants for independence (Grossman *et al.*, 1985).

These are, however, relatively minor differences and it should be remembered that the claim of attachment theory is that babies have a biological need to form an attachment and to seek a secure base from which to explore the world.

Changing patterns of childcare and their impact on attachment

Although the early work on attachment emphasised the importance of attachment to the mother, it has become clear that many infants develop secure attachments to a number of different people. Fathers now often play a much larger role in the lives of young infants than they did at the time Bowlby and Ainsworth were developing their ideas about attachment; and older brothers and sisters and other family members can also play important roles in the lives of young children. More recent developments of attachment theory have emphasised the possibility of multiple attachments in infancy and have also considered the effects of mothers going out to work and involving other people as major carers for their child (Vaughn, Deane, & Waters, 1985).

It is not straightforward to identify the potential effects of childcare on the formation of attachment because of the many different factors that are involved, not least the age of the child, the quality of the day care and the kind of measures of attachment that are used (Vaughn *et al.*, 1985). One of the most comprehensive studies was completed in the USA by Belsky (Belsky, 2001). His study showed evidence of an interaction between maternal style and the effects of childcare. As in Ainsworth's original study in Baltimore (Ainsworth, 1969), the strongest predictor of insecure attachment at 15 months of age was insensitive mothering (which Belsky observed at ages six and 15 months). However, this effect was amplified by any one of three distinct childcare conditions occurring in the first 15 months of life: (a) an average of more than ten hours per week in any type of care, irrespective of quality; (b) enrolment in more than a single childcare arrangement and (c) low quality care (Belsky, 2001). The first of these – amount of care – predicted insecurity of attachment at 36 months, again in interaction with insensitive mothering.

What these findings suggest – and those from similar studies in Israel (Sagi, Koren-Karie, Gini, Ziv, & Joels, 2002) and Australia (Harrison & Ungerer, 2002) – is that good quality day care does not impact on the development of attachment security. However, poor quality care – especially a high ratio of children to carers and a long period of day care – can exacerbate the effects of insensitive mothering. The Australian study also highlighted the fact that placing a child in day care before the age of five months was also a risk factor.

6.5 DEVELOPMENT OF THE SELF-CONCEPT

Having seen that infants become increasingly sophisticated and individuated in their interaction with others, we now turn to the question of how infants develop a sense of self. Since a sense of self is complex and multi-faceted, it is not surprising to find that there are many strands of evidence relevant to this question. There are also a number of different views about how the sense of self develops.

Rochat provides a good overview (Rochat, 2010). He notes that one view is that the sense of self in infancy develops primarily through relationships with other people. On this view, the early sense of self is moulded into an adult-like sense of self through interaction with other people. Meltzoff's view about the important of imitation is one such view as are the views of Fogel and Lewis (Fogel, 1993; Lewis, 1999). Other theorists, notably Stern, have argued against the importance of the social environment for the emergence of the self-concept. He proposes that, during the first two months of life, infants develop a sense of the emergent self as they learn about the inter-relation of their various sensory experiences. On this view, the sense of self grows from developing perpetual abilities (Stern, 1985).

A third view, expounded by Eleanor Gibson, is that it is the environment in general – rather than the social environment in particular – that is important for the development of a sense of self. In her view the development of self-knowledge is just part of a wider process of learning about the actions that can be undertaken with physical and social objects – affordances, as they are called (Gibson, 1988). Gibson argues that infants first learn about their own ability to perceive and act on the world by responding to the affordances of people and objects and engaging effectively with them.

Rochat (2010) argues that a full account of the development of the self concept needs to take account of both perceptual and social factors, reflecting the fact that our sense of self includes, among other things, an awareness of the way in which we can have an effect on the objects and people in the world, an awareness of the movement of our own bodies and an ability to recognise ourselves.

We have already seen in this chapter how babies become increasingly sophisticated in their interactions with other people. In this section we focus on the other two important abilities that form part of the developing self-concept.

Perceptions of bodily movements

As Rochat (2010) notes, the infant's own body is a primary object of perceptual exploration. When we perceive or act on an object or person in the world we also perceive ourselves in relation to that object or person. We also perceive ourselves in relation to the movements that we make. The same is true for infants, though their awareness of being at the centre of their own movements is something that takes some months to develop. One clear sign of this developing awareness is hand regard. At about the age of three months, infants can be observed spending sustained periods looking at their hand as it is held above their body while they lie on their back (White, Castle, & Held, 1964). Over the next few weeks, infants bring both hands to the midline more and more frequently, often watching their hands as they move in front of them. This experience allows them to link the look and feel of these movements.

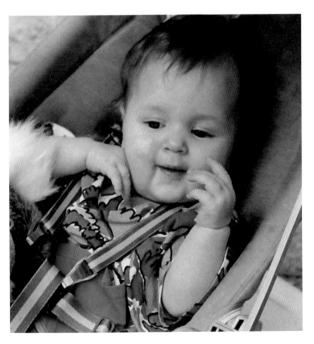

Francesca looking at her hands at five months.

Experimental studies by Rochat showed a similar developmental trend. The studies, which used preferential looking, compared the preferences of three- and five-month-old infants for two different views of their own body (see Rochat 2010 for more detail). In one study, infants were shown a number of different views of their lower body on a TV monitor. All were live, that is, they showed the infant's body in real time so when the infant moved her legs this could be seen in all of the views. The difference between them was that, in each comparison, one view was as the infant would normally see it – the ego view – and the others were modified in various ways. For example, one view was reversed so that the right leg appeared on the left and, in another view, the infant's legs were seen from the perspective of an observer looking at the baby.

Rochat wanted to find out if infants could tell the ego view from other views and, if so, which they preferred. He found that, by three months of age, infants looked longer at the unfamiliar view. They were especially attracted to the views that reversed the direction of movement by 180 degrees (observer view) or reversed the way in which one leg moved in relation to another. Not only did the infants look more at these unusual views of their own legs, they also moved their legs much more as though testing out the relationship between the familiar feeling of their leg movements and the unfamiliar view of these movements.

Self-recognition

Young babies, like almost all animal species, do not recognise themselves when they look in a mirror. Being able to recognise oneself in a mirror is seen as an important advance because it is taken as evidence of possessing a concept of self. One problem is assessing mirror recognition in young babies is that they cannot explain what they can see. One way of testing mirror recognition is to use a 'rouge removal' task – a simple but effective way to see whether someone recognises their own reflection. The idea is that if someone looks at their reflection and sees a strange mark on their face, they will reach up to remove it. However, if they do not recognise the face in the mirror as their own they will not attempt to do this.

In the **rouge removal task**, a small amount of rouge is surreptitiously placed on a child's face. Then the child is allowed to look in a mirror. Some infants as young as 15 months notice the strange mark on their face in their reflected image and reach up to remove it; and by the age of 24 months all normally developing children will respond in this way. Of course rouge removal is a tricky task and younger children, who do not yet attempt to remove the rouge, may respond to their own mirror image. For example, babies from the age of ten months will reach up to grasp a hat lowered just above their head when they see the hat in the mirror although they would not attempt to remove the rouge (Bertenthal & Fischer, 1978).

The fact that the ability to remove a dab of rouge occurs rather late in infant development suggests that there is a substantial cognitive component in mirror self-recognition. It has been found that children with Down's syndrome (who have learning difficulties) are delayed on the rouge removal task until the age of three or four years (Mans, Cicchetti, & Sroufe, 1978). Chimpanzees (at about eight years) and orangutans (age unknown) can also perform the rouge removal task but this ability does not appear to be present in any other species (Suarez & Gallup, 1981).

The rouge removal task probably requires a combination of perceptual and cognitive abilities that include detection of the contingent nature of the mirror image and the infant's own actions, monitoring the position of the hand and fingers in relation to the rouge mark, as well as recognising oneself. However, even though the rouge removal task may overestimate the age at which children first recognise images of themselves, evidence from recognition of photographs also suggests that self-recognition does not reliably appear until around the middle of the second year. Interestingly, infants often recognise other familiar people (such as parents and siblings) in photographs and videos before they recognise themselves in the same images.

KEY TERMS

Rouge removal task
A small amount of rouge is surreptitiously placed on a child's face. Then the child is allowed to look in a mirror. This task tests mirror recognition.

Young babies do not recognise themselves when they look in a mirror. Self-recognition does not appear until around the middle of the second year, and is considered evidence of having a concept of self.

Social referencing
The gauging of others' emotional reactions before deciding one's own reaction.

6.6 RESPONDING TO EMOTIONS

One important aspect of interaction with other people involves responses to their emotions. Newborns can imitate emotional expressions (Field, Woodson, Greenberg, & Cohen, 1982) and they also cry in response to the prolonged crying of other babies (Hay, Pedersen, & Nash, 1982). Towards the end of the first year, infants start to use adults' expressions as a guide to their own actions – a process known as **social referencing** (Campos & Stenberg, 1981). Social referencing can most easily be observed when infants are in an unfamiliar situation in which they are not sure how to proceed. They will look to their mother to check her reaction before carrying on with an activity. For example, when babies who can crawl are placed on a 'visual cliff' – a clear, rigid toughened glass surface that goes over the top of what appears to be a steep drop – they behave differently according to their mother's expression. Babies pause when they reach the apparent drop but will continue crawling if their mother looks happy or interested. However, if mothers look sad or angry, most infants do not venture over the drop (Campos, Bertenthal, & Kermoian, 1981). Similarly, babies' reactions to a potentially frightening toy – such as a jack-in-the-box – are strongly affected by their mother's reactions (Hornik, Risenhoover, & Gunnar, 1987).

Social referencing is not only to the mother. Babies who spend a lot of time with other caretakers will also use their emotional reactions as a guide (Camras & Sachs, 1991). Clearly, the use of an experienced adult as a point of reference is very useful since it means that babies do not have to deal with every new situation on a trial and error basis.

More recent research has investigated the emotional understanding of infants directly. These studies test to see whether infants can relate emotional displays to particular objects or activities. In a recent study (Hepach & Westermann, 2013), infants watched short video clips of an actor showing a happy or angry demeanour. The actor then either patted a toy tiger (happy action) or thumped the toy tiger (angry action). There were several different trials in which the actor, emotion and action were systematically varied (see the following photos for some examples). The infants' responses to the various video clips were measured by looking at pupil dilation. The idea was that, if infants were surprised by the events in a particular video clip, their pupils would dilate. Hepach and Westermann predicted that the clips where the action and the emotion were mismatched (i.e. incongruent) would elicit greater pupil dilation than the clips where the two were congruent. This is what they found in the older infants – aged 14 months – who took part in the study. However, the younger infants, who were only ten months old, did not show this pattern. What this suggests is that, by 14 months, infants have already learned about the link between emotions and actions.

Examples of stimuli from Hepach and Westermann.

One final study we should mention, which brings together many of the issues we have considered in this chapter, shows that early experience plays an important part in channelling the way that young children respond to emotional expressions. This research looked at the way that children who have been maltreated respond to threatening expressions (Masten *et al.*, 2008; Pine *et al.*, 2005). Although this study was carried out on older children it shows how long lasting the effects are of early maltreatment on children's perceptions of emotions (see Box 6.3).

BOX 6.4: THE IMPACT OF MALTREATMENT ON CHILDREN'S PERCEPTION OF EMOTIONS

Recent research has shown that development of a normal ability to process emotional expression is largely dependent on normal experiences with emotions in daily social interactions. As we saw, infants learn that particular facial expressions are associated with particular actions (Hepach & Westermann, 2013). Most infants will experience a wide range of emotions and over the first few years of life they gradually develop an increasingly sophisticated understanding of a wide range of emotions and how they are likely to affect the way someone behaves. Infants and young children who are maltreated will have a very different kind of experience. They will typically be exposed to many negative adult emotions and few positive ones; and they will soon observe that negative emotions are often associated with negative behaviours.

Victims of child maltreatment respond to facial emotions, particularly negative ones, differently from children who have not been maltreated. In particular, they show enhanced sensitivity to negative facial expressions, especially those associated with threat (Pine *et al.*, 2005). The technique used in the Pine *et al.* (2005) study was to present pairs of pictures on a computer screen. In each pair one picture was of a face with a neutral expression while the other was a face with either a happy or an angry/threatening expression. Attention to the faces was measured by reaction time to a probe (an asterisk) that appeared on the screen immediately following a pair of faces. Children (aged 7–13 years) who had been exposed to physical or emotional abuse were more likely to direct their attention away from angry/threatening faces than non-abused children and so were slower to react to the probe when it appeared in the same location as a threatening face. The avoidance effect was strongest for children who had been subjected to the most serious abuse.

In another study (Masten *et al.*, 2008), maltreated children, ranging in age from eight to 15 years, were recruited through Connecticut's largest child protection service agency (the Department of Children and Families: DCF). These children had been removed from their homes because of severe neglect and/or physical or sexual abuse. At the time the study was carried out, approximately three quarters of the maltreated children were in DCF custody – some in foster homes and some awaiting placement in foster homes – and one quarter had returned to their biological homes. Control participants were carefully matched children from the same residential areas as the maltreated children, but had no known history of neglect or abuse, or exposure to domestic violence.

All the children and their parents were interviewed and the children also undertook a range of tasks while they were at summer camp. One key task involved the recognition of facial expressions from photographs presented on a computer. The facial expressions were created using a morphing technique so that they ranged from 100 per cent happy though neutral to 100 per cent fearful. An exaggerated fearful face was also included.

Children were asked to identify each of the stimuli as happy, neutral or fearful by pressing an appropriate button as quickly as possible after each face was presented. The results were striking. Overall, maltreated children were faster than control children in identifying the depicted emotions but the most clear cut differences were in the identification of the fearful faces.

6.7 SUMMARY

In this chapter we have seen that infants rapidly become familiar with the people who interact with them on a daily basis. Infants not only learn what other people look like, smell like and how they talk, but they also build up a complex picture of how other people respond to them. They rapidly detect when someone is not interacting with them in the normal way, as shown by the still-face paradigm and experiments on imitation. They also respond with increased attention when adults imitate the infant's own actions and, as they progress through the first year of life, they become increasingly capable of varying their own actions to elicit a reaction from the adult. The infant's own reactions to other people, especially smiling and vocalisations, have a very positive effect on adults and serve to ensure that adult and infant spend protracted periods in interaction.

The social behaviours of infants and the responses that these elicit in adults are an important component in the development of attachment. The work of John Bowlby and Mary Ainsworth provided a framework for understanding the vital role of attachment in infancy and its long-term consequences as well as the external signs of secure attachment in infant behaviour and the relationship with maternal behaviour. The characteristics of maternal behaviour that support the development of secure attachment in the infant – sensitivity and responsiveness – are now well understood and more recent work has explored the impact of changing social patterns and cultural traditions on attachment.

Relationships with other people during infancy also provide one important source of knowledge about the self. The other important source is infants' developing perceptual awareness of their own bodies. Over the first months of life infants gradually become aware of their ability to control their own body movements and will spend long periods observing and systematically varying the movements of their own hands, arms and legs. By the middle of the second year of life infants are beginning to recognise themselves in the mirror and in photographs.

Emotional understanding also develops during infancy. Towards the end of the first year, infants will use adult emotions as a cue to how they should respond to a new situation and they are also able to detect cases where an adult emotion and action are inconsistent.

Overall it can be seen that infants have a sophisticated knowledge of how other people interact with them and they can use this to predict behaviour in familiar situations. This social knowledge is important not only for future social development but also as a rich context for much of the learning about language and cognition that takes place during infancy. So it is important to recognise that social, physical, linguistic and cognitive development during infancy are closely inter-twined.

FURTHER READING

Hepach, R., & Westermann, G. (2013). Infants' sensitivity to the congruence of others' emotions and actions. *Journal of Experimental Child Psychology, 115*(1), 16–29.

Posada, G., & Kaloustian, G. (2010). Attachment in infancy. In J. G. Bremner & T. D. Wachs (Eds), *The Wiley-Blackwell handbook of infant development*. Chichester: Wiley-Blackwell.

Turati, C. (2004). Why faces are not special to newborns: An alternative account of the face preference. *Current Directions in Psychological Science, 13*, 5–8.

ESSAY QUESTIONS

1. Why are infants attracted to faces?
2. Discuss the role of imitation in early development.
3. What is attachment and how can infant attachment be assessed?
4. Why is a secure attachment important for development?
5. How does experience affect children's perception of emotion?

CHAPTER 7

CONTENTS

Introduction to the preschool years

7

After reading this chapter you will be able to

- explain why the period from two to six years is treated as a single period of development
- understand how the brain develops during the preschool years and what the implications are for children's physical and mental development
- describe the main changes in motor ability that occur during the preschool years
- describe the way in which children's ability to draw develops during this period and explain why this occurs.

The period of childhood that we describe as the preschool years begins with the end of infancy (at two years) and ends at the age of six years. You might ask whether there is a clear rationale for a period for development that covers the period from two to six years. The answer to this question is that a number of important changes in cognitive abilities take place between the ages of six and seven years – as we see in Chapter 8 – so it makes sense to treat the preschool years as a discrete period of development. However, in the United Kingdom, the developmental picture is complicated by the fact that formal schooling begins in the year that children reach their fifth birthday. This means that most children in the UK actually start school when they are only four years old.

Such an early starting age for formal schooling is unusual. Within Europe, half of the countries list six years as the official age to start school and in a number of other countries (including three in Scandinavia) formal schooling does not begin until the age of seven years. In line with Europe, most countries of the world favour a school starting age of six years.

You might wonder why the UK has such an unusually early age for starting school and why six years is a more common age. The term after a child's fifth birthday was set out as the compulsory age to begin school in the 1870 Education Act. There was little parliamentary debate at the time and the reasons set out for adopting an early starting age had nothing to do with educational readiness. There was a

KEY TERMS

Corpus callosum
A thick bundle of nerve fibres in the centre of the brain that acts as the major connection between the left and right hemispheres, transferring information between them.

well-meaning intention to take children away from exploitation at home and unhealthy conditions on the streets and, at the same time, a need to appease employers by allowing education to be completed as soon as possible (i.e. to have a correspondingly early school leaving age) so that children could enter the workforce (Woodhead, 1989). So it turns out that the practice in the UK was not based on any developmental or educational criteria, whereas there are strong educational and developmental criteria for beginning school at age six when important developments in cognitive abilities are taking place.

7.1 BRAIN DEVELOPMENT

There are significant developments in children's brains from infancy to adolescence that can help to explain the basis for their increasing intellectual abilities.

It is not, however, an easy matter to chart brain development because there is considerable individual variation. So while it is clear that there are age-related changes in a number of regions of the brain it is equally clear that there is wide variation in the size of specific brain regions (Evans, 2006). Cross-sectional studies are therefore of limited value in providing a clear picture of brain development over time and longitudinal studies are the best way to show patterns of both typical and atypical brain development.

As we noted in Chapter 1, longitudinal studies are both time-consuming and expensive to carry out so, while there are many cross-sectional studies of brain development, there are few longitudinal studies. However, in the last few years, repeated brain scans of the same children have begun to appear. Magnetic Resonance Imaging (MRI) is the most commonly used technique. In Chapter 1 (see 1.2) we described Functional Magnetic Resonance Imaging (fMRI), which is used to measure blood flow in specific regions of the brain. Structural MRI can be used to provide a detailed picture of the anatomy (size and shape) of particular brain regions so that changes in and over time can be measured by comparing a scan taken at one time with a scan of the same child taken some time later.

One study carried out repeated MRI scans of children over a four-year period (Thompson *et al.*, 2000). The youngest children included in the study were three years old and the oldest were 15 years by the end of the study. The most striking finding was that, between the ages of three and six years, rapid growth was detected in the frontal circuits of the anterior **corpus callosum**. The corpus callosum is a thick bundle of nerve fibres in the centre of the brain that divides the cerebral cortex into left and right hemispheres. It acts as the major connection between the two hemispheres, transferring information between them, and it contains more than 200 million nerve fibres.

The importance of the corpus callosum for cognitive and social development can be gauged by looking at the kind of problems that are experienced by children whose corpus callosum shows incomplete development. Such children are likely to show

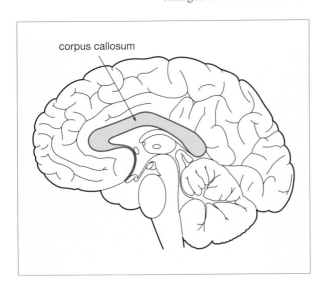

Figure 7.1
A diagram of brain to show the corpus callosum.

delay in reaching developmental milestones in physical development, in language, literacy and problem solving and in social interactions. Incomplete development of the corpus callosum has been linked to number of developmental disorders, including **autism** (see Chapter 8) (Alexander *et al.*, 2007) and **Attention Deficit/Hyperactivy Disorder** (ADHD: see 11.3) (Catherine, 1994).

Co-ordinating information from the two hemispheres is important in many tasks so it would be expected that an impaired ability to transfer information from one hemisphere to the other will lead to developmental delays in a number of areas. Equally, the growth of the corpus callosum will mean that children's ability to perform a range of tasks will show significant advances over the preschool period as they become better able to optimise the use of the two hemispheres of the brain.

Another scanning method that has been used to study the brain functioning of young children is **Positron Emission Tomography** (PET). PET scans show glucose metabolism and they are another way of indicating the amount of activity that is taking part in a particular area of the brain. The rate of glucose metabolism in the frontal cortex doubles between the ages of two and four years. As we explain in Chapters 11 (see 11.2) and 15 (see 15.2), the frontal cortex continues to develop until well into adolescence but it is notable that significant development begins at the end of infancy. The frontal cortex is involved in many aspects of cognition and a marked increased activity suggests that children will rapidly develop new cognitive abilities as they move from infancy into early childhood. This is indeed the case, as we see in Chapter 8.

7.2 MOTOR DEVELOPMENT

One of the most striking developmental changes to occur in the preschool years is in children's physical abilities. Figure 7.2 shows how the relative proportions of the head, trunk and limbs change from birth to adulthood. You can see that, between the age of two and five years, the proportions of children's bodies undergo a major

KEY TERMS

Autism
Childhood autism is a rare developmental disorder, often manifest before the second year of life, which involves a profound failure in social, linguistic and imaginative development.

Attention Deficit/Hyperactivity Disorder
This is one of the most common developmental disorders. It is characterised by a triad of difficulties: chronic and pervasive inattention, impulsive behaviour and hyperactivity.

Positron Emission Tomography (PET)
A brain scanning method that shows activity in the brain by measuring blood flow to different brain areas.

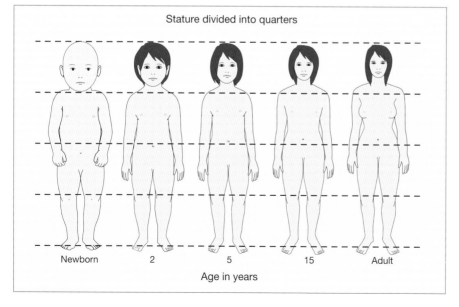

Stature divided into quarters

Newborn   2   5   15   Adult

Age in years

Figure 7.2
Changes in body proportion with age. Adapted from Sinclair (1978).

Between the age of two and five years, the proportions of children's bodies undergo a major change as the relative size of the limbs increases and the relative size of the head decreases.

change as the relative size of the limbs increases and the relative size of the head decreases.

Along with the changes in body shape come significant developments in motor skill. By the end of infancy, children will have mastered basic locomotor and manual skills but, by the end of the preschool period, they will have mastered all the fundamental motor skills to some degree (Sugden & Wade, 2013). The achievements of the period from two to six years can best be seen by considering a number of key motor skills, such as walking, running, jumping, and throwing and catching.

Most children begin to walk around the end of the first year of life but they continue to increase their proficiency in walking until the age of five or six, at which point their walking pattern is virtually indistinguishable from an adult's. One important change is from flat-footed contact with the ground to heel-strike contact, followed by a heel raise and push off from the toe. Children's increasing control over walking can be illustrated by asking them to walk in a straight line with their heels raised. This is one of the tasks used to assess motor skills in a standardised test, *The Movement Assessment Battery for Children – 2* (Henderson, Sugden, & Barnett, 2007). At three to four years of age children can manage about seven steps but, by four to five years, they can manage 14 steps. Over the same period children's overall co-ordination and posture during walking improves and they adopt a more upright posture, rather than leaning forward. This improved balance is also evident in children's ability to descend stairs with ease – one of most difficult locomotor skills to master – and also in their ability to run, which is well developed by the age of five years (Sugden & Wade, 2013). Effective walking and running require the development of a number of inter-linked movement patterns and abilities and these have been modelled using dynamic systems theory (see 2.6).

Jumping skills also improve in the preschool years as one of the tasks in *The Movement Assessment Battery for Children – 2* illustrates. Children are asked to jump from one floor mat to another, without stopping. Children aged between three and four years can, on average, manage to make three jumps although their feet are often not together when they jump. By five years of age, children can manage to jump from one square to the next five times, landing with their feet together on each jump.

Manual dexterity improves considerably over the preschool years and this has many practical benefits as children become increasingly independent and able to wash and dress themselves and brush their teeth. Most children can dress and undress themselves without supervision by the age of four years and also brush their teeth. *The Movement Assessment Battery for Children – 2* includes a number of manual dexterity tasks that show how these skills develop. Tasks include posting coins through a small aperture, threading beads onto a lace and tracing a simple pattern, keeping within guidelines. All of these tasks require children to co-ordinate their two hands. For example, in the posting task, one hand is used to steady the posting box while the other places the counter in the aperture. Children's skill at all of these tasks improves steadily between the ages of three and six years as they become increasingly good at co-ordinating their two hands. This fits in with the fact that, as we noted in the previous section, there is marked development in the corpus callosum between the ages of three and six years.

7.3 DRAWING

Another way to view children's unfolding abilities through the preschool years comes through their drawings. In *Strategies of Representation in Young Children* (Freeman, 1980), the author showed that the planning strategies used in children's drawings revealed a developmental progression in the acquisition of the various subskills that are required for successful drawing. These included sequencing, organisation and orientation.

This view of the cognitive significance of children's drawing emerged relatively recently in developmental psychology compared to some of the other traditional markers of cognitive development that we discuss elsewhere. The main reason for this relatively recent interest in drawing is that there had previously been a strong tendency to treat children's drawings 'as if they were direct translations of mental states and images onto paper' (Thomas, 1995). On this (mistaken) view a picture is considered merely as a copy of the scene that it represents. Such a view is clearly not adequate to explain children's drawings since they not only look very different from what they are representing but they vary according to the age of the child.

Freeman's (1980) view – and that of later researchers such as Thomas (1995) – is that a more accurate way to think of children's drawing is as a pictorial construction of what they observe. Thomas (1995) argues that pictorial constructions are often copied from memory or from other pictures so that, at a given point in development, children will tend to draw in a rather similar way.

Children's ability to draw develops significantly during the preschool years and this can be seen most clearly in their drawings of people. Circles usually play an important part in children's early drawings of people. The simplest drawing of a person is a 'tadpole figure' comprising a circle for the head and two vertical lines for legs (see Figure 7.3). A little later a differentiated head and trunk will be drawn, sometimes with arms added. Gradually, as children get older, more features are added and the figure becomes more accurately proportioned. Figure 7.4 shows a typical sequence of development. It is remarkable that congenitally blind children, when asked to draw the human figure, also do so using combinations of circles and straight lines, just like sighted children (Millar, 1975).

As Thomas (1995) points out, it seems unlikely that children's knowledge of the human body develops in line with their drawings. Four-year-old children do not believe that people really have arms growing out from their heads even though they often depict people in this way. Indeed when discrepancies between a child's drawing and a real person are pointed out children will often admit that the picture is not an accurate reflection of reality (Freeman, 1987). Perhaps the best way to think about children's drawings of people – and of familiar objects such as a house or a tree – is that they are 'schematic'. Children tend to follow the same general plan every time they make a drawing. Thus a four year old might distinguish a person from a cat by the addition of hair to the former and a tail to the latter hair while using identical body outlines as in the example in Figure 7.5.

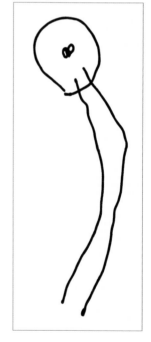

Figure 7.3

A tadpole person.

Figure 7.4
Drawings of a man and a dog at different ages. From Silk and Thomas 1986, © British Psychological Society, reproduced with permission from Wiley-Blackwell.

Thomas (1995) argues that young children have only a small number of schema available and, equally importantly, a limited capacity to adapt them. When asked to draw a man and a dog, three-year-old children tend to draw both figures according to the same basic formula (see the top line in Figure 7.4). However, children's drawings of the two figures show increasing differentiation with age. In the bottom line of Figure 7.4 you can see the drawings made by six year olds. Interestingly, the dog often displayed human features (such as eyebrows) but the man was never depicted with doglike features.

Even the youngest children differentiated the dog and man by size, with the dog being drawn as smaller than the man. This suggests that the children were fully aware of a need to distinguish the two. Size appears to be one of the first ways in which children begin to make an accurate distinction in their drawing. Arguably this is because a drawing can be changed in size without modifying the schema.

It is interesting to note, however, that in the drawing shown in Figure 7.5 of Francesca (the first author's daughter) and her cat, the two figures are shown of equal size. This may well be because the cat in question was the family pet and a very important companion to Francesca. His significance was also evidenced by the fact that a simplified form of his name – Ta-Ta (Tarquin) – was Francesca's first word, which was produced when the cat came into the room. It would be interesting to compare children's drawings of cats and dogs in general with ones that they made of valued family pets.

Figure 7.5
A four-year-old's drawing of her cat and herself. The cat and the child have been drawn with identical bodies, arms and legs, but the cat has been given pointed ears and a tail, while the little girl has a hair band and hair.

BOX 7.1: HOW TO IMPROVE CHILDREN'S DRAWING OF THE HUMAN FIGURE

The actual sequence in which the parts of a drawing are executed can affect the accuracy of children's drawing. When they are drawing a person most children start at the top and then work down to the bottom of the page since this allows them to see what they have already drawn. Thomas and Tsalimi (1988) were interested in the possibility that this pattern of working might contribute to children's tendency to exaggerate the size of the head. They observed that children would invariably begin with the head and work down if asked to draw a person. Many of the children did not leave sufficient space to complete the rest of their picture to scale. Some of the children were persuaded to start by drawing the trunk instead and, in every case, their second drawing was more accurate than their first (Thomas & Tsalimi, 1988). Some examples are shown in Figure 7.6.

Figure 7.6

Drawings of a man and a dog at different ages. From Thomas and Tsalimi 1988, © British Psychological Society, reproduced with permission from Wiley-Blackwell.

Headfirst
Girl
(5:5)

Trunkfirst
Girl
(5:4)

Headfirst
Girl
(7:9)

Trunkfirst
Girl
(7:10)

7.4 SUMMARY

The period of the preschool years lasts from two to six years of age. The period begins with toddlerhood and ends as children are beginning formal schooling. Worldwide, the most common age for starting school is six years and this corresponds with a major transition in cognitive abilities.

During this period there are significant changes in the brain, most notably in the corpus callosum. This is a thick bundle of nerve fibres that forms the major connection between the two hemispheres. Co-ordinating information across the two hemispheres is important in many tasks and children who have incomplete development of the corpus callosum experience deficits in a number of areas.

One area where the effects of the changes to the corpus callosum are particularly noticeable is motor development. Motor skills require good co-ordination between the hemispheres and, during the preschool period, children become adept at running, jumping, throwing and catching. This increasing physical prowess is aided by the change in body shape occurring between two and six years, as the limbs grow and the head becomes proportionately smaller in relation to the trunk and limbs. Manual dexterity also increases as children become competent at tasks that require the co-ordination of two hands, such as threading beads or posting shapes through a letterbox.

Advances in drawing ability through the preschool years are visible evidence not only of manual dexterity and control but also of increasing cognitive ability. Children's drawings tend to be schematic with the schema that is adopted becoming more sophisticated with age. The tadpole-shaped figures that children produce at the beginning of the preschool years have, by the end of the period, been replaced by a figure that is accurately proportioned and depicts all the relevant features.

FURTHER READING

Sugden, D., & Wade, M. (2013). *Typical and atypical motor development*. London: Mac Keith Press.

ESSAY QUESTIONS

1. Describe the main developments in the brain that take place in the preschool years and explain how these affect children's developing cognitive and motor abilities.
2. What are the major changes that take place in children's motor abilities in the preschool years?
3. Consider whether a child's drawing is 'a copy of the scene that it represents'.

CHAPTER 8

CONTENTS

Cognitive development in the preschool years

8

After reading this chapter you will be able to

- critically discuss Piaget's claims about development during the preschool years

- characterise the development of reasoning and problem solving and the tasks that have been used to assess these abilities in children

- discuss the development of the distinction between appearance and reality

- explain different viewpoints on the development of a theory of mind and its relation to autism.

In this chapter we will discuss some of the major changes that occur in the cognitive abilities of preschool children. We take 'preschool' as the range from two to six years although, as we noted in Chapter 7, the ages at which children start formal schooling vary between countries.

The major changes in cognitive abilities that occur during the preschool years were first described by Piaget, and much subsequent research has evaluated and criticised Piaget's work. We begin this chapter with a brief description of Piaget's account of pre-operational reasoning and then turn to more recent work on reasoning and problem solving. We also discuss children's ability to separate fact from fiction, that is, reality from appearance or fantasy. Finally we discuss the development of theory of mind, the ability to understand that other people have thoughts, feelings and desires that are different from ours.

8.1 PIAGET'S THEORY OF PRE-OPERATIONAL REASONING

In Piaget's theory, the period from two and a half to six years is known as the pre-operational stage. According to Piaget, the pre-operational period is a time during which children gradually acquire systematic, logical thinking although many important developments do not occur until after the age of six when children move into the next stage of concrete operations.

According to Piaget, the main changes that occur during the pre-operational period are in the organisation of thinking into a system of mental operations, and the key feature of preschool thinking is that the child is able to focus only on one salient feature of a problem at a time. Piaget argued that the child is dominated by the immediate appearance of things and, as a consequence, thought is pre-logical. The limitations of thinking in the pre-operational stage are best illustrated by children's performance in conservation tasks. These were invented by Piaget as a way of showing the limitations of preschool children's thinking. The conservation tasks are so effective at demonstrating the difference between a pre-operational child and one who has acquired concrete operations that they have become one of the most well-known aspects of Piaget's very extensive research.

Conservation tasks test children's ability to understand that the basic properties of matter – volume, number and weight – are not altered by superficial changes in their appearance. The best-known example is probably conservation of volume, which involves judgements about the amount of water in three glasses, A, B and C.

In Piaget's original conservation task the experimenter begins by showing two glasses with equal amounts of water in them. Children will tell you that the amount of water is the same. Then, in full sight of the child, the water from one glass is poured into a third one that is narrower and taller, so that the water level is higher than before. Preschool children will now say that there is more water in the glass with the higher level. This is because they have failed to compensate a change in the height of the liquid by the change in the width that results from the water being poured into a differently shaped glass. Nor can children of this age understand the important principle of **reversibility**, that is, if the water is poured back into the original jar then the levels will once again be the same. Pre-operational children are said not to be able to imagine the sequence of changes in the appearance of the water in the successive jars that would accompany a reversal of the height of the liquid to its original level.

The same lack of conservation is evident in other domains, including the case of conservation of number. In the classic conservation task, two rows of coins are first equally spaced so they have the same overall length and then one of them is spread out so that now the second row looks longer. Preschool children will now claim that the more spread out row contains more coins. Figure 8.1 shows some examples of Piagetian conservation problems.

Further evidence of pre-operational children's inability to compare different views comes from Piaget's studies of **egocentrism**. At its simplest, egocentrism can be defined as looking on the world only from one's own perspective. It implies an inability to differentiate between one's own point of view and other possible points of view. In general, egocentrism means that the child is unable to differentiate what is *subjective* (this means what is strictly private or personal) from what is *objective* (i.e. a matter of public knowledge, something we know for certain to be true). It is just as well to be clear that egocentrism does not refer to selfishness as a personality trait. It is simply the unconscious adoption of one's own perspective through failure to realise that other perspectives exist.

Piaget's most famous demonstration of egocentrism comes in preschool children's performance in the three mountains task (Piaget & Inhelder, 1956). The task involves children assessing both their own viewpoint of a mountain and that of

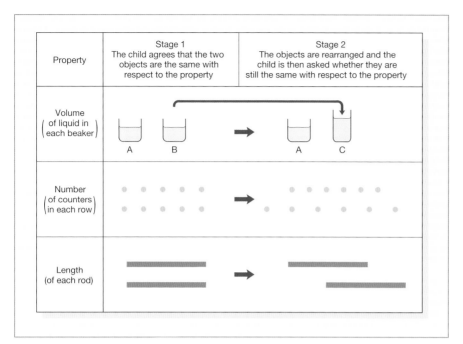

Figure 8.1

Examples of Piagetian conservation problems.

an observer who has a different view. Children's performance in the three mountains task is described in Box 8.1.

8.2 CRITICISMS OF PIAGET'S TESTS OF PRE-OPERATIONAL THINKING

At first sight, then, preschool children appear quite illogical in their failure to reason about simple conservation problems or to differentiate their own point of view from that of others. However, we can ask an important question about Piaget's conclusions: is children's inability to do certain tasks a result of their pre-operational frame of thinking, or does it have to do with how they are asked and how the tasks are designed?

This possibility, that it might be task demands that make children perform poorly on some Piagetian tasks, has received a lot of attention. It may not be the case that children actually believe that the volume of a liquid changes when it is poured from one container to another. Piaget's results might have other explanations. One possibility is that young children, who have limited experience with the physical world, may not yet understand relatively complex terms such as 'same' and simply make a guess when confronted with an adult's question that they do not fully understand. If this is the case then simplified versions of the same tasks – involving more familiar scenarios and less complex language – might reveal abilities to succeed in these tasks much earlier than Piaget thought.

Critics of Piaget, especially Donaldson (1978) and, more recently, Siegal (1997), have taken precisely this view. Donaldson has argued that the traditional Piagetian tasks make little sense to the preschool child while Siegal has shown that performance may be strongly affected by relatively subtle changes to the wording of

BOX 8.1: PIAGET'S 'THREE MOUNTAINS TASK'

Piaget and Inhelder (1956) developed the three mountains task in their laboratory on the shores on Lake Geneva. A large mountain, called Mont-Salève, is visible across the lake from the city of Geneva and it is known to everyone locally, including the children tested by Piaget and Inhelder. The three mountains task uses a 3D model of the mountain and surrounding peaks. In the diagram in Figure 8.2 a child is seated at position A and asked to represent both her own view and the view of a doll placed at positions B, C and D. Children can answer about their own perspective and that of the doll either by arranging three pieces of cardboard shaped like the mountains, selecting the doll's view from one of ten pictures depicting different points of view, or by choosing one picture and deciding where the doll must sit with respect to the model to have that view.

Piaget and Inhelder described a sequence of stages in the development of perspective taking ability. Children who are not yet four years old simply do not understand the meaning of the questions. Between four and five years children cannot distinguish between their own view and a doll's view, and they always choose their own view whatever the perspective of the observer. The first signs of discrimination between viewpoints occur at about six years when children show that they are aware of the distinction but cannot specify what it is. Between seven and nine years, when children are already in the stage of concrete operations, they are able to understand some relationships between their own viewpoint and that of the doll. Initially it is the relationship between being in front of or behind the mountain that they can recognise but transformations in the left–right perspective remain problematic. Only by eight years do children become capable of dealing with all changes in perspective.

In this classic demonstration, then, children below eight years are considered egocentric because they are 'rooted in their own position' and cannot imagine any position other than their own.

Figure 8.2

Piaget's three mountains task: one mountain has a cross on top, another a house, and another a peak covered in snow. Children of various ages had to choose an appropriate photograph for the view of a person standing at locations A, B, C, and D.

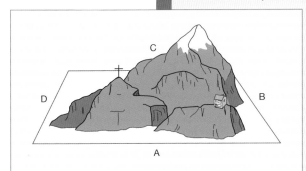

questions that children are asked. It is not just that children lack knowledge of language, which leads them into error: children's errors arise in an active attempt to discover what the adult actually means by the questions being asked in the social context established for the task. Children don't expect adults to ask questions that do not make any sense.

In her landmark book, *Children's Minds* (1978), Donaldson argues that preschool children are much more competent than Piaget gives them credit for. She suggests that Piaget's testing situations are too abstract and do not connect with young children's everyday, social experience. Why would adults ask if water becomes more or less when poured from one jug to another when it's clear that it doesn't? Is children's failure to respond correctly really due to their failure of the logical operations of conservation, or are they just being co-operative in trying to make sense of the adult? If this interpretation is correct, then performance in the standard Piagetian tasks underestimates children's ability to reason. Donaldson suggests, instead, that children should be tested in situations that make 'human sense' to them. By human sense she means that the child should be tested on problems that are couched in the social terms familiar to the child in everyday life, rather than in the abstract rather unfamiliar ways that Piaget used.

Donaldson argues that young children understand other people's feelings and therefore, socially-based tasks that tap this ability will give a rather different estimate of preschoolers' thought processes than Piaget's rather abstract tests of intellectual development. One well-known example, which shows how social knowledge can improve children's performance, is an experiment on childhood egocentrism by Hughes & Donaldson (1979). The task is shown in Figure 8.3 and it involves a model with two intersecting walls, in cross formation. Children aged from three to five years played a game in which they were asked to hide a boy doll in one of the quadrants formed by the walls, so that the boy doll could not be seen from the position of a policeman doll. The task varied in difficulty. In the example shown in Figure 8.3a, there was one policeman and two quadrants were visible and two hidden. The boy could therefore be hidden in either position and not be visible to the policeman. The task in Figure 8.3b involves two policemen so that only one hiding place (location C) is concealed from the gaze of the policemen.

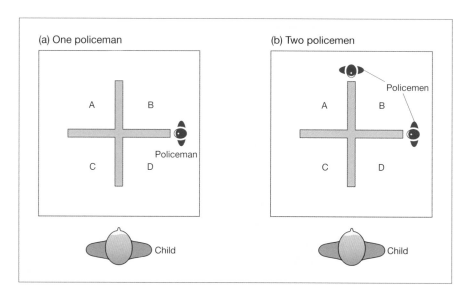

Figure 8.3

Hughes' perspective-taking task, showing the experimental set up for (a) the one-policeman condition and (b) the two-policemen condition. Adapted from Hughes & Donaldson (1979).

This task taps into the same cognitive abilities as Piaget's three mountains task in that children need to take another person's perspective and see the world from their view in order to choose the correct location for the boy doll. As we have seen, children are not able to solve the three mountains task until they are at least six years old. In contrast, even the youngest children (aged three years) were 90 per cent correct in placing the boy doll in a position where the policeman could not see him. Even when the task became more complicated, with up to six sections of walls and three policemen, four-year-olds were still 90 per cent correct. These results seem impossible to reconcile with Piaget's theory that young children are egocentric and cannot understand the viewpoint of another person.

However, in order to evaluate Donaldson's claims about the implications of this task, we need to be aware that children could fail in the three mountains task for two rather different reasons: (1) they might not be aware that the viewpoint of other people may be different from their own, or (2) they might know that other viewpoints exist but they may not be able to work out what someone with a different viewpoint would actually see.

Donaldson's results provide convincing evidence that even the youngest children could appreciate that different viewpoints from their own exist. This must mean that preschool children cannot be considered completely egocentric. However, there is an important procedural difference between the three mountains tasks and the policemen task that makes it easier for children to choose the correct viewpoint in the latter task. In the three mountains task Piaget asked the children what the doll in each position could see, whereas in the policeman task children are asked whether or not the policeman can see the boy doll.

Piaget's task requires children to describe a scene as seen from another viewpoint – and therefore a full representation of that viewpoint – whereas the policeman task only requires a yes/no answer, which may not require such a detailed representation. As we discussed earlier (see Chapter 5), babies can work out where someone else is looking or pointing. So, the ability shown by children in the policeman task could be explained by a relatively basic understanding of lines of sight and how one object can hide another. For example, children may understand that, if a policeman's line of sight is blocked by a wall, he will not be able to see the boy. If this is the case, the superior performance of children on the policeman task can be explained by the use of a simpler strategy that does not involve the comparison of viewpoints.

This discussion of the policeman task is a good example of a more general point about how difficult it is to compare the performance of children on different tasks that do not make the same cognitive demands. Simplifying the task may make it clearer and more relevant to young children but it may also fundamentally change the nature of what they are required to do.

Another source of criticism of some of Piaget's findings concerns his extensive reliance on verbal questioning. In giving children instructions or asking them questions in a task, it is essential that they understand what they are being asked. Young children have a limited vocabulary and they may rely heavily on context in order to understand what is meant, especially where a word has more than one meaning.

A good example of the problems that can arise from misunderstanding a key word comes from a study by Annette Karmiloff-Smith. Karmiloff-Smith (1979) showed that terms such as 'same', 'different' and 'all' are not fully understood until children are around the age of six years. For example, many three-year-olds interpret *same* as meaning 'the same kind'. When they were given toys to act out a sentence in which a boy pushed a cow and then 'a girl pushed the *same* cow', they first touched one cow and then a different but identical cow. Understanding of *same* – and of *other* – gradually developed over the next three years so that, by the age of six years, children could reliably interpret both terms correctly.

Siegal (1997) discusses how children's responses can be influenced not only by how questions are worded but also by the conversational context. He points out that the repeated questioning that characterises standard conservation tests violates the normal rules that govern conversation. Siegal cites a study by Siegler (1995) in which children aged between four and a half and six years were given a series of con-servation problems. All the children were unsuccessful on the conservation tasks – as you might expect – but then they were given one of three kinds of training. One group received feedback on whether their answer was correct or not. A second group also received this feedback but in addition they were asked to explain their reasoning. The third group was asked to explain the reasoning behind the experimenter's judgement of their own answer. The children in the third group performed best and Siegler suggested that being encouraged to take on the perspective of the experimenter contributed most to children's developing insights into the nature of conservation. Siegal argues that the reason for the efficacy of this third condition is that it sets a context for the repeated questioning since it enables children to understand the behaviour of the experimenter in the task. Siegal argues for an experimental context in which the child and experimenter can collaborate in their search for the correct answer rather than the traditional relationship in which children may be induced to provide an answer that they know to be incorrect.

McGarrigle and Donaldson (1975) devised the now famous **'Naughty Teddy' study** to provide a more naturalistic context for the number conservation task. As in the original task, the experimenter sets out two rows of coins and these are adjusted until children agree that both contain the same number. Then, under the control of the experimenter, a glove puppet known as 'Naughty Teddy' rushes in and moves the coins in one row so that it is now longer than the other row. Children are then asked whether the two rows contain the same or a different number of coins. In the standard conservation task most children between four and six years say that the number of coins has changed. However, in the Naughty Teddy study the children correctly said that the number of coins remained the same in the two rows.

When the adult moves the coins around and asks repeated questions about their number, the child is likely to assume that the adult asks the questions because the answer has changed. However, when the rearrangement is made to appear accidental, children are less likely to assume that teddy's action is directly related to the question that is being asked and so will say what they think the answer is.

Despite the new insights into children's thinking that were offered by the Naughty Teddy task, it turned out that the original story about how it affected children's behaviour was not complete. Moore and Frye (1986) compared the performance of five-year-olds in the standard task (where Naughty Teddy rearranges the coins), with an alternative version in which the teddy added additional coins instead of just rearranging the existing coins. In the standard task the children behaved as they had done in the original McGarrigle and Donaldson study and said that the number of coins had not changed. However, they also said this when in fact

KEY TERMS

'Naughty Teddy' study
McGarrigle and Donaldson's (1975) study where the experimenter sets out two rows of coins, which are adjusted until children agree that both contain the same number. Then, under the control of the experimenter, a glove puppet known as 'Naughty Teddy' moves the coins in one row so that it is longer than the other row. Children are then asked whether the two rows contain the same or a different number of coins.

coins were added! Thus it would appear that, at five, children are still having significant problems in distinguishing length from number in this type of conservation task.

Expertise and reasoning

More recent work on reasoning has investigated children's ability to reason within a specific domain. Often the performance of preschool children in their domains of expertise is quite impressive. For example, a study by Inagaki (1990) cleverly capitalised on the fact that Japanese parents will often buy their preschool children goldfish. This study compared children aged five years ten months who had raised goldfish at home for at least six months, with an equal number who had not. The children were given factual questions about goldfish such as 'Suppose someone is given a baby goldfish and wants to keep it forever the same size because it is so small and cute. Can he do that?'; 'What will happen to a goldfish if we feed it ten times a day?' Unsurprisingly, the children who had kept goldfish at home knew a lot more about the facts of raising them than a control group who had not had the experience. But they also had a better conceptual understanding of biological processes, such as growth, illness, digestion and excretion as revealed by questions on the effects on the fish of over-feeding or of failure to change the water. Almost all these children made analogies with people in offering their explanations. For example, a goldfish should not be overfed 'because it will feel a pain in its stomach'.

Another example of context-specific reasoning comes from a study by Siegal (1997). His examples concern the young child's knowledge of the causes of health and illness. Siegal showed preschoolers (aged 4 years and 11 months) a glass of milk, with a dead cockroach floating on top. The children were asked, for example, 'Would you want to drink milk with a cockroach in it, even if an adult told you you could?' The children said they would not drink the milk, even with the dead cockroach removed. This finding reveals a basic understanding of contamination. It also shows an ability to distinguish appearance from reality because, once the contaminant has been removed, the milk looks wholesome but the child knows it remains contaminated. Siegal (1988) also showed that preschoolers understand that a scraped knee is non-contagious and that toothaches are not sent as a mysterious punishment. In these highly salient and familiar contexts, preschool children *do* show appropriate reasoning. Siegal points out that such early causal knowledge might be used as a basis for preventative health education.

These examples of what quite young children can actually do in specific contexts suggest that intellectual development in the preschool child is rather patchy. Instead of Piaget's assumption that deficits in reasoning are due to a domain general inability of formal reasoning, it appears that reasoning ability depends on the child's specific knowledge about certain domains (Willatts, 1997).

8.3 PROBLEM SOLVING

The philosopher Karl Popper wrote a book entitled *All Life Is Problem Solving* (Popper, 1999). And so it is. Consider the following examples: the young child trying to retrieve an object from a jar or to open a door; the older child crossing the road safely or building a Lego spaceship; the student considering how to take notes from a book and deciding how to study for an exam; the engineer planning a bridge, the doctor a treatment, the author a book section. All these examples contain the features of problems that need to be solved: one's current situation is assessed, a plan is made to achieve a goal, and then one works toward this goal.

Children's ability to solve problems undergoes significant change between the ages of two and six years. While young infants can only use trial-and-error to reach a goal (for example, swiping their hand towards a rattle to make it produce a noise), slightly older children begin to employ **means-ends analysis**: they can perform intermediate steps (sub-goals) to achieve the goal. For example, seven-month-old babies will pull on a cloth in order to retrieve a toy that they cannot reach directly (Willatts, 1990), but six-month-olds will not. However, in this simple task it is not clear that sub-goals need to be represented; this task can reasonably be considered to consist of just a single task (Willatts, 1997). It is only by around nine months of age that infants seem to display genuine means-end analysis. With age, the number of sub-goals that can be represented gradually increases.

Developmental change in the number of sub-goals was shown in a study by Bullock and Lütkenhaus (1988) who asked children to complete a puzzle involving a tower made up from three painted blocks. Before the children tried to complete the task the experimenter showed them the correct solution. Although the youngest children, who were 17 months old, stacked different blocks they were not able to solve the task. Twenty-six-month-old toddlers were able to build a tower with three painted blocks, but they mostly did not use the correct blocks. Even at 32 months of age only half of the toddlers produced the correct solution.

A similar pattern of development was evident in the children's monitoring of their own performance and their correction of mistakes. At 17 months, just under half the children corrected the position of a single block on at least one trial but only 9 per cent showed evidence of carefully stacking a complete tower of three blocks. By 26 months almost all children corrected the position of at least one block and 85 per cent carefully stacked all the disks on at least one trial.

The most interesting aspect of this study was the children's reaction to their own performance. Only 36 per cent of 17-month-olds smiled or frowned after building their tower but among the oldest children, aged 32 months, such reactions were evident in 90 per cent of cases. This suggests that, as children approach the age of three, they are beginning to understand that there is a correct solution to a problem.

Means-ends problem solving clearly develops significantly in the early toddler years but many important changes in children's ability do not occur until the preschool period. For older children the **Tower of Hanoi** puzzle is often used to study means-ends problem solving (Piaget, 1976). The puzzle (shown in Figure 8.4a) can be made more or less difficult and in its most challenging form is difficult even for adults. In this puzzle there are three pegs. On the first peg there is a series of disks of increasing size, placed with the largest disk at the bottom. The child's task is to move the blocks to the last peg so that they end up in the original order. This seems a simple task, especially when there are only a few disks, but it is made more difficult by the rules of the puzzle: these are (1) that only one disk may be moved at a time and (2) a larger disk may not be placed on top of a smaller one.

The Tower of Hanoi puzzle requires means-ends analysis because it is necessary to identify and achieve the sub-goals that are required to achieve a solution. Disks have to be moved back and forth to the middle and last pegs in order to move the entire stack from the first to final peg (you can try this yourself using three different

Figure 8.4

(a) The initial state and the goal state in the Tower of Hanoi problem. (b) The three-disk Tower of Hanoi problem using cans instead of disks. The goal is to have the three cans on the child's side match the three on the experimenter's side by putting larger cans on top of smaller ones. The problem can be solved in seven moves.

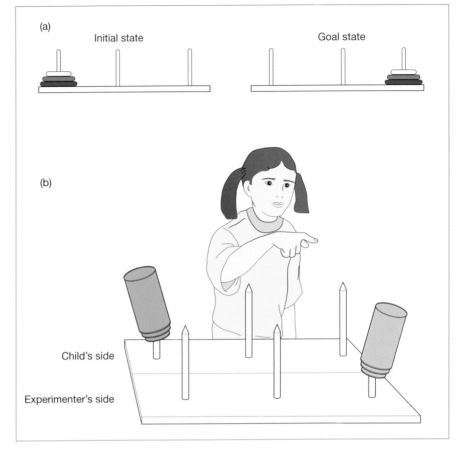

sized coins). The task becomes more difficult as the number of disks increases. The simplest version of the puzzle has only two disks. This can be solved by moving the smaller disk to the middle peg, then the larger disk to the final peg and, finally, the smaller disk to the last peg (three moves in total). Piaget (Piaget, 1976) found that five- and six-year-olds could eventually solve the two-disk problem but they were not aware of the relationship among the moves from one peg to another. Children of this age were still not able to solve a three-disk problem.

As with Piaget's views on reasoning discussed in the previous section, more recent research suggests that Piaget's version of the task may again have under-estimated children's abilities. The task could seem harder than it is because it is so abstract and the child has to remember the rules that make it arbitrarily more difficult (without the rules the task would be very easy). Klahr and Robinson (1981) investigated this issue by developing their own version of the Tower of Hanoi puzzle using cans of increasing size rather than disks (see Figure 8.4b). This change gives a clear physical basis for the rule that – in this case – a smaller item cannot be placed on top of a larger one since it would simply fall off. Therefore, there was now no need for children to remember an abstract rule. In order to give even more meaning to the task, Klahr and Robinson labelled the cans as a monkey family with the big 'daddy' can, a smaller 'mummy' can and the smallest 'baby' can. The task was for the family to move to a different pole, and the goal state was shown to the children and remained in view while they tried to solve the task.

Klahr and Robinson asked children to describe the entire set of moves that would be necessary to move the cans from the start to the finish. In this simplified, more intuitive and engaging version of the Tower of Hanoi task, most five-year-olds and nearly all six-year-olds could produce perfect four-move solutions and most six-year-olds could produce perfect six-move solutions. Like other examples, this study highlights the fact that children's failure to complete a specific task might not be due to their in principle inability to do so, but may be due to task demands that are not central to the studied ability. In the simplified 'monkey cans' version of the Tower of Hanoi task, the children show that they can identify sub-goals and keep them in mind while solving the task. In the original task it appears that it is the need to remember abstract, arbitrary rules and not the inability to process sub-goals that prevents success for this task, even in six-year-olds.

DeLoache, Miller and Pierroutsakos (1998) point out that means-end analysis of a problem imposes a daunting cognitive load because the child needs to identify the current state and the goal state and reason backward from the goal state to consider the obstacles to achieving the goal, and then identify the sub-goals of removing each obstacle. A simpler way to solve problems that often works is called **hill climbing**. The idea here is that if you want to reach the top of a hill, a good way to achieve this is to go uphill with every step. In this way it is not necessary to keep the 'grand picture' in mind; merely following an uphill direction is sufficient. To solve a problem in this way, at each point of the solution you would choose an action that takes you closer to the goal. This strategy does not impose such a large cognitive load because it simply requires the problem solver to reason forwards from the current state towards the desired goal. With a hill climbing strategy, unlike a mean-end strategy, all the sub-goals and their solutions do not have to be determined at the outset.

Klahr (1985) presented children aged between four and six with a puzzle that could be solved using a hill climbing strategy. The puzzle was to move three animals (dog, cat and mouse) to their favourite food (bone, fish and cheese). Klahr found that the children preferred to make moves that took them towards their goal and resisted moves that appeared to take them further away from the solution. The children also looked only two moves ahead. All these preferences are consistent with use of a hill climbing strategy rather than a means-ends analysis. Interestingly the tendency to prefer hill climbing strategies is not restricted to preschool children. Even adults are often very reluctant to make a move that appears to take them away from rather than towards their ultimate goal (Mayer, 1992). Nevertheless, sometimes it is necessary to do just this. Imagine that you are walking through a maze. If your strategy is to always choose the path that leads towards the direction of the exit it is likely that you will end up in a dead end and will have to walk back, away from the exit. Hill climbing therefore is a useful heuristic that works in many, but not all cases.

8.4 REASONING BY ANALOGY

Another important facet of developing reasoning skill lies in the ability to use analogies. Analogies can be very helpful in problem solving because they allow us to use knowledge we already have to solve a problem in a new domain instead of trying to find a solution from scratch. For example, knowing how to open a jar

KEY TERMS

Hill climbing
A method for solving problems – at each point of the solution you would choose an action that takes you closer to the goal.

(by unscrewing its lid) can help us to open a bottle. This is a simple analogy, and, unsurprisingly, other analogies can be much more complex.

Inhelder and Piaget (1964) believed that children are not very good at making analogies. However, once again, the tasks they used to assess this ability were quite complex. For example, they asked children to complete analogies such as 'A bicycle is to handlebars as a ship is to ... '. This difficult analogy was too hard even for most ten-year-olds. It is possible, however, that the children didn't know enough about ships to draw an analogy. Indeed, other researchers have argued that the main limiting factor in children's analogy making is the lack of knowledge about the relevant domains. When domains are used of which the children have good knowledge, even three-year-olds can draw analogies. One example is provided in Goswami's studies of item analogy. In item analogy (like in Inhelder and Piaget's bicycle: handlebars example) children are given two related items such as *bird: nest* and a third item such as *dog*. The children have to find a fourth word that is related to the third item in the same way that the second item is related to the first (in this case – *doghouse* or *kennel*). Goswami and Brown (1990) asked four-year-old children to make analogies by picking out the appropriate picture from a set of four (see Figure 8.5).

Goswami (2008) (p 323) quotes an example of a four-year-old boy, called Lucas, trying to solve the *bird: nest – dog:?* analogy that we have already mentioned:

> Bird lays eggs in her nest – dog – dogs lay babies and the babies are – um – and the name of the babies is puppy!

Lucas was so sure of his response that he initially did not want to look at the possible choices represented by the pictures shown in Figure 8.5. However, when he was finally persuaded to study them he was able to pick out the intended answer. Thus, at age four years, Lucas not only understood the principle of making an analogy but he was also flexible enough to use a different basis for his analogy – homes rather than offspring – when confronted with the picture choice.

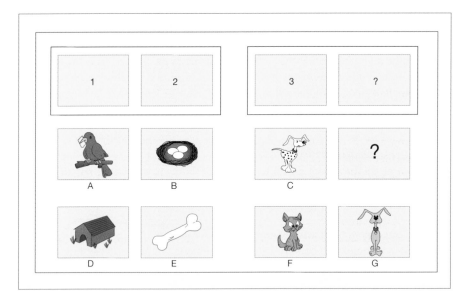

Figure 8.5

The gameboard (top row), analogy terms (middle row), correct answer and distractors (bottom row) used for the analogy bird : nest : dog : doghouse. Adapted from Goswami and Brown (1990).

Goswami and Brown (1990) have shown that reasoning by analogy is well established by age four and very simple analogies (e.g. apple: cut apple – playdoh: cut playdoh) can even be completed by three-year-olds. Much of the difficulty of an analogy lies in recognising the correspondence between the new problem and that encountered earlier. This was well illustrated by Brown, Kane and Long (1989) who gave four- and five-year-old children the 'Genie' problem invented by Holyoak, Junn and Billman (1984). In this task a genie needs to move some precious jewels to a new location. In order to avoid damaging the jewels he must move them by rolling his magic carpet into a tube and then rolling the jewels through it. In the study by Brown *et al.* the children were shown the Genie problem with the aid of toy props. The magic carpet was represented by a sheet of paper. The children and experimenter together acted out the solution. One group of children also answered questions that were intended to allow them to extract the goal structure of the problem: 'Who has a problem?'; 'What did the genie need to do?' and 'How does he solve this problem?' A control group did not receive these questions.

Having gone through the solution to the Genie problem the children were then given another problem involving an 'Easter bunny' who needed to deliver a lot of Easter eggs to children. He needed the help of a friend, as he had left the delivery rather late, but the friend was on the other side of the river from the bunny. This meant that the eggs had to be transported across the river but they had to be kept dry. The bunny had a blanket (represented by a piece of paper) and the solution, by analogy with the Genie problem, was to roll up the paper into a tube so that eggs could be rolled across to the other side of the river.

Brown *et al.* found that 70 per cent of the children who had answered the questions while seeing the solution to the Genie problem spontaneously saw the analogy between the earlier problem and the new one whereas only 20 per cent of the children in the control group, who had not answered the questions, did so. This highlights the difference between merely having appropriate experience and realising that this experience is relevant to a new problem. Brown *et al.* argue that what is important is for children to have represented the relational structure of the previously encountered problems in memory. The questions asked by the experimenter allowed children to uncover the relational structure.

8.5 APPEARANCE, FANTASY AND REALITY

Discovering that not everything is as it appears to be, and understanding the difference between things and people that are real and things and people that are only pretend, are important challenges for children in the preschool period.

The appearance–reality distinction was notably investigated by Flavell and his colleagues (Flavell, Miller, & Miller, 1993). They showed children a piece of sponge that had been carefully painted to look like a rock. The child was allowed to squeeze the 'rock' and discover that it was actually spongy. The child was then asked two questions. One was an appearance question ('When you look at this with your eyes right now, does it look like a rock or does it look like a piece of sponge?'), and the other was a reality question ('What is this really, really? Is it really a rock or really a piece of sponge?').

The majority of three-year-olds gave a similar answer to both questions: they thought that the object was really a sponge and that it looked like a sponge, or sometimes, that the object really was a rock and looked like a rock. It was not before four years of age that the children gave the correct answers: that it looked like a rock but was in fact a sponge.

Flavell and his colleagues explained the failure of three-year-olds to answer correctly by suggesting that at this age children cannot hold more than one representation of objects in their mind. By four years, however, children are beginning to acquire a notion of misrepresentation and they can understand how the sponge can look 'as if' it is a rock (Perner, 1991).

As with other aspects of preschool children's cognitive abilities, scientists have asked whether the children in appearance–reality tasks could not succeed because they were not 'developmentally ready' (e.g. in terms of being able to hold multiple representations for an object), or whether it was the way in which the task was set that led to the observed results. Several researchers have therefore tried to make the task easier for the children while still testing the appearance–reality distinction. One example is a study by Sapp, Lee and Muir (2000), who distinguished between verbal and nonverbal responses in an appearance–reality task. The idea was that if the poor performance is caused by the linguistic complexities of verbalising the distinction between reality and appearance, then three-year-olds should succeed in the nonverbal version of the task. In their study the verbal response task was similar to the one by Flavell *et al.*, but in the nonverbal task they asked questions such as 'I want to take a picture of my teddy with something that looks like a rock. Can you help me?' and 'I want a sponge to wipe up some spilled water. Can you help me?' Sapp *et al.* found that, as in previous studies, three-year-olds could not do the verbal task. In contrast, in the nonverbal task, the children performed much better and almost all responded correctly to the reality and appearance requests by handing the experimenter the correct object. While these results provide evidence that, yet again, the complexities of the traditional task led to an underestimation of young children's true abilities, other researchers maintain that three-year-olds nevertheless have certain conceptual limitations that prevent them from fully succeeding in the reality–appearance distinction (Moll & Tomasello, 2012).

Another key issue about representation concerns the difference between fantasy and reality. Young children often invent complex fantasies, and they are confronted with fantastical creatures such as Santa Claus and cartoon characters all the time. An important question is whether children in the preschool period draw a firm line between fantasy and reality.

Traditionally the view had been that children confuse the boundary between fantasy and reality (Piaget, 1955). More recent research, however, suggests that they have at least some ability to make this distinction. One line of evidence suggests that preschoolers reliably distinguish between things that they imagine and those that are real. In one study (Woolley & Wellman, 1993) three- to five-year-olds were able to draw a clear distinction between real physical objects and objects that they had imagined: they understood that you can see, touch and act upon a real object but you cannot do any of these things to an object that is imaginary. Woolley and Wellman also found that, when three- to four-year-olds were asked to judge whether an object that they had imagined really existed, most correctly said that it did not.

However, other studies suggest that preschoolers' understanding of the difference between reality and fantasy is not so reliable. In an investigation of children's beliefs in monsters and witches (Harris, Brown, & Marriott, 1991) children aged between four and six years were asked to imagine that there was either a bunny or a monster inside a real box. The experimenter then left the children alone in the room with the box and observed their behaviour with a hidden video camera. Although the children had earlier denied that the monster or bunny were real, a number of them went to look inside the box after the experimenter had gone out. When the children were later questioned about their behaviour they admitted to wondering about the contents of the box.

More recent work has studied on what basis children come to assign reality status to objects. In one study (Woolley & Van Reet, 2006) children listened to descriptions of 'surnits' and 'hercs'. Some of the children heard fantastical descriptions such as 'Dragons hide surnits in their cave'. Others heard everyday descriptions ('Grandmothers find surnits in their garden'), and a third group heard science-based descriptions such as 'Doctors use surnits to make medicine'. In this study four-, five- and six-year-olds were able to use the context of the description to assign reality status to the novel objects. The five- and six-year-olds were able to explain their reasoning, for example by saying 'Surnits are real because doctors use surnits and doctors are real'. It therefore seems that there is a gradual development in the ability to evaluate evidence and to use context when deciding whether something is real or fantastical.

8.6 SOCIAL COGNITION AND THEORY OF MIND

During the preschool period children begin to develop an understanding of what other people think, feel and want and how this will affect their behaviour. This knowledge is referred to as social cognition. As the term suggests, social cognition can be viewed as being on the boundary of social and cognitive development. The preschool period marks an important milestone in children's social cognition because between the ages of three and four children acquire what has become known as a '**theory of mind**'.

The notion of 'theory of mind' came to prominence in psychology following a seminal experiment (Premack & Woodruff, 1978) that attempted to test whether chimpanzees have a theory of mind. According to Premack and Woodruff, someone has a theory of mind if they 'impute mental states' to themselves and others. Discussion of the Premack and Woodruff paper led to the suggestion by a number of philosophers that chimpanzees and children could be tested to see if they had a 'theory of mind' by giving them a **false belief task**. The essence of the false belief task is that a child is given some crucial information that a second person does not have. Without a theory of mind children would not be able to understand that the other person might know different things from themselves, and they would expect the other person to have the same information that they do. In contrast, if children have a theory of mind, then they will realise that the behaviour of the second individual will be consistent with their lack of information.

There are now a number of classic false belief tasks that have been developed for use with preschool children. In one well-known task (Wimmer & Perner, 1983), known as the **Smarties task**, children are shown a Smarties tube that (disappointingly) contains pencils rather than Smarties. Children are asked what another child, who has not seen inside the Smarties tube, will think is inside. The correct answer is, of course, 'Smarties' since this is what the appearance of the tube suggests. However young children typically say that another child will think that the tube contains pencils even though there is no way of telling this without looking inside.

KEY TERMS

Theory of mind
The ability to think about other people's mental states and form theories of how they think.

False belief task
A test to see whether a child will act on a knowingly incorrect belief, or be aware that a second person who is not in possession of a certain piece of information may act 'incorrectly'.

Smarties task
A false-belief task in which children are shown a Smarties tube that contains pencils rather than Smarties. Children are asked what another child, who has not seen inside the Smarties tube, will think is inside.

Another task that has been used in many studies is the **Sally-Ann task** (Baron-Cohen, Leslie, & Frith, 1985) in which a girl doll (Sally) hides a marble and then goes for a walk. A second doll (Ann) then moves the marble while Sally is still away and so cannot see what has happened. The children are asked where Sally will look for the marble. In this task, as in other tests of theory of mind designed for children, it is important to ask a series of control questions to ensure that they remember the real location of the marble as well as being able to predict where Sally will look.

Three-year-old children almost always fail classic theory of mind tasks that involve a false belief. In the Sally-Ann task they say that Sally will look in the new location for the marble rather than the original location in which she placed it and where she would expect it to be. In the Smarties task three-year-olds say that another child will expect pencils in the tube. Four- and five-year-olds, however, normally pass both the Sally-Ann and Smarties tests indicating that they are able to distinguish between their own knowledge and that of another person.

However, it is possible that the standard false belief task is too cognitively demanding for young children: in order to pass it a child has to remember the sequence of the events as they happen, correctly understand the experimenter's (complex) question and inhibit their (natural) response to indicate the actual location of the object (Birch & Bloom, 2004). It may be that children fail in this task despite being able to represent the fact that other people have a different perspective.

Nevertheless, performance in other tasks provides a similar picture to the false belief task. For example, three-year-old children are not able to learn a game involving two boxes, one empty and the other containing sweets. In order to succeed at the game the children must deceptively point to the box that does not contain sweets rather than to one that does, otherwise another child will be given the sweets. Attempts to train three-year-olds to deceptively point to the 'wrong' box were a failure but four-year-olds soon picked up the rules of this deception game (Russell, Mauthner, & Sharpe, 1991).

Since the original research was carried out into theory of mind a number of researchers have turned to a consideration of its earliest beginnings. One issue concerns social influences on the development and theory of mind and the other focuses on its origins in infancy.

Social influences on theory of mind

As we will see in Chapter 10, children's early social skills are strongly influenced by their early social experiences. Researchers have asked whether theory of mind might also be subject to the effects of social experience. One obvious place to look is the quality of the interaction between mother and infant since, for most children, this provides the first opportunity to learn about the thoughts and wishes of another person.

In one of the first studies to explore this link (Meins *et al.*, 2002), mother–infant pairs were observed in free play when the infants were six months old. The interactions were coded for the mother's use of mental state language that appropriately commented on her infant's mental state. The other measures were security of attachment, assessed using the Strange Situation procedure and maternal sensitivity during free play (see 6.4).

An independent coder classified the mother's mental state comments as appropriate or inappropriate, according to a coding scheme. In essence, a mental state comment was considered appropriate if the coder judged that the mother had correctly interpreted her child's behaviour or commented on something related to an ongoing activity or to a likely future activity. For example, if the mother commented that her baby wanted a particular toy and the coder judged that this was what the baby wanted the comment was classed as appropriate.

When the children were aged 45 months they were given an appearance–reality task in which they were given four different objects, including a cat-shaped salt shaker, and asked both what the object looked like and what it was 'really and truly'. They were also given a version of the Smarties task (Wimmer & Perner, 1983). At 48 months the children were additionally given a standard false belief task.

The children were also given a verbal intelligence score and this was used to ensure that relationships among scores were not simply the result of differing levels of verbal ability. Although there were a large number of correlations among the measures, rigorous statistical analysis showed that only two factors were reliable predictors of theory of mind ability (using a composite score from the theory of mind tasks at 45 and 48 months). These were verbal intelligence and the proportion of mothers' appropriate mental state comments at six months. Neither security of attachment nor quality of the interaction at six months was related to theory of mind scores and neither was the proportion of inappropriate mental state comments. The relationship was a very specific one.

Meins has coined the term 'mind mindedness' to describe the way in which parents appropriately interpret their infants' desires and intentions. She argues that early experience of mind mindedness provides an infant with relevant experience that can help to develop a theory of mind. Of course, we cannot assume from this study that it is only experience at six months that is crucial since mind mindedness tends to be a stable quality. Mothers who are mind minded with young infants will invariably continue to be mind minded throughout the early years of development and will continue to supply appropriate comments about the mental states of the child and other people; these will, in turn, aid the child's understanding of the beliefs, desires and intentions of other people.

Early cognitive origins of theory of mind

Other evidence about the possible beginnings of theory of mind comes from studies of infant abilities. In one such study (Moll & Tomasello, 2007), infants aged 12 and 18 months played with an adult and two novel toys in succession. Then the adult left the room while the infant played with another adult and a third toy. The first adult then returned and looked at all three toys lined up on a tray, exclaiming excitedly 'Oh look! Look at that one! Can you give it to me?'

In such a situation another adult or older child would suppose that this request is for the novel toy although, from the infant's perspective, none of the toys is novel since they have all been played with. What Moll and Tomasello found was that both the 12- and 18-month-old infants handed the adult the one object that she had not already played with thus showing that they were aware of which object was novel to the adult and that this object was the one he or she would like.

The ability to discriminate between what is novel to you and what is novel to someone else could be seen as laying the foundations for the development of a theory of mind, although it is important to note that considerably more development is necessary before children can respond appropriately in the classic theory of mind

KEY TERMS

Mind mindedness
Describes the way in which parents appropriately interpret their infants' desires and intentions.

tasks involving false belief. If there is a relationship between these early and later abilities, there should be a longitudinal relationship between performance in infancy and the ability to succeed in classic theory of mind tasks. This possibility was investigated in a longitudinal study (Wellman, Lopez-Duran, & LaBounty, 2008). The study began with an initial preferential looking experiment that took place when infants were aged between 10 and 12 months.

During the habituation phase of the experiment, infants saw an actor looking at one of two objects with a positive expression. During the test phase infants saw two different events. In one – the consistent event – the actor looked positively at one object and then picked it up. In the other – the inconsistent event – the actor looked positively at one object and then went on to hold the other. The infants' looking behaviour was used to compute two measures that assessed the speed of habituation and the difference in looking times for the two kinds of test event. The first measure, speed of habituation, has been shown to be an early indicator of intelligence since it measures speed of processing information. The other was taken to be an indicator of the extent to which an infant could distinguish between consistent and inconsistent actions.

At four years of age the same children were given a battery of theory of mind tasks as well as an IQ test. Analysis of the relationship between infant performance in the habituation task and four-year-old performance in theory of mind tasks showed that the speed of habituation measure was related to theory of mind scores. Novelty preference, as measured by the difference in looking times for the consistent and inconsistent conditions, did not predict theory of mind scores. However, Wellman *et al.* argue that this finding suggests a specific link between early social attention and later theory of mind rather than a more general link with early intelligence. The

BOX 8.2: AUTISM AND THEORY OF MIND

One special group of children appear to have a more specific difficulty with theory of mind tasks. These are children who are diagnosed as falling on the autistic spectrum. Childhood autism is a rare developmental disorder, often manifest before the second year of life, that involves a profound failure in social, linguistic and imaginative development. Autism occurs more frequently among boys and it is accompanied by severe learning difficulties in approximately 75 per cent of cases. However, a minority of children with autism have intelligence in the normal range and this latter group can be tested on theory of mind tasks.

Many studies have now shown that the great majority of high functioning children with autism fail theory of mind tasks. For example, in an early study (Baron-Cohen *et al.*, 1985), only 20 per cent of such children were successful in a classic theory of mind task compared with 80 per cent of typically developing children and children with Down syndrome who were of a similar ability level. Such findings have led to the proposal that children with autism have a specific deficit in understanding the mental states of other people, that is, they lack a theory of mind.

As we have noted, a key element in classic theory of mind tasks is the ability to understand false belief. Subsequent research has demonstrated that children with autism have wide-ranging problems in understanding false beliefs. For example, they find it difficult to lie to a thief – which involves the creation of a false belief – even to help a friend although they are able to physically block the thief when prompted (Sodian & Frith, 1992). They also find second-order theory of mind tasks, which involve understanding of what someone thinks that someone else thinks, to be impossible and the small percentage of children with autism who can pass a standard theory of mind task do not pass second order tasks (Baron-Cohen, 1989). However, in spite of their well-documented problems in understanding false beliefs, there is evidence that the difficulties of children with autism go well beyond this.

Leslie (1991) has argued that autistic children lack the ability to suspend belief in order simultaneously to consider the real and symbolic properties of objects. Typically developing children know that a banana remains a banana, even when they are pretending that the banana is a telephone. Leslie argues that autistic children cannot 'decouple' the properties of the real object from its mental representation, so that the object can take on pretend properties. This basic deficit makes autistic children excessively literal in their understanding since they cannot consider reality 'as if' it were different (Leslie, 1991). On a related point, Happé (1993) argues that children with autism, even when they are high functioning, have difficulties in understanding non-literal language such as irony.

Another area in which children with autism show atypical development is in joint attention (see 5.3). In a longitudinal study, the siblings of children with autism were followed up from infancy (Baron-Cohen, Allen, & Gillberg, 1992). Such children are at increased risk of being on the autistic spectrum because there is a strong genetic component to the disorder. A small number of the children were identified as having atypical patterns of both joint attention and pretend play at 18 months and later went on to receive a diagnosis of autism. We have already considered the possibility that difficulties in pretence may be a characteristic of children with autism. What might be the significance of a problem with joint attention?

We can argue that there might be both direct and indirect effects. First, a difficulty with joint attention may be a marker for autism because it involves the co-ordination of attention with another person and the picking up of social signals. Second, following on from the work of Meins, we can also see that difficulties with joint attention could make it very difficult for mothers to be mind-minded (Meins et al., 2002). Commenting appropriately on what a young child wants or needs often relies on being able to tell on what a child is focusing attention. This will be difficult where joint attention does not develop in the normal way.

rationale for their conclusion is that, at the same time as the theory of mind tasks, the children were given an IQ test and a test of executive function. The relationship between the rate of habituation and theory of mind scores remained even when both IQ and executive functioning were accounted for.

8.7 SUMMARY

Piaget laid the foundations for research on many aspects of preschool cognitive development. For him the deficits that children at this age showed – in the conservation task, the three mountains task, in reasoning and analogy making – suggested a specific stage of logical development (the pre-operational stage) in which the ability for abstract logical reasoning had not yet developed. However, subsequent research has shown that, in virtually all domains, Piaget seriously underestimated children's abilities, usually by using tasks that were too complex or abstract for preschool children to solve. By using simple, concrete tasks with objects that are familiar to children of this age researchers have shown that preschool children can do many of the things that Piaget claimed they could not. Often it seems that the limiting factors in children's performance are their lack of familiarity with objects and situations, and that development proceeds as they gain more familiarity. A more general limiting factor might be children's memory development. Several of the tasks we have discussed require children to keep several different and sometimes conflicting pieces of information in memory (such as different perspectives in the three mountains task), and there seems to be gradual development of this ability.

As we have seen repeatedly, doing developmental psychology is about studying the abilities of children, but it is at least as much about carefully considering how to interpret the results of a study. In Chapter 4 we discussed 'rich' versus 'lean' interpretations of infants' abilities, and again in this chapter, we have seen something similar: Piaget believed that the ability to solve a task (e.g. the three mountains task) requires a sophisticated ability, and thus, failure in the task shows that this ability is absent in preschool children. Donaldson (1978) argued against Piaget's interpretation and showed that the failure in the task can be explained with how it was set up. In a simpler version of the task, children can do much better. However, as we have discussed, it is possible that Donaldson's task was in fact measuring a somewhat different and simpler ability than Piaget's task.

We have also seen that the preschool years witness important developments in understanding what other people know and how this differs from one's own knowledge. This kind of understanding has its origin in infancy and it grows out of interactions with other people.

Preschoolers are also beginning to understand the boundaries between what is real and what is not real although, as with other abilities that develop during this period, how children perform in tests of theory of mind and in judgements of fantasy, appearance and reality is very dependent on the task that they are given in a particular experiment.

With each new study we learn something about children's abilities, but we also learn that we need to carefully consider what each study actually measures and, thus, what failure in a task means for understanding how children's abilities develop through the preschool years.

FURTHER READING

Apperly, I. (2010). *Mindreaders: The cognitive basis of theory of mind.* Hove: Psychology Press.

Goswami, U. (2010). Inductive and deductive reasoning. In U. Goswami (Ed.), *The Blackwell handbook of childhood cognitive development* (2nd edition) (pp. 399–419). Oxford: Blackwell.

Meins, E., Fernyhough, C., Wainwright, R., Das Gupta, M., Fradley, E. & Tuckey, M. (2002). Maternal mind–mindedness and attachment security as predictors of Theory of Mind understanding. *Child Development*, 73, 1715–1726.

Wellman, H. M. (2010). Developing a theory of mind. In U. Goswami (Ed.), *The Blackwell handbook of childhood cognitive development* (2nd edition) (pp. 258–284). Oxford: Blackwell.

ESSAY QUESTIONS

1. Discuss, using examples, how changes in experimental procedures have given different answers about preschool children's cognitive abilities.
2. Critically discuss different methods for assessing children's theory of mind.
3. Explain what is meant by 'mind mindedness' and discuss its influence on children's development during the preschool years.

CHAPTER 9

CONTENTS

Language development in the preschool years

9

After reading this chapter you will be able to

- explain the key differences between Inside-out and Outside-in theories of language development
- outline the nativist theories of Chomsky and Pinker
- evaluate evidence about the relationship between grammatical development and the language input that children receive
- explain what overregularisation errors are and why they have been considered theoretically significant for theories of language development
- describe how a preferential looking paradigm can be used to understand early grammatical understanding
- describe the main features of specific language impairment
- explain what the FOXP2 gene is and describe its likely role in human language.

When we discussed language development in infancy (see Chapter 5), our main focus was on how children begin to understand and use words. In this chapter the main focus will be on how children learn about grammar, that is, how they learn to combine and modify words in systematic ways to form larger units of meaning. Mastering the grammar of a language is key to being able to use it effectively to communicate and children are still developing their grammatical skills through the early school years. We begin the chapter by considering two rather different views of the processes that underlie the mastery of grammar.

9.1 THEORETICAL ACCOUNTS OF LANGUAGE DEVELOPMENT

There are many different theories of language development – or language acquisition as some theorists prefer – but one useful way of grouping theories together is to divide them into Inside-out and Outside-in theories (Hirsh-Pasek & Golinkoff, 1996; Roy

Table 9.1 A comparison of Inside-out and Outside-in theories of language development (Adapted from Hirsh-Pasek & Golinkoff, 1996)

	Inside-out theories	Outside-in theories
Initial structure	Linguistic	Social or cognitive
Mechanism of language development	Domain-specific	Domain-general
Source of structure	Innate	Learning procedures
Key theories	Chomsky 1965/ 1986 Hyams 1986 Landau & Gleitman 1985 Pinker 1999	Bates & MacWhinney 1989 Bruner 1975/ 1983 Nelson 1977 Snow 1989

& Chiat, 2012). The main difference between the two types of theory is that Inside-out theorists claim that children acquire language according to the innate linguistic constraints of a 'language faculty' while Outside-in theorists place a much greater emphasis on the role of experience, also arguing that the mechanisms underpinning language learning are general-purpose rather than language-specific. The two kinds of approach place very different emphases on the role of language experience with nativist – Inside-out – theories minimising the role of children's own experience. The main differences between the Inside-out and Outside-in approaches are summarised in Table 9.1. You may also have recognised that the contrast between these two major types of theory has its origin in the nature versus nurture debate that we outlined in Chapter 1.

Nativist theories

The first, and most famous, of the nativist theorists is Noam Chomsky. Since Chomsky first published his influential critique of Skinner's *Verbal Behavior* in 1959, he has gone on to spell out his views on the nature of language acquisition in a series of influential monographs culminating in *Knowledge of Language* (Chomsky, 1986). Although these developments mark an important change in Chomsky's thinking, the essence of his fundamental view of the nature of language acquisition has remained unchanged. Chomsky's claim is that

> language is only in the most marginal sense taught and that teaching is in no sense essential to the acquisition of language. In a certain sense I think we might even go on and say that language is not even learned . . . It seems to me that, if we want a reasonable metaphor, we should talk about growth. Language seems to me to grow in the mind rather as familiar physical systems of the body grow. We begin our interchange with the world with our minds in a particular genetically determined state. Through interaction with experience—with everything around us—this state changes until it reaches a mature state we call a state of knowledge of language . . . this series of changes seems to me analogous to the growth of organs.
> (Chomsky in conversation with Brian McGee, 1979)

This quotation encapsulates one key tenet of the Inside-out view – experience and the language environment have only a minimal influence on the innately driven processes of language development in the child. In the quotation Chomsky talks of 'interaction with experience' but this is only in the sense that children need exposure to the particular language used in the local language community. This minimal contribution for language experience is necessary even in Chomsky's theory in order to explain why a child who grows up surrounded by people speaking English will learn to speak English rather than, say, French, Italian or Japanese. We should note, in passing, that what Chomsky is concerned about is the learning of grammatical rules. Clearly learning about individual words has to be rooted in experience since these are language specific. For this reason it can be argued that this kind of account is, in effect, a two-process account since it assumes that acquiring the vocabulary and the grammar of a language involve rather different kinds of learning (Tomasello, 2006).

The other main tenet of the Inside-out view is that the processes involved in language acquisition are language-specific and thus distinct from those involved in other aspects of cognitive development. The main reason why Chomsky argues for this uniqueness of language processes is that, for him, acquiring a language involves the acquisition of a body of language-specific knowledge. In Chomsky's early theory (Chomsky 1965), this knowledge was characterised as a set of syntactic rules but, in his more recent theorising, Chomsky (1986) has argued for a set of principles and parameters.

One aim of the principles and parameters account is to explain how the many different languages of the world can be acquired from a common starting point. Each language parameter has a number of settings that vary from one language to another. For example, one of the most widely discussed parameters, called 'pro-drop', has two possible settings. One setting is for languages such as Italian, where sentences without a grammatical subject are allowed and the pronoun can be omitted – hence 'pro-drop' – and the other setting is for languages, such as English, where sentences without subjects are not permissible. This difference between languages that allow subjectless sentences and those that do not can be seen in an English sentence such as '*It's* raining', which is translated into Italian simply as the verb 'Piove'. In Chomsky's theory, exposure to a few sentences of Italian would produce one setting of the pro-drop parameter and exposure to a few sentences of English the other. Chomsky makes it clear that, in his theory, parameter settings are 'triggered' by exposure to a particular language rather than being learned.

As a linguist, Chomsky has been concerned with the general mechanism by which children acquire language rather than with providing a detailed theory. However, a number of psychologists have developed their own Inside-out theories of innate, language-specific processes underpinning language development. One such theory is that of Pinker, who argues for a words and rules approach in which the periphery of linguistic competence, including words, is learned but the core, i.e. grammar, is innately given (Pinker, 1999). Pinker argues, for example, that children have innate knowledge of grammatical word classes, such as noun and verb, and syntactic categories such as subject and object. On his view, this information is then used to 'bootstrap' grammatical development in different ways.

In '**semantic bootstrapping**', children are able to link certain semantic categories such as 'person' or 'thing' to their corresponding grammatical word class and syntactic categories by a series of 'linking rules'. The linking rules described by Pinker are complex but a simple example will serve to illustrate the general idea. Suppose that a child hears the following sentence while, at the same time, seeing her pet cat playing: 'Fluffy is chasing the ball.' It will be clear from the context that

KEY TERMS

Semantic bootstrapping
The linking of certain semantic categories such as 'person' or 'thing' to their corresponding grammatical word class and syntactic categories by a series of 'linking rules'.

Fluffy is the actor (i.e. carrying out the action), that 'chasing' refers to an action and 'ball' to an object or thing. Thus, through linking rules, 'Fluffy' and 'ball' can both be interpreted as nouns and 'chasing' as a verb. Additionally 'Fluffy' can also be identified as the subject of the sentence and 'ball' the object.

The use of linking rules together with innate knowledge of word categories would only get children so far in discovering syntactic rules so, according to Pinker, there is also '**syntactic bootstrapping**'. This involves inferring information about the syntactic properties of words from their position in the sentence and extending these inferences to new cases that occur in similar syntactic positions. For example, if a particular verb always has a noun occurring both before and after it, as would be the case for a transitive verb such as 'chases', it would be treated differently from an intransitive verb, such as 'run', which always occurs with a preceding noun but never has a following noun.

Pinker has shown that children are able to generalise morpho-syntactic information in a way that suggests they are capable of syntactic bootstrapping. In a well-known study (Pinker, Lebeaux, & Frost, 1987), four-year-old children were taught nonsense verbs that described unusual actions. For example, children were given two contrasting sentences: 'The pig is *pilking* the horse' and 'I'm *mooping* a ball to the mouse'. The critical difference between these sentences lies in the type of verb that they contain. The first sentence uses a verb – such as 'brush' or 'rub' – in which one animal (the pig) does something to another animal (the horse). The verb in the second sentence is different because it is performed on an inanimate object (a ball). This kind of verb functions in the same way as 'roll' or 'throw'.

Children were asked to explain what had happened in the pictures – a technique that was designed to see whether they could form a past tense for the nonsense verbs. If they understood the distinction between the two types of verb they should produce different responses for the two pictures. This was what happened. The children produced descriptions such as 'The horse is being pilked by the pig' and 'I mooped the mouse a ball' but not, for example, 'The mouse is being mooped by the ball'. This latter form would not be correct.

Pinker, Lebeaux and Frost's study shows that, by four years of age, children have already developed a good understanding of the difference between verb classes. The question is whether this understanding grows out of innate knowledge or whether it emerges from children's experience with language. Preschool children can certainly add morphemes to real words in order to create (or 'coin') novel words. Clark (1995) has described a large number of examples including cases where a child coins a verb from a noun (*Is Anna going to babysitter me?*) or an adjective from a verb (*Try to be more rememberful, Mom.*) Such examples show that preschool children are aware of some of the rules of word formation, for example how to form a verb infinitive using an ER ending or an adjective using the common FUL ending as in 'careful'. However the fact that children can respect word class distinctions – and use them in novel ways – does not tell us anything about the source of their ability to do this. They could be using a language-specific ability underpinned by innate knowledge (as Pinker proposes) or they could be using a more general kind of distributional analysis in which they separate out word classes on the basis of their particular patterns of occurrence within different sentence types. We saw an example of this kind of statistical learning in 5.4 when we discussed the research of Johnson and Jusczyk (2001).

Outside-in theories

In Chapter 5 we considered Bruner's theory about the way that the child's experience of social interaction provided a springboard into language. This theory is one example of an Outside-in theory that emphasises the role of experience and argues for general-purpose rather than language-specific processes in language learning. A key tenet of Outside-in theories is that language structure emerges from language use. In other words, children learn the regularities of language by slowly putting together more and more complex utterances that grow out of their attempts to communicate effectively. These word combinations grow out of the language that they hear and from which they extract consistent patterns.

As we have already noted, one important feature that distinguishes Inside-out from Outside-in theories is the emphasis that they place on children's language environments as a significant contributory factor in their language development. Many studies have attempted to establish the extent to which linguistic input – the language children hear – directly influences language development. As we saw earlier there are very strong links between early language experience and early vocabulary development (see Chapter 5). It has been more difficult to determine whether such links exist for grammatical development although, as with the case of early word learning, it is clear that learning about grammar involves the extraction of regularities in spoken language in relation to familiar, everyday activities.

This was the conclusion of a longitudinal study carried out in Bristol (Ellis & Wells, 1980). The study found very little relationship between syntactic measures of maternal speech (i.e. length and complexity of maternal utterances) and children's language development. What proved to be important was the relationship between what mothers said to their children and what the children were doing at the time. Most notably, the group of children in the Bristol study who showed the most precocious development – Early Fast Developers – were asked more questions and given more instructions by their mothers than children with less precocious development. The mothers of this group were also more responsive to their children's own utterances, which they tended to acknowledge and imitate more often than the mothers of children whose language development was less precocious. Finally, the Early Fast Developers had more opportunity to hear speech that referred to activities in which they were currently involved.

What binds these apparently disparate features of maternal speech together is that they are all concerned with the relationship of individual utterances to the prevailing nonverbal context. In other words, the mothers of children with more precocious language development were more likely to ask questions, give instructions and generally comment on the activity in which their child was currently engaged. The Bristol study thus demonstrated that, in the very early stages of learning to talk, mothers who relate their language very specifically to their children's ongoing activity have children with more precocious development.

Other evidence of the role of language experience in children's language learning comes from cross-linguistic comparisons. Children learning English as a first language tend to have a predominance of object names in their early vocabulary. This contrasts with children learning Korean, for whom verbs appear earlier and form a greater proportion of early vocabulary (Gopnik & Choi, 1995). Similarly, 21-month-old children who are learning Mandarin Chinese have as many different verbs as

BOX 9.1: CORRECTING CHILDREN'S GRAMMATICAL ERRORS

Another effect of input to emerge in recent studies concerns adult correction of children's grammatical errors. The traditional view had been that parents rarely correct grammatical errors and respond mainly to the content of what children say (Brown & Hanlon, 1970). Attempts to correct grammatical errors were considered to be rare and doomed to failure: many textbooks quote a well-known example from McNeill (1966) of a mother's repeated, but unsuccessful, attempt to correct a child:

Child: Nobody don't like me.
Mother: No, Say 'Nobody likes me'.
Child: Nobody don't like me.
(8 repetitions of this sequence)
Mother: Now listen carefully. Say 'Nobody likes me'.
Child: Oh! Nobody don't likes me.

(McNeill, 1966, p. 69)

Saxton (2000) has shown that children do, in fact, receive more direct evidence about their errors than was previously thought. This is either in the form of what Saxton has called 'negative evidence' or 'negative feedback'. Negative evidence is provided when a child produces an incorrect utterance that is immediately followed by an adult utterance modelling the correct form:

Child: I *losed* my hands (pulling up hands inside pyjama sleeves)
Adult: You *lost* your hands.
Child: I *lost* my hands.

Negative feedback is when an adult queries a child utterance:

Child: The pirate *hitted* him on the head.
Adult: What?
Child: The pirate *hit* him on the head.

Saxton has shown that children often reformulate their own utterance following both types of negative input. He argues that the adult model of the correct form is providing children with a contrast between the correct and incorrect forms. One might suggest that such an effect will only be of short duration, with the child reverting to the incorrect form when there is no adult model to follow. However, Saxton, Kulcsar, Marshall and Rupra (1988) have shown, in an experimental setting, that preschoolers will learn the irregular past tense of nonsense verbs (*pell/pold* and *streep/strept*) better when they are presented with negative evidence over a five-week period rather than only the correct form. The methodology of this study was similar to that of Pinker, Lebeaux and Frost (1987) in using puppets to depict the novel action.

Verb form	Action
Pro/prew (cf. throw/threw) Twisting motion applied with a cross-ended stick.	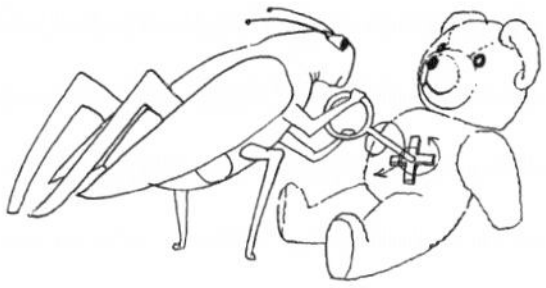
Neak/noke (cf. speak/spoke) Repeated clapping motion in which target is trapped between the palms.	
Jing/jang (cf. sing/sang) Striking a target with a beanbag flipped from a spoon.	
Streep/strept (cf. creep/crept) Ejection of a ping-pong ball from a cone-shaped launcher towards target.	
Sty/stought (cf. buy/bought) Prodding action performed with a plastic stick which concertinas on contact to produce a honking noise.	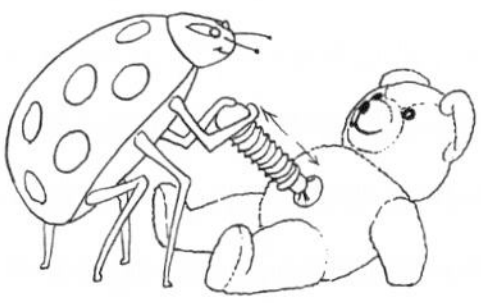
Pell/pold (cf. sell/sold) Striking action achieved by swinging a beanbag on the end of a string towards target.	

Figure 9.1
Meanings and past tense alternations of Saxton's novel verb forms. Drawings by Colin Saxton. Reproduced with permission from Matthew Saxton.

nouns in their vocabulary (Tardif, 1996). These patterns reflect a greater preponderance of verbs in the maternal speech of Korean and Mandarin speaking mothers compared to English speaking mothers.

9.2 EARLY WORD COMBINATIONS

Most children are combining words into simple utterances by the time that they are two years old and some children will be doing so well before their second birthday. Children use their early multi-word utterances to talk about many of the same things that they talked about when they were only able to produce one word at a time. The length of children's utterances is measured by the **Mean Length of Utterance** (MLU). This measure is calculated by taking a sample of 100 or so utterances and working out their average length in morphemes. One word may also be one **morpheme** but, where a child produces a word that is not in its stem (or basic) form, this counts as more than one morpheme. So *Baby cry* is two words and also two morphemes but *Baby cried* is three morphemes because the stem form 'cry' has been modified to the past tense form by adding the ED morpheme. Similarly, *Babies cry* also contains three morphemes as babies is the plural form of baby.

Data collected using the **Communicative Development Inventory** (CDI) have shown that children vary very considerably in the age at which they first begin to combine words. Figure 9.2 shows the maximum length of utterances produced by children aged between 16 and 30 months (Fenson *et al.*, 1994). The maximum length of utterances per sentence rose from just under two morphemes at 16 months to around eight morphemes at 30 months. Girls were slightly ahead of boys but this difference was not significant.

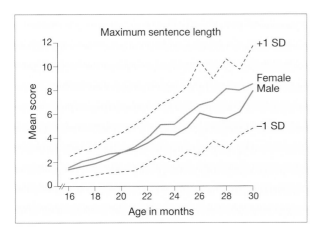

Figure 9.2
The purple and blue lines mark the mean scores for maximum sentence length on the toddler scale reported to be produced by females and males at each month. The dotted lines indicate the range at each month for ±1 SD for the sexes combined.
From Fenson et al. (1994), © The Society for Research in Child Development Inc, reproduced with permission from Wiley-Blackwell.

Pioneering analyses of children's early multi-word combinations revealed that many of them had a systematic structure in which one event word was used in conjunction with a wide variety of object labels (Braine, 1976). For example, a child might combine 'more' with many other object names as in, *More juice, More milk, More nana* (banana) or use the word 'no' in a similar way. Braine called these systematic combinations, pivot schema.

More recent experimental research has confirmed that young children are able to combine words productively according to a pivot schema. In order to demonstrate this, 22-month-old children were taught a novel object label such as 'wug' (using a nonsense word to ensure that the word was entirely unfamiliar). Children were able to use this new word in combination with their existing pivot words, producing such utterances as 'More wug' and 'Wug gone' (Tomasello, Akhtar, Dodson, & Rekau, 1997). However, children were not able to move beyond combinations that were similar to ones in their existing schema. For example, children were taught a novel word such as 'meeking' as they watched someone acting out a novel action and heard. 'Look! Meeking!' Children found it very difficult to use the novel verb in response to questions such as, 'what did you do?'.

Tomasello (2006) concludes that, although early word combinations are systematic, each pivot schema operates in isolation and children do not have an overarching grammar of their language. He makes similar arguments about the early use of verbs, showing that new uses of a verb tend to be very similar to old uses. This view is supported by experimental evidence in which children are taught novel verbs. Typically children are not able to use a new verb in a construction that has a different form from the one in which they have been taught the verb.

All this suggests that children have a lot to learn about the general principles underlying the combination of words and that they move very gradually from having isolated pockets of knowledge towards a wide-ranging understanding of grammar.

9.3 THE BEGINNINGS OF GRAMMAR

One of the sections in the CDI Toddler Scale asks parents about the length and complexity of their children's utterances. Rather than asking parents to report actual utterances that their children had produced, parents are given choices between pairs of sentences and asked to indicate which one is more like the kind of utterances that their child is currently saying. The sentence pairs are graded from very simple sentences to increasingly complex ones. At the simplest end of the scale, parents are asked to decide whether their child says sentences such as *two shoe* or *two shoes*. At the most complex end of the scale they have to decide between *I sing song* and *I sing song for you* and between *Baby crying* and *Baby crying cuz she's sad*.

You can see that in all cases, the second option is the more complex utterance. There are 37 sentence pairs in all and a child scores between 0 and 37 according to the number of second options that are chosen by the parents.

Figure 9.3 shows the average sentence complexity score from the CDI study. The score is around zero at 16 months and has risen to around 24 by 30 months. The sharpest increase in sentence complexity occurs after 24 months indicating that this is the age at which most children begin to show rapid syntactic development. You will also see from Figure 9.3 that girls produced more complex sentences than boys of the same age. This difference was significant.

Two factors contribute to sentence complexity. One is the number of words that children can combine in a single utterance and the other is the number of morphological endings (grammatical morphemes) that they use. For example, *two shoes* is considered to be more complex than *two shoe* because the former includes the plural *s* morpheme on the noun. Again the CDI data can tell us about children's developing ability to use grammatical morphemes.

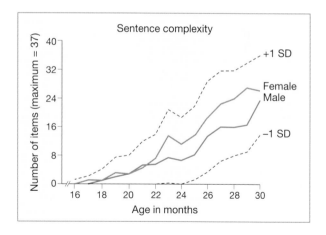

Figure 9.3

The purple and blue lines mark for females and males the mean number of sentence pairs on the toddler form for which the parent selected the more complex option as typical of their speech. The dotted lines indicate the range at each month for ±1 SD for the sexes combined. From Fenson et al. (1994), © The Society for Research in Child Development Inc, reproduced with permission from Wiley-Blackwell.

The CDI concentrates on four morphemes that children tend to acquire early on. Two are used to modify nouns – the regular noun plural (*s*) and the possessive (*s*) – and two are used to modify verbs – the progressive (*ing*) and the past tense (*ed*). The CDI data show that, at 16 months, few children were able to use any of these grammatical morphemes. By the age of two, most children were using two of them and by two and a half most children were able to use all four. The majority of children used the two noun morphemes before they used the two verb morphemes and the *ed* ending proved to be the most difficult of all.

Not all nouns are made plural by the addition of the *s* morpheme and not all past tenses of verbs end in *ed*. However, once children start to use these two morphemes, they sometimes incorrectly apply them to words that have an irregular pattern. For example a child might say *mouses* or *teeths* (instead of 'mice' and 'teeth') and *blowed* and *comed* (instead of 'blew' and 'came'). These kinds of errors are known as *overregularisations*.

The CDI Toddler Scale contains a list of common **overregularisation errors** (14 occurring with nouns and 31 occurring in past tense verbs) and parents are asked to indicate which of these their child has produced. Children generally make very few of these overregularisation errors before their second birthday. By two and a half, about 25 per cent of the children in the sample were reported as using eight or more of the overregularisations but the majority of children used fewer than five out of the total of 45 items. This finding is consistent with other studies (Marcus *et al.*, 1992) showing that children make overregularisation errors much less often than was originally thought.

Overregularisation errors have been seen as theoretically important in child language development because they provide evidence that children are developing an awareness of morphological rules. It has often been argued that children apply newly derived morphological rules very strictly to all nouns and verbs even if they are irregular. However, it now seems that, as with other aspects of language development, there is considerable individual variation and by no means all children go through a stage of overregularisation.

9.4 EXPERIMENTAL STUDIES OF EARLY GRAMMATICAL UNDERSTANDING

One important development in the study of early grammatical understanding has been the use of the preferential looking paradigm. To investigate grammatical understanding a spoken sentence is presented at the child's midline while two events are presented on television screens at either side (see Figure 9.4). If children understand something about the spoken sentence, they should look longer at the screen depicting the event described in the sentence.

In one early series of studies (Hirsh-Pasek & Golinkoff, 1996) toddlers heard sentences such as 'See? Big Bird's hugging Cookie Monster' while seeing *Big Bird hugging Cookie Monster* on one screen and *Cookie Monster hugging Big Bird* on the other. The choice of the events depicted on the television screens is critical for demonstrating understanding of grammar. In this example, both screens showed the two characters mentioned in the sentence so a simple recognition of their names would not be enough to distinguish *Big Bird hugging Cookie Monster* from *Cookie Monster hugging Big Bird*. If the children look significantly longer at the screen showing the

Figure 9.4

The intermodal preferential looking paradigm showing a sample stimulus set from Experiment 1. On the left screen a woman is kissing keys while holding a ball in the foreground. On the right screen she is kissing a ball while holding keys in the foreground. Reproduced with permission from Hirsh-Pasek and Golinkoff (1996), with permission from MIT Press.

event described in the sentence this would be an indication that they associated the sentence with that event and thus were sensitive to the grammatical contrast (in this case, word order) being tested.

The studies of Hirsh-Pasek and Golinkoff (1996) showed, among other things, that 18-month-old children could distinguish word order (as in the Big Bird–Cookie Monster example). However, the more complex contrast between transitive and intransitive uses of a verb (as in 'Look at Cookie Monster turning Big Bird' versus 'Look at Cookie Monster and Big Bird turning') was not distinguished until several months later. Interestingly, children first showed a preference for the 'correct' event only with familiar verbs, supporting the view that much early verb learning is verb-specific (Tomasello, 1992). This pattern occurred at 23 months but, by 27 months, children preferred the correct event even with unfamiliar verbs.

Overall the results of Hirsh-Pasek and Golinkoff show that, by the age of 24 months, children are beginning to use syntax as a guide to meaning but they are not doing so six months earlier, at 18 months. These findings using the preferential looking procedure thus support evidence from many other studies showing that that there is a significant period of grammatical development towards the end of the second year.

Grammatical development continues throughout the preschool years. As we saw in the previous section, mastering verb endings such as -ed and -ing is an important step in being able to understand tense. In another study that used preferential looking (Wagner, Swensen, & Naigles, 2009), three-year-olds were presented with two versions of four familiar events such as picking a flower and drinking juice. All of the events were filmed using an actor and presented on television screens. In one version of the events, the event carried on throughout the video whereas, in the other, the event began and was completed. For example in one version the actor was picking flowers throughout the trial and in the other she picked flowers for two seconds and then held up the resulting bouquet for four seconds.

After some familiarisation trials the children were presented with a test trial in which they saw the two versions of the event side-by-side on television screens and heard either 'Look, she's picking the flowers' or 'Look, she's picked the flowers'. If the children understood that the *-ing* morpheme referred to an ongoing event and the *-ed* morpheme to a completed event they should have looked more to the relevant screen. This is exactly what happened. For example, when children heard 'picked' they looked longer at the screen showing the completed event than when they heard 'picking'.

In this first study the four verbs were chosen to be highly familiar to three-year-olds. However, developing language is about being able to generalise what has been learned to unfamiliar words. Wagner *et al.* (2009: Experiment 3) went on to ask another question about children's understanding of the two morphemes. In order to see how good children were at generalising their understanding of verb endings, Wagner *et al.* used unfamiliar actions and novel words to describe these actions. For example, one action was icing a cake with blue icing. The two nonsense verbs were *geed* and *krad*. Each verb could have either the *-ing* or *-ed* ending added. As in Experiment 1, the children (who had a mean age of 29 months) were initially shown familiarisation trials in which they saw the familiar events from Experiment 1 and the novel events. The children also heard the nonsense verbs in both a progressive (i.e. ongoing) and past form.

Analysis of the children's looking pattern during test trials showed that, for the familiar actions, they looked longer at the matching screen as they had done in Experiment 1. The key comparison was for the novel verbs. In order to ensure that any differences in looking times could be attributed to children's understanding of the verb endings, the main analysis considered children's looking patterns to verb forms that they had not heard during the familiarisation trials, that is, *geeded* and *kradding*. The analysis showed that, in two conditions of the study, children looked longer at the completed action when they heard *geeded* and longer at the ongoing action when they heard *kradding*. In the other two conditions, which used different actions, there was no difference in looking pattern for the two verb forms and children generally had a preference for the ongoing action.

These experiments show that, around the age of two and a half years, children are capable of understanding the meaning of English verb morphology. However, it is also clear that their understanding at this early age is fragile and that it is strongest for verbs that are familiar. This pattern illustrates the more general point that language development, like so much of early development, initially generalises from familiar instances.

9.5 SPECIFIC LANGUAGE IMPAIRMENT

The term **specific language impairment** (SLI) is used to describe cases in which children's language skills are much worse than would be expected from their level of nonverbal intelligence and where the difficulties with language cannot be explained by other known causes such as deafness or a pervasive developmental disorder such as autism. As with many of the other developmental disorders that we discuss in this book, there are a number of different patterns of difficulty. Some children with SLI have difficulties in both the understanding of spoken language and in their own production of speech. For others the main problem may lie in understanding what

KEY TERMS

Specific language impairment
This term is used to describe cases in which children's language skills are much worse than would be expected from their level of nonverbal intelligence and where the difficulties with language cannot be explained by other known causes such as deafness or a pervasive developmental disorder such as autism.

other people say rather than in their own spoken language. Some children may be good at understanding and producing syntax but poor at understanding the social aspects of language.

The precise criteria for identifying a child as suffering from SLI vary but the general principle is that of discrepancy, that is, performance on language tasks is lower than would be expected. For example, in the diagnostic criteria published by the World Health Organization (1993), known as ICD-10, the discrepancy is either one standard deviation below nonverbal IQ or two standard deviations below chronological age. Depending on the diagnostic criteria, the incidence of SLI ranges from 3 per cent to 6 per cent and the ratio of boys to girls from 3:1 to 4:1 (Hulme & Snowling, 2009).

A number of longitudinal studies have tracked children identified with SLI over time. Many children are first identified as having SLI in the early years at school. For some of these children, early difficulties with language will resolve over time but, for a considerable number, problems will persist. In a study of 87 children who had difficulties with speech and language at the age of four (Bishop & Edmundson, 1987), an initial classification was made of either SLI (that is a specific difficulty with language and nonverbal IQ within normal range) or of a speech–language difficulty coupled with an impairment of nonverbal IQ. After 18 months there was a rather different pattern in the two groups. For almost half of the SLI group (44 per cent), the language difficulties at age four had resolved. However, for the children with the more general delay, language problems had resolved in only 11 per cent of cases.

In a follow-up study (Bishop & Adams, 1990), 83 of the original sample of 87 children were re-assessed when they were eight years old. The majority of children whose language difficulties had resolved at the second assessment were still doing well and had good oral language and reading skills. Interestingly, however, this group showed some mild difficulties on two measures of oral language comprehension that assessed, respectively, understanding of grammar and social understanding. This suggests that these children, who had a good nonverbal IQ, had largely been able to compensate for their language difficulties and so had only very minor problems that would not have been evident from everyday speech.

The group of SLI children whose language difficulties had not resolved after 18 months showed a different pattern. Their oral language skills and reading ability, especially reading comprehension, were significantly below chronological age level. The children with general delay at five and a half months showed the most serious problems in that they continued to have severe difficulties with all the language and cognitive tests that were administered.

Specific language impairment often co-occurs with other developmental disorders. This is known as **comorbidity**. There is a substantial comorbidity between SLI and dyslexia (see Chapter 13) and also SLI and developmental co-ordination disorder (DCD). As the study by Bishop and Edmundson (1987) suggests there is also an association between language difficulties and general learning difficulties for many children. More recent evidence (Botting, 2005) suggests that some children who satisfy the diagnosis of SLI when they are young (because they have language difficulties but nonverbal IQ within normal range) show a decline in nonverbal IQ as they get older.

KEY TERMS

FOXP2 gene
Mutation of this gene, among others, in humans causes speech and language impairments.

These various patterns of comorbidity of SLI with other disorders suggests that language impairment is often an indication that children are experiencing serious and pervasive developmental problems. As Hulme and Snowling (2009) so rightly conclude, 'children who really do satisfy the strict criteria for a "specific" language impairment may be quite unusual'.

Some recent evidence about the genetic factors that underpin SLI gives an indication of the complexity of factors involved. It has been clear for some time that SLI is a highly heritable disorder. Among monozygotic (MZ) twins, that is, twins who have identical genes because they developed from a single fertilised egg that divided, there is a high level of concordance for SLI. In other words, if one MZ twin has SLI the other twin is very likely to have SLI or a non-specific language impairment (that is a language deficit and low nonverbal skills). The concordance rate for dizygotic (DZ) twins, who share the same degree of genetic similarity as siblings, is considerably lower (Hayiou-Thomas, Bishop, & Plomin, 2005).

At a more detailed level, twin studies have shown that a wide range of linguistic abilities appear to be affected by genetic factors. Interestingly, vocabulary appears to be less affected than phonology or syntax and, overall, expressive language difficulties are more susceptible to genetic effects than receptive language skills (see Hulme & Snowling, 2009 for a review).

Over the last decade a number of genetic mutations affecting language development have been identified and these also provide evidence of the complexity of genetic factors in SLI. One of the first discoveries came about when a large three-generational family in the UK – known as the KE family – was identified as having a history of language problems (Lai, Fisher, Hurst, Vargha-Khadem, & Monaco, 2001). Analysis showed that all members of the family who had a speech or language problem had a mutation on chromosome 7 that was labelled FOXP2. None of the other members of the family had this mutation. Subsequent investigation of the family showed that their speech and language impairments were unusual in that they involved problems with motor control of the face and mouth; and the FOXP2 mutation has not been found in children with a more typical pattern of SLI (Hulme & Snowling, 2009).

Another important point to note about the **FOXP2 gene** is that it is not unique to humans and it can be found, for example, in the mouse where its form is almost identical. Since mice do not have language it is clear that the FOXP2 gene cannot be responsible for language in any simple way (Fisher, 2006). Furthermore, further research has suggested that FOXP2 is involved in the development of the heart, lung and gut in the embryo as well as in the development of pathways that are important for language. As Fisher puts it: 'FOXP2 is a well conserved regulatory gene with multiple roles during development (and perhaps also in adulthood) and is likely to influence patterning/function of several regions of the CNS in all mammals' (Fisher, 2006, p. 288).

It is now clear from studies of adults and children with SLI that the idea of 'a single gene for language' does not appears to be correct (Fisher, 2006). Instead, it appears that there are many different genes associated with language development and language disorder. To date, four potential chromosomal regions have been identified and it is likely that more will be discovered with further research.

9.6 LANGUAGE DISORDER AND LANGUAGE DISADVANTAGE

One final issue to consider in relation to language development is the contrast between language disorder and language disadvantage. In the previous section we considered cases where children appeared to have either a specific difficulty with developing their language skills or a more general delay that also affected language ability. In this final section of the chapter we consider how the development of language skills might be affected by social factors.

In an extensive study of the prevalence of SLI in the United States, Tomblin and colleagues (Tomblin, Records, Buckwalter, Smith, & O'Brien, 1997) reported an overall incidence of 7 per cent. However, the incidence varied across ethnic subgroups with the highest rates occurring among Native American and Afro-American children and lower rates among Hispanic and White children. Interestingly, there was not a single case of SLI among the Asian community. Tomblin *et al.* interpret their findings as indicating that SLI was more prevalent in groups with lower levels of parental education and income. However, another interpretation is possible as argued in a recent chapter (Roy & Chiat, 2012) in which the authors point to the possibility that children growing up in households with low socio-economic status (SES) are more at risk of language disadvantage. In other words, they see the greater prevalence of poor language skills among children from low SES groups as arising from social conditions – and specifically impoverished language input – rather than from greater genetic susceptibility to SLI.

Roy and Chiat (2012) argue that children who grow up in disadvantaged communities are at particular risk of reduced language input and experience. They are less likely to have a rich experience of story-telling and books or rich and varied conversation (Tizard & Hughes, 1984). Roy and Chiat carried out language assessments on a sample of preschool children who were divided into a low SES group and a mid-high SES group. Although there was no statistical difference in the incidence of SLI across the two SES groups, there was a considerably greater incidence of speech problems that could be classed as 'delay' in the low SES group. The speech and language therapists who assessed the children reported that the spontaneous speech of some children in the low SES group was difficult to understand. Another, related, difference between the two groups was that 40 per cent of the low SES children had difficulties with repeating nonwords compared to fewer than 10 per cent in the mid-high SES group. Such a difficulty indicates that children have a poor level of phonological representation since repeating a nonword requires the remembering and reproduction of a novel sequence of sounds.

Poor phonological skills among preschoolers are often predictive of continuing language problems and a future diagnosis of SLI. Nevertheless, Roy and Chiat found that the language skills of many of the children from the low SES backgrounds caught up over time, suggesting that their language development was merely delayed. They conclude that the children from a low SES group are more likely than peers from higher SES groups to show evidence of language delay and they argue for the importance of ensuring that children growing up in a disadvantaged environment receive optimal language input.

9.7 SUMMARY

Theories about how children learn to understand and produce language can usefully be grouped into Inside-out and Outside-in theories. Inside-out (nativist) theories emphasise innate linguistic abilities and language-specific learning while Outside-in theorists emphasise the role of experience and general-purpose learning mechanisms (such as statistical learning). Two leading exponents of linguistic nativism are Chomsky and Pinker. Chomsky argues for innate principles and parameters that are set with very minimal exposure to a particular language. Pinker agues for innate knowledge of grammatical word classes, such as noun and verb, that 'bootstraps' grammatical development. Alternative theories, such as that of Bruner, point to the importance of children's language experience (including its social context) as providing the springboard into language. Studies of the relationship between children's language development and language input (including feedback about language errors) suggest that children's experience of language is important for language development.

Children vary considerably in the rate at which they develop language and this variation is present in the emergence of word combinations just as it is in the age at which the first words are spoken. Early combinations tend to follow particular patterns, called a pivot schema. However, initially the ability to combine words is very limited and isolated but eventually children come to use very general schema that become grammatical rules.

Grammatical ability increases steadily beyond the age of two years with most children producing overregularisation errors, such as *mouses* or *blowed*. These kinds of errors have been seen as evidence that children are building up their own grammatical rules. Linguistic nativists see these rules as emerging from innate constraints whereas non-nativists see them as emerging from statistical learning.

Developing awareness of grammatical structure in sentences, and especially an understanding of morphological endings such as *ing* and *ed,* can help children to work out the meaning of new words. Children who suffer from specific language impairment (SLI) often have difficulty in understanding morphological endings like this. SLI is defined as a discrepancy between language abilities and IQ. SLI varies in severity and, in less severe cases, early problems with language are resolved before children begin school. In more severe cases, language difficulties last throughout the school years and are often comorbid with other developmental disorders such as dyslexia and developmental co-ordination disorder.

Recent research on genetics suggests that difficulties with expressive language are more subject to genetic effects than difficulties with receptive language. The FOXP2 mutation on chromosome 7 has been proposed as a major contributor to risk for SLI. However, subsequent research has shown that there is no single gene for language but that many different genes are associated with language development. Social factors also affect children's language development and children growing up in households where there are few opportunities to listen to stories or read books are at risk of delayed language development.

FURTHER READING

Roy, P., & Chiat, S. (2012). Teasing apart disadvantage from disorder: The case of poor language. In C. R. Marshall (Ed.), *Current issues in developmental disorders* (pp. 125–150). Hove: Psychology Press.

Saxton, M. (2010). *Child language: acquisition and development.* London: Sage.

Tomasello, M. (2006). Acquiring linguistic constructions. In D. Kuhn & R. S. Siegler (Eds), *Handbook of child psychology Volume 2* (pp. 255–298). Hoboken, NJ: Wiley.

ESSAY QUESTIONS

1. Outline the main differences between Inside-out and Outside-in theories of language development, giving one example of each type.
2. What are 'overregularisation errors' in early language development? What do they reveal about possible mechanisms in children's language development?
3. When do children begin to combine words? How can their developing ability to combine words be assessed?
4. What have experimental studies revealed about young children's understanding of language?
5. To what extent can the FOXP2 gene be described as a language gene?
6. What factors can affect how well children develop language?

CHAPTER 10

CONTENTS

Social and emotional development in the preschool years

10

After reading this chapter you will be able to

- understand how children's friendships develop over the preschool years and be able to explain the key skills that underpin successful interactions with peers
- explain why and how preschool children show an increased awareness of gender
- describe how children's understanding of the self can be assessed experimentally and explain what such experiments reveal
- understand the developmental significance of pretend play
- explain why learning who to trust as a reliable source of information is valuable for learning.

Earlier in the book, when we were discussing the social development of infants and toddlers, we mainly focused on dyadic interactions, that is, interactions involving the child and one other person. This is because during this early period much of social interaction involves just one other person and often that person is an adult or an older child. Between the ages of two and five years, there is a significant change in the pattern of interactions as children spend increasing amounts of time with peers. They begin to spend more time interacting with other children – children whom initially they do not know – and they often interact in small groups.

10.1 FRIENDSHIPS AND PEER INTERACTION

During the preschool period, many children come into contact with their peers in playgroups and at nursery. At the start of this period the notion of a friend is closely bound up with having someone to play with. Indeed, compatibility of play style seems to be a key ingredient in decisions about which children to spend time with. In general, preschoolers are attracted to other children who are similar to them in some way and,

Between the ages of two and five years children spend increasing amounts of time interacting with peers, often in small groups.

in addition to similarities in behaviour, children tend to choose playmates who are similar in age and gender (Dunn, Cutting, & Fischer, 2002).

By the age of three and a half years, children behave differently towards their friends and other children who they know but have not singled out as friends. They engage in more social interaction, more initiation of interaction and in more complex play with friends. They also show more positive social behaviours, including co-operation, with friends than non-friends (Dunn *et al.*, 2002). A key component of friendship even at this young age is reciprocity. In cases where two children independently nominate each other as friends, they are likely to spend more time together. More friendships tend to be reciprocal as children move through the preschool years.

Friendships are often volatile in the preschool period and studies by Hartup and his colleague (Hartup & Laursen, 1992) have shown that there are more conflicts between friends than other peers. Presumably this is because friends spend much more time together than non-friends. However Hartup's work also shows that friends make more use of negotiation and disengagement in their resolution of conflicts than do non-friends; and conflicts are more likely to be resolved to mutual satisfaction. This is reflected in the finding that, after conflicts are resolved, friends will tend to stay close to each other and to carry on interacting whereas disputes between non-friends usually end in separation. We discuss the development of friendships in more detail in Chapter 14 when we consider how friendships develop over the school years.

Not all children have reciprocal friendships in the preschool years and approximately 25 per cent do not have a reciprocally nominated best friend. There are a number of factors associated with having one or more friends. These include social-cognitive and emotional maturity. A recent review (Rose-Krasnor & Denham, 2009) identifies three key skills that underpin the ability to engage in successful peer interactions and to create and maintain friendships. These are self-regulation, social problem solving and prosocial behaviour.

Self-regulation

Self-regulation is the ability to actively control levels of arousal and emotional responses. The ability to regulate one's own behaviour and to respond in a socially-appropriate manner is an important skill for achieving social competence and avoiding social problems. One of the most common forms of socially undesirable behaviour is physical aggression. This first appears in infancy in response to other children grabbing an object of interest or invading a child's personal space. By 12 months, infants respond to such peer provocations by protests and physical retaliation. During a peer group observation of 21-month-old children in a laboratory for only 15 minutes, 87 per cent participated in at least one conflict with another child (Hay & Ross, 1982).

Children's ability to self-regulate increases significantly over the toddler period as they understand more about the causes and consequences of their own behaviour (Wigfield, Eccles, Schiefele, Roeser, & Davis-Kean, 2006). In part this increasing understanding develops with increasing cognitive ability but parents have an important influence on the extent to which young children regulate their own behaviour. Positive parenting, involving the use of indirect commands and reasoning to induce compliance as well as the more general fostering of children's autonomy, supports the development of self-regulation. Supporting autonomy, that is encouraging young children to act independently and to make their own choices about how to behave, has been shown to have generally positive effects including the engendering of higher self-esteem (Grolnick, Gurland, Jacob, & Decourcey, 2002).

There are, however, considerable individual differences in the ability to self-regulate that appear to be of genetic origin and these interact with effects of parenting. For example, 18-month-old children who showed high levels of distress and resistance in frustrating situations were likely to behave similarly at 24 months when their mothers were low in positive parenting but not when their mothers were highly positive (Calkins, 2002). One very important role for parents is to provide good models of self-regulation since children learn effective self-regulation strategies from other people. Initially they imitate adult models closely but, over time, they learn to become less and less dependent on the adult model to the point where they can use successful strategies in a highly flexible manner, suited to their own purposes (Wigfield *et al.*, 2006).

10.2 SOCIAL PROBLEM SOLVING

Children who are to be socially successful and liked by other children have to become good at social problem solving. Young children have to learn to process complex social information as they encounter their peers in a variety of settings. Processing social information includes a number of different components such as the encoding and analysis of a social situation, the setting of social goals and the development and completion of plans to attain these goals. Studies that have sought to improve social problem solving skills have shown that better skills lead to improved social behaviour (Rose-Krasnor & Denham, 2009).

Much of the research on the development of social problem solving skills has focused on the differences between aggressive and non-aggressive children. For example, a comparison of aggressive and non-aggressive preschoolers found differences both in the type of strategy they preferred and in their social goals. Aggressive children tended to favour intrusive strategies and to have as their goal the stopping or preventing of other children's behaviour whereas non-aggressive children saw the gathering of information about other children and the enhancement of relationships as a goal (Neel, Jenkins, & Meadows, 1990). There are also differences in the way that social information is encoded with children who are aggressive being less good at interpreting the social cues of other children (Rose-Krasnor & Denham, 2009).

Prosocial behaviour

Prosocial behaviour is voluntary behaviour that is intended to help someone else. Once children go to school, considerate behaviour towards other children is actively encouraged and is normally part of the school ethos. However, well before explicit

KEY TERMS

Prosocial behaviour
Altruistic behaviours such as sharing, helping, caregiving and showing compassion.

admonitions to engage in prosocial behaviour at school, there is evidence that children will act in a kindly way towards others, for example, by sharing toys or food or comforting a child who is crying. In the preschool years, it is natural to look for links between the prosocial behaviour of young children and that of their parents. There are also interesting differences in prosocial behaviour depending on the position that a child occupies in a family.

Laboratory based studies of prosocial behaviour have investigated social modelling. Children see a model perform a prosocial act – such as donating the winnings from a game to other children – and their own behaviour is then compared to that of a control group who did not observe the modelling. An overview of these studies (Eisenberg, Fabes, & Spinrad, 2006) concludes that children who observe a generous or helpful model are more generous and helpful themselves. Not all adults are equally good models, though, and preschool children are more likely to model the prosocial behaviour of the adults who care for them over extended periods. For any preschoolers, then, parents will provide important models for interaction with others – a point that we have already noted in our discussion of self-regulation.

Children who have a younger sibling have an ideal opportunity to learn about caring for others. Birth order is important because older siblings are often encouraged to care for their younger siblings who, in turn, learn to co-operate in these ministrations. Preschoolers who have a younger sibling will often comfort them if they show signs of distress (Howe & Ross, 1990) and even one- and two-year-olds have been found to exhibit prosocial behaviour towards their siblings (Dunn & Kendrick, 1982). Several studies have found that older sisters are particularly likely to engage in prosocial behaviour (Eisenberg *et al.*, 2006). Interestingly, the caring attitude of an older sibling towards a newly arrived younger sibling is strongly affected by the mother's preparation for the arrival of the baby. Dunn and Kendrick (1982) found that when mothers discussed the feelings and needs of the newborn with the older child, that child was more nurturant towards the new baby. The positive, nurturant attitude engendered at birth tended to persist, with behaviour following the birth predicting prosocial behaviour three years later. This finding underlines the view, that for young children, parental influence on this kind of behaviour is very important.

10.3 GENDER DEVELOPMENT

The preschool period is a time when children begin to show an increased awareness of gender. By the age of three years, children can accurately label children by gender and they are already showing a positive bias towards same-gender children. This preference comes through in the choice of play partners and friends and in children's perceptions of similarity between themselves and peers. For example, in one recent study (Bennett & Sani, 2008), five-year-olds were asked to judge their similarity to five male and five female classmates. Initially they were questioned as to whether they felt they were like/different from a named child in their class and, if they responded 'yes', they were asked whether they were 'a little bit', 'quite' or 'very' like/different. Each child was separately asked both a similarity and difference question about each named classmate. The five-year-olds consistently judged same-gender classmates as more similar to themselves than opposite-gender classmates. Interestingly, their feelings of similarity were greater than those of seven-year-olds, who also took part in the experiment, while the judgements of ten-year-olds did not differ according to gender.

Another study looked at preschool children's preferences indirectly, through acting-out with dolls (Kurtz-Costes, DeFreitas, Halle, & Kinlaw, 2011). In addition to looking at same-gender preferences, this study also looked at same-race preferences. The children taking part were all girls, aged either three years or five years and either white or black. They were asked to organise a birthday party for dolls, placing dolls in line to take part in party games, arranging seating for a puppet show and giving out refreshments and party favours. The dolls varied in gender and race with two dolls (one male, one female) having a similar skin tone to the child and the other two (also one male and one female) having a different skin tone. The favouritism shown to each of the four dolls was measured by looking, among other things, at the order in which they were selected to take part in a game and the amount of food and number of party favours they were given. White girls treated the female, white doll most favourably but did not distinguish between the black girl doll and the white boy doll. This was the pattern of a preference for same-gender, same-race that Kurtz-Costes *et al.* had expected to find. However, a different pattern was evident among the black girls. They also favoured the white, female doll with the black, female doll being favoured less. The black, female doll was, however, preferred to the black, male doll. Although unexpected, this pattern of preferences was consistent with the fact that, when asked, 'Which doll is most like you?' a large percentage of black three-year-olds chose the female, white doll. White girls were equally likely to show favouritism according to gender as race whereas black girls were more likely to favour a same-gender doll than a same-race doll.

It is difficult to be sure exactly what this pattern of preferences in relation to race means and the authors urge caution is assuming that this is evidence of young black children preferring white people. The majority of dolls are white so it could well be that this pattern of preferences is limited to dolls. What is clear – and consistent with other studies – is that a same-gender preference is already well established in the preschool period.

10.4 UNDERSTANDING THE SELF

As well as learning more about interacting with other people, the preschool years also see continuing developments in children's understanding of themselves. We saw in Chapter 6 that, by the time they reach the age of two years, children will remove a dab of rouge from their face when they see their own reflection. This has been taken as evidence that children are able to recognise their own reflection by this age. However, more recent research has shown that the process of self-recognition continues to develop over the preschool period as children begin to learn about their continuing identity over time (Povinelli & Simon, 1998).

Povinelli and Simon tested children on two successive occasions, one week apart. On the first visit, one experimenter surreptitiously placed a sticker on the child's head and then a video recording was made of the child playing an unusual game. The sticker was then removed without the child's knowledge. One week later the same children were filmed playing a different game in a distinctively different location from their earlier visit. Again a sticker was surreptitiously placed on the child's head. Then, after a three-minute delay, half the children were shown the recording made at the previous visit and half were shown the recording made only three minutes before. The point of the two contrasting locations and the choice of different games for each visit was that the two visits should be easily distinguishable.

After the brief delay the majority of four- and five-year-olds (but not three-year-olds) reached to remove the sticker from their head when they had been shown the recording made a few minutes earlier. However, when shown the recording made on the previous visit, they were unlikely to try and remove the sticker. Four- and five-year-olds often referred to the video image using the first pronoun 'me' or their own name. In contrast, the three-year-old often said that sticker was 'on his (or her) head', implying that they did not recognise the continuity of self. This is in marked contrast to their ability to recognise themselves in a mirror – which is well established by two years – when they can rely on the spatio-temporal contiguity between their own action and that in the mirror.

Three-year-olds were equally likely to try to remove the sticker when the film was of the previous week's session than when it was of the immediately preceding play session. This suggests that they recognised themselves on the video recording but did not take into account the contextual information – location and game – that distinguished between the recent recording and the one made a week ago. They treated both older and more recent images as equivalent.

A series of developmental changes may underlie these differences in performance between two and five years. As we have noted, children can recognise themselves in mirrors (and photographs) by the age of two, but, even at three, young children have difficulty in relating the present self to the past self in delayed visual feedback. This latter situation requires the child to consider two simultaneous perspectives on self – self as it is now and self at a previous time. The capacity to link the present and past self is still incompletely developed at three years (Povinelli, 1995). Three-year-old children lack the 'duplicated self' that enables older children to connect 'me experiencing now' with 'me experiencing then'. Such an autobiographical self emerges at four. At this age children can simultaneously consider the present and immediately past states of self; and previous states of the self can be linked to present states. Thus, by the end of the preschool period, children have developed a sustained view of themselves.

10.5 PLAY, IMAGINATION AND PRETENCE

During infancy, pretending mainly tends to revolve around object play but, during the preschool years, pretend play becomes an increasingly important and elaborate activity. It is common to class pretend play as a cognitive activity – as indeed it is – but what is often overlooked is that the great majority of pretend play is also social. Young children engage in *shared* pretence in which they and a partner move from the real into an imaginary world. From this perspective, pretend play can be viewed as an important social activity.

One reason why there has traditionally been an emphasis on the cognitive significance of pretend play is that Piaget's seminal account is very much concerned with this aspect. Piaget (1952) made extensive observations of his own three children at play in early childhood. We mention some examples below. Piaget used the examples to highlight stages in what he describes as 'symbolic play'. However, if you read Piaget's examples carefully you can see that his children's imaginary play was often part of a complex social interaction. This is an aspect that Paul Harris (Harris, 2000) highlights and we will return to this important dimension of pretend play at the end of this section.

Piaget was the first person to highlight the essential difference between the physical play of infancy and the symbolic play of early childhood in an influential book, *Play Dreams and Imitation in the Child* (Piaget, 1962). He also traced the development of symbolic play from infancy to the age of seven years. **Symbolic play** always involves some element of pretending but the complexity and abstractness of the pretending increases with age. Initially symbolic play revolves around objects as in the example Piaget gives of his daughter, Jacqueline, imitating a previously observed action. When Jacqueline was nearly 22 months old she rubbed the floor with a seashell, then with a cardboard lid, imitating her previous observation of the cleaner scrubbing the floor.

As children develop they engage more frequently in more complex symbolic play that does not always involve objects. Piaget records that another of his daughters, Lucienne, at the age of four, stood absolutely still as she imitated the sound of bells. Piaget put his hand over her mouth in an attempt to stop the noise. Lucienne pushed him away angrily, saying 'Don't! I'm a church'. Play with objects becomes increasingly imaginative. At three and a half, Jacqueline constructed an imaginary ants' nest from pine needles, complete with imaginary furniture, a family of ants and imaginary macaroni in the cellar.

Piaget argued that, over time, symbolic play becomes more orderly and children show an increasing desire for exact imitation of reality as in the example we have just considered. The social roles of the participants in symbolic play become increasingly complementary. In one of Piaget's observations, Jacqueline (aged four and a half) decided that she and her sister, Lucienne, would pretend to be Joseph and Therese, two of their local friends. In the course of the play Jacqueline reversed the roles so that she was Therese and Lucienne was Joseph. The play continued with mealtime scenes and other imaginary activities. At this age children spend a great deal of time acting out their everyday activities such as being taught at nursery school, going shopping or going to hospital.

Given that pretend play has such an important role in the preschool period, it is legitimate to ask what function it serves: why do young children enjoy pretending and why do they engage in increasingly elaborate games with age? Harris (2000) points out that Piaget saw pretend play as an immature form of thinking that eventually gives way to logical thought. He argues for a very different account, beginning with an important reminder that pretend play does not emerge until the end of infancy – as Piaget observed – by which time young children already have a surprisingly sophisticated understanding of the relationship between make-believe and reality. In other words, 'pretend play is not an early distortion of the real world but an initial exploration of possible worlds' (Harris, 2000, pp. 27–28).

Harris describes a number of studies that show the extent to which young children can engage in pretence. For example, two-year-olds can interpret the same prop – a toy brick – as standing for one thing in one game of make believe – food – and as something else – soap – in a new game. They can also interpret pretend actions as though they have actually happened and so are able to wipe up pretend spillages; and to determine what an animal would look like after being covered with imaginary talcum powder. An even more impressive finding was that, when two-year-olds watched an adult acting out imaginary episodes such as making a naughty teddy pour tea over a toy monkey's head, they described the imaginary action rather than what had actually happened. So they said that naughty teddy had 'poured tea over the monkey' rather than saying that teddy had lifted up an empty teapot, lifted

Pretend play has an important role in the preschool period. This type of play is rewarding for young children because not only are they pushing the boundaries of reality and entering the realm of the imagination, they are doing so with a play partner with whom there is a mutual suspension of belief.

it above the monkey, tilted it and put it down. They also said, when questioned, that the monkey's head was 'wet'.

Harris argues that young children apply their knowledge of cause and effect in the real world to the play situation. Yet, at the same time, they are aware that the way that cause and effect work during pretence is different from reality. For example, in pretend pouring, no liquid is involved. However, children are easily able to join in games of pretence with a play partner where they are engaging in shared pretence in which reality is temporarily suspended. What makes such play rewarding for young children is not only that they are pushing the boundaries of reality, and entering the realm of the imagination, but that they are doing so with a play partner with whom there is a mutual suspension of belief.

10.6 DEVELOPMENT OF TRUST

The final topic that we will consider in this chapter is one that has been an increasing focus of research. This is children's development of selective trust in other people during the preschool period. Much of what we know about the world comes not from our direct experience but from what we read and hear from other people. In order to learn effectively, we need to discover the people we can trust and those who will give us reliable information.

Much of the research on this topic has been stimulated by the work of Harris (Harris, 2006). He has shown that children increasingly show selective trust over the preschool period. At the age of three, children can distinguish between a previously accurate informant and one who professes ignorance. However, they cannot reliably choose between a previously accurate and a previously inaccurate informant. By the age of four years they are able to do this. For example, when shown an unfamiliar object and provided with different names for that object by two informants, four-year-olds will choose the name provided by a previously reliable informant and ignore the name given by an ignorant or previously unreliable informant (Koenig & Harris, 2005).

Subsequent experiments have demonstrated that preschoolers are sensitive to a number of parameters that indicate the reliability of an informant, including the familiarity and expertise of the informant (Corriveau & Harris, 2009). In other words preschoolers are more likely to trust someone they know rather than someone they don't know, providing that person does not give them inaccurate information. Preschoolers also show a preference for information that is independently provided by a number of different informants rather than a single informant (Corriveau, Fusaro, & Harris, 2009) and for an informant who knows the answer unaided rather than one who seeks information from someone else (Einav & Robinson, 2012). This

BOX 10.1: EINAV AND ROBINSON (2012)

The Einav and Robinson (2012) study used childlike hand puppets (Blue Puppet and Green Puppet) in order to engage preschool children. In the first part of the study, the puppets labelled pictures that were familiar to preschool children (cow, elephant and rabbit). Although both puppets were correct in their labelling, one puppet produced the correct label without assistance whereas the other was given help by a teddy bear.

Einav using puppets.

In order to make the aided and unaided trials as similar as possible, the puppet *always* paused after being shown a picture. The teddy then asked, 'Would you like some help?' The unaided puppet refused help and then produced the correct label whereas the aided puppet asked for help and the teddy whispered the answer into the puppet's ear.

In the test phase of the study, the teddy was removed and children were told that he couldn't provide any more help. They were then shown a picture of an unfamiliar animal (a mongoose) and asked which of the two puppets could tell them what the animal was. As a memory check, and once children had chosen which puppet could give them the answer, children were asked which puppet had been helped by the teddy. All of these controls ensured that the children's experience of the aided and unaided puppets was similar and that they had remembered which puppet had produced the correct answer unaided and which had required help. It was thus possible to determine at what age children could recognise the greater reliability of the puppet who had not received assistance.

latter level of discrimination requires children to take into account how someone previously arrived at a correct answer. When faced with two previously accurate informants, four- and five-year-old children in the Einav and Robinson study were more likely to seek guidance from an informant who had previously given the answers unaided than from an informant who had always relied on help from a third party.

Experiments to test children's trust in others have to be carefully designed since it is important to ensure that the judgement a child is required to make is not influenced by anything other than what is taking place during the experiment. See Box 10.1 for more details of the Einav and Robinson (2012) study.

10.7 SUMMARY

During the preschool years children develop increasingly complex relationships with their peers as more of their time is spent in the company of other children and away from parents. Self-regulation, social problem solving and prosocial behaviour are all key skills that underpin the successful negotiation of peer interactions and the building of relationships. Children learn these skills from others, especially family members. Parents act as role models for social behaviour and children with younger siblings have the opportunity to learn about caring. Increasing cognitive capacity means that preschoolers can engage in more complex analysis of social situations. Awareness of gender increases as do positive biases towards same-gender children.

At the same time that preschool children are developing their social skills, they are also developing a sense of self. By the age of four or five years, children have become aware that they have continuity over time and they can distinguish past events in which they were involved from current events. A sense of the autobiographical self is emerging by the age of four years.

Social play is very important in the preschool years and it often involves pretending. Piaget saw pretence as an immature form of thinking but Paul Harris argues that pretend play allows young children to push at the boundaries of reality and to engage in a mutual suspension of belief with a play partner.

During the preschool period children also develop an understanding of who to trust as a reliable informant. Although much can be learned through direct observation, children often need to learn from other people. Between the ages of three and five years, children become increasingly accurate at judging who is giving them reliable information and, by the time they begin formal schooling, they are able to take account of factors such as the reliability of an informant and their ability to provide an answer without help from anyone else.

FURTHER READING

Einav, S., & Robinson, E. J. (2012). When being right is not enough: Four-year-olds distinguish knowledgeable informants from merely accurate informants. *Psychological Science, 22*(10), 1250–1253.

Eisenberg, N., Fabes, R. A., & Spinrad, T. L. (2006). Prosocial development. In N. Eisenberg (Ed.), *Handbook of child development* (pp. 646–718). Hoboken, NJ: Wiley.

Kurtz-Costes, B., DeFreitas, S. C., Halle, T. G., & Kinlaw, C. R. (2011
Gender and racial favouritism in Black and White preschool girls. *Britis*
Journal of Developmental Psychology, 29(2), 270–287.

ESSAY QUESTIONS

1. What is important for early friendships?
2. Explain what is meant by 'prosocial behaviour' and explain how it develops in young children.
3. Review the evidence for the contention that children develop an increased awareness of gender in the preschool period.
4. Discuss the claim that the 'autobiographical self' emerges in the preschool period.
5. Is pretence merely a product of immature thinking?
6. How has preschoolers' trust in others been studied experimentally?

CONTENTS

CHAPTER 11

Introduction to middle childhood

11

After reading this chapter you will be able to

- describe the development of motor skills during middle childhood and explain where there are gender differences in performance
- understand the continuing processes of brain development during this period
- describe the main characteristics of attention deficit/hyperactivity disorder (ADHD) and explain how this condition can be diagnosed
- describe the main features of developmental co-ordination disorder (DCD) and explain the difficulties that children with DCD have in planning their movements.

Middle childhood is the period from six years to the onset of puberty and adolescence. During this period, relationships within the family – with parents, siblings and grandparents – continue to be very important but relationships with other children take on increasing significance. One estimate is that 40 per cent of the waking time of 6- to 12-year-olds is spent with peers (Cole & Cole, 1993).

In many societies, the beginning of middle childhood coincides with the start of formal schooling. Starting at school brings with it many new experiences and challenges as children learn to adjust to the rhythm of the school day and the new expectations that are placed on them. School presents new cognitive challenges as children learn to read and write and to do mathematics. It also presents new social challenges as children learn how to interact successfully with their peers, many of whom will be unfamiliar at first, and to co-operate on shared tasks.

Physical growth continues apace during middle childhood, with a gain in height of four to six centimetres per year for both boys and girls. Children take a great interest in their own growth and marking year-on-year increase in height on a wall or growth chart is a popular activity. Another physical change that children regard as very important is the loss of milk teeth, as adult teeth erupt. The loss of milk teeth is often marked by special events such as the arrival of the Tooth Fairy.

11.1 MOTOR SKILLS

Motor skills develop significantly during middle childhood. Children become better at catching and throwing, better at balancing and they can run faster and jump further than they could before. The physical characteristics of boys and girls during this period are very similar: boys and girls are very similar in body type and body composition – they have similar ratios of muscle to fat – and also limb length. It is not until puberty, when boys begin to produce increasing amounts of testosterone, that this changes. Testosterone produces an increase in the amount of muscle and, by the end of puberty, the proportion of muscle has doubled for males while remaining at a similar level for females.

In spite of the physical similarity of boys and girls in middle childhood there are some gender differences in motor abilities. In a meta-analysis of 64 studies (which in total included over 30,000 children), there were clear difference in performance for boys and girls on a number of abilities (Thomas & French, 1985). The most striking difference was for throwing. Boys were able to throw harder and over a greater distance from as early as four to seven years of age and, by 12 years of age and the onset of puberty, boys' performance exceeded that of girls by three or more standard deviations. What this means is that, by the age of 12 years, there was almost no overlap between the throwing ability of girls and boys. There was also a smaller but significant difference between boys and girls in balance by the age of ten years (in favour of boys) but younger boys and girls performed at similar levels.

From the age of about six years until the onset of puberty boys and girls are physically quite similar.

Other abilities – such as running, jumping over a distance, grip strength and sit ups – followed the most typical pattern for motor development. There were small gender differences in performance in early childhood, a slightly larger difference in middle childhood and a much larger difference after puberty. In each case, boys performed at a higher level than girls. Interestingly, catching ability showed a different, U-shaped pattern, with boys being better than girls in the preschool period but no difference in middle childhood. With the onset of puberty, boys were again better than girls.

There were two motor skills at which girls were consistently better than boys. These were flexibility and fine hand–eye co-ordination (including the ability to move pegs on a board, turn a screw and punch holes).

Thomas and French (1985) argue that gender differences occurring in early and middle childhood are largely the result of environmental influences whereas those occurring post-puberty are the result of the larger size of boys and their greater proportion of muscle tissue. They suggest that teachers and parents often have different expectations of the motor capabilities of boys and girls and place greater emphasis on these skills for boys. However, it should also be noted that children's

BOX 11.1: ATTITUDES OF BOYS AND GIRLS TO PHYSICAL ACTIVITY

The differing attitudes of boys and girls to physical activity is highlighted in a study in which nearly 500 children, aged between 9 and 11 years, completed a questionnaire to determine which criteria were most important in determining popularity (Chase & Dummer, 1992). Children were asked what would make them popular with their classmates, and also what would make a girl or boy popular. Boys reported sports to be the most important determinant of both personal and male popularity, and appearance as the most important determinant of female popularity. Girls reported appearance to be the most important determinant of personal, male and female popularity. For girls, appearance became more important with each year at school. The findings of this study support the view that boys see participation in sport as more valuable than girls do.

Chase and Dummer (1992) found that boys and girls have different attitudes to physical activity – boys valued sport participation more than girls, who valued appearance more.

choice of activities to do with friends also differs. Boys are more likely to spend time in physical activity with their friends than girls, especially in playing team games. For girls, a major part of socialising during middle childhood (and beyond) is the development of relationships (Baines & Blatchford, 2009).

11.2 BRAIN DEVELOPMENT

As we have seen in earlier chapters, there are marked changes in the brain during infancy when the rate of development is most rapid. However, the brain continues to develop throughout childhood, until at least the end of adolescence. Almost all of the 100 billion neurons in the human brain have developed before birth and, until fairly recently, it was thought that virtually no new neurons were added after birth. However, more recent research has shown that, in certain areas of the brain, new

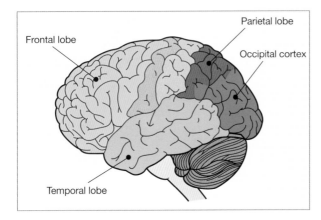

Figure 11.1

This diagram of the brain shows the position of the different lobes and the occipital cortex.

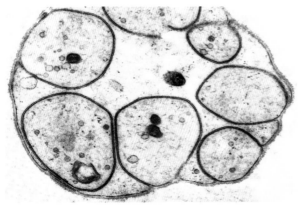

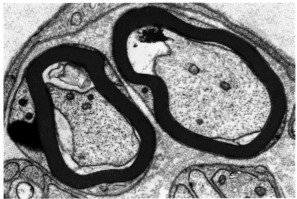

Composite transmission electron micrographs (TEMs) showing unmyelinated nerve fibers (top) and myelinated ones (bottom).

cells are added for many years after birth (Nelson, Thomas, & de Haan, 2006). There is also evidence that the addition of new neurons during childhood is affected by experience, although much remains to be discovered about this aspect of neural development.

The major changes that take place in the brains of children in middle childhood are in *synaptogenesis*, that is, the forming of new connections between neurons and in the loss of connections that are not used (*synaptic pruning*). The forming of new connections and especially the loss of unused connections is the basis for learning and development. The time course of **synaptogenesis** and synaptic pruning varies from one region of the brain to another. For example, the number of synapses in the occipital cortex – an area at the back of the brain – is at a maximum in early infancy (between four and eight months) and has been pruned to adult levels by four to six years of age (Nelson *et al.*, 2006). The occipital cortex is the visual processing centre of the brain and, as we have seen in earlier chapters, there are important developments in visual processing during infancy. So it makes sense that synaptogenesis and synaptic pruning in the occipital cortex are complete early in life. By contrast, the number of synapses in part of the prefrontal cortex does not reach its peak until the end of infancy (at around 18 months) and synaptic pruning continues well into adolescence. The prefrontal cortex is involved in complex cognitive activity and decision-making as well as complex social behaviour. These abilities develop throughout middle childhood and well into adolescence, as we see in later chapters.

Another important feature of brain development is **myelination**. Myelin is a liquid/protein substance that wraps itself around axons, forming insulation and thereby improving conductivity. Axons are the long, slender fibres that carry the electrical impulses from one neuron to another. The effect of myelination is to make this process more efficient and so to make the brain function more effectively.

The process of myelination begins prenatally and ends in young adulthood. Advances in imaging have meant that it is possible to gain a much more detailed understanding of the time course of myelination. What the imaging studies have shown is that the most dramatic changes occur in frontal lobes during adolescence. However, from birth onwards there are steady increases in myelination that, together with the continuing processes of synaptogenesis and synaptic pruning, mean the brain becomes increasingly efficient as children develop through the preschool period and middle childhood. These changes are gradual and so we might expect to see a correspondingly gradual development in ability. We consider changes in cognitive capacity in 12.3 (where we focus on changes in working memory during middle childhood) and also in 16.3 (where we discuss the development of executive function during adolescence).

11.3 DEVELOPMENTAL DISORDERS

The increasing demands that are placed on children once they begin formal education mean that it is often in middle childhood that certain developmental difficulties are first diagnosed. We discuss a number of specific developmental disorders in the following chapters, relating to skills that are developing during the school years. These include problems with reading and spelling words (developmental dyslexia), difficulties in understanding text (**reading comprehension impairment**), difficulties in writing, and problems in developing mathematical skills (dyscalculia). Two other developmental disorders that become particularly noticeable during middle childhood are **attention deficit/hyperactivity disorder (ADHD)** and **developmental co-ordination disorder (DCD)**.

ADHD

ADHD is one of the most common developmental disorders. It is characterised by a triad of difficulties: chronic and pervasive inattention, impulsive behaviour and hyperactivity. Children who are diagnosed with ADHD show signs of all three difficulties (Cornish & Wilding, 2010). Unlike a number of other developmental disorders that have a known genetic basis – such as Down syndrome, Williams syndrome and Fragile X syndrome – the genetic underpinnings of ADHD are still not well understood. Furthermore there are no outward physical signs of ADHD as in the case of Williams or Down syndrome. This means that ADHD is not easy to identify (Williams & Lind, 2013) especially since it often co-occurs (i.e. it is comorbid) with other developmental disorders such as conduct disorder, oppositional defiance disorder, learning disability, Fragile X syndrome and also anxiety and depression (Cornish & Wilding, 2010). The common pattern of comorbidity also means that it has been difficult to determine which aspects of cognition are specific to ADHD and which to a comorbid condition.

Epigenetic factors (see Chapter 1) seem to be particularly implicated in children's vulnerability to ADHD. The environmental factors that affect gene expression and increase susceptibility to ADHD include exposure to chemical or environmental toxins both before and after birth and early complications immediately following birth, such as hypoxia (lack of oxygen). Environmental toxins that have been linked to increased susceptibility to ADHD include lead pollution and foetal alcohol exposure (Cornish & Wilding, 2010) (see also Chapter 3).

Low levels of *dopamine* have been identified as a major contributor to ADHD. Dopamine is an important neurotransmitter that is produced in many parts of the brain, including the thalamus and substantia nigra, located in the mid brain (see Figure 11.2).

KEY TERMS

Synaptogenesis
The forming of new connections between neurons.

Myelination
The production of the myelin sheath that surrounds axons, forming insulation and improving conductivity.

Reading comprehension impairment
A disorder in which children have significant difficulty in understanding text even though they can read individual words.

Attention Deficit/Hyperactivity Disorder
This is one of the most common developmental disorders. It is characterised by a triad of difficulties: chronic and pervasive inattention, impulsive behaviour and hyperactivity.

Developmental Co-ordination Disorder (DCD)
Developmental co-ordination disorder is diagnosed in children who, for no medical reason, fail to acquire adequate motor skills.

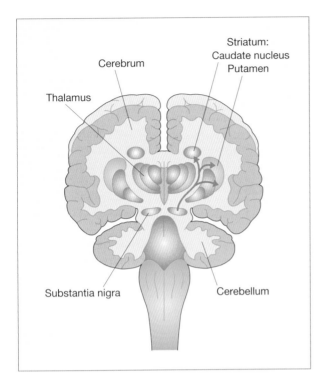

Figure 11.2

A section through the brain showing the substantia nigra and thalamus.

Dopamine plays a critical role in cognition, reward and emotion, and low levels of dopamine will result in impaired cognition. The most widely used treatment for ADHD is Ritalin and this acts to significantly increase the levels of dopamine in the brain, allowing individuals to maintain their attention more effectively.

The clinical dignosis of ADHD is not usually made until at least the age of seven years. There is no suggestion that ADHD suddently appears at this point in development but, rather, that the early symptoms are dfficult to spot. The attentional abilities of preschool children are variable and there is also more tolerance of poor attention at this age. The demands of formal schooling, however, require children to attend for long periods, to sit still and to follow instructions. These are precisely the kinds of demand that will be difficult for children with ADHD. Furthermore, the tests that are used to identify children with ADHD require abilties that do not begin to develop until the early school years. These are tasks that test the maintenance and control of attention as well as inhibition. These kinds of tasks are important for executive function and they show clear developmental trajectories throughout middle chidlhood and into adolescence. (See Cornish & Wilding, 2010, Chapter 8, for a detailed discussion and also 16.3.)

DCD

Developmental co-ordination disorder is diagnosed in children who, for no medical reason, fail to acquire adequate motor skills. Typically, the milestones of motor development are achieved rather later than would be expected and a range of different motor abilities are affected, including dexterity in fine motor tasks – such as tracing, writing and fastening buttons – and in gross motor skills such as jumping, hopping, catching a ball and balancing (Zoia, Barnett, Wilson, & Hill, 2006).

As we noted earlier in this chapter, motor skills develop significantly during middle childhood and competence in motor abilities – or lack of competence – can become a subject of evaluation by other children. The marked impairment of motor skills that are evident in children with DCD has a significant, negative impact on a range of day-to-day activities, such as dressing, eating, riding a bicycle or taking part in team games. DCD can also have an impact on academic achievements, primarily as a result of poor handwriting skills (see 13.3). DCD affects around 5 per cent of school-aged children and, as with many other developmental disorders, it occurs roughly three times as often in boys than in girls. Its onset is apparent in the pre-school years but it is not usually diagnosed formally before the age of five years (Zoia *et al.*, 2006).

There is a high degree of comorbidity between DCD and a number of other developmental disorders, including autism spectrum disorder, ADHD, dyslexia and specific language impairment.

Research into the nature of the motor difficulties of children with DCD suggests that they have particular difficulty in planning their motor movements and in modifying a movement once it has begun (Wilmut & Wann, 2008). In the Wilmut and Wann (2008) study, children with DCD, aged from 6 to 12 years, were asked to reach towards a specific location on a tabletop, either following a cue or without a cue. The correct location was indicated by the illumination of one of a number of toy bugs and, in the cue condition, the children were given a visual cue as to which bug would be illuminated. Their task was to grab the correct bug as soon as it lit up. The children had reflective markers placed on the index finger, knuckle and wrist of their hand and their hand movements were recorded with special cameras that picked up the movement of the reflective markers.

The performance of the children with DCD was compared with that of typically developing peers and two main differences between the groups emerged. First, the children with DCD were less effective in correcting their movement if they initially began to reach for the wrong bug. Second, the typically developing children made much more effective use of the visual cue that alerted them to the location of the next bug to be illuminated. When there was no cue, both groups of children showed a lag of around 400 milliseconds between looking at the illuminated bug and beginning to move their hand towards it. When there was a cue, the typically developing children began to move their hand less than 100 milliseconds after they moved their eyes to the correct location, showing that they had benefitted substantially from the cue. However, the performance of the children with DCD did not change when they were provided with the same cues. Wilmut and Wann (2008) conclude from this study that typically developing children as young as six years of age can program movements in advance if they have a relevant cue whereas children with DCD do not appear to be able do this to the same extent.

You might wonder why being able to rapidly program a movement in response to a visual cue is important. The answer is simple. Imagine a ball coming towards you or a pencil that is about to slip off the desk. In order to catch the ball or stop the pencil from falling to the floor, you have to produce precisely the right sequence of movements at exactly the right time. It seems that children with DCD have particular difficulty in programming and executing such finely-tuned sequences of movements in response to environmental cues.

11.4 SUMMARY

The beginning of formal schooling coincides with the beginning of middle childhood. We have seen that formal schooling places new demands on children and both their cognitive and social skills go through significant changes as the efficiency of brain function continues to increase. There are also new-found physical skills and, for the first time, differences in the ability of boys and girls begin to emerge. Girls and boys also show increasing social differences in middle childhood with the majority of friendships being formed with children of the same gender and the majority of free time being spent in activities with same-gender peers.

Middle childhood is often the period in which children with atypical development are first identified. The demands of school in relation to literacy and numeracy, and also attention, highlight problems for some children. In the next set of chapters we consider the development of cognitive and social abilities as well as the development of skills in literacy and numeracy. We also consider why some children find it very difficult to develop these school-based skills that will prove so essential for education in the period beyond middle childhood.

FURTHER READING

Cornish, K., & Wilding, J. (2010). *Attention, genes, and developmental diorders*. New York: Oxford University Press.

Nelson, C. A., Thomas, K. M., & de Haan, M. (2006). Neural basis of cognitive development. In D. Kuhn & R. S. Siegler (Eds), *Handbook of child psychology Volume 2* (pp. 3–57). Hoboken, NJ: Wiley.

Williams, D. M., & Lind, S. E. (2013). Comorbidity and diagnosis of developmental disorders. In C. R. Marshall (Ed.), *Current issues in developmental disorders* (pp. 19–45). London: Psychology Press.

ESSAY QUESTIONS

1. Describe the main changes that occur in motor skills during middle childhood.
2. In what ways does the brain develop during middle childhood and how do these changes affect children's cognitive abilities?
3. What is ADHD and how can children with this conditon be identified?
4. What impact is DCD likely to have on children's performance at school?

CHAPTER 12

CONTENTS

Cognitive development in middle childhood

12

After reading this chapter you will be able to

- describe and evaluate Piaget's account of concrete operational reasoning
- explain how and why children's ability to solve balance beam problems develops over middle childhood
- understand the changes that take place in working memory during this period
- explain some of the challenges that children face in learning to do mathematics
- describe the main features of dyscalculia
- understand why there are cross-cultural differences in mathematical ability.

In this chapter we review a number of different aspects of cognitive development in middle childhood and we consider how children's ability to think progresses beyond the achievements of the preschool period. We begin with reasoning abilities, which lie at the heart of Piaget's account of cognitive development.

12.1 REASONING

Piaget's theory of concrete operational reasoning

As with the earlier periods of development that we have considered, Piaget's account of reasoning in middle childhood has been highly influential. As we saw in Chapter 8, preschoolers are more competent in reasoning tasks than Piaget originally suggested but, nevertheless, there are many problems that preschool children find difficult but children of school age readily solve.

Concrete operational stage
Piaget's third developmental stage in which children begin to use logical rules to solve problems. They can deal with more than one salient feature of a problem at a time and are no longer dominated by appearance. However, they are not yet able to deal with abstract problems. This stage lasts from the ages of six or seven to 11 or 12.

Piaget described the stage of thinking that follows on from the pre-operational thinking of the preschool period as concrete operational reasoning. The key features of the thinking of preschoolers, according to Piaget, are an inability to focus on more than one aspect of a problem at a time and a tendency for judgements to be dominated by immediate appearance. For these reasons, Piaget saw the thinking and reasoning of preschool children as pre-logical. These limitations of thinking in the pre-operational stage – and the superior abilities of school-aged children – are well illustrated by children's performance in conservation tasks.

As we saw in Chapter 8, conservation tasks test children's ability to apply the principle of conservation. To have the concept of conservation means that children understand that the basic properties of matter – volume, number and weight – are not altered by superficial changes in their appearance. One of the best-known examples of a Piagetian conservation task is conservation of volume. This involves judgements about the amount of water in three transparent containers. Children are initially shown two tall, thin containers with identical dimensions and with water at the same level. They recognise that the two containers have equal amounts of water. Then the water from one container is poured into another container of a different shape so that the water level is no longer the same as in the other container.

As we also saw in Chapter 8, preschool children fail to recognise that the amount of water remains unchanged (i.e. it is conserved) when it is poured from one container to another. They are unable to recognise that changes in both height and width need to be considered together. They also do not understand the important principle of reversibility, that is, if the water were to be poured back into the original container then the level would return to what it had been before. Understanding the interrelationship of two dimensions and the principle of reversibility are core aspects of concrete operational reasoning.

In contrast to preschoolers, school-aged children are able to understand conservation and will say, in the conservation of liquid volume, that the amount of water in the two differently-shaped jars remains the same because nothing was added or taken away when the water was poured into the differently shaped container. Furthermore, if the water in the short flat jar were to be poured back into the tall thin one, children know that the levels in the two tall thin jars would once more be the same. Children also understand that the change in the height of the liquid was accompanied by a correlated change in its width and this accounts for the change in appearance.

According to Piaget, the stage transition from pre-operational to concrete operational reasoning is a shift from reliance on perception to reliance on logic. The conservation problems, which caused such difficulty before, are now solved because children can reason that, if nothing was added or taken away, the amount must be the same. Similarly, mentally reversing the sequence of steps (i.e. imagining the water being poured back into the original container) enables children to conclude that nothing can have changed simply as a result of pouring the water into a new container.

The logical thinking that children acquire during the period of middle childhood is also evident in their understanding of seriation, classification and numeration. Classification refers to the hierarchical ordering of objects into superordinate classes and subclasses. Piaget's famous example is the class inclusion problem where children are questioned about a necklace made up of seven brown and three white beads. When six-year-old children are asked whether there are more beads

BOX 12.1: LOGICAL OPERATIONS

Piaget defines a logical operation as an internalised, mental action that is part of a logical system. According to Piaget, thought during the concrete operational stage is more flexible than in the pre-operational stage because children can mentally retrace their steps within an internally consistent set of mental operations. However, cognitive development is not yet complete. The thinking of children who are in the concrete operational stage remains limited because of the need for concrete objects to support their thinking. According to Piaget, it is not until adolescence that purely hypothetical problems can be solved (see 16.1).

The system of logical concrete operations involves two different sets of rules that allow children to reverse imagined sequences of actions and their observed consequences. These are Identity (I) and Negation (N) (I/N rules) and Reciprocal (R) and Correlative (C) (R/C rules). Children at the stage of concrete operations can solve concrete problems that involve *either* I/N *or* R/C rules. For example, children who can conserve volume in the water conservation task know the volume is the same and often justify their judgements by saying things such as, 'If you poured the water back, the levels would be just the same as before' (justification by the Negation rule) or 'The water in this jar is taller but this one is wider' (justification by the Correlative rule).

The I/N and R/C operations can be illustrated in the conservation of water task as follows:

I = *Identity:* It is the same water poured into a new jar.
N = *Negation:* The water is poured back into the original jar.
R = *Reciprocal:* Two sets of operations, such as pouring the water and then pouring it back are the reciprocal of each other.
C = *Correlative:* Changes in one aspect (e.g. the height of the liquid) are compensated by change in another aspect (e.g. the width of the liquid).

As we see in Chapter 16 (see 16.1) the final stage of cognitive development, according to Piaget, is formal operational thinking. This involves the integration of these four operations into a single coherent logical structure.

(superordinate class) or more brown beads (subordinate class) they typically reply that there are more brown beads than beads. However, by eight years, children understand that the questions refer to different aspects of the problem, the set and the subset.

Numeration emerges from the combination of classification and seriation. Pre-school children understand something about number and may be able to count small sets of objects. According to Piaget the main advance during the concrete operational stage is that the ability to understand serial ordering and classification enables children to comprehend numbers as a sequence and to classify them as a set of classes and subclasses. For example, a group of eight counters can also be understood to comprise two groups of four, or four groups of two counters; and this provides the logical foundation for learning about multiplication and division. We discuss these aspects of numerical understanding in 12.4.

Seriation refers to the understanding of relationships of position both in space and in time. Acquiring the logic of seriation allows children to order objects according to spatial dimensions such as height, length, width or according to when events occurred in time. Seriation, in turn, enables the logical operation of **transitive inference** where, for example, children can work out the relative length of two sticks by employing a third stick of intermediate length.

Here is a typical transitive inference problem: if stick A is longer than stick B, and stick B is longer than stick C, which is the longest? The logic of this problem is that if A>B and B>C, then A>C. In other words, we can deduce that A must be the longest stick from the dual relationship of B with both A and C. To solve transitive inference problems like this, children must be able to store all the relevant information in memory and compare the relationship of the common item, B, with the two other items A and C.

Piaget argued that children cannot solve transitive inference problems until they are capable of concrete operational reasoning and are then able to infer the logical relationship of the A and C terms from their relationship to a common term (B). As we see in Chapter 16, there is a further advance in understanding when children become capable of formal operational reasoning. This allows them to go beyond understanding transitive inference for the case of physical objects, such as sticks, to understanding the relationship for more abstract cases (see 16.1).

Criticisms of Piaget's account of concrete operational reasoning

Over the years there have been many criticisms of Piaget's account of concrete operational reasoning. One of the earliest and very influential critiques came from Bryant and Trabasso (1971). They showed that children could solve transitivity tasks at a rather younger age than Piaget proposed (Bryant & Trabasso, 1971; Stevenson *et al.*, 1990). Bryant and Trabasso used a version of the transitive inference task with five rods of different lengths and colours. The rods were kept in a block of wood with holes drilled into it, so that the longest rod (which was red) was at the left, with successive rods of reducing length to the right. Each rod protruded by exactly the same amount above the surface so children could only see how long the rods actually were when the experimenter took them from the block, in pairs, and showed them to the child. The relationship of the five rods was A > B > C > D > E.

Four-year-old children were given extensive training in which pairs of rods were removed in turn from the block and they were shown that the red rod was longer than the white one next to it, the white rod longer than the yellow one next to it, and so on. The children were tested on their knowledge of the relative lengths of adjacent pairs when the rods were replaced in the block and children could no longer see their actual length.

After training the children had learned all the relationships between adjacent pairs i.e. that the red rod A was longer than the white one B; the white one B was longer than the adjacent yellow one C; the yellow one C was longer than the blue one D;

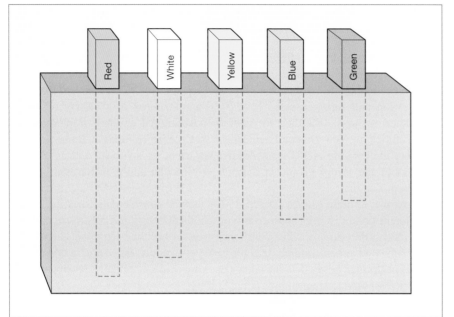

Figure 12.1

A diagram of the apparatus used by Bryant and Trabasso (1971).

and the blue rod D was longer than the green one E. In other words the children knew that A > B, B > C, C > D and D > E. Then came the critical tests in which the children were asked about non-adjacent pairs. Children correctly deduced that A > C and C > E. They also correctly deduced that B>D. This relationship is particularly important because, in the training phase, children had named the B and D rods as being both longer and shorter than the adjacent rods on an equal number of occasions. Therefore if they correctly understood the relationship of rod B to rod D, this could not be explained away as a simple repetition of a verbal label they had heard during training. Bryant and Trabasso concluded that young children's problem is not that they do not understand transitive inferences but, rather, that they are subject to memory limitations that conceal their underlying capacity for logical reasoning.

As we see later in the chapter, there are significant changes in memory capacity that occur as children move through the school years and these will have an impact on the amount of information that can be processed. Indeed, the prevailing view is that age differences in the successful solution of deductive reasoning problems, such as those involving transitive inference, are largely dependant on developmental differences in the capacity of working memory, the effectiveness of executive function and the ability to retrieve information from long-term memory (Goswami, 2011).

A final point to note is that, as is so often the case with post-Piagetian experiments, the task used by Bryant and Trabasso is not exactly the same as the one used by Piaget to measure transitive inference. Russell (1978) has argued that more recent tasks, used to demonstrate transitive inferences in pre-operational children, actually structure the problem space for the child. This contrasts with Piaget's tasks, where children are expected to come up with the right solution without this kind of structuring. Structuring the problem-space will inevitably help children to work out what to pay attention to and thereby enable them to solve a particular problem that they might otherwise not be able to solve.

Cross-cultural comparisons of concrete operational reasoning

The timing of children's progression from preoperational thinking to concrete operational thinking appears to be influenced by the children's experiences, including their schooling. Since they were first developed, many of the standard Piagetian conservation and seriation tasks have been administered in a variety of different cultural settings, including to Australian Aboriginal children from rural and urban settings, to New Guinea Highlanders, to Chinese children in Hong Kong, to Canadian Eskimos, to adults from Amazonian tribes, to schooled and unschooled members of the Wolof people in Senegal, to illiterate adults in Sardinia, and to children in Zambia.

A review of these studies (Dasen, 1972) showed considerable variation among the different groups. For example, rural, unschooled Aboriginal Australian children can, with a little training, solve conservation tasks but they lag about three years behind schooled, urban children. In some tasks, even adults failed and in other tasks, children performed better than the adults, as if the adults eventually developed quite different reasoning strategies in different cultures.

Dasen suggests that a combination of two major factors can explain this variation in performance. The first is whether or not the children had attended school and the second is the extent of their contact with Western culture. Thus, children in New Guinea and Senegal, who attended Western type schools, were comparable to Western children in the attainment of concrete operations whereas unschooled children from the same cultures were much slower in attaining a similar level of performance. This might suggest that schooling has a special effect on the attainment of concrete operations. Alternatively, it may be that schooling simply serves to bring children into contact with the kind of Western intellectual values that are inherent in standard conservation tasks and other tasks that are used to assess the acquisition of concrete operation thinking. Where the society already holds such intellectual values – ways of thinking – schooling may not significantly influence the onset of concrete operations. For example, unschooled Chinese children in Hong Kong, which has for long been heavily influenced by European culture, performed comparably to schooled Western children on Piagetian tests of concrete operational reasoning.

These kind of findings about cross-cultural differences in children's performance on standard tests of concrete operational thinking suggest that, to some extent, Piaget's account of the emergence of concrete preoperational thinking is rooted in the cultural and intellectual norms of Western societies. It is for this reason that the sociocultural context of cognitive development has become a topic of legitimate concern in developmental psychology. The idea is a simple one – and one that we have noted at various points in this book. Behaviour does not occur in a vacuum 'but in a meaningful confluence of material, social, and individual resources organized to accomplish a goal' (Gauvain, 1995, p. 29). We return to this issue later in this chapter when we discuss mathematics and we also touch on this important aspect of cognitive development in the next section.

12.2 PROBLEM SOLVING

One of the main tasks that has been used to investigate the development of problem solving in middle childhood, and beyond, is the balance beam or balance scale. Like a number of the other tasks we have considered in this chapter, this task was initially developed by Piaget (Inhelder & Piaget, 1958).

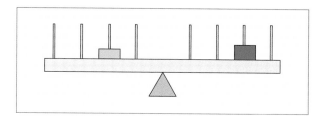

Figure 12.2

A diagram of the balance beam used by Siegler (1976).

The balance scale is pivoted in the middle and it has a number of pegs spaced at equal intervals on either side of the fulcrum. Weights are placed at different peg positions and children are asked to predict which side of the balance will go down. The answer to this question is determined by two factors – the total amount of weight on each side of the balance and the distance of those weights from the fulcrum. Solving the balance scale task, and making the correct prediction about which side will go down, therefore depends on combining information about two different dimensions.

Children's ability to solve **balance beam** problems has been extensively studied by Siegler (Siegler, 1976b). Given that pre-operational children often have difficulty in combining information about two different factors, Siegler predicted that five-year-olds would make incorrect predictions because they would only be able to attend to one dimension. Siegler assumed that this dimension would be weight rather than distance from the fulcrum since this is a more obvious variable in the balance scale task.

Siegler predicted that children would use one of four rules to predict which side of the balance beam would tip down. These are shown in Table 12.1. These different rules are increasingly successful in solving a range of balance beam problems but, interestingly, improvement in success rates is not uniform across specific balance beam tasks. For example, the least sophisticated rule (Rule 1) will produce the correct answer only when both weight and distance from the fulcrum are equal or when distance is the same but one side has a heavier weight than the other; and only the most sophisticated rule (Rule 4) will make the correct prediction with all possible combinations of weight and distance. However, children who are following Rule 3 actually perform *less* accurately than those who are following Rule 1, in situations where there is a conflict between weight and distance but the side with more weight is the one that will go down. Presentation of a range of different weight × distance combinations can therefore reveal which rule children are following.

In Siegler's original study (Siegler, 1976b) more than 80 per cent of 5- to 17-year-olds consistently used one of the four rules. Five-year-old children most often used Rule 1. Nine-year-olds most often used either Rule 2 or Rule 3 and those over 13 usually used Rule 3. Very few children used Rule 4. Since Siegler's original study a number of other studies have shown similar sequences of rule-following in this task (Jansen & van der Maas, 2002).

Overall, performance in the balance scale task can be seen as providing evidence for the claim that there is a major change in children's ability to deal with two conflicting task dimensions between the ages of five and nine as Piaget originally claimed. However, appropriate training can improve performance.

Siegler (1976) gave children, aged between five and eight, feedback on balance scale problems. The children were asked to predict which side of the beam would

Table 12.1 Rules for solving balance scale problems (from Siegler 1976)

Rule 1	If the weight is the same on both sides, predict that the scale will balance. If the weight differs, predict that the side with more weight will go down.
Rule 2	If one side has more weight, predict that it will go down. If the weights of the two sides are equal, choose the side with the greater distance (i.e. the side with the weight furthest from the fulcrum).
Rule 3	If both weight and distance are equal, predict that the scale will balance. If one side has more weight or distance, and the two sides are equal on the other dimension, predict that the side with the greater value on the unequal dimension will go down. If one side has more weight and the other side more distance, muddle through or guess.
Rule 4	Proceed as Rule 3, unless one side has more weight and the other side more distance. If so, calculate torques by multiplying weight × distance on each side. Then predict that the side with the greatest torque will go down.

go down and were then shown what would actually happen when the beam was released by unlocking it. Feedback was given on three types of problem. Some children received only problems where Rule 1 would always make a correct prediction. Other children were given problems where the weights were the same but distance varied (distance problems). These can only be solved using Rule 2. A third group received problems where there was a conflict between weight and distance (conflict problems). These can only be solved using Rule 3.

As predicted, children who were given only problems that could be solved with Rule 1 continued to use this rule after the feedback session whereas children who had received distance problems were able to use Rule 2 in new problems. The most interesting results came from the third group to whom the most difficult problems – involving conflict between weight and distance – had been presented during the feedback session. The younger children – aged five years – did not make any progress in their solutions of balance scale problems but many of the eight-year-olds were able to advance to Rule 3. This is a very significant advance since it involves taking account of both dimensions.

Siegler was interested in trying to pinpoint what is was that enabled the older children, but not the younger, to make this impressive developmental progression. Videotapes of the children solving problems, where weight and distance were in conflict, showed an important difference between the five- and eight-year-olds. The younger children – still in the preoperational stage – seemed to treat each side of the fulcrum as two separate piles of weights whereas the older children – who were capable of concrete operational thinking – seemed to encode information both about weight on either side of the fulcrum and the distance between each pile of weights and the fulcrum. This is exactly what Piaget's theory of concrete operational thinking would predict.

Siegler (1976) showed children an arrangement of weights on pegs, which was then hidden behind a board. The children were asked to 'make the same problem' with their own balance scale and set of weights. The eight-year-olds could usually put the correct weights onto the correct pegs – showing that they had encoded both weight and distance – but the five-year-olds usually selected the correct weights but put them on the wrong pegs. This confirmed that the younger and older children were encoding the balance scale array in a different way. Siegler then taught a group of five-year-old Rule 1 users to encode distance as well as weight before giving them feedback training on balance beam problems where weight and distance were in conflict. This time, 70 per cent of the five-year-olds were able to benefit from their experience with conflict problems and were able to use Rule 3 after the feedback session. This impressive finding highlights the importance of encoding appropriate information in problem solving as well as the importance of providing the right kind of experience to promote learning.

In a more recent article (Siegler & Chen, 2002), Siegler has pointed out that rule following is not typical of all problem solving. Rule-following provides a good explanation of children's performance in many of the standard Piagetian tasks, including the balance scale, liquid and solid quality conservation, probability estimation, and comparisons of time, speed and distance. In particular, children appear to follow a rule if they are faced with an unfamiliar task that includes two or more relevant dimensions and requires a quantitative comparison. On tasks like this, children usually follow systematic rules such as relying on one, perceptually salient dimension – weight in the case of the balance scale task – to the exclusion of other dimensions. However, the majority of problem-solving tasks that children encounter are not like this. On problems of arithmetic, spelling, telling the time or moral reasoning, among others, children's performance is inconsistent. They may use one approach on one trial and then shift to another approach on a subsequent trial, a day or so later.

Siegler notes that children may adopt a different approach to two similar problems even when they correctly solved the first problem. He argues that it is important to distinguish between rule following (the consistent use of one approach over trials) and strategy use. His overlapping waves model (Siegler, 1996) captures the idea that children know and use multiple strategies in problem solving and also, less frequently, consistently employ a single rule.

One final point to make about problem solving is that, like other aspects of cognitive development during the school years, experience plays an important role in children's performance on particular tasks. During the school years children show considerable development in their ability to plan and monitor their solutions to problems. By five years of age children are planning recurrent daily activities such as laying out their clothes for the morning (Kreitler & Kreitler, 1987). However the ability to plan ahead in solving a problem seems to be a relatively late acquired skill, especially when the problem is unfamiliar.

One task that involves careful planning is route finding (Fabricus, 1988). The task that Fabricus devised was a route-planning task in which children were asked to plan a route that would allow them to retrieve a specified set of objects without any backtracking. Route-planning ability seems to vary from culture to culture and relates to experience. Most Western children have relatively little experience of needing to find their own routes. The dangers of modern traffic and worries about 'stranger danger' mean that younger children are invariably taken from place to place by an adult or in the care of older children. Navajo Indian children spend much more time finding their own way round their neighbourhood and this explains why eight-year-old Navajo Indian children proved to be much better at solving route-finding problems than their non-Navajo peers (Ellis, 1997).

KEY TERMS

Working memory
The system for attending to, processing and remembering information over short periods of time in a temporary store.

Central executive
A component of Baddeley and Hitch's working memory model. It is a mechanism for controlling attention – its main function is to ensure that the limited resources of working memory are used as effectively as possible in a given task.

Phonological loop
A component of Baddeley and Hitch's working memory model. It is used for holding speech-based information.

Visuospatial scratchpad
A component of Baddeley and Hitch's working memory model. It is used for holding visual and spatial information.

Memory span
The number of items that can be accurately recalled in the correct order.

12.3 WORKING MEMORY

Another important perspective on cognitive development during middle childhood comes from research into working memory. **Working memory** is the name given to the short-term storage of information. You may have come across the term 'short-term memory' memory before, which also refers to a temporary store for remembering information over a short period of time. The difference between the terms is that working memory describes a whole system for attending to, processing and remembering information over short periods of time in a temporary store (Henry, 2012).

The original model of working memory was devised by Baddeley and Hitch. It was originally a model of adult processing but, since the theory was proposed (Baddeley & Hitch, 1974), it has proved to be a very fruitful source of ideas about the way that children's capacity to process information changes with age. The original model proposed that working memory was composed of three components. The most important one is the **central executive**, which is a mechanism for controlling attention. Its main function is to ensure that the limited resources of working memory are used as effectively as possible in a given task. There are also two temporary storage systems. The **phonological loop** is used for holding speech-based information and the **visuospatial scratchpad**, as its name suggests, is used for holding visual and spatial information. The two storage systems are described as 'slave systems' because they passively store information. The central executive is the active part of working memory.

The phonological loop is divided into two subcomponents, a phonological store and an articulatory rehearsal mechanism. The phonological store is a rapidly-fading (decaying) store for speech-based information. However, the contents of the store can be refreshed through verbal rehearsal, that is, repeating the contents of the phonological store. Rehearsal is usually silent but, if you hear someone repeating a telephone number that they are trying to remember, that is an example of audible rehearsal. In a later version of the working memory model (Baddeley, 2000), a new component was introduced. The episodic buffer acted as an interface between working memory and long-term knowledge and also integrated the information within working memory (Henry, 2012).

There has been an enormous amount of research on the development of the various components of working memory (Henry, 2012). In this chapter we will focus on memory span and verbal rehearsal. In Chapter 16 (see 16.3) we discuss the development of the central executive.

Memory span – the number of items that can be accurately recalled in the correct order – increases with age over middle childhood. At the age of five, children can typically recall only three words in the correct order. This increases to four words by the age of 9 years and to five words by the age of 11 years (Henry, 2012). This is a relatively slow increase over time but it has not been easy to explain exactly what causes the increase.

One explanation for the increase in memory span is that children's rate of articulation increases as they get older. The idea is that the rate of articulation, that is, the speed at which children can say words or syllables, affects the efficiency of rehearsal. Remember that information in the phonological store fades away very rapidly, over a period of seconds. So the speed at which information can be rehearsed, and so refreshed, affects how many items can be remembered. A large number of studies have found evidence for this view, showing a linear relationship between the rate at which children can say words aloud and their memory span (Hulme, Thomson, Muir, & Lawrence, 1984) (see Henry, 2012 for a review).

Although this account is both simple and elegant, it has a number of problems. One major problem is that the existence of a linear relationship between two variables, that are themselves both varying with age, does not necessarily imply a causal relationship. After all, as children develop, many of their abilities change and they generally become more physically and mentally competent. So, in order to establish a causal link between aspects of development it is, at a minimum, necessary to show that there is a relationship that is independent of age. When age is removed from the correlation between rate of articulation and memory span, through the use of a partial correlational analysis, the relationship between the two becomes non-significant (Henry, 2012).

There is another problem with using an increase in rate of articulation to account for an increase in memory span. This concerns rehearsal. Remember that memory span increases systematically from the age of 4 years to the age of 11 years. However, a series of experiments, beginning with an often-cited study by Flavell and colleagues (Flavell, Beech, & Chinsky, 1966), has reliably established that verbal rehearsal does not appear to occur in children until they are seven years old. Furthermore, if children are prevented from using verbal rehearsal, through articulatory suppression (see Box 12.2), this does not eliminate age differences (Hitch, Halliday, & Littler, 1989).

BOX 12.2: ARTICULATORY SUPPRESSION

One important technique for looking at the effects of verbal rehearsal on memory is articulatory suppression. This involves a participant in repeating a meaningless syllable such as 'blah' over and over, while carrying out a memory task. The idea is that repeating a syllable fills up the articulatory rehearsal mechanism and so does not allow it to be used for rehearsing information that is to be remembered. Articulatory suppression also disrupts the phonological coding of visually-presented words or sentences.

The effects of articulatory suppression are striking. The amount of information that can be remembered is significantly reduced (see Henry, 2012, for a detailed discussion).

Henry (2012) concludes that articulation rates may have some role in the development of memory span for spoken items but that other factors are also relevant, including access to long-term knowledge.

12.4 LEARNING TO DO MATHEMATICS

A main focus of schooling in middle childhood is the teaching of core skills in literacy and numeracy. We discuss literacy in Chapter 13. Here we focus on core skills in numeracy and also consider why some children experience difficulties in mathematics learning.

Understanding and representing numbers

As we saw in Chapter 4, the first understanding of numbers begins in infancy (see 4.3). At this stage, infants can discriminate numbers of items that are relatively far apart (e.g. 8 from 16 or 16 from 32) but not 1 from 2 or 8 from 12. The exact basis of embryonic numerical knowledge in infancy remains controversial but there is general agreement that an ability to count is essential for true mathematic skills. A seminal paper (Gelman & Gallistel, 1978) described three principles that children have to master in order to count objects correctly. These are the principles of **one-to-one correspondence**, stable order and **cardinality**.

One-to-one correspondence requires children to understand that, when they count, they must count each object only once but also count all the objects. Stable order requires that number words be produced in their canonical sequence. If children do not use the correct sequence of number words when they count – saying, for example, 1, 2, 3, 5, 4 when counting five items – then they will arrive at an incorrect answer even if they respect the one-to-one principle. The third of Gelman and Gallistel's principles, cardinality, refers to the fact that, in counting, the final number word reached is equal to the total number of items that have been counted. Thus, if the final number that is counted is 7, this means that there are seven items. Of course, this will only be true if both the one-to-one and stable order principles have been respected.

Most children first experience the concepts of addition and subtraction through the counting of objects (Nunes & Bryant, 1996). However, learning to do mathematics

BOX 12.3: WAYS TO REPRESENT NUMBERS

Systems for representing number can be divided into formal systems that use written numerals, and more informal systems that make use of objects or body parts to represent numbers. The most widely used formal system, now utilised across the world, employs Hindu-Arabic numerals in which the underlying base of the counting system – 10 – is explicitly represented. This is the number system that is used in the West even though, as its name suggests, it was developed in the East.

The Hindu-Arabic number system has many advantages for mathematical calculations. This can be seen by contrasting it with the Roman number system, in which the counting base is not explicitly represented. Consider the way that the Roman system represents the numbers 10 and 100. Ten is represented by the letter X, and the number 100 by the letter C. The use of these two letters does not reveal anything about the numerical relationship between the two numbers, notably that the second (C) is ten times as big as the first (X). By contrast, the equivalent Hindu-Arabic numerals, 10 and 100, tell you a great deal about the relationship between the two numbers once you understand the convention that the column furthest to the right represents units (the numbers from 0–9), the adjacent column represents tens, and the third, hundreds. The transparency of number representation in the Hindu-Arabic numeral system facilitates simple mathematical operations and also allows complex operations with large numbers to be carried out.

Of course, children have to learn the conventions of the way that numbers are represented in the Hindu-Arabic numeral system and, as we will see, the value of numbers in each column – what is called *place value* – can be a source of difficulty in mathematical understanding. For example, in a number such as 254, children must learn that the 2 stands for two hundreds, the 5 for five tens, while the 4 represents four units.

In some societies more informal systems for representing number are used. These do not have a corresponding written form but they may, nevertheless, allow simple arithmetic calculations to be carried out. As with written number systems, the form of the representation can affect how children learn about numbers.

The Oksapmin, who live in a remote part of New Guinea, use body locations to represent numbers (Saxe, 1981). They starting counting on the thumb and fingers of the right hand, work up the right arm and round the head, and finishing by working down the left arm and finally using the fingers of the left hand. In this way the Oksapmin are able to represent numbers up to 27 in sequential order ending with the little finger of the left hand. Numbers greater than 27 are represented by continuing to count down the left wrist and then ascending back up the body. A similar system to represent numbers is used by the native people of the Torres Straight (see Figures 12.3a and 12.3b).

Saxe (1981) found that Oksapmin children's understanding of numerosity was influenced by the way that numbers were represented. He tested children, aged between 7 and 16, and found that the younger children tended to treat different numbers that were located on the same body part as being equivalent. This is because numbers on the equivalent left and right sides had similar names e.g. the numbers represented on the ears are known as 'nata' (right ear) and 'tan-nata' (left ear). It was not until the children were more than nine years old that they were able to treat numbers as independent of their physical location on the body. Saxe also found evidence of another confusion. Some of the younger Oksapmin children began counting from the left side of the body, rather than the right side. Even when it was explained that counting always started on the right, some children remained confused.

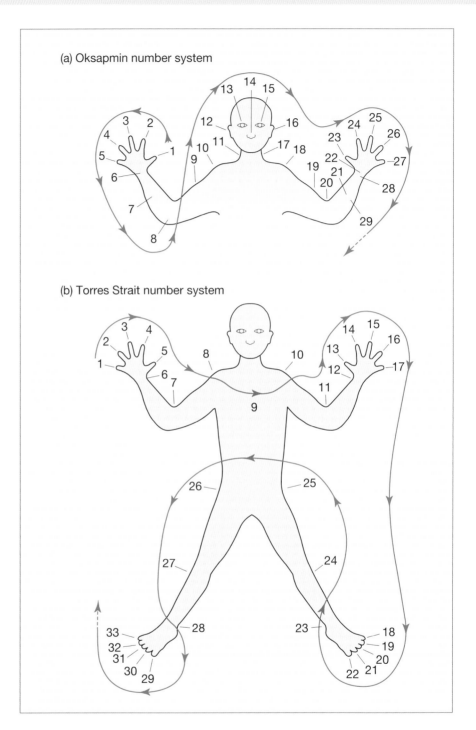

Figure 12.3
Two alternatives to our number system; (a) shows the Oksapmin number system, and
(b) shows the number system used by Torres Straight islanders.
(a) reproduced with permission from Saxe (1981), (b) reproduced with permission
from Ifrah (1985), John Wiley, © 1985 John Wiley & Sons.

in primary school involves learning how to represent numbers in a more abstract way so that addition and subtraction, and more complex mathematical operations, can be carried out in the absence of objects.

Adding and subtracting

Although formal mathematics requires children to understand written numbers, their first exposure to the arithmetic operations of addition and subtraction usually relies on oral counting and often makes use of objects.

The most straightforward way to use counting for simple addition and subtraction is to use a *counting all* strategy. For example, if children are shown two sets of sweets and asked to find out how many sweets there are altogether, they can do this by counting all the sweets in the first set (e.g. 1, 2, 3, 4) and then continuing the count for the sweets in the other set (e.g. 5, 6, 7). Studies of five-year-old children show that this is the strategy they most often apply when asked to add up two sets of objects (Nunes & Bryant, 1996).

A counting all strategy can also be used for subtraction problems using objects (Riley, Greeno, & Heller, 1983). Riley *et al.* gave simple addition and subtraction problems to six-year-old American children. The subtraction problems were of this kind: 'Joe had eight marbles. Then he gave five marbles to Tom. How many does he have now?' The children proved to be successful at both kinds of problem providing that they were able to use blocks to represent the numbers involved and providing that the numbers were small.

The use of physical markers to assist in addition and subtraction continues once children move on to formal operations involving written numbers. The counting all strategy can be applied to fingers just as to objects and this is often how children first solve simple addition problems using numbers. Thus to work out 3 + 4 children hold up three fingers and then, while still holding up the first set of fingers, they hold up another four fingers (often on the other hand). The total number of fingers is then counted to give the answer, 7.

Children who have poor representation of their fingers are likely to have poor mathematical understanding and there is a rare disorder, Gerstmann's syndrome, whose symptoms include a deficit in finger representation (finger agnosia) and dyscalculia (Butterworth, Varma, & Laurillard, 2011) (see Box 12.4).

The counting all strategy cannot easily be applied to addition where the sum is greater than ten. Children thus move on to a *counting on* strategy in which they can still use their fingers but now they count upwards from the one of the addends. Now, to work out the solution to 3 + 4 the child would start from three, hold up four fingers and count 4, 5, 6, 7. In the counting on strategy, it is more efficient to count on from the larger number rather than the smaller as it involves less counting. Primary school children naturally count on from the larger number, for example, counting on from 7 rather than 2 in 7 + 2 (Groen & Parkman, 1972). However, it is possible that, when children first employ the counting on procedure, they always start with the first number in an addition and count on according to the size of the second number. Selecting the larger of two numbers as the starting point in an addition requires children to realise the numerical equivalence of, say, 15 + 7 and 7 + 15. This equivalence is obvious to someone who is familiar with arithmetic, but it is not immediately apparent to children who are at the early stage of understanding mathematical operations.

Counting aloud is usually replaced by subvocal (silent) counting as children reach the end of primary school. It is more difficult to study the use of subvocal counting in the solution of arithmetic problems but reaction time studies, comparing the time taken to solve addition problems involving numbers of different magnitudes, show that subvocal counting continues to be used to solve arithmetic problems throughout the early school years (Gallistel & Gelman, 1991). This method is later supplemented by the retrieval of number facts from memory in which the addition of numbers is carried out by recalling the answer from previous additions.

In the case of subtraction, the most common method used by primary school children is the choice algorithm (Woods, Resnick, & Groen, 1975). This can be seen as analogous to the counting on method used for addition. There are two ways of employing the choice algorithm. The first involves counting the number of steps required to get from the subtrahend (the number to be subtracted) to the minuend (the number from which the subtraction is to take place). For example the solution to the sum 8 − 6 is obtained by counting up from 6 to 8 (7, 8) and seeing how many steps are involved (2). In the second method the child counts down from the minuend the number of steps specified by the subtrahend. The answer to 8 − 2 is obtained by counting down from 8 two steps, thus 7, 6 (6 being the correct answer). The use of the choice method is demonstrated both by reaction time data (which shows that reaction time increases with the difference in size between the minuend and the subtrahend) and by interviews with children, in which use of these methods was spontaneously reported (Gallistel & Gelman, 1991). As in the case of addition, these counting methods are finally replaced by the use of retrieval of number information.

Understanding place value and place holders

Success in addition and subtractions, as well as the more complex operations of multiplication and division, requires children to understand the basis of written number representation. In the first instance, children have to learn about **place value**, which is an important convention in the Hindu-Arabic system for writing numbers. They must learn that the rightmost column represents numbers from 0 to 9 (units), the column to the immediate left represents tens, the next left hundreds and so on (see Box 12.3).

One important aspect of place values that can be especially difficult to grasp is the significance of 0. Zero is used as a **place holder**, that is, it indicates the presence of an empty column. For example, in 204 the 0 indicates that there are no tens. If the 0 were omitted, giving 24, a very different value would be indicated. The conceptual difficulty of zero is underlined by that fact that it was not introduced into Hindu-Arabic notation until one century after the concept of place value.

Having understood place values and the importance of zeros, the next step is for children to learn how these are maintained when multi-digit numbers are added, subtracted, multiplied and divided. This is a complex problem and many of the difficulties that children experience in mastering formal arithmetic stem from failures to understand the maintenance of place values, especially the significance of zeros.

Six- and seven-year-old French children did not understand place value even for two digit numbers and were not aware that in a number such as 16 the first digit stood for 1 ten (i.e. 10) rather than 1 one (Sinclair, 1988). Nunes and Bryant (1996) gave five- and six-year-old children in England a series of tasks that assessed understanding of place value. These included reading and writing numbers containing from one to four digits as well as round numbers (10, 60, 100, 200, 1,000). The children found it relatively easier to read and write the round numbers than other numbers with the same number of digits. Thus 200 was easier than 202 and 1,000 than 1,237. Nunes and Bryant suggest that this is because of the relatively greater familiarity of the round numbers.

Problems with writing numbers again reflected confusions in understanding the value of 0 as a place holder. Some children added additional zeros as in two examples reported by Nunes and Bryant of one child who wrote 108 as 1008 and another who wrote 2,569 as 200050069. The logic of such a representation is clear: thousands and hundreds are each followed by the correct number of zeros to act as place holders. What had confused the children is that place holders are only necessary when lower place values are empty. In all, 40 per cent of the five- and six-year-old children described by Nunes and Bryant used an incorrect number of noughts (either too many or too few) to write the numbers 108 and 2,569.

Overall, there was an interesting difference between the children who were good at writing numbers and those who were not. Children in the former group were generally better at understanding how numbers could be decomposed and added. This was tested in a task where children were given pretend coins of different values that they were required to give to a shopkeeper to pay for a particular item. Both single denomination (1p) and multiple denomination (10p and 20p) coins were used and the children were required to use combinations of these. Thus to pay for an item that cost 11p a child would require one 10p and one 1p coin. In order to select the correct coins, children had to realise the relation between single and multiple denomination coins and understand how a combination of coins could produce the correct amount. Additive composition – as this ability is called – clearly has a great deal in common with understanding place value and Nunes and Bryant suggest that understanding the additive composition of numbers provides a basis for subsequent understanding of place values in written numbers (Bryant & Nunes, 2011).

Difficulties with place values and place holders are a major factor in children's problems with multi digit arithmetic (Dockrell & McShane, 1992). Summarising the findings of an extensive earlier study that analysed nearly 20,000 multi digit additions and subtractions carried out by school children (Brown & Burton, 1978), Dockrell and McShane noted that the most common errors occurred when children had to deal with zeros, for example, borrowing from 0 in order to subtract a larger number from a smaller but failing to carry the borrowing over to the next column; or writing the bottom digit in a column as the answer whenever the top digit was 0. Another common error was to subtract the smaller from the larger digit regardless of which was on the top line and which on the bottom.

Although the Brown and Burton study was carried out over 30 years ago, the difficulties that children experience with addition and subtraction of large numbers remain the same. What has become clear, however, is that there are significant cultural differences in performance in mathematics.

Cross-cultural differences in mathematical ability

Many studies have shown that children in East Asian countries (China, Japan, Korea and Taiwan) perform at a consistently higher level on tests of mathematical ability than their contemporaries in the West. One of the most extensive cross-cultural

KEY TERMS

Developmental dyscalculia
A disorder of mathematical understanding. The core feature is a severe disability in learning arithmetic.

BOX 12.4: DYSCALCULIA

Developmental dyscalculia is a disorder of mathematical understanding. It has roughly the same prevalence as developmental dyslexia (around 5 per cent) but, whereas you will almost certainly have heard of dyslexia, you will probably not have heard of dyscalculia. In a recent article, Butterworth points out that the consequences of having dyscalculia are just as severe as the consequences of having dyslexia (Butterworth et al., 2011). However, dyslexia is considerably better understood than dyscalculia; and, as a consequence, there is a much better understanding of how to support children who are identified as having difficulties with reading and spelling than there is of how to support children who have a specific difficulty with mathematics.

Recent research in genetics and neuroscience suggests that dyscalculia is a coherent syndrome – in other words, there are certain features of this difficulty that tend to occur together. The core feature is a severe disability in learning arithmetic. The disability may be highly selective and children who are diagnosed as having dyscalculia may have normal intelligence and normal working memory. However, like many other developmental disorders, dyscalculia can also co-occur with other disorders such as dyslexia and attention deficit/hyperactivity disorder (ADHD) (Williams & Lind, 2013).

Mathematical abilities have a high degree of specific heritability. Twins studies, in which the mathematical ability of monozygotic and dizygotic twins are compared (see Chapter 1), have suggested that about 30 per cent of variance in mathematical ability is due to genetic factors. Furthermore, although dyscalculia and dyslexia often occur together, some of the genetic factors involved are specific to mathematics.

The core difficulty that is experienced by children who have significant difficulty with mathematics is a poor understanding of

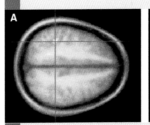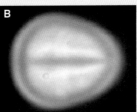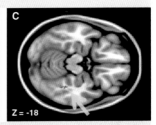

Structural abnormalities in young dyscalculic brains suggesting the critical role for the intra-parietal sulci. This diagram shows areas where the dyscalculic brain is different from that of typically developing controls. (A) There is a small region of reduced grey-matter density in left IPS in adolescent dyscalculics. (B) There is right IPS reduced gray-matter density (yellow area) in nine-year-olds. (C) There is reduced probability of connections from right fusiform gyrus to other parts of the brain, including the parietal lobes.

> numerosity. According to Butterworth *et al.* (2011), 'Numbers do not seem to be meaningful for dyscalculics – at least, not meaningful in the way that they are for typically developing learners. They do not intuitively grasp the size of a number and its value relative to other numbers' (Butterworth *et al.*, 2011, p. 1050).
>
> There are a number of lines of evidence to support this view. First, children with dyscalculia are impaired in their ability to count the number of objects in a set or compare the number of objects in two sets. Second, brain scans have shown that, when they are carrying out mathematical tasks such as comparing numerosities, comparing number symbols or doing simple arithmetic, children with dyscalculia have decreased activation in the parts of the brain that are particularly involved in these kind of tasks. The intra-parietal sulci seem to be areas of the brain that are particularly important for processing numerosity.

comparisons of mathematical ability was carried out by Stevenson and his colleagues (Stevenson *et al.*, 1990). They tested over 4,000 primary school children in Taiwan, Japan and the United States. All the children in the three countries came from large cities and attended schools that were representative of their local area. Half the children were in grade 1 (age 6 years) and the others were in grade 5 (age 11 years). All children were given a wide range of tests to assess different aspects of mathematical ability and also reading.

There were no overall differences between the three groups on the reading tests although more American fifth graders performed at the extremes (i.e. reading well above or well below their chronological age) than their peers in Taiwan and Japan. (This could be explained by differences in reading strategies for English and the other two scripts – see Chapter 13.) However, for maths, there was a clear overall difference with the Japanese and Taiwanese children having significantly higher scores on almost all of the tests.

One clear indication of the extent of the superiority of the Japanese and Taiwanese children over their peers in the United States came from a comparison of the highest and lowest scorers across the entire sample. In the first grade, only 14 children from the US were in the top 100 while 56 were in the bottom 100. By the fifth grade, only one American child was in the top 100 while 67 were in the bottom 100. Had the ability of the children in the three countries been the same, there should have been around 33 American children in both the top and bottom 100 since an equal number from each country was tested. However, Stevenson's data show that, particularly in fifth grade, the American children were significantly under-represented in the group of high achievers and significantly over-represented in the group of low achievers.

Accounting for the mathematical superiority of East Asian children has proved difficult because there are many possible factors that could contribute to this differ-ence (Towse & Saxton, 1998). An obvious starting point is to consider whether there are differences in the educational experiences of the children that might explain the superior performance of children being educated in Asia.

There have been a number of studies looking at the way that mathematical concepts are taught in school. American textbooks devote a great deal of space to series of exercises that the children are expected to work through while Japanese textbooks spend more time in explaining underlying concepts and providing worked out examples for the children to follow (Mayer, Sims, & Tajika, 1995). This finding has been echoed in other studies showing a more conceptual approach to mathematics teaching in East Asia (Siegler & Mu, 2008). For example, a comparison between Japanese and American mathematics lessons for ten-year-olds showed that, in Japan, children were encouraged to offer their own argument to the whole class and evaluate arguments proposed by other students. Teachers seldom gave direct evaluation. In contrast, American teachers often gave individual elaboration as well as direct evaluation to the students' responses, and some of the teachers offered their own opinions about mathematics (Inagaki, Morita, & Hatano, 1999).

There are also striking differences between American and Asian children in the amount of time spent on mathematics education. Considerably more class time is spent on mathematics in Japan and Taiwan and many children have additional private tuition to supplement school teaching. Stevenson *et al.* (1990) found that, in grade 1, Japanese children spent an average of 5.8 hours per week on mathematics, Taiwanese children spent 4 hours and American children only 2.7 hours. By grade 5, these figures had increased to 7.8, 11.7 and 3.4 hours.

This greater emphasis on mathematics reflected a finding from the Stevenson *et al.* (1990) study that Taiwanese and Japanese children and their families saw success in mathematics as closely related to hard work and effort whereas American children and their families were more likely to attribute success to natural ability rather than hard work. This difference in attitude has also been highlighted by Hatano, who writes of the experience of children in Japan:

> children have almost no choice than to seek mastery of . . . culturally prescribed skills. In contrast, there are also many skills that are viewed as culturally provided alternatives and for which freedom of choice is allowed. I think that school mathematics is a national intellectual pursuit in Asian countries, but not in the United States. Whereas students cannot escape from it in the former, in the latter they are told . . . that, if they are poor at or dislike mathematics, they are free to seek achievement in some other area.
>
> (Hatano, 1990, pp. 111–112)

It is not only school experience that is relevant to the development of mathematical understanding because cross-cultural differences in mathematical ability are evident even in kindergarten. Siegler and Mu (2008) tested Chinese and American children, aged between five and six years, on two mathematical tasks. One task was addition of single-digit numbers – a task that the children had practised at school – while the other was number-line estimation. This second task was unfamiliar to the children. It involved looking at a number line, marked with 0 at one end and 100 at the other, and then estimating the location of a particular number within this range.

The number-line estimation task is an interesting one to use for comparing mathematical understanding. Children in the United States show a clear progression in ability from age five to age seven. Accurate number-line estimation should be linear, that is, the total line should be mentally divided into equal sections so that the estimation of the position of low numbers and high numbers is equally accurate. In the case of five-year-olds, estimates of low numbers tend to be too spread out while estimates of high numbers are too compressed. However, seven-year-olds adopt a more linear approach, like adults. Six-year-olds show a mixed pattern, with some children adopting a linear approach and some performing like five-year-olds (Siegler & Mu, 2008).

Siegler and Mu compared the performance of two groups of children, matched for age, type of school and socioeconomic background. On the number-line task, there were clear differences in the performance of the Chinese and American children. The Chinese children produced more accurate estimates than the American children and their estimates were more linear. The Chinese children also performed better on the addition tasks. Within both samples of children, performance on the two tasks was positively correlated.

Siegler and Mu point to the greater practice that Chinese children have at home in preschool activities, such as counting on fingers and counting objects, as contributing to this difference (Pan, Gauvain, Liu, & Cheng, 2006). Another factor may be the greater transparency of the system of number names in Chinese and other East Asian languages.

English is not consistent in its number names (see Towse & Saxton, 1997) especially for numbers between 11 and 19 where some, but not all, numbers end with the suffix 'teen' and some numbers have their unit value expressed in full (as in *four*teen) while others have a reduced form of their unit value (as in *fif*teen rather than *five*teen). Similar inconsistencies exist with the use of full and modified forms to describe the tens in numbers from 20 to 100. Thus we have 'fifty' rather than 'fivety' and the suffix 'teen' becomes 'ty'.

The East Asian countries, where mathematical superiority has been documented, all have Chinese-based number names. These are highly regular for numbers up to 100 and, importantly for the concept of place value, the number of tens is made explicit. For example, in Japanese, 2 is 'ni', 10 is 'juu' and 20 is ni-juu (i.e. two-ten). The number of units is stated after the number of tens so 21 is ni-juu-ichi (i.e. two-ten-one).

Japanese children develop a more precocious understanding of the composition of numbers (Miura *et al.*, 1994). Seven-year-old children in China, Japan and Korea and in three Western countries (Sweden, France and the United States) were asked to represent written numbers using single-unit blocks (representing one unit) and multiple-units blocks that represented ten units. Miura *et al.* found that six- and seven-year-old Chinese, Korean and Japanese children produced significantly more responses in which they correctly used a combination of single and ten-unit blocks. The Western children mainly used only single unit blocks to represent numbers.

As we have already noted, parents also play an important role in supporting the development of their children's mathematical skills in Japan and China (Hatano, 1990; Pan *et al.*, 2006) and, as with many other aspects of cognitive development, it appears that the right kind of experience can support children to develop their mathematical skills.

12.5 SUMMARY

We began this chapter by considering Piaget's account of concrete operational reasoning, which spans a period from the age of six years to the onset of adolescence. The major logical operations that children acquire during this extended period are conservation, seriation, classification and numeration. A key aspect of the new-found abilities that characterise concrete operational reasoning is the dealing with more than one variable at a time. In conservation tasks, preschoolers can only focus on one dimension (such as the height of a liquid in a container) but six- and seven-year-olds can look at the relationship between two key variables in a task. They realise, for example, that a change in height can be compensated by an increase in width (in a conservation task) or an increase in distance can compensate for a decrease in weight (on a balance scale).

For many tasks, appropriate training can improve performance as Siegler (1976) showed for balance scale problems and Bryant and Trabasso (1971) showed for a transitivity task. What appears to be particularly important is to cue children about the appropriate variables to consider in a particular problem and, in this way, help them to structure the problem space.

Age differences in the successful solution of deductive reasoning problems, such as those involving transitive inference, are largely dependent on developmental differences in the capacity of working memory, the effectiveness of executive function and the ability to retrieve information from long-term memory. We saw in this chapter that there is an increase in the capacity of working memory during the period of middle childhood and this will enable children to hold and manipulate more complex information.

Learning to do mathematics is a key activity during middle childhood and an understanding of numbers and how they are represented in written form are key skills for developing a sound understanding. Children with dyscalculia have been shown to have difficulty in understanding what numbers represent and they have difficulty in making simple numerosity judgements, such as comparing the number of items in two sets. Learning how to count accurately – and how to apply counting to perform simple mathematical operations – lays the foundation for understanding how to multiply and divide and to work with large numbers.

Finally, in this chapter, we saw that there are notable cross-cultural differences in mathematical ability with children from East Asian countries tending to outperform their peers in the West. There appear to be a number of contributing factors including teaching methods, the amount of time spent on teaching mathematics in the classroom and the greater transparency of Chinese-based number names.

FURTHER READING

Bryant, P. E., & Nunes, T. (2011). Children's understanding of mathematics. In U. Goswami (Ed.), *Childhood cognitive development, 2nd edition* (pp. 549–573). Chichester: Wiley-Blackwell.

Butterworth, B., Varma, S., & Laurillard, D. (2011). Dyscalculia: From brain to education. *Science, 332*, 1049–1053.

Goswami, U. (2011). Inductive and deductive reasoning. In U. Goswami (Ed.), *Childhood cognitive development, 2nd edition* (pp. 399–419). Chichester: Wiley-Blackwell.

Henry, L. (2012). *The development of working memory in children*. London: Sage.

ESSAY QUESTIONS

1. How does Piaget explain the cognitive changes that take place during middle childhood?
2. What have experimental studies of children's ability to solve balance beam problems revealed about cognitive development in middle childhood?
3. Why does working memory span increase during middle childhood?
4. What is dyscalculia?
5. Explain some of the factors that can affect children's achievement in mathematics.

CHAPTER 13

CONTENTS

Literacy

13

After reading this chapter you will be able to

- describe the main factors that determine how well children learn to read
- explain the difference between decoding skills and reading comprehension
- understand why learning to read some scripts is more difficult than others
- explain the strategies that children use in spelling
- describe the main features of developmental dyslexia and compare this disorder with reading comprehension impairment
- explain why difficulties with handwriting can affect children's performance at school.

Much of the time that children spend in the classroom during their early years at school is devoted to the mastering the art of reading and writing. In this chapter we consider how children learn to read, write and spell, and some of the problems that they may encounter.

13.1 LEARNING TO READ

Theories of learning to read

There are a number of different theories of how children learn to read but the most common view is that the process of learning to read develops through a series of stages. One of the first stage theories was that of Frith (1985). She proposed that children begin to read by initially building up a sight vocabulary of words that they recognise on the basis of their overall appearance. Frith called this kind of early reading logographic (Frith, 1985; Pacton, Fayol, & Perruchet, 2002). Children who read using a **logographic strategy** recognise whole words and do not pay attention

Logographic strategy

Reading by recognition of whole words.

Alphabetic strategy

Reading by recognition of individual letters.

Orthographic strategy

Reading by recognition of groups of letters, or orthographic units.

to individual letters. This means that children can only read words they already know and cannot attempt to read unfamiliar words. When children are taught to read words on 'flash cards' – cards with single words printed on them in large letters – they are being encouraged to use a logographic strategy.

In this early stage, when children make a reading error they tend to say one of the words in their reading vocabulary. However, their choice of word is often not arbitrary and so, for example, they may incorrectly choose another word that is similar in length or shares some letters in common. For example, one child read 'policeman' as 'children' explaining that 'I know it's that one because it's a long one'; and another read 'smaller' as 'yellow', swayed by the presence of the double l (Seymour & Elder, 1986).

Children soon begin to notice that there are systematic relationships between the letters in a word and its pronunciation and they begin to learn the associations between graphemes (letters and letter strings) and phonemes using what Frith calls an **alphabetic strategy**. This new strategy of using grapheme-to-phoneme rules enables children to make a guess about how to pronounce an unfamiliar word by looking at the sequence of letters it contains. This strategy works well for words in which the sound of individual letters gives a good indication of the pronunciation of a word as in the case of 'cat' or 'dog'. However, for a language such as English using letter-to-sound relationships alone will not always produce the correct pronunciation. Consider, for example, what happens the first time a children comes across a word such as 'might'.

To deal with words that have an irregular spelling pattern Frith proposed a final stage of reading that she described as orthographic. This involves the recognition of orthographic units – strings of letters that commonly go together such as IGHT. By using an **orthographic strategy** children are able to pronounce irregular words that are similar in structure to words that they already know. For example, if a child can already read 'light', then it is possible to make a good guess about the pronunciation of words such as 'might' and 'sight'. The orthographic strategy does not, however, replace the alphabetic strategy and children will continue to use this for pronouncing new regular words. Words with a very unusual spelling pattern, such as 'yacht' or 'ogre', will have to be learned logographically so, for English, all three strategies will continue to be used.

There has been some debate about the extent to which children make use of letter–sound relationships in their early reading. As we just saw, Frith (1985) argues for a distinct logographic stage and this view is shared by Seymour and Elder (1986). However, Ehri (Ehri & Robbins, 1992) has argued that children begin to make use of letter–sound knowledge as soon as they have it available.

To some extent the use that children make of letter–sound knowledge in the early stages of learning to read depends on the way that reading is taught. Unlike many other aspects of development that we have considered so far, literacy is explicitly taught. If early teaching emphasises a whole word approach to reading then children are more likely to use a logographic strategy when they first begin to read as Seymour and Elder (1986) found in their study, carried out in Scotland. However, if children are taught through a phonics approach in which they sound out letters when they first begin to read, they will pay much more attention to individual letters in words and will not use a purely logographic strategy (Connelly, Johnston, & Thompson, 2001). Children taught to read using a phonics approach will also make more attempts to read words that they do not know.

Longitudinal studies of learning to read

One of the best ways to find out about how children learn to read, and why some children are much better than others, is to carry out a longitudinal study in which a group of children is followed up over time to see what kinds of ability predicts individual progress. Two of the earliest studies to look at contributions to reading success were carried out in Scandinavia (Lundberg, Olofsson, & Wall, 1980) and in Oxford (Bradley & Bryant, 1983). Both studies included a training element and it is interesting to note that such an approach has been a feature of much reading research.

Lundberg *et al.* (1980) trained preschool children in Sweden on a wide range of tasks involving phonological knowledge. These included recognition of rhymes, finding the initial phoneme in a word and segmenting words into their constituent syllables. Lundberg *et al.* found that children who were trained in these tasks made better reading progress than comparable children who had not received this training.

Bradley and Bryant (1983) investigated pre-reading children's sensitivity to rhyme and alliteration by presenting them with sets of monosyllabic words (such as 'hill', 'pig' and 'pin') and asking them to say which was the odd one out. (The correct answer is 'hill' because the other two words both begin with the sound 'pi'.) Words either had their first sound in common, their middle sound or final sound. When the children's subsequent reading performance was measured after three years of schooling, those children who had initially been good at judging the odd word out were better readers than those children who had been less good at this task.

In a second study, Bradley and Bryant randomly allocated children to one of three training conditions: sorting words by meaning; sorting words according to their initial and final sounds (phonological analysis); phonological analysis plus training in identification of letters of the alphabet. The children who were given training in phonological analysis alone learned to read more successfully than the group who had been trained to classify words by meaning. However, the third group, who had received training in phonological analysis and had also been taught about letter–sound relations, made even greater progress.

Bradley and Bryant's study was taken as strong evidence that preschool children, who have a high level of phonological awareness and are good at making judgements about similarities in rhyme and initial sound, have a head start when they begin learning to read. More recent studies have provided detailed information about the precise phonological skills that are important for reading.

One key study, which was carried out in York (Muter, Hulme, Snowling, & Stevenson, 2004), followed 90 children over their first three years at school. At the initial assessment, which took place on school entry, children were tested on their ability to detect and produce rhymes and to manipulate and isolate phonemes. Rhyme skills were assessed by asking children to produce words that rhymed with a target (e.g. words that rhymed with 'day') or to pick out the non-rhyming words from a set such as 'sand, hand, bank'. Phoneme skills were assessed by means of a phoneme deletion task in which children were given a word and asked what would be left when one sound was deleted. For example, 'tin without the /t/ says . . . ?' The other task – phoneme completion – involved the presentation of the beginning of a word and asking the child what sound was needed to complete the word. All of the tasks used relevant pictures so the child was always clear what the intended word was.

In addition to the phoneme deletion and completion tasks, the children were also assessed to see how many letters they could give the name or sound for, how many common words they could read and how large their spoken vocabulary was.

Two kinds of skill on school entry predicted the number of words that children could read after 12 months. These were letter knowledge and phoneme manipulation. Rhyme skills did not predict reading. In order to establish causality, the researchers at York also carried out a training study (Hatcher, Hulme, & Snowling, 2004) in which children were given a highly systematic phonics-based reading program during their first two years at school. For some groups the reading program was supplemented with explicit phonological training involving phonemes, rhymes, or a combination of the two. For children who were identified as being likely to have difficulties in learning to read (see 13.3), the addition of explicit phoneme-level training was found to be more effective than was rhyme-level training in improving reading. However, such training only appeared to be important for children who were deemed to be at risk because the systematic phonics-based approach was sufficient for most children to learn to read successfully.

Reading comprehension

Learning to sound out words is only one aspect of reading. The other key skill is being able to understand what you read. The simple view of reading (Hoover & Gough, 1990) argues that two components, decoding and linguistic comprehension, underpin the development of skilled reading. As we have just seen, the development of decoding skills relies on good letter knowledge and good phonological skills. Reading comprehension relies on rather different skills. In the Muter *et al.* (2004) study we discussed earlier, vocabulary knowledge and grammatical awareness were significant predictors of reading comprehension (even when the effects of early word recognition, phoneme sensitivity and letter knowledge were controlled). In other words, in order to understand what they were reading, children relied on their knowledge of spoken English both in terms of the meaning of individual words and the meaning of sentences.

This wider knowledge of the spoken language becomes even more important as children progress through school since they are required to deal with increasingly complex texts. A meta-analysis of studies examining the correlations among reading comprehension, listening comprehension and decoding skills over a wide range of ages (Gough, Hoover, & Peterson, 1996) showed that the correlation between reading comprehension and decoding decreased over time (i.e. reading comprehension became less influenced by variations in decoding skill) whereas the correlation between reading comprehension and listening comprehension increased. What this shows is that a good knowledge of the spoken language is essential if you are going to become a fluent reader.

Another important factor in continued reading progress across the later years at school is that children continue to read. Many studies have shown that early reading levels are a good predictor of later levels. For example, in a longitudinal study that followed a group of children from first to eleventh grade (Cunningham & Stanovich, 1997), reading in first grade was a strong predictor of reading ten years later even after individual differences in cognitive ability had been accounted for. However, a key factor in the sustained development of reading ability was children's continuing exposure to print.

Stanovich famously coined the term 'Matthew effect' to characterise these later stages of learning to read where it is the process of reading itself that drives further progress: children who read a lot become increasingly competent readers (Stanovich, 1986). (The term 'Matthew effect' refers to a famous passage in Saint Matthew's Gospel in the New Testament: 'For everyone who has will be given more, and he will have an abundance. Whoever does not have, even what he has will be taken from him.')

As predicted by the 'Matthew effect', children who read a lot in the Cunningham and Stanovich (1997) study continued to develop their reading skills. This highlights the fact that children who find it easy to learn to read will most naturally spend time reading and so will become even better while, conversely, children who find reading difficult will be less inclined to read and so will fall even further behind their peers.

Learning to read in other languages

So far we have only considered what happens when children learn to read English. Like the majority of modern languages, English is written using an alphabetic script in which a relatively small number of letters is used to write words. The Roman alphabet is used for writing English and many other European languages. Other European languages are written using a Greek or Russian alphabet. In all alphabetic scripts the sounds in a word are represented through letters but the relation between sound (phonology) and spelling (orthography) is very variable. In languages such as Italian or Spanish, the relationship between phonology and orthography is very consistent and (with very few exceptions) a particular sound always has the same spelling. This means that once children have learned all the relations between letters and sounds it is possible for them to spell any word that they hear and to read any word that they see written down. Languages such as Italian or Spanish are described as having high **orthographic transparency** for both reading and spelling.

The orthographic transparency of reading and spelling do not always mirror one another. Modern Greek has high orthographic regularity for reading, comparable to that of Italian or Spanish. However, unlike Italian or Spanish, Greek has much greater orthographic irregularity for spelling because vowels can be spelled in more than one way. English differs from Italian, Spanish and Greek because it is highly irregular for both reading and spelling.

The speed with which children learn to read is strongly influenced by the degree of orthographic transparency (Seymour, Aro, & Erskine, 2003). Italian children learn to read much faster than English children of comparable ability and are reading fluently by the end of their first year at school (Cossu, 1999; Thorstad, 1991). Thorstad also found that all the Italian children he studied, even those who were ten years old, used an alphabetic strategy and converted letters to sounds in order to read an unfamiliar word. Since such a strategy is always successful in a transparent orthography, children who are learning to read Italian do not need to acquire other strategies that will allow them to read irregular words.

Interestingly, for a transparent orthography like Italian, there is no such thing as a graded reading test in which children are presented with increasingly difficult

KEY TERMS

Orthographic transparency
A consistent relationship between the sounds of a language and the spelling so that a particular sound always has the same spelling.

words. For English, such tests are used to assess reading age and so to indicate whether a child is reading at an age-appropriate level. After a few months of instruction, children who learn to read a transparent orthography can read aloud any word they see with near perfect accuracy. What changes over time for such children is therefore not reading accuracy but reading fluency, in other words, the speed with which they can read.

In spite of differences in the time it takes for children to become fluent readers of scripts with varying orthographic transparency, comparisons between scripts suggest that similar core skills are important. For example, in a direct comparison of Czech (which is highly transparent) and English (Caravolas, Volín, & Hulme, 2005), the reading fluency of children in both groups was predicted by phonological skills, assessed by phoneme deletion (which we mentioned earlier) and spoonerisms. In this latter task, children are required to transpose the initial consonant in two nonwords e.g. *sor, nep* to *nor, sep*. This is one of the most difficult phoneme manipulation tasks and it is often used with older children and adults as it is sensitive to individual differences in ability.

As Greek is highly regular for reading but not for spelling we might expect that children will make very rapid progress in learning to read Greek – comparable to that in Italian or Czech – but that progress in spelling will be slow and comparable to that in English. In a study of beginning readers (Harris & Giannouli, 1999), Greek children were found to be fluent readers at the end of their first year of reading instruction and, even after only six weeks at school, they were showing clear evidence of the use of an alphabetic strategy. However, the same children were relatively poor at spelling and continued to make a large number of errors until they were 11 years old. As in the case of other alphabetic scripts, phonemic skills predicted reading progress in the first years at school (Nikolopoulos, Goulandris, Hulme, & Snowling, 2006).

13.2 LEARNING TO WRITE

Spelling

As in the case of reading, the relative difficulty of learning to spell depends on the level of orthographic regularity in a given script. Where there is a similar degree of transparency for both reading and spelling, as in Italian, the two skills will tend to develop in tandem. Where there is higher regularity for reading than for spelling then spelling tends to lag considerably behind reading as in the case of Greek (Harris & Giannouli, 1999).

Spelling typically lags behind reading in English. This is because there is considerably greater ambiguity about the spelling of an unfamiliar word than there is about its pronunciation. As for Greek, the main reason for this asymmetry in English lies in the spelling of vowels. When reading there are typically a number of spelling-to-sound correspondences although, in most cases, one particular pattern is more common than the others. For example, the sequence EA is most commonly pronounced as /i:/ as in EAT or READ. Words in which EA is pronounced in a different way (such as SWEAT or GREAT) are much less frequent. This means that, when an unfamiliar word containing EA is encountered for the first time, a good reader can make a plausible guess that it is pronounced /i:/.

When we turn to spelling, the picture is much more ambiguous especially for vowels. Consider the sound /ou/, which can be spelled in at least 13 different ways including DOLE, BOWL, COAT, FOLK, SEW and BROOCH (Barry, 1994). The most common spelling pattern for the /ou/ sound is O_E (as in DOLE, MOLE, HOLE, HOSE etc.) but this occurs in only 32 per cent of words. The next most common spelling is O, which appears in 26 per cent of words and OW and OA both occur in about 15 per cent of words. Given that all of these spelling patterns are relatively common, it is difficult to guess how an unfamiliar word with an /ou/ sound might be spelled.

One reason for the complexity of English spelling is historical change. Before the Norman Conquest in 1066, when Old English was in use, there was almost perfect one-to-one correspondence between graphemes and phonemes and little orthographic irregularity (Scholfield, 1994). With the Norman Conquest, the sound of many words changed and the close link between spelling and pronunciation weakened. Many spellings were adopted unchanged from the French and, at the same time, new letters were introduced into English spelling from Latin, French and elsewhere.

The spelling of words in Old English directly reflected the way they were spoken so that words that sounded the same were written the same, even though they were quite unrelated in meaning, and words that were related in meaning were spelled differently. Thus, in Old English, the spelling of the singular form of the word for small was SMAEL while the plural form was SMALU. This is quite different from modern English spelling, which tends to preserve meaning relations at the expense of pronunciation as in the case of CHILD, CHILDREN and CHILDHOOD or PHOTOGRAPH and PHOTOGRAPHY where the spelling of the root word remains the same in derivations.

Children adopt different strategies for English spelling as they become more proficient. Initially, children spontaneously write words using a letter sequence that bears no relation to the target word, suggesting that they have no awareness of the relation between letters and sounds. In the next stage, children begin to take some account of this relationship and they begin to include some letters that reflect the sounds in a word (e.g. LEFT for *elephant*). Gentry calls this the pre-phonetic stage (Gentry, 1982). Gradually spelling becomes phonetic until the point where all the sounds in a word are represented by letters. However, phonetic spelling will often be incorrect in English because of the many possible ways in which particular sounds – especially vowels – may be spelled. Thus 'come' might be spelled as KOM, 'type' as TIP or 'eagle' as EGL. In the next – transitional – stage, children begin to take account of English spelling patterns. They start to include a vowel in every syllable (e.g. *eagle* is now spelled as EGUL) and to incorporate common English letter sequences such as AI, EA and EE and the silent E at the end of words into their spellings. Finally children move towards correct spelling where they are able to take account of the many different rules that are reflected in English spelling including the use of silent and double consonants.

As in the case of reading, good phonemic skills appear to be important in becoming a proficient speller in English and other alphabetic scripts (Caravolas *et al.*, 2005; Nikolopoulos *et al.*, 2006). Surprisingly, however, the link between phonemic skills and spelling seems to be equally strong for scripts with low and high orthographic transparency (Caravolas *et al.*, 2005), suggesting that accurate spelling in an alphabetic script always requires good phonemic analysis.

As we noted earlier English spelling tends to preserve the spelling of root words in derivational forms as in CHILD and CHILDHOOD. Often the pronunciation of the root form changes so that the phoneme–grapheme correspondence becomes inconsistent. For example, CHILD has a long vowel whereas the same vowel becomes short in CHILDREN. Knowing about the morphological structure of words can help with English spelling and with spelling other languages where the written form reflects meaning as well as sound.

Children learning to write both French (Pacton *et al.*, 2002) and Greek (Chliounaki & Bryant, 2002) make some use of morphology fairly early on in the development of spelling. In both languages, the spelling of the morphological ending in verbs and nouns is determined by grammatical rules and the way these endings sound does not indicate how they will be spelled. Indeed, in French, many of these endings are not pronounced so, for example, 'il marche' (he walks: singular) and 'ils marchent' (they walk: plural) sound exactly the same. Understanding that these different spellings reflect singular and plural forms is essential for correct spelling. Initially children spell such words more or less as they sound but gradually they learn about the morphological endings. In the case of French (Pacton *et al.*, 2002), children go from phonetic spelling to an intermediate stage where they begin to incorporate morphological endings but do not always add them appropriately. For example they

Handwriting competency is essential; it is a skill taught in primary school, along with learning to read and spell.

BOX 13.1: HANDWRITING

In addition to learning to read and spell in their early years at school children also receive instruction in handwriting. Handwriting proficiency is essential for children's success and participation in school and it is used in many classroom activities. It is has been estimated that 30–60 per cent of activities during the school day involve writing so it is not surprising to find that handwriting skill is one of the factors associated with self-esteem (Rosenblum & Livneh-Zirinski, 2008).

Systematic research into children's handwriting has begun relatively recently and it has been facilitated by the development of techniques for measuring key aspects of the way that children write. Many studies now use a graphics tablet and a special pen that allows automatic collection of information about the movements that children make as they copy out a passage or write the letters of the alphabet. This includes information about the amount of time that children take to make individual strokes in letters and the time they spend with the pen raised above the paper. This detailed analysis has highlighted the fact that some children are particularly prone to handwriting difficulties that can have a major impact on their ability to produce written text.

correctly add 's' to plural nouns but also, incorrectly, to plural verb forms and later, when they become aware of the 'nt' verb ending, they may incorrectly add it to verbs. Eventually all of these confusions are resolved.

Similar patterns have been observed in children learning to spell English words (Nunes, Bryant, & Bindman, 1997). When morphological endings such as 'ed' are first used they are not only correctly used to indicate past tense in regular verbs such as 'pulled' but also incorrectly at the ends of other words. One example from Nunes *et al.* (1997) is the spelling of SOFT as *sofed*. Later children restrict the use of the 'ed' ending to verbs but incorrectly use the ending for irregular verbs as in *keped* for KEPT and *heared* for HEARD. Finally children homed in on the correct pattern of usage but this was often not until their second or third year at school.

13.3 DIFFICULTIES IN LEARNING TO READ AND WRITE

Reading disorders are the most researched and best understood cognitive deficits. There are two main kinds of reading disorder, affecting each of the two main components described in the simple model of reading (Hoover & Gough, 1990) that we described earlier. These are decoding (i.e. reading accuracy and fluency) and reading comprehension. DSM-IV (The Diagnostic and Statistical Manual of Mental Disorders, published by the American Psychiatric Association, 2004) classifies someone as having a reading disorder when their 'reading achievement, as measured by individually administered standardised tests of reading accuracy or comprehension, is substantially below that expected given the person's chronological age, measured intelligence, and age-appropriate education'.

There are a couple of points to note about this definition (Hulme & Snowling, 2009). First, the DSM-IV classification does not separate reading accuracy from reading comprehension even though problems in these two areas have distinct profiles. Second, it is not clear that the reading difficulties of children who have an IQ within normal range are fundamentally different from those of children with below average IQ. This latter issue is similar to the one that has been raised in relation to specific language impairment (SLI; see Chapter 9).

Developmental dyslexia

The most common form of reading difficulty in children is **developmental dyslexia**, which can be defined as 'a problem in recognising printed words at a level appropriate for a child's age' (Hulme & Snowling, 2009). It is a relatively common disorder with between 3 per cent and 6 per cent of children being affected, of whom the great majority are boys. Most children with developmental dyslexia have problems with spelling as well as reading.

Children who are diagnosed with developmental dyslexia often have problems that persist into adulthood. Typically they can become relatively good at reading words accurately but their spelling remains poor and they often read slowly. Dyslexia may occur together with SLI, developmental co-ordination disorder (DCD) and attention deficit/hyperactivity disorder (ADHD).

We have seen that success in learning to read is heavily dependent on phonological skills. It comes as no surprise to discover that poor phonological skills appear to be a major cause of developmental dyslexia. Numerous studies have shown that children with developmental dyslexia are poorer at tasks that require awareness of phonemes, using the kind of task that we considered earlier in this chapter (Hulme & Snowling, 2009).

Another task that highlights the differing abilities of children with and without developmental dyslexia is nonword repetition. Nonword repetition – as the name suggests – involves repeating carefully chosen nonwords (Gathercole, Willis, Baddeley, & Emslie, 1994). This task involves the perception, memorising and reproducing of an unfamiliar sequence of phonemes and, as such, it is similar to the learning of a real word. Children who have poor performance on a nonword repetition task tend to have problems in acquiring new vocabulary (Gathercole, 2006).

Children with developmental dyslexia also have problems with nonword repetition. In one study, a group of children with dyslexia were given words and nonwords to repeat (Snowling, 1981). Their performance was compared with that of younger, typically developing children, who were reading at the same level. The words were all polysyllabic (e.g. pedestrian, magnificent) and the nonwords were derived from them (e.g. kebestrian, bagmivishent). As you might expect, both groups of children found the nonsense words more difficult to repeat than real words. However, the children who had developmental dyslexia had particular difficulties with the nonwords and most especially, with four-syllable nonsense words like the ones in the examples. These kind of items have a very high level of phonological complexity, suggesting that children with dyslexia have increasing difficulty as they have to deal with phonologically complex stimuli. Part of the problem seems to lie in their ability to produce the precise sequence of phonemes required to pronounce an unfamiliar word. Such a difficulty is likely to present problems not only for learning to read but also for the development of spoken language.

Longitudinal studies of children, who are at risk for dyslexia because of a family history, have revealed that phonological problems are present before children start learning to read and have an impact on spoken language. In one study (Snowling, Gallagher, & Frith, 2003), 56 children who were at high risk of reading difficulty were followed from just before their fourth birthday until they were eight years old. Not all the children went on to become dyslexic but, in those who did, there was evidence of difficulty in a number of oral language tasks on the first assessment. These included object naming, which is a measure of spoken vocabulary, and nonword repetition. The same children also had poor letter knowledge. At six years, the same children had noticeable difficulties with spoken language and poor phonological awareness.

As these results suggest, problems with the development of spoken language often go hand in hand with dyslexia. Many children with speech–language problems in the preschool period go on to experience later reading problems and many children who are diagnosed as dyslexic appear, from retrospective reports, to have experienced delays in their early speech and language development (Hulme & Snowling, 2009).

Reading comprehension impairment

While children with developmental dyslexia show a general difficulty with reading and spelling, another group of children have a more specific problem with reading.

These are children with poor reading comprehension. Unlike children with developmental dyslexia, they are good at reading individual words and their performance on single-word reading tests is age-appropriate. However, they have significant difficulty in understanding text. The profile of a poor comprehender is easy to spot because of the discrepancy in their reading performance. They will do well at single-word reading, where the task is to read words aloud, and considerably less well on a test that involves reading a passage and answering questions about it.

Three different aspects of text comprehension appear to be particularly problematic for poor comprehenders (Oakhill & Yuill, 1996). The first of these is the ability to draw inferences, that is, to link together related ideas and to draw on more general knowledge to interpret what is being read. The second is the ability to understand the structure of what is being read. In the case of stories, which children frequently encounter in their early reading, this may require identification of main characters and their motives and understanding of key components of the plot, being able to understand why something happened and being able to predict what will happen next. The third problem that poor comprehenders may show is in 'comprehension monitoring'. This is the ability to keep track of what has been understood or not understood as reading proceeds. Oakhill and Yuill argue that poor comprehenders typically have problems in all three areas.

Understanding the meaning of words, as distinct from being able to pronounce them, is key to being a good comprehender. It is also important to be able to be able to understand what is read at the sentence level. Longitudinal studies show that a range of language skills predicts reading comprehension ability. In one study that we mentioned earlier (Muter et al., 2004), children were followed over the first two years of learning to read. They were given a wide range of assessments but three are of particular interest in relation to poor reading comprehension. These were all assessments of spoken language and they focused on vocabulary, syntax and morphology. The test of syntactic awareness required children to reorder a sequence of words so that they formed a meaningful sentence. For example children heard 'Ben throwing was stones' and were expected to say 'Ben was throwing stones'. The test of morphological knowledge involved the child in producing the appropriate morphological ending for nouns and verbs to describe a picture. In each case, the experimenter said one sentence and prompted the child to produce an analogous sentence to describe a picture. For example, the experimenter said, 'The burglar steals the jewels, here are the jewels he _____ [stole]'.

Reading comprehension was assessed using the Neale Analysis of Reading Ability in which children read passages of increasing complexity and answer comprehension questions. Until very recently, this test has been the standard test for comprehension of text.

Muter et al. (2004) found that word reading skills, assessed at age five years nine months, were a powerful predictor of reading comprehension one year later. This is what you might expect because children have to be able to read individual words in order to understand a text. However, once the effects of word reading skill had been taken into account, all three spoken language measures (words, syntax and morphology) predicted reading comprehension. Together, the three measures of spoken language ability and single-word reading accounted for 86 per cent of the variability in reading comprehension.

As we noted earlier, spoken language skills seems to become even more important as children begin to read more complex materials. The study by Gough *et al.* (1996), showing the importance of the 'Matthew effect' (see 13.1), also found that reading comprehension becomes progressively less dependent on decoding skills and more dependent on spoken language skills.

It should also be noted that good reading comprehension is important for learning new vocabulary as children progress through secondary school. Early reading vocabulary development relies on spoken language since children will be learning to read words that are already familiar in the spoken language. Later-acquired vocabulary comes mainly through exposure to complex text. Consider as an example some of the later items from the British Ability Scales II (Elliott, Smith, & McCulloch, 1996) word reading test. At the age of 14, children are expected to read words such as GENERATION and CHARACTER. By the time they are 17, they are expected to read CATASTROPHE and METICULOUS and to attain a reading age of 18 years they need to know words like MNEMONIC and ARCHAIC. Words like these are going to be encountered most often when reading rather than in everyday conversation.

Difficulties with handwriting

We introduced developmental co-ordination disorder (DCD) in Chapter 11 where we saw that this disorder is characterised by motor impairment that interferes with a child's activities of daily living and academic achievement (Barnett, 2008). Problems with handwriting are listed as one of the possible areas of difficulty for a child with DCD in the DSM-IV diagnostic criteria.

Research into children's handwriting has been facilitated by the development of techniques for measuring key aspects of the way that children write. Many studies now use a graphics tablet and a special pen that allows automatic collection of information about the movements made as the participant writes.

One study of seven- to ten-year-old-children compared the writing of a group who had been diagnosed as suffering from DCD with a group of typically developing children of similar age and gender (Rosenblum & Livneh-Zirinski, 2008). Three different writing tasks were used – writing one's name, writing the alphabet sequence from memory and copying a paragraph. Children wrote on a piece of A4 lined paper, placed on a graphics tablet.

Children with DCD required significantly more on-paper and in-air time per stroke in both the alphabet sequence and paragraph copying tasks. In other words, they took more time to write each letter and took more time between each letter stroke. There was also significant difference in the mean amount of pressure applied while writing in both the paragraph copying and name writing tasks, with the DCD children exerting less pressure when writing than their typically developing peers. The amount of pressure used by children in the DCD group was also considerably more variable.

Given that children with DCD take more time to write individual letters and spend more time with their pen lifted off the paper, it is not surprising to find that they generally write more slowly that typically developing peers. This was evident in the Rosenblum and Livneh-Zirinski (2008) study, which looked at children writing Hebrew. Slow handwriting has also been found in many other studies across a number of different languages (Barnett, 2008). The handwriting of children with DCD also tends to be difficult to read.

Problems with handwriting tend to be identified during secondary school but they have been found to persist beyond the end of the school years. A study of university students (Connelly, Dockrell, & Barnett, 2005) found that slow handwriting was particularly problematic when students were writing under the pressure of a timed examination. Students with slow handwriting tended to produce worse examination answers than those with faster handwriting. The authors suggest that, if handwriting is effortful, the physical act of writing words on a page takes up a large amount of cognitive resource, thereby leaving less resource for the planning activities that are essential for the production of a coherent text.

A major intervention study carried out in the United States (Berninger *et al.*, 2002) showed that the skills of children who were slow in producing text could be improved. The study focused on eight-year-olds who were given instruction over a four-month period in either spelling, composing text or spelling plus composing. Instruction in composing text involved reflective discussion with a teacher and structuring of ideas by the teacher, thereby assisting the planning and revision of text. In a control condition children practised writing but did not receive any explicit instruction. Instruction in spelling improved spelling, instruction in composing improved children's ability in persuasive essay writing and combined instruction improved both aspects of writing and brought about the greatest improvement in the children's writing ability.

13.4 SUMMARY

In this chapter we have considered how children learn to read and write, an activity that, together with mathematics, takes up a significant part of the school day during middle childhood. We saw that mastering the relationship between sounds and letters is key to becoming a good reader although, in a language like English where the written form has a large number of irregular spellings, it is also important to learn about orthography.

Phonological awareness, as well as knowledge about letters, is an important skill that underpins learning to read and children who have difficulty in learning to read and spell (dyslexia) often have poor phonological skills. Appropriate early intervention in the recognition and manipulation of phonemes has been shown to support the literacy development of children who are at risk of experiencing difficulty.

Children who are learning to read and spell English have a more challenging task than children who are learning an orthographically transparent script such as Italian or Spanish. However, as for English, phonological awareness and phonemic skills are important predictors of success. Reading and spelling tend to develop hand-in-hand in highly transparent orthographies but, for children who are learning to spell English, spelling poses an even greater challenge than reading since there are many possible ways to spell an unfamiliar word. Knowledge of morphology may be useful for learning about spelling in cases where the way that a word is spelled captures something about its meaning and derivation.

Children can have difficulties in learning to read for two main reasons – poor decoding skills (so that recognising and reading individual words is difficult) and poor comprehension skills (so that understanding the meaning of what is read is difficult). The more common reading difficulty is developmental dyslexia in which a major problem is in the accurate reading of individual words, typically caused by poor phonological skills. Children with dyslexia often develop strategies to help them read words although they often continue to have marked problems in spelling and to be slow readers. Other children have difficulties with text comprehension and these tend to be related to more general language skills. Finally, some children have difficulties with writing because of motor problems and poor handwriting is common in children with DCD.

FURTHER READING

Barnett, A. L. (2008). Motor assessment in developmental coordination disorder: From identification to intervention. *International Journal of Disability, Development & Education, 55*(2), 113–129.

Hulme, C., & Snowling, M. J. (2009). *Developmental disorders of language learning and cognition*. Chichester: Wiley-Blackwell.

Muter, V., Hulme, C., Snowling, M. J., & Stevenson, J. (2004). Phonemes, rimes, and language skills as foundations of early reading development: Evidence from a longitudinal study. *Developmental Psychology, 40*, 663–681.

ESSAY QUESTIONS

1. What are the main factors that predcit how well a child will learn to read?
2. Why is learning to read and spell English more difficult than learning to read and spell Italian?
3. How can children's handwriting be studied experimentally?
4. Describe the main types of developmental reading disorder and explain how they can be identified.

CHAPTER 14

CONTENTS

Social and emotional development in middle childhood

14

After reading this chapter you will be able to

- understand how children's interaction with their peers develops over the period of middle childhood
- explain how children's ideas of 'fairness' and 'harm' develop over this period
- evaluate the accounts of moral development from Piaget and Kohlberg
- explain what is meant by 'display rules' and describe the way in which children's responses to negative social situations change over the period of middle childhood
- explain how accounts of gender development have changed since the 1970s.

14.1 INTERACTING WITH PEERS

As we saw in Chapter 10, during the school years children spend increasingly large amounts of time with their peers, unsupervised by adults. Even at the age of two years children prefer to spend time with playmates of the same gender but this preference becomes noticeably stronger with age. In a longitudinal study (Maccoby & Jacklin, 1987) children were found to spend nearly three times as much time playing with same-gender peers as with as with other-gender peers when they were between four and five years old. When the same children were observed two years later, this ratio had gone up to ten times. So, during the years of middle childhood, girls are choosing to spend almost all of their time with other girls and boys with other boys. This preference for spending time with children of the same gender does not appear to be specific to particular cultures or nationalities since it has been observed in many different settings (Pasterski, Golombok, & Hines, 2011).

Children tend to interact rather differently in same-gender and opposite-gender pairs. In one study (Leman, Ahmed, & Ozarow, 2005) 120 children, whose average age was eight years seven months, were paired with either a classmate of the same gender or the opposite gender. Children knew the other child with whom they were paired but they were not close friends. Pairs were judged by their teacher to have similar levels of mathematical ability. This was an important consideration in view of the task they were required to undertake. Each pair was given a set of counters, of different values, and the task was to select a combination that would add up to 100. The task was deigned to provoke different solutions from each member of the pair because the two children had previously been taught different values for each counter. The conversations that the children had while trying to agree on a solution were recorded and analysed.

Overall, boys made more controlling remarks and engaged in more controlling behaviour than girls and they also made more negative interruptions when paired with a girl than with a boy. Controlling behaviours included directing a partner in a dogmatic manner, building on an answer without engaging with a partner, disagreeing with a partner in a hostile or aggressive way, snatching shapes from a partner and forceful physical acts (e.g. moving a partner's hand away). Overall, girls were more collaborative in their interactions and did things like helping their partner build an answer using the shapes together, counting shapes together or suggesting a course of action without a dogmatic or hostile manner. However, all children were more collaborative when paired with a child of the opposite gender. Interestingly the rather different interactional styles of the boys and girls did not affect the outcome in the sense that the views of girls and boys predominated equally often in the agreed solution.

Friendship

Best friends are invariably of the same sex but children's expectations of their best friends change significantly with age. In a study of 480 children aged between 6 and 14 years (Bigelow, 1977), teachers asked children to think about their best friend and to write about their expectations. Answers revealed that initially ideas about friendship were anchored in the here-and-now and typically tied to particular social situations, such as being in the same class or attending swimming lessons together. In their first years at school children had a fairly pragmatic view about the nature of friendship since a best friend was someone convenient in the sense of being available (typically living nearby or attending the same school) who had interesting toys and possessions and wanted to engage in similar kinds of play.

By the age of 10 or 11 years, there was a significant development in what children reported as their expectation of best friends. They were expected to share values and rules and to show public loyalty, and there was disapproval of friends who broke the rules. The notion of social acceptance is very important at this age. Children want to be popular and to feel accepted by their peer group. Unquestioning acceptance by a best friend is seen as essential.

During the school years, friendships have positive effects on experiences at school. Children benefit from having a friend who affirms their

In middle childhood best friends are invariably of the same sex, and often tied to social situations e.g. being in the same class or attending swimming lessons together.

positive attributes and minimises their shortcomings since this means that they tend to see themselves more positively and to feel better supported and less lonely (Ladd, Kochenderfer-Ladd, & Rydell, 2011).

Social withdrawal

Although having friends is such an important part of children's social experiences during middle childhood and beyond, not all children are successful in making friends. Some children show signs of social withdrawal and spend a large amount of time engaged in solitary behaviour. Children who are characterised as socially withdrawn spend the majority of time playing alone and they are invariably on the edge of the social scene in which their peer group is engaged. Longitudinal research suggests that social withdrawal is relatively stable over time with socially withdrawn children often being shy or socially anxious. Rubin and colleagues (Rubin, Chen, McDougall, Bowker, & McKinnon, 1995) found that children who frequently engaged in solitary play at age five were likely to show a similar pattern at the age of ten years and that the perception of such children by their peers also tended to be stable. When asked to nominate 'someone who is shy' or 'someone who likes to play alone' children tended to nominate the same children across the period of middle childhood (Rubin et al., 1995; Wonjung et al., 2008).

As you might perhaps expect, being socially withdrawn has been identified as a risk factor for psychosocial adjustment and children who are identified as socially withdrawn are more likely to experience low self-esteem, feelings of social incompetence and anxiety. In addition socially withdrawn children are more likely to be rejected by their peers and to experience depression and loneliness in adolescence (Rubin et al., 1995). However, there is considerable individual variation in social withdrawal over time with some children showing increasing levels and others becoming more successful in interacting with peers. This raises the question of what factors contribute to these differences over time and which ones might be associated with more positive outcomes.

A pattern of social withdrawal is likely to arise from a combination of factors arising from the predispositions of an individual child, the members of their immediate peer group and the individual's experiences of interaction. When starting at a new school some children will be socially anxious and withdrawn. If such children are welcomed by their peers and supported by their teacher, they may then find it easier to engage in social interactions and so become less socially withdrawn. However, if children with similar anxieties and tendencies towards social withdrawal are excluded by their peers and not supported by their teacher, their patterns of social withdrawal are likely to persist.

One key to having a positive experience is the establishment of friendships as we saw in the previous section. In a large longitudinal study of children in the Washington DC area in the United States, a number of assessments were carried out on the same children between the ages of 10 and 14 years (Wonjung et al., 2008). The assessments included observations and questionnaires as well as nominations of same-sex friends. Children were asked to give the name of same-sex friends in their year group. Only reciprocated nominations (i.e. where a nominated child also nominated the nominee) were considered *best* friendships. A questionnaire was used to assess the quality of the relationship with the nominated best friend. The Revised Class Play (RCP) paradigm (Wojslawowicz Bowker, Rubin, Burgess, Rose-Krasnor,

& Booth-La-Force, 2006) was used to find out about children's perceptions of classmates. Children are asked to pretend that they are casting for a school play and to nominate classmates for each role. Roles reflect a number of different behaviours such as aggression, social isolation and withdrawal as well as more positive behaviours.

Wonjung *et al.* identified three different developmental trajectories of social withdrawal. The majority of children (85 per cent) showed a stable pattern of low social withdrawal across the duration of the study, indicating that they were generally well-integrated into the social network of their year group. The remaining 15 per cent of children were divided almost equally into two further groups. In one group, children had a high level of social withdrawal at the start of the study but this decreased over time, showing increasing levels of social engagement. In the other group, there was a relatively high level of withdrawal at the start of the study and this steadily increased over time so that by the end of the study these children had the highest level of social withdrawal of all the participants.

Differences between children in these two latter groups provide some insight into factors that affect social withdrawal. Children in the decreasing social withdrawal group had the highest level of social withdrawal at the age of ten years. However, if they experienced less exclusion and victimisation after their transition to middle school they were likely to show a decrease in social withdrawal over time. Having a best friend who was not socially withdrawn was an important protective factor in that children were likely to become less withdrawn if their best friend was not socially withdrawn. Children who showed increasing withdrawal over time were likely to have experience of negative peer relationships in middle school and also to have a friend who was socially withdrawn. In other words, having a socially withdrawn friend after the transition to middle school was likely to increase social withdrawal; having a friend was not in itself a protective factor. What was important was to have a friend who was socially included.

Wonjung *et al.* (2008) speculate about the positive and negative role that friends appear to play in ameliorating social withdrawal. They suggest that, when best friends are both socially withdrawn, their discussions are likely to focus on negative thoughts and feelings about themselves and their peer group whereas if one child is not socially withdrawn they can present more positive views. Given how important group membership is in middle school, and how much of children's time is taken up in reflecting on their own social standing and the behaviour of their peers, this seems a very plausible explanation.

Aggression and bullying

Aggressive behaviour towards other children is another common feature of life during the period of middle childhood. During the first decade of life there is a steady decline in physical aggression with the most noticeable drop occurring during the transition to middle childhood. However, physical aggression tends to be replaced by verbal and other kinds of aggression as children's understanding of other people and how to upset them becomes more sophisticated (Murray-Close, Ostrov, & Crock, 2007). It is ironic that precisely the same developing skills of language, theory of mind, empathy and emotional understanding that underpin the emergence of positive social behaviours also enable children to produce more sophisticated forms of aggression. In other words with better verbal skills and a more sophisticated understanding of the needs, anxieties and emotions of other children, children can fine tune behaviours so that they have the maximum impact: they become adept at saying or doing things that will upset someone else.

Another important component of developing patterns of aggression in middle childhood is the emergence of strong and intimate friendships. They provide a fertile ground for what is known as 'relational aggression'. This can be defined as 'intentionally harmful behaviours that use the manipulation of *relationships* as the vehicle of harm' (Murray-Close *et al.*, 2007). Perhaps surprisingly, children tend to use relationally aggressive behaviours most often against their close friends so the emergence of close friendships in middle childhood sets the scene for both supportive and aggressive behaviours.

Relational aggression tends to increase over middle childhood but, given that friendships are the focus for relational aggression, it is not entirely surprising to find that this kind of behaviour is more evident in girls than boys (Murray-Close *et al.*, 2007), as by the age of ten, girls tend to be involved in a small number of intimate friendships whereas boys tend to participate in larger friendship groups (Maccoby, 1990). Intimate friendships involve high levels of self-disclosure and such disclosures can provide potential ammunition for relationally aggressive children who can, for example, threaten to pass on shared secrets.

14.2 MORAL DEVELOPMENT

As children progress through the school years they develop an increasingly sophisticated understanding of the societal rules that govern morally acceptable behaviour. They begin to understand the notion of 'fairness' and 'harm' and also how someone's behaviour should be judged not only on the outcome but also on intention.

As with many other aspects of development during the school years, Piaget was the first author to develop a systematic account of children's moral development. His aim was to apply his theory of cognitive development to aspects of social knowledge, publishing his theory in *The Moral Judgement of the Child* (Piaget, 1932). There he argued that children's cognitive development underpins moral reasoning. Piaget's work was subsequently extended by Kohlberg (1963), whose theory, while differing in some details from that of Piaget, agreed with the key claim that moral reasoning progresses through a universal sequence of stages that are not affected by the culture or context in which a child is growing up. His argument was that, following Piaget, there is a close link between moral reasoning and intellectual development and, since intellectual development is universal, so is moral reasoning.

Before considering the extent to which more recent research has challenged this view of moral development, it is worth considering one of the key methods that both Piaget and Kohlberg used to uncover children's moral reasoning. This is the posing of dilemmas. One of the classic dilemmas posed by Piaget was the following:

> John accidentally broke 15 cups.
> Henry purposely broke one cup.
> Who is naughtier, John or Henry?

Piaget found that, aged seven years, children choose John on the grounds that he was naughtier because he caused more damage. Nine-year-olds, however, choose Henry because he was deliberately naughty.

Kohlberg's dilemmas were rather more sophisticated:

> A woman is near death from cancer. One drug might save her, a form of radium discovered by a chemist living in the same town, who is selling the drug at 10 times what it costs him to manufacture it. The sick woman's husband tried to borrow the money but could raise only half the price. He told the chemist that his wife was dying and asked him to sell the drug more cheaply or, at least, let him pay later, but the chemist refused. The desperate husband broke into the chemist's shop to steal the drug for his wife. Should he have done that?

Figure 14.1
Kohlberg's six stages of moral development.

From the various responses to this dilemma Kohlberg described six stages of moral development, extending from childhood to adulthood. The six stages are made up from three levels each with two sub-stages. Each level corresponds to a stage of cognitive development in Piagetian theory, beginning with the preoperational stage and ending with formal operations. The levels are Preconventional, Conventional and Postconventional. The Preconventional level corresponds to the preoperational stage. In Sub-stage 1 of the first level, children judge actions to be good or bad by their outcome as in the example of the broken cups we considered earlier. An action is good if it is rewarded and bad if it is punished. In Sub-stage 2, behaviour is judged as good if it satisfies a need. The Conventional level coincides with Piaget's concrete operational stage and is most relevant to the period of middle childhood. Children

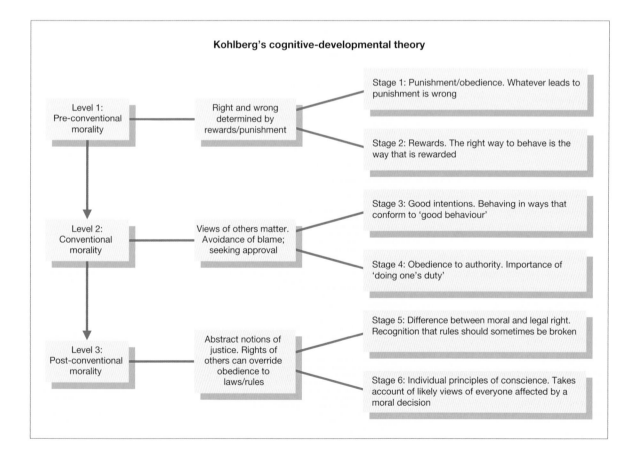

Kohlberg's cognitive-developmental theory

Level 1: Pre-conventional morality → Right and wrong determined by rewards/punishment

Stage 1: Punishment/obedience. Whatever leads to punishment is wrong

Stage 2: Rewards. The right way to behave is the way that is rewarded

Level 2: Conventional morality → Views of others matter. Avoidance of blame; seeking approval

Stage 3: Good intentions. Behaving in ways that conform to 'good behaviour'

Stage 4: Obedience to authority. Importance of 'doing one's duty'

Level 3: Post-conventional morality → Abstract notions of justice. Rights of others can override obedience to laws/rules

Stage 5: Difference between moral and legal right. Recognition that rules should sometimes be broken

Stage 6: Individual principles of conscience. Takes account of likely views of everyone affected by a moral decision judge actions to be good or bad according to the intentions of the actor, within a framework of social rules. In Sub-stage 3 children consider that whatever pleases or helps others is good and they are able to take into account the points of view and intentions of other people. By Sub-stage 4 children take the view that maintaining the social order and doing one's duty is good. The third level is Postconventional. This corresponds to Piaget's formal operational stage and so is assumed to coincide with adolescence. The adult judges actions to be good or bad according to transcendent moral principles. In Sub-stage 5 what is morally correct is determined by values agreed upon by society, including individual rights. Laws are no longer viewed as fixed but as relative. Finally, in Sub-stage 6, what is morally correct is a matter of personal conscience guided by morally transcendent principles. (See Chapter 17 for a discussion of the later stages of moral development.)

More recent research has suggested that moral development is not a unitary phenomenon. In the theories of Piaget and Kohlberg, morality is intertwined with social norms and self-interest in the earlier stages but morality becomes intertwined with justice in the later stages and this displaces social convention (Nucci & Gingo, 2011). Turiel and his colleagues (Turiel, 1983) have argued for there being separate strands of moral development pertaining to morality and convention. Morality covers non-arbitrary features of social relationships and concerns matters such as fairness and human welfare whereas convention concerns issues that are social determined and dependent on context (Nucci & Gingo, 2011). Turiel summarises many of these studies in a review (Turiel, 2006) and he concludes that even during the preschool period – as early as three years in some instances – children are able to differentiate between matters of convention and matters of morality.

Children are typically required to make judgements about different social acts that relate to either morality or convention. Moral acts pertain to physical harm (e.g. pushing another child), psychological harm (e.g. name calling) and fairness or justice (e.g. failing to share or stealing). By contrast, conventions concern socially prescribed behaviours that are seen as desirable but where, in contrast to moral actions, non-compliance will not cause harm to another person. Conventions include such things as adherence to table manners, forms of address and dress codes. Across cultural groups and social class, children reliably consider moral transgressions to be wrong but do not take the same view about transgression of convention.

Drawing this distinction between morality and convention provides the basis for a more subtle account of moral reasoning than that of either Piaget or Kohlberg. Moral development is seen as beginning in early childhood with a focus on issues of harm to the self and to other people. Up to about the age of seven years, children's moral judgements are not yet able to take account of fairness and so they find it hard to make a judgement that requires them to take account of the needs of more than one person. This problem is well illustrated by the work of Damon (1977, 1980). He has been concerned with children's judgements about how goods should be shared and distributed – a problem that regularly confronts children in real life. Damon used both real life and hypothetical situations. One hypothetical scenario concerned the distribution of money that a class of children had made from selling paintings at a school fair. Damon gave children examples of different ways in which the money could be distributed (e.g. on the basis of merit, need, equality and sex of the children) and asked what they thought of them.

Damon found that children's thinking about 'distributive justice' progresses through four levels. For preschoolers, views about distribution are initially tied to their own desires and perspective, very much in line with what would be predicted from other aspects of their intellectual functioning during this period. However, towards the end of the preschool period children begin to bring in external criteria such as size or ability. Such considerations are the first stage in developing other-orientated concepts.

Primary school children, who are at the next of Damon's levels, base their judgements on equality. Their view is that everyone should be given the same regardless of either need or merit. Such a view is echoed in the frequent comments of children of this age along the lines of 'It's not fair. She had more than me'. Gradually this insistence on equality gives way to increasing considerations of merit and the idea of reciprocity. Children begin to argue for a distribution based on a need to acknowledge the good deeds, merits and achievements of others. In the fourth stage, which children reach at 10 or 11 years, a larger range of factors is considered, which can be seen overall as comprising a notion of 'fairness'. So by this age, children will take account of merit (e.g. how hard someone worked or how talented they are) and advantages and disadvantages as well as other particular factors that might apply to a specific situation e.g. inheritance.

Similar age-related changes have been found in children's judgements of the fairness of classroom practices (Thorkildsen, 1989). In one study, Thorkildsen asked children from the age of six years upwards to judge the fairness of different behaviours of students who finished their work before others. For example, students who finished could go on to other learning tasks or they could help the children who had not yet finished their work. In line with the studies of sharing, the younger children focused on equality in their answers while older children focused on equity. Within the younger group, the youngest children judged a situation to be fair if it produced an equality of rewards whereas slightly older children considered fairness to reside in equality of work completed. Older children considered learning practices to be fair if they resulted in an equality of learning. The final stage in this judgement was to recognise equity in learning. The oldest children considered that classroom practices were fair if they enabled students to learn as much as much as they could i.e. more able students would learn more than less able.

14.3 EMOTIONAL DEVELOPMENT

Another important aspect of developing social maturity involves the understanding of emotions. Emotional understanding is a complex issue for children, involving both the understanding of their own emotions and those of other people. Successful functioning in society also requires children to know when to display their real emotions and when to hide them.

Very young infants have emotional states and can imitate the emotional expressions of others. They also engage in social referencing, where they use the emotional expressions of adults as a cue to their own behaviour in a potentially stressful situation (see 6.6). Preschool children use emotional labels to talk about their own feelings and those of others (Saarni, Mumme, & Campos, 1988). At this age, they tend to anchor their emotions in an appraisal of the person, object or event that has given rise to the emotion (Harris, 1989) and typically talk about being scared of spiders or excited that their birthday is approaching.

During the school years, children develop a much more sophisticated understanding – and conscious awareness – of their own emotions. One clear sign of emotional sophistication is the ability to distinguish between internal emotional experience and the external expression of emotion. Different cultures have their own rules about displaying emotions, known as display rules. One study (Saarni, 1984) investigated the ability of children aged between 6 and 11 years to follow display rules in a study where children were given a disappointing present. Western display rules demand that someone should look pleased with a present even if they do not like it. The children in Saarni's study met with an experimenter who posed as a market researcher. At an initial session they did a small task and were rewarded with sweets and money. This session provided baseline data about how the children reacted when they were given a desirable gift. Then, two days later, the same children did another task and, this time, they were given an inappropriate baby toy as a reward.

There was an interesting developmental trend in the children's disguise of their disappointment. The youngest boys – aged six – were uniformly negative in their reaction to the baby toy. However six-year-old girls and older boys and girls (aged eight and nine years) showed, what Saarni described as, 'transitional behaviour'. This was not clearly negative but was not positive either. Children at this transitional stage appeared uncertain how to react and tended to look from the gift to the experimenter and back again, apparently seeking social guidance on an appropriate response. Only the oldest children, who were aged 10–11 years, were likely to express a positive

BOX 14.1: GENDER DIFFERENCES IN DISPLAYING EMOTIONS

Evidence that girls are often better than boys at concealing negative emotions comes from a study of American children (Davis, 1995). The children who took part were highly motivated to conceal their true emotions because they were asked to play a game in which there were two possible prizes. One was highly desirable while the other was not. Each prize was placed in a box that allowed the child, but not the experimenter, to see what was inside. Before the game started, the children were told that, if they were able to trick the experimenter into believing that they liked both prizes, then they would be allowed to keep both. However, if they failed, they would not receive either prize.

Davis found that girls were better than boys at masking their negative emotions about the undesirable prize. The girls also engaged in more social monitoring than the boys – glancing at the experimenter to gauge her reaction. Davis concluded from her study that girls are better at managing the expression of negative emotions. However, there may well be cultural norms at work here because another study found that Indian girls were three times more likely than their English peers to acknowledge that children might conceal a negative emotion from an adult (Joshi & MacLean, 1994). The same study found no differences between Indian and English boys. Joshi and MacLean argue that these differences reflect the fact that Indian girls experience a strong cultural pressure to adopt a deferential attitude to adults, in which negative emotions are suppressed.

reaction when being presented with the baby toy. Interestingly, the girls were rather more consistent than the boys in their adoption of a positive response, in line with other findings that girls tend to be better at boys in masking negative feelings (see Box 14.1).

A later study (Cole, 1986), using the same disappointing gift paradigm, has shown that young, preschool children will make an attempt to cover up disappointment by smiling when the giver of the gift is present but they make no attempt to hide their disappointment when they are alone. Saarni *et al.* (1998) suggest that social cues can guide younger children to produce a socially appropriate response. This is consistent with Saarni's finding that six-year-olds looked to the gift giver to provide a cue about the expected emotional response. Older children did not appear to require social cues in order to produce an appropriate response.

Four- and five-year-olds can deceive others by adopting a misleading expression when lying (Cole, 1986). They could also pretend that a glass of fruit juice was sweet, in order to trick an adult, and took delight in anticipating how the adult would react upon discovering that the juice was really sour. Preschoolers often giggled or covered their mouth with their hands in an attempt to disguise a smile when they were deceiving the adult about the sour juice. Children become noticeably better at deceiving others about their emotions in the early school years.

14.4 GENDER DEVELOPMENT

We have seen evidence of a number of areas in which girls and boys behave differently, especially in the ways that they interact with other people. Over time there has been a radical shift in prevailing views about the nature of gender development within developmental psychology (Leaper, 2011). Until the 1970s there were two dominant theories about children's gender socialisation. One was psychoanalytic theory, notably that of Freud, and the other was social learning theory. According to psychoanalytic theory (Freud, 1927), children's relationships with their parents are crucial determinants of gender development. The view was that children identified with the same-gender parent and, in doing so, imitated gender-appropriate behaviour. Social learning theory, such as the account of Mischel (1966), also saw relationships with parents as pivotal although the claim was that the behaviour of same-gender parents acted as a direct model for behaviour without positing the need for identification of the child with the parent. Social learning theory also highlighted the importance of the differential treatment of boys and girls by their parents and other significant adults, and the rewarding of gender-appropriate behaviour (Mischel, 1966).

As Leaper (2011) points out in a recent review, the publication of a highly influential book in the mid 1970s, *The Psychology of Sex Differences* (Maccoby & Jacklin, 1974), challenged views about the centrality of parents in gender role development. Maccoby and Jacklin carried out a systematic review of the evidence concerning both children's imitation of same-gender parents and the differential treatment of children by their parents according to gender. They found little evidence for either pattern, thus casting doubt on the basis for both psychoanalytic accounts and social learning theory. Maccoby and Jacklin concluded that there was a 'surprising similarity' in the way that boys and girls were reared (at least in Western cultures). A more recent meta-analysis arrived at a similar conclusion (Lytton & Romney, 1991).

Leaper (2011) argues that a more plausible view of the importance of parents in gender development is that they can influence aspects of children's gender development but not to the extent proposed by either psychoanalytic theory or social learning theory. Effects are often subtle. For example, there is a general tendency for parents to give their children gender-stereotyped toys and to encourage gender-typed play (Lytton & Romney, 1991). Girls tend to be given dolls and toy food sets while boys tend to be given sports equipment and vehicles. However, most parents will not continue to give their children particular toys unless they respond positively to them; and, although parents with strong views about gender equality are less likely to encourage gender-typed toy play, this does not necessarily mean that their children will not show clear preferences for gender-typed toys.

It is important to recognise that, as in so many areas of development, children's gender identity and behaviour is affected both by their own predispositions and the behaviour of their parents and other adults; and it is not only the case that children respond to their parents' treatment but also that parents' behaviour is affected by their children's own behaviour. We discuss the role of parents in shaping adolescents' views of gender roles in Chapter 17 (see 17.5).

Another important context for the development of gender identity is peer relationships. As we saw earlier in this chapter, the period of middle childhood is one is which relationships with peers, and especially with close friends of the same gender, become increasingly important. Maccoby and Jacklin's (1974) book emphasised the importance of peer relationships for gender development and, in subsequent studies, Maccoby (1990) went on to highlight the particular importance of gender-segregated relationships. The key idea is that spending the majority of time with other children of the same gender will tend to enhance preferences for taking part in particular activities and dressing in a particular way.

A recent study (Zosuls *et al.*, 2011) asked whether the prevalence of gender-segregated interactions in middle childhood reinforces positive feelings about own-gender peers while leading to more negative views of other-gender peers. The study asked children, aged between 9 and 11 years, questions about interacting with boys and girls of the same age. These included, 'How do you fees about girls/boys?' and 'How many girls/boys make you feel happy/sad/like you want to be their friend/angry/shy?' In addition the children were asked to imagine that they had to join a group of either same-gender or other-gender peers for a variety of activities including playing a fun game and working on a group project in class. Children were asked whether they would expect to have fun and whether they would be accepted into the group.

Zosuls *et al.* found that both boys and girls had more positive feelings about own-gender peers than other-gender and also higher expectations about both the satisfaction and the ease of interacting in a new same-gender group. Children who had a more positive attitude to other-gender children had higher expectations of what would happen when they joined a new group of other-gender children. However, although girls generally preferred other girls and boys other boys, they did not feel negative about the other gender. Zosuls *et al.* suggest that, although children in middle childhood prefer the company of same-gender peers, they do not actively dislike other-gender peers.

14.5 SUMMARY

Middle childhood is a period of development in which relationships with peers, and especially friends, assume a huge importance. Children of this age tend to spend most of their time with same-sex friends and the quality of friendships contributes to feelings of self-worth and to feeling part of the peer group. Patterns of social inclusion or withdrawal that are established towards the end the primary school years tend to persist into adolescence.

Negative behaviour towards other children tends to become less physical and more psychological as the understanding of relationships becomes more sophisticated. Increasing levels of self-disclosure serve both to enrich friendships but also to provide potential ammunition for relational aggression.

There are important changes in moral understanding as notions of fairness, intention and potential harm to others are developed. We saw that the theories of moral development set out by Piaget and Kohlberg were closely tied to cognitive development and correspondingly argued for clear stages that mirrored the stages of cognitive development. More recent theories have argued that moral development is not a unitary phenomenon and a useful distinction can be drawn between morality and convention. Children in middle childhood do not treat adherence to moral values and conventional values in the same way, recognising that not adhering to the former is wrong. However, judging what is fair takes some time to develop as it involves a number of factors that have to be weighed against each other. Studies of distributive justice show that children in the early years of primary school seek solutions in which everyone receives the same, irrespective of merit. However, as they near the end of their time in primary school, children begin to develop notions of fairness that take into account such concepts as the contribution and achievements of other children.

During middle childhood children also become much more conscious of their own emotional responses and they learn to disguise their real feelings when appropriate, for example, when a relative gives a well-intended but inappropriate present. From the parents' perspective it often becomes more difficult to tell whether children are telling the truth as the tell-tale cues of preschoolers, such as giggling or looking away, are more likely to be disguised.

FURTHER READING

Ladd, G. W., Kochenderfer-Ladd, B., & Rydell, A.-R. (2011). Children's interpersonal skills and school-based relationships. In P. K. Smith & C. H. Hart (Eds), *The Wiley-Blackwell handbook of childhood social development, 2nd edition* (pp. 181–206). Chichester: Wiley-Blackwell.

Nucci, L. P., & Gingo, M. (2011). The development of moral reasoning. In U. Goswami (Ed.), *Wiley-Blackwell handbook of childhood cognitive development, 2nd edition* (pp. 420–445). Chichester: Wiley-Blackwell.

Pasterski, V., Golombok, S., & Hines, M. (2011). Sex differences in social behaviour. In P. K. Smith & C. H. Hart (Eds), *The Wiley-Blackwell handbook of childhood social development, 2nd edition* (pp. 281–298). Chichester: Wiley-Blackwell.

Saarni, C., Mumme, D. L., & Campos, J. L. (1988). Emotional development: Action, communication and understanding. In N. Eisenberg (Ed.), *Handbook of child psychology vol. 3: Social, emotional, and personality development (Editor in chief W. Damon)* (pp. 237–309). New York: Wiley.

ESSAY QUESTIONS

1. How do children's interactions with their peers change over the period of middle childhood?
2. Discuss the distinction between morality and convention as it relates to children's development of notions of 'fairness' and 'harm'.
3. Explain how children's ability to disguise their emotions develops over the preschool period.
4. 'There has been a radical shift in prevailing views about the nature of gender development.' Discuss.

CHAPTER 15

CONTENTS

Introduction to adolescence

15

After reading this chapter you will be able to

- understand why adolescence can been seen as a paradoxical stage of development
- be able to describe the main changes that occur in brain development during adolescence and explain how these can explain some typical adolescent behaviours
- understand how cultural factors can affect behaviour in adolescence.

15.1 THE PARADOX OF ADOLESCENCE

Adolescence is the period of development that is least well researched by psychologists. Indeed there may appear to be an almost inverse relation between the age of children and the amount of research that is carried out, with the greatest number of recent studies focusing on infancy and the preschool period. Perhaps one reason for this imbalance is that it is tempting to think that adolescence is well understood and that there is not much more to learn. However, there are many challenges to understanding adolescent development.

As we have seen in the earlier chapters, new techniques have opened up the possibility of studying infancy experimentally and there is no doubt that the understanding both of infancy and the preschool period have advanced considerably as new experimental methodologies have emerged. The same is true of adolescence. In part, as we see later in this chapter, what has really changed is that it is now possible to see the characteristics of adolescence in the light of a growing understanding about changes to brain function that are occurring during this period.

Traditionally, following the work of Hall over 100 years ago, adolescence was viewed as a time of 'heightened storm and stress' (Hall, 1904), reflecting the view that this was a period of high emotion and tensions between parents and their teenage children. Several decades later, in the 1960s and 1970s, this was still the prevailing view and attempts were made to explain the heightened storm and stress in terms of 'raging hormones'. However, as the twentieth century neared its end, systematic reviews of the empirical evidence about the relationship between hormones, behaviour and puberty showed that this early picture was too simplistic. Notably, in Western society, it is only a minority of adolescents who experience major difficulties as they negotiate the transition from childhood to adulthood and up to 80 per cent of adolescents have very few problems (Arnett, 1999). As Dahl points out, 'most adolescents get along quite well with their parents and teachers most of the time, succeed in school, have positive relationships with peers, do not become addicted to drugs and alcohol, and become productive and healthy adults' (Dahl, 2004, p. 7).

It is clear, however, that although major problems are not the norm in adolescence, a minority of young people experience stress and emotional turmoil during this developmental period. There is an essential paradox in adolescence that is eloquently captured in the following summary by Dahl (author's own italics):

> This developmental period is marked by rapid increases in physical and mental capabilities. . . . Compared to young children, adolescents are stronger, bigger, faster, and achieving maturational improvements in reaction time, reasoning abilities, immune function, and capacity to withstand cold, heat, injury, and physical stress. . . . Yet, despite these robust improvements in several domains, overall morbidity and mortality rates increase 200% over the same interval of time. . . . The major sources of death and disability in adolescence are related to difficulties in the control of emotion and behaviour. . . . Adolescence is strongly associated with an increase in risk-taking, sensation-seeking and reckless behaviour – all of which lead, far to often, to actions with dire health consequences.
>
> (Dahl, 2004, p. 3)

Dahl goes on to argue that, in addition to the 'reckless' nature of adolescence, there is a second level of paradox. As we see in Chapter 16, on many levels the reasoning and decision-making capabilities of adolescents are at adult levels as they become capable of formal operational thinking. Yet, in spite of these sophisticated mental abilities, adolescents are often prone to erratic and emotionally influenced behaviour. Understanding how the brain develops in adolescence can help in understanding some aspects of this paradox.

KEY TERMS

Prefrontal cortex
Part of the frontal cortex, its primary function is to co-ordinate a wide range of neural processes. The PFC serves a key function in cognitive control in maintaining information about the current goal of a task and the means to achieve that goal.

15.2 BRAIN DEVELOPMENT IN ADOLESCENCE

Much of the evidence about brain development in adolescence has come from brain scans. The most common techniques for scanning the brain are not appropriate for use with young children unless they are very ill. However, by the time of adolescence, it is more common to carry out techniques such as functional Magnetic Resonance Imaging (fMRI) for research purposes. These techniques have been used for a number of years to study adult cognition. The detailed picture of brain function, which modern imaging can provide, sheds light on the way that adolescents process information and how this compares with adult performance.

One area of the brain that has attracted particular interest is the prefrontal cortex. This is a neocortical area right at the front of the brain. As the term neocortex suggests, the **prefrontal cortex** (PFC) is a relatively new part of the brain in evolutionary terms and it is most developed in primates. The PFC is a collection of interconnected areas that send and receive information from sensory systems (auditory, visual, touch), motor systems and other neocortical structures. There is good evidence that its primary function is to co-ordinate a wide range of neural processes (Miller & Cohen, 2001). This co-ordination is particularly important when behaviour is not automatic but must be guided by internal states or intentions. Miller and Cohen (2001) argue that the PFC serves a key function in cognitive control in maintaining information about the current goal of a task and the means to achieve that goal.

Patients who have damage to the PFC find particular standard cognitive tasks difficult. Performance on the Stroop task (see Box 15.1) has been shown to be particularly vulnerable (Miller & Cohen, 2001). Another standard task that patients with damage to the PCF find difficult is the **Wisconsin Card Sorting Task**. This task involves sorting a standard set of cards according to a particular dimension such as shape, colour or number. The key feature of the task is that the rule for sorting changes as the sort progresses and so success requires the ability to move flexibly from one sorting rule to another.

Inhibiting distraction and focusing on the information that will lead to a correct response is key to performing successfully in both the Stroop task and the Wisconsin Card Sorting Task. It has been known for some time that children are more susceptible to attentional interference than adults, due to the immaturity of their PFC (see 7.1). More recently it has become clear that the PFC is continuing to mature through adolescence and so adolescents and adults will show differences in behaviour that are controlled by this area of the brain. In other words, adolescents would be expected to show less control and more distractibility in cognitive tasks that place high demands on attention.

Emotionally charged events can be particularly distracting and difficult to ignore and it appears that adolescents are very susceptible to distraction by information with an emotional content. This was demonstrated in a study in which adolescents, aged between 10 and 15 years, were presented with neutral and emotionally-charged photographs while in an fMRI scanner. Their pattern of brain activation, while completing a specific task, was compared with that of adults, carrying out the same task (Wang, Huettel, & De Bellis, 2008).

The task was to identify a very infrequent target (a circle) within a stream of photographs. The majority of the photographs (90 per cent) were scrambled and contained no recognisable information. However, some of the photographs depicted recognisable scenes and these were designed to be distracters. The distracters were either happy (neutral) or sad. The sad distracters depicted scenes of people crying

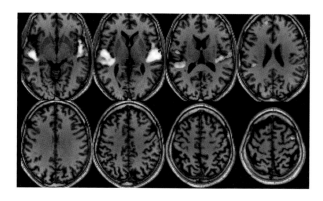

Functional Magnetic Resonance Imaging (fMRI) scans in axial section through the brain of a healthy patient hearing the sounds of atmospheric music. Highlighted areas show activity in regions of the cerebrum associated with hearing such as the auditory area in the temporal lobe.

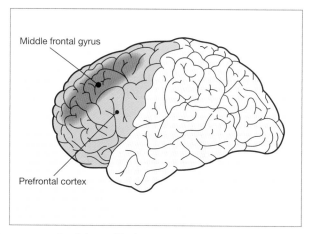

Figure 15.1
A diagram of the brain showing the prefrontal cortex and middle frontal gyrus.

The Stroop effect

GREEN

RED

GREEN

RED

Figure 15.2

BOX 15.1: THE STROOP TASK

This classic paradigm, invented in 1935 by Stroop, has become one of the most widely used tasks in cognitive psychology (MacLeod, 1991). There are now a number of variations but the standard task involves presentation of words that are written in different colours. The task becomes demanding when the presented word is a colour word (e.g. GREEN) and it is written in a different colour, such as red. Participants are asked either to read aloud the word or to name the colour of the letters. In either case, a correct response involves selecting from two competing alternatives. When naming the colour of the letters, there is an automatic tendency to say the colour named in the word (i.e. green) and this has to be inhibited in order to produce the correct answer (i.e. red).

or showing other sad facial expressions. The neutral distracters were visually very similar except that the people in the scenes had happy expressions. The target circles and the happy and sad distracters occurred equally often (10 per cent in all) in a random sequence of 150 photographs. Figure 15.3 shows the experimental design. The adolescents who took part in the study lay in an fMRI scanner. The stimuli were

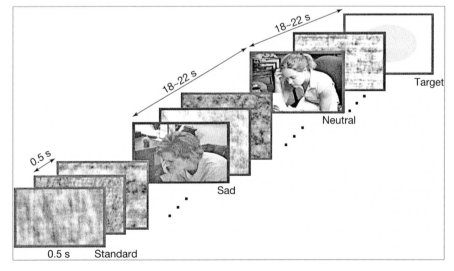

Figure 15.3

The design of Wang et al.'s (2005) study. Participants were presented with rare circle targets (oddballs) and frequent phase-scrambled pictures (standards) interspersed with rare sad and neutral distractors. Copyright © American Psychological Association.

projected onto a screen and they were asked to press a response button whenever they saw a target circle.

The fMRI images showed that a number of different brain regions were active during the task. This is what you would expect given the relative complexity of a task that involves, among other things, vision, motor activity, pattern recognition and face processing. Two aspects of the pattern of activation were of particular interest in the study: would there be any differences in responses to the target stimuli and to neutral and emotional stimuli and would the responses of adolescents and adults differ?

There were a number of key findings. The processing of target stimuli was very similar in adolescents and adults in terms of the major regions of the brain that were activated. However, the processing of the sad distracters showed a different pattern for the two groups. There were some areas in common – as you would expect – but adolescents showed activation in two additional areas of the brain. One area where there was additional activation was the PFC. The other area of additional activation was some of the same area that was active during response to the targets. In other words, compared to adults, the adolescents responded more similarly to sad distracters and targets.

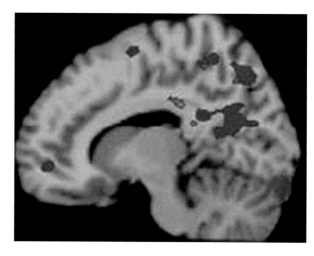

A brain scan from the Wang *et al.* (2008) study to show activity in the VmPFC (on the left). From Wang *et al.* (2008), reproduced with permission from Wiley-Blackwell.

The particular part of the PFC that was activated when adolescents processed sad stimuli is called the ventromedial prefrontal cortex (VmPFC). You can see this area on the left of the scan shown in the photograph above. This area of the brain has been shown to be particularly active when people are feeling sad and the increased activation shown by the adolescents suggests that they were more engaged with the sad stimuli than the adults, even though these stimuli were irrelevant to the task of looking for the target circles.

Another result from this study is also relevant to understanding the final phases of brain development that take place during and beyond adolescence. This is the finding that activation in the VmPFC was related to activation in the middle frontal gyrus (MFG). Adolescents who had greater activation in VmPFC to sad distracters had lower activation in the anterior MFG to attentional targets. Put simply, what this means is that greater attention to the emotional component of the sad stimuli was at the expense of attention to the targets. Or, to put it another way, paying too much attention to irrelevant emotional stimuli detracted from the ability to process the targets.

15.3 PUBERTAL AND MATURATIONAL CHANGES IN ADOLESCENCE

The study by Wang *et al.* (2008) illustrates the way in which the brain of adolescents is still developing. In order to understand the broader significance of this finding it is helpful to understand something about interactions between brain development and puberty.

Some brain changes precede the increase in hormones occurring in puberty. Indeed, pubertal maturation actually starts in the brain in the sense that some neural changes lead directly to the hormonal cascade at the beginning of puberty. Other changes in the brain are the consequence of puberty. For example, a recently-identified oestrogen receptor comes into play with the hormonal changes of puberty (Cameron, 2004). Finally, some changes in the brain are independent of puberty and continue long after puberty is over. The developments described in the Wang *et al.* (2008) paper appear to be of this latter kind. It turns out that many brain developments within the cognitive domain seem to be like this. That is, they are maturational in relation to age rather than puberty.

Interestingly, some changes in behaviour seem to be linked very specifically to the physical changes of puberty. Martin and colleagues (Martin *et al.*, 2002) investigated the development of smoking and other risky behaviours such as drug-taking and alcohol consumption in adolescents aged between 11 and 13 years. One of the measures they looked at was sensation seeking. Within this age range there was a significant correlation between pubertal maturation and sensation seeking but not between chronological age and sensation seeking. In other words it was the physical progress into puberty that predicted sensation seeking.

Dahl (2004) notes that a number of developmental domains are associated with puberty rather than with maturation. These are romantic motivation, sexual interest, emotional intensity, changes in sleep/arousal regulation, appetite, increase in risk taking, novelty seeking and sensation seeking. The age at which puberty occurs has been decreasing over time with advances in health and nutrition and so these linked changes in drives, appetites and emotional intensity are also occurring at a younger age. However, most aspects of cognitive development – including developments in reasoning ability and capacities for self-regulation – are still developing slowly and they continue to develop long after puberty is over. Dahl (2004) likens this asynchrony between developments associated with puberty and maturational developments to 'starting the engines with an unskilled driver'. He goes on to explain:

> This metaphor is one way to capture the relatively earlier timing of these 'igniting passions' – passions that refer not only to romantic and sexual interests, but also to the intensification of many kinds of goal-directed behaviors that emerge in adolescence. . . . when these passions flare up to intense levels, these young people have often not yet developed the skills that can harness these strong feelings (nor have they yet achieved the neural maturation of underlying control systems).
>
> (Dahl, 2004, pp. 17–18)

Historical changes in the timing of puberty can be seen in data plotting the onset of menstruation (menarche) in girls. The plot shows that, across a number of European countries and the USA, the average age of menarche fell from around 15 years in

1860 to around 13 years in 1960 (Tanner, 1990). Menarche is not the beginning of puberty and other physical and hormonal changes will have occurred some time before. What this fall in the age of pubertal onset suggests is that, over time, the asynchrony between cognitive maturational and pubertal maturation has become more extreme. In other words, while the physical changes associated with puberty are beginning at an earlier, the rate of cognitive maturation has not changed and will continue for some years after the main physical changes are complete.

15.4 A CROSS-CULTURAL PERSPECTIVE ON ADOLESCENCE

If we think of adolescence as the interval that begins with the physical changes of puberty and ends with the taking up of adult roles in society we can see that there have been important historical changes in the developed world in the experience of adolescence. However, there are considerable cross-cultural differences in the way that society recognises adolescence.

In most societies, there is a developmental period that can be recognised as adolescence, marking the transition from the status of a child to the status of an adult. Becoming an adult in traditional societies tends to be defined in terms of roles or status. For example it may involve becoming a hunter, owning property or marrying. The interval between entering into puberty and becoming an adult tends to be relatively brief in traditional societies. For example, girls are likely to marry within two years of the onset of puberty, as they did in Western society up until the last few hundred years. The interval between puberty and recognition as an adult tends to be longer in boys and to be associated with the achievement of particular skills, such as the ability to hunt. Nevertheless, in most traditional societies, boys are married within four years of puberty. Marriage is an important marker of a transition from childhood to adulthood because it brings with it personal responsibility for the welfare of other people.

This pattern of a relatively short gap between puberty and adulthood is in marked contrast to the typical pattern of Western society where there is a clearly defined and extended period between the end of middle childhood and the beginning of adulthood. This period of adolescence sees a transition from childhood to adulthood, with independence from parents and economic contribution to society increasing only gradually. One indicator of the relative length of adolescence in Western society is the gap between puberty and marriage for girls. In the USA, the average age of menarche is 12 years but the average age of marriage is 26 years – a gap of 14 years. Similar trends are evident across Western society.

There are a number of reasons for this change in the relationship between puberty and independent adulthood. A major factor has been the evolving needs of society in the developed world. Over the last 100 years expectations about education have increased considerably as can be seen in changes to the school leaving age. In the UK, the school leaving age has gradually increased since 1918 when compulsory education from the age of 5 to 14 years was first introduced. The school leaving age was raised to 15 in 1944 and then again to 16 in 1972. Similar changes have occurred across the developed world. They reflect the need to provide an extended education that will serve as a preparation for entry into a skilled job.

The continuing trend is for the period of education to expand as more young people go on to study beyond school, entering a college or university or undertaking an apprenticeship. Even for those young people who do not go on to study beyond school leaving age, the demands of society require relatively high standards of literacy and numeracy. These are very different from the demands of a traditional society.

The need for an extended period of education inevitably means that independence is delayed. At the same time, expectations about lifestyle have changed so that young people are delaying marriage and parenthood and even choice of careers in order to explore options. In traditional societies there are clear-cut roles for individuals and typically girls will adopt the same role as their mother and boys the same as their father. Western society offers much more choice and the protracted period of adolescence offers an opportunity for exploration of different possibilities.

15.5 SUMMARY

The development of advanced techniques for studying brain activity has shed new light on adolescence. Brain scans have shown that significant developments in brain function continue through adolescence, especially in the prefrontal cortex. This area of the brain is involved in cognitive control in complex tasks. Brain scanning also shows that adolescents respond more strongly than adults to emotionally-charged stimuli, and that these responses to emotion can make cognitive processing less efficient.

The time course of the intellectual maturation that takes place during adolescence appears to be age dependent. Other changes, including a greater tendency to engage in risky behaviours and to seek sensation, as well as changes in sleep and arousal patterns, are linked to puberty. The gap between puberty and intellectual maturity has widened over time as improvements in health and nutrition have resulted in an earlier onset of puberty. At the same time, the increased demands of a post-industrial society have meant that the period of adolescence has gradually extended as young people take an increasingly long time to become financially independent from their parents.

In the next chapter we consider how the ability to reason develops through adolescence and in the final chapter we explore the complex socio-emotional development that take place during this period.

FURTHER READING

Dahl, R. E. (2004). Adolescent brain development: A period of vulnerabilities and opportunities. *Annals of the New York Academy of Sciences, 1021*(1), 1–22.

Wang, L., Huettel, S., & De Bellis, M. D. (2008). Neural substrates for processing task-irrelevant sad images in adolescents. *Developmental Science, 11*(1), 23–32.

ESSAY QUESTIONS

1 Why can adolescence be described as a paradoxical period of development?
2 To what extent can behaviour in adolescence be seen as a function of the particular culture in which an adolescent is growing up?

CHAPTER 16

CONTENTS

Cognitive development in adolescence

16

After reading this chapter you will be able to

- describe Piaget's account of formal operational reasoning and some of the key tasks that Piaget and Inhelder devised to assess adolescent reasoning
- evaluate Piaget's account in the light of more recent research into moral reasoning and understanding of conditional probability
- describe the development of executive functioning in adolescence and relate this to brain development.

In this chapter we consider the main cognitive changes that occur as children move towards adulthood. From the contemporary perspective of Western society in the early twenty-first century it is hard to believe that the psychological study of cognitive development in adolescence is a relatively recent phenomenon. In a *Manual of Child Psychology*, published in 1954, Horrocks devoted barely one page to the mental growth of adolescents. However, in 1955, Inhelder and Piaget published *The Growth of Logical Thinking from Childhood to Adolescence,* which was translated into English almost immediately (Inhelder & Piaget, 1958; Moshman, 1998). This book fundamentally changed the way that psychologists and educationalists viewed cognitive development in adolescence and firmly established the view that adolescence was a structurally distinct period of cognitive development in which thinking advanced well beyond the achievements of middle childhood.

16.1 PIAGET'S THEORY OF FORMAL OPERATIONAL REASONING

Although it was the writing of Piaget and Inhelder that revolutionised views of adolescent cognition, the idea that cognition progresses beyond childhood was first advanced by James Mark Baldwin, writing at the end of the nineteenth century. Baldwin argued that there was a 'hyper-logical' stage of mental development. Piaget and Inhelder took up Baldwin's view, arguing that there was a final stage of mental development, emerging around the age of 10 or 11 years. They described this final stage as formal operational reasoning.

We saw in earlier chapters that Piaget's account of cognitive development focuses on children's ability to reason and on the kind of mental operations that they can carry out. For Piaget, the key mental operation that characterises the formal operational stage is the ability to carry out formal deduction. Piaget defines formal deduction as an ability that enables

> drawing conclusions, not from a fact given in immediate observation . . . but in a judgement which one assumes.
>
> (Piaget, 1972, p. 69; cited in Moshman, 1998)

This ability to engage in formal deduction opens up a huge range of new intellectual possibilities. Children who have reached the stage of concrete operations have acquired some organised systems of thought but they are able to proceed only from one concrete link to the next. By contrast, being capable of formal operational reasoning allows for a systematic consideration of all possible combinations in relation to a whole problem. Equally importantly, it enables reasoning about entirely hypothetical situations. These new found abilities enable abstract scientific thinking and the discussion of issues in philosophy and theology. In educational terms, the development of thinking and problem solving beyond the concrete operational stage of middle childhood paves the way for the educational demands of secondary school education.

To get a feeling for the way that Piaget viewed formal operational thinking, and the way that it differed from concrete operational thinking, it is useful to consider the kinds of experimental tasks that Piaget and Inhelder (1955) devised to study the cognitive abilities of adolescents. Moshman (1998) points out that all of the 15 studies reported in Piaget and Inhelder involve some kind of physical apparatus – flexible rods, a pendulum, an inclined plane, communicating vessels, a hydraulic press and a balance beam. These are, of course, the kinds of basic apparatus that are used in scientific investigations.

Piaget and Inhelder tested children between the ages of 5 and 16 years. Participants were asked to manipulate the various sets of apparatus and to derive an understanding of the underlying physical phenomena that determined the behaviour of the apparatus. The point about these kinds of task is that they require children to determine a general principle from a series of observations.

One well-known task involves understanding the movement of a pendulum. The length of the pendulum can be varied and the task is to discover the relationship between the speed of movement of the pendulum and its length. Over the centuries, the pendulum has been used in a number of important scientific observations. One of the most famous people to observe the movement of a pendulum was Galileo. He was able to show that the rate at which a pendulum swings back and forth is a function of its length: the longer a pendulum, the more slowly it oscillates. Note that the way to discover the precise relationship between length and oscillation is to systematically vary pendulum length and observe how this affects oscillation.

Inhelder and Piaget interviewed children individually and recorded the experiments they carried out with the apparatus and the conclusions that they drew. In the case of the pendulum task, deducing the underlying principle involves being able to observe the two variables of pendulum length and oscillation and understand the relationship between them. Inhelder and Piaget found that children who were still at the stage of concrete operational thought could only think about one variable at a time and so had great difficulty in determining the general principles that governed the operation of the pendulum. However, children who were capable of formal operation reasoning, from about the age of 11 years, were able to carry out a systematic analysis of the relationship between the two key variables of pendulum length and oscillation.

Piaget explained the transition from concrete to formal operations in terms of the construction of second-order operations that involved the trans-formation of first-order (i.e. concrete) operations. These second-order operations are hierarchically integrated into a totally internally coherent logi-cal structure known as the Identity–Negation–Reciprocity–Correlative (INRC) group. This advance enables the child to take into account two frames of reference at the same time.

The cognitive effects of this new found ability to co-ordinate information can be seen very clearly in children's performance in a complex conserva-tion task. Performance changes as children move from concrete operational thought to formal opera-tional thought. Take the case of the height of water in jars in the classic conservation of liquid volume task. The task begins with two identical jars with identical levels of water that are clearly of identical volumes. When the contents of one tall, thin jar are poured into a second, short, fat jar the level of water drops. Children are asked, 'Does the water in each glass take up the same amount of room?' Children who are at the stage of concrete operations will say 'yes' (see Chapter 12).

Then children are given a new test in which a ball of clay is dropped into the water and they observe how the water level rises. The new, higher, level of water is marked on the side of the glass. Then the clay ball is taken out and flattened into a

Figure 16.1
The pendulum problem.

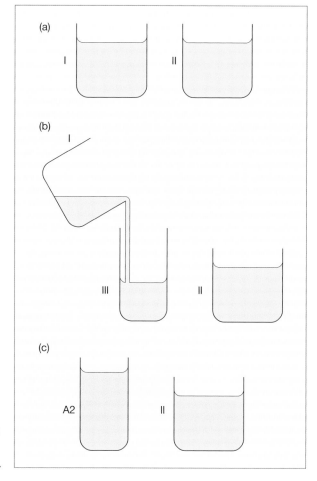

Figure 16.2
Piaget's study on conservation of quantity.
(a) Children agreed that I and II both contained the same quantity of liquid, but when I's liquid was poured into a taller, thinner glass (b and c), the pre-operational children argued that the quantities differed.

pancake. Children are asked to predict where the water level will be when the pancake-shaped clay is put back. Children are not able to accurately predict this until the age of 11 or 12 years.

Piaget argues that it is only when children can co-ordinate information from two sub-problems (conservation of the volume of the liquid and conservation of the volume of clay) that they can draw the correct conclusion that the change in the height of liquid must be proportionate to the volume of clay dropped into the water.

Children's performance on balance beam problems follows a similar pattern, as we saw in Chapter 12 (see 12.2). Emergent understanding of the relationship between weight and distance from the fulcrum does not come about until age 13. At this age, most children tested by Siegler (1976) were able to use Rule 3, which recognised the need to take into account both the weights on the balance and their distance from the fulcrum. (Rule 3 was: if both weight and distance are equal, predict that the scale will balance. If one side has more weight or distance, and the two sides are equal on the other dimension, predict that the side with the greater value on the unequal dimension will go down. If one side has more weight and the other side more distance, muddle through or guess.)

Using Rule 3 is, however, evidence of only a partial understanding of the relationship between weight and distance from the fulcrum. Full understanding enables prediction of what will happen with any combination of the two variables. Very few adolescents showed understanding of what Siegler calls Rule 4 (compare weight x distance on either side of the fulcrum), even if they had explicit training on very similar tasks (Siegler, 1976). This shows that, as Piaget himself found, the more complex relations that form part of formal operational thinking are not always mastered in early adolescence even though some important advances in thinking have taken place, beyond concrete operations.

Other examples of the difference between formal and concrete operational thought can be seen in the ability to carry out transitive inference (see Chapter 12). Children, who are in the stage of concrete operations, can infer that if A = B and B = C then A = C. This type of logic enables children to use a ruler to measure the relative lengths of two rods. They are able to look at the relationship between the ruler and each rod in turn and then draw an inference about the relative length of the two rods. However, although children who function at the concrete operational stage can solve transitive inferences that involve physical objects, they are unable to solve transitive inference problems that are more abstract. Given a relatively simple problem, such as *John is taller than Mary, Mary is taller than Jane. Who is the tallest?*, it is only children who are capable of formal operational thinking who can arrive at the correct answer.

16.2 CRITICISMS OF PIAGET'S THEORY

We saw in the previous chapter that a number of different developmental processes are occurring in adolescence. Some are linked to puberty while others are linked to maturation that is independent of puberty. The most recent evidence suggests that cognitive changes tend to be of the second kind and, furthermore, that they extend well beyond the period in which the main pubertal changes are occurring. This more recent view of adolescence casts some doubt on aspects of Piaget's account of the development of formal operational thought.

Piaget makes two main claims about thinking in the period after concrete operations. The first is that developmental changes continue through early adolescence and the second is that formal operational thinking is the final stage of development. Both of these claims have been challenged.

The first claim relates to the timing of the changes that Piaget describes. As we have seen in earlier chapters, there is considerable evidence that many important cognitive skills emerge rather earlier than Piaget proposed. Equally, the most recent evidence suggests that cognitive changes are occurring into late adolescence. This suggests that there is not a clear cut off between concrete operational thinking and formal operational thinking but, rather, a gradual change in ability that takes place over a number of years. We also saw in the previous chapter that there are interactions between responses to emotion and cognitive abilities that gradually change over adolescence.

Piaget's claim that the attainment of formal operations marks the final stage of cognitive development has been challenged by those who argue for later advances in cognition that occur towards the end of adolescence and into adulthood. There is now a growing body of research that has charted the developments in cognition occurring in late adolescence and adulthood (see Dahl, 2004). If we move beyond cognition to think about social reasoning, there are other examples.

A longitudinal study of prosocial moral reasoning (Eisenberg, Miller, Shell, McNalley, & Shea, 1991) investigated changes occurring over an 11-year period, covering middle childhood and adolescence. Several modes of higher-level reasoning did not emerge until late childhood or adolescence. The kinds of reasoning that occurred relatively late are illustrated by another study, looking at adolescents' and young adults' views about civil liberties and their application to various hypothetical situations (Helwig, 1995). The study compared three age groups of 12-, 16- and 19-year-olds, living in the San Francisco Bay area in the United States. Helwig was interested not only in beliefs about civil rights but also in the much more complex question of how civil rights were viewed when they came into conflict with other moral concepts such as physical harm, psychological harm and equality. From the perspective of formal operational thinking, this is a very pertinent issue to consider because it is concerned with complex reasoning in which differing and competing values have to be integrated.

Here is an example of the kind of scenarios that the participants in Helwig's study were asked to judge. It presents a conflict between the right to freedom of speech and the risk of psychological harm:

A resident of a surrounding neighbourhood gives a speech in an area of a public park, which has been designated as a place where people can freely express their opinions. The speech contains racial slurs, aimed at a minority group. Although the majority of the audience are white, like the speaker, a number of people from the minority group are present. They might be very offended by the racial slurs in the speech.

Other scenarios presented conflicts between freedom of speech and physical harm or equality of opportunity and between freedom of religion and psychological or physical harm or equality of opportunity. The latter involved a religion in which low-income individuals were excluded from the priesthood.

Participants were interviewed to see how they resolved the competing moral imperatives depicted in the scenarios. Justifications were coded according to the kind of argument that was made about the importance of freedoms. These included mention of general psychological needs (such as people's need to practise their religion) and the right to self-expression, the value to society, democratic principles, tradition, and government authority. What is of particular interest is how justification changed across the three age groups.

Across all age groups, civil liberties were often subordinated to other issues. Decisions in the complex scenarios reflected several sources of variation, some of which were age related. The younger adolescents (age 12 years) tended to affirm freedoms of speech and religion less often than the older groups, when these freedoms were in conflict with other social and moral concepts. However, even among this age group, there was unanimous agreement that freedom of religion outweighed psychological harm. What changed with age was that older adolescents and young adults applied and prioritised civil liberties across a wider range of situations. The changes focused around judgements of freedoms and rights in relation to the demands of freedom and equality.

One of the clearest examples from Helwig's data concerns judgments about civil liberties. Around half of the youngest group argued that it would be wrong for individuals to violate laws restricting civil liberties even when these laws were seen as unjust. As Helwig reports,

> younger adolescents were able to use concepts of abstract rights to evaluate laws and social systems that restrict basic freedoms, [but] many . . . resorted to a purely legalistic perspective when considering the legitimacy of acts embedded within social systems [that were] held to be unjust. Older adolescents and young adults, by contrast, tended to judge both legal restrictions on rights and acts violating restrictive laws from the perspective of abstract rights alone.
>
> (Helwig, 1995, p. 163)

Although there were clear developmental trends in Helwig's study, there were also significant individual differences. We return to the possible origins of such differences when we discuss the development of moral reasoning in more detail in the final chapter. However, it is notable that reasoning abilities in adolescence are considerably more variable than in earlier periods of development. Indeed, there is good evidence that the attainment of formal operational thinking does not appear to be universal.

Consider the understanding of correlation or covariation, one of the second-order operations in the INRC group. One of the tasks that Inhelder and Piaget (1958) used was judgement about the co-variation of hair and eye colour. For example if there are four combinations of hair and eye colour – dark hair/dark eyes; dark hair/light eyes; light hair/dark eyes; light hair/light eyes – it is possible to determine whether occurrence of the colour of hair and eyes is correlated. Inhelder and Piaget found evidence that the ability to understand co-variation continued to develop through adolescence. However, subsequent research has shown that there is considerable variation among adults in the understanding of the nature of co-variation (Shaklee, Holt, Elek, & Hall, 1988). Furthermore, unlike the earlier stages of cognitive development that Piaget proposes, there would appear to be an important role for formal

BOX 16.1: UNDERSTANDING CO-VARIATION

Among the general public there appears to be a poor understanding of co-variation. The most reliable way to determine the extent of a relationship between two variables is to use the *conditional probability rule*. Shaklee et al. (1988) give the example of the relationship between the health of a plant and plant food. There are four relationships that you need to consider in order to fully understand the co-variation of the two variables. You can think of these as forming a 2 x 2 contingency table. The example of the eye colour–hair colour relationships used by Inhelder and Piaget (1958) is like this. In the case of the plant health–plant food example, the table looks like this:

A Frequency of healthy plants with plant food	B Frequency of healthy plants without plant food
C Frequency of unhealthy plants with plant food	D Frequency of unhealthy plants without plant food

There are a number of possible rules to determine the strength of the relationship between the two variables. The Cell A rule is the least sophisticated and involves only looking at the frequency of Cell A. If this is the largest of the four frequencies, the relationship is judged to be positive. Another strategy is to compare the A and B frequencies, that is, looking to see whether there are more healthy plants with plant food than without. However, a more sophisticated strategy is to compare the number of events confirming a positive relationship between plant health and plant food (A and D) with the number disconfirming the relationship (B and C). This is sometimes called a *sum of the diagonals* strategy.

Inhelder and Piaget (1958) proposed that children who were at the formal operational stage of reasoning would use this sum of the diagonals rule to judge event contingency. This rule has the advantage of making use of all four pieces of evidence but it can be misleading when the frequencies of the two main conditions are substantially different. If you are familiar with the use of Chi Square to analyse contingency tables then you will be aware of this problem. Arriving at the correct judgement about the strength of a relationship requires the use of conditional probabilities, that is, comparing the likelihood of plant health in two populations of plants, with plant food and plants without, that is, comparing, A:B with C:D. Again, this idea will be familiar if you understand how Chi Square calculates the strength of the relationship between two variables.

Use of the conditional probability rule is not common even among well-educated adults. Shaklee *et al.* (1988) set out to train 13-year-olds and college students to use this rule, using three different training conditions. The problems they used related to the health of plants and raising agents for bread. Here is an example of one of the problems:

> A plant grower had a bunch of sick plants. He gave some of them special plant food, but some plants didn't get special food. Some of the plants got better but some didn't.

There was a 2 × 2 table for each problem, with a number of variations in which the frequency of the four cells differed. Each participant was given 12 different problems.

Before training the majority of 13-year-olds (54 per cent) used the A versus B rule, comparing the frequencies of these two events, and 38 per cent used the sum of the diagonals rule. Among college students, 57 per cent used the A versus B rule and 30 per cent used the sum of the diagonals rule. After training, in which participants worked through examples and were shown how to compare outcomes in two conditions, both the younger and older groups improved their performance. As you might expect, the training was most effective for the college students. The majority were able to use the conditional probability rule after training. The 13-year-olds showed improvements but these were significantly less marked.

This study shows two important things about formal operational thinking. First, it is clear that developments in reasoning ability are continuing throughout adolescence. This is why training had a much greater impact on the 20-year-old college students than on the 13-year-old school children, even though they were both in the stage of formal operational thinking. Second, it is notable that none of the college students was spontaneously using the conditional probability rule even though they could do so with appropriate training. Clearly they had the cognitive potential to engage in such reasoning but this was not something that spontaneously emerged.

education in supporting the development of formal operational thinking. The study by Shaklee *et al.* (1988) illustrates both the difficulties inherent in understanding and employing the logic of formal operational reasoning and the benefits of training (see Box 16.1).

16.3 THE DEVELOPMENT OF EXECUTIVE FUNCTIONING

So far in this chapter we have viewed cognitive development in adolescence from the perspective of formal operational thinking. Another useful framework for considering how the ability to think matures as children move from middle childhood to adolescence is that of executive functioning.

We saw in Chapter 12 that there are important changes in working memory during the preschool period. The central executive is one component of working memory, as described by Baddeley and Hitch (Baddeley & Hitch, 1974). We need not concern ourselves here with all of the subtleties of the various accounts of executive functioning. We will follow the definition given by Henry (2012):

> Executive skills are a constellation of abilities required to deal with unfamiliar situations or novelty. These skills include being able to plan ahead (planning); generate new solutions (fluency); switch attention from one thing to another (switching); ignore readily available information that is not currently useful (inhibition); and remember important details relevant to the task (executive-loaded working memory). In short, these are higher-level thinking and attentional skills for dealing with complex problem solving and behaviour regulation . . .
>
> (Henry, 2012, p. 114)

In the previous chapter we saw that adolescence is a period in which the prefrontal cortex develops. This is area of the brain that plays a large part in the control of executive skills and so we might expect to find that executive functioning continues to develop throughout adolescence and into adulthood. Research into the development of executive skills suggests that this is indeed the case, although there are some differences among the various sub-skills that go to make up executive functioning.

The clearest evidence for development of executive functioning from middle childhood into adolescence comes from studies of executive-loaded working memory. There are a number of tasks that measure this aspect of executive function but they all require a combination of remembering some information over a short period of time while, at the same time, manipulating that information in some way. The important point is that, unlike short-term memory tasks such as the recall of digits, executive-loaded working memory does not merely require the recall of information.

One executive-loaded working memory task requires children to supply the correct word to complete a series of sentences that they read aloud – such as 'with dinner we sometime eat bread and [BUTTER]' – and then to recall the final word in each sentence (Slegel & Ryan, 1989). This is a demanding task but it is a classic test of executive functioning. The task requires a very careful allocation of cognitive resources between listening to each sentence, supplying the correct final word, remembering that answer as well as all preceding answers in the trial. The data from Siegel and Ryan's study shows a clear increase with age in the total number of sentence-final words that can be remembered. This rose from a mean of just under three sentences at age seven to eight years, to a mean of just under four sentences at 9–20 years, and a mean of just over five sentences at 11–13 years.

There has been considerable debate about exactly why, from a cognitive perspective, the ability to handle information in executive-loaded working memory tasks improves with age from middle childhood to adolescence (Henry, 2012). A number of different factors appear to be involved. One is the development of more efficient rehearsal and attentional strategies and more effective allocation of resources between the different demands of a particular task (Tam, Jarrold, Baddeley, & Sabatos-DeVito, 2010). Furthermore, younger children take longer to process information than older children and this means that more stored information will have

The Wisconsin Card Sorting Task, which tests the participants' ability to flexibly switch the sorting rule.

decayed to the point where it can no longer be retrieved from memory (Towse & Hitch, 2007). The effect of this is that younger children can retain less information than older children.

Other components of executive function also improve with age. One study (Levin *et al.*, 1991) compared the performance of children aged seven to eight years through to adolescence. They tested participants on a range of tests including the Wisconsin Card Sorting Task, The Tower of London, word and design fluency, the Go/No-Go task, and the California Verbal Learning Task.

As we saw in the previous chapter, the Wisconsin Card Sorting Task is a measure of the ability to switch from one sorting rule to another (see 15.2). The Go/No-Go Task is a measure of the ability to inhibit incorrect responses. It involves responding to one type of stimulus and not responding to another. Levin *et al.* found that performance on both these tasks had reached adult levels by the age of 12 years.

However, the pattern for other tasks was different. The Tower of London is a complex planning task that becomes increasingly difficult across trials. It is very similar to the Tower of Hanoi task described in Chapter 8 (see 8.3) except that it uses balls rather than disks. Performance on this task and also on the fluency and memory strategy tasks (California Verbal Learning Task) continued to develop through adolescence.

What these results suggest is that the various executive skills mature at somewhat different rates, with the skills relating to attentional control and inhibition maturing sooner than the high-level skills involved in planning, retrieving and organising information. These latter skills are not mature in early adolescence but mature slowly over a period of years. They are examples of the slow-maturing cognitive skills that we identified in the previous chapter.

16.4 SUMMARY

Piaget saw adolescence as a period in which the final cognitive stage, formal operational thought, was attained. We have seen that this kind of thinking entails the ability to deal with logical deduction and the ability to consider the behaviour of two or more variables at the same time. The work of Piaget and Inhelder was the first to characterise, in detail, how logical thinking developed and they devised a series of novel experimental tasks that were designed to tease out the various thinking skills that emerged after the period of concrete operations.

This characterisation of logical thinking, that enables adolescents to engage in scientific thinking and to consider abstract hypotheses, has been of great importance for the understanding and assessment of adolescent thought and it has had a huge impact not only on developmental psychology but also on education. However, formal operational thinking is only one aspect of higher-level thinking and it could be seen as somewhat abstracted from what people actually do in daily life. As such, Inhelder and Piaget's account does not explain everything about the cognitive capabilities of adolescents and adults. More complex kinds of reasoning, such as the ability to weigh competing moral imperatives or to understand the relationship between two potentially associated variables, develops over later adolescence into early adulthood.

Finally, in this chapter, we saw that there are very specific developments in the various sub-skills that go to make up executive functioning, with the ability to plan complex tasks and retrieve and organise information developing only gradually through adolescence.

FURTHER READING

Helwig, C. C., Arnold, M. L., Tan, D., & Boyd, D. (2003). Chinese adolescents' reasoning about democratic and authority-based decision making in peer, family, and school contexts. *Child Development, 74*(3), 783–800.

Henry, L. (2012). *The development of working memory in children*. London: Sage.

Kuhn, D. & Franklin, S. The second decade: What develops (and how). In D. Kuhn & R. S. Siegler (Eds), *Handbook of child psychology* (Vol. 2) (pp. 953–993). Hoboken, NJ: Wiley.

ESSAY QUESTIONS

1. How do Piaget and Inhelder explain the transition from concrete to formal operational thinking?
2. To what extent does Piaget's account of formal operational reasoning capture the full range of cognitive development in adolescence?
3. Explain what is meant by 'executive functioning' and describe the changes that occur in executive functioning through adolescence.

CHAPTER 17

CONTENTS

Social and emotional development in adolescence

17

After reading this chapter you will be able to

- understand how adolescents' moral judgements are affected by socio-cultural factors
- explain the importance of relationships with family and friends during adolescence
- understand the long-term consequences of attachment
- explain how the friendships of boys and girls differ
- describe gender differences in aggression and patterns of bullying
- understand how expectations about family roles are influenced by parental roles.

17.1 MORAL REASONING

We saw in Chapter 14 that there are important changes in children's abilities to form moral judgements during middle childhood. During adolescence further changes take place as the use of implicit principles gives way to the application of explicit principles (Moshman, 1998; Sinno & Killen, 2011). Moshman argues that there is a set of metalaws which justify a range of moral rules. He has suggested that children use such principles implicitly in middle childhood but, as they become adolescents and move on into adulthood, these principles become the object of reflection. This account can explain why many adolescents become concerned about issues to do with natural justice such as animal rights and third world debt.

Socio-cultural context

The way that adolescents reason about human rights is heavily dependent on the cultural context in which they are growing up. Recent research has begun to study adolescent reasoning about human rights in different cultural settings. One study compared the attitudes of Muslim and non-Muslim adolescents who were attending schools in the Netherlands (Verkuyten & Slooter, 2008). The focus of the study was attitudes to free speech and minority rights. Participants were aged between 12 and

18 years and they were all attending the same, integrated schools. One group was made up of non-Muslim adolescents, who had two ethnically Dutch parents, and the other comprised Muslim adolescents whose parents had come to the Netherlands as immigrants from such countries as Turkey, Morocco, Iran, Iraq and Bosnia.

All the participants in the Verkuyten and Slooter study were given scenarios to consider that concerned the endorsement of free speech in the media and Muslim minority rights, such as the right to wear certain forms of dress and the separation of the sexes for activities such as education. For example, one of the scenarios that concerned free speech asked, 'Should it be allowed that on the internet people can call for the Jihad?' and one relating to Muslim minority rights asked, 'Should people have the right to found Islamic schools to which only Muslims can go?' Participants were also asked about the wearing of headscarves and the rights to home education, to carry out female circumcision, to burn the Dutch flag during a demonstration and to ridicule religion. All of these issues were chosen because of their relevance to recent events and to life in the Netherlands. Participants were also asked to indicate the importance of religion in their lives.

As you might expect there was a considerable difference between the two groups in the importance of religion in their lives. The mean score on a 5-point rating scale (where 5 indicated strongly agree that religion was important and 1 indicated strongly disagree) was just over 4 for the Muslim adolescents and just over 2 for the non-Muslims. Differences and similarities between Muslims and non-Muslims in their responses to the scenarios indicated that the adolescents who were questioned took into account a number of different issues, including whose freedom of speech and rights they were being asked to endorse and what the social implications were of acceptance. Religious beliefs entered into these considerations so that, for example, the rejection of freedom of speech was stronger among Muslims than non-Muslims when it involved offending God or religion; and non-Muslims more strongly rejected the right to burn the Dutch flag or to have separate schools. There were some interesting differences between male and female Muslim participants. Muslim girls more strongly rejected female circumcision, differential gender treatment and home education than either Muslim boys or non-Muslims. Presumably this was because these issues are most relevant to Muslim girls since they affect their lives.

What these findings show is that attitudes to human rights in adolescence are strongly affected by group membership. Where particular rights were of greater or lesser relevance for a particular group, there were group differences. However, where particular rights were not of relevance to one group rather than another, the judgements of Muslim and non-Muslim adolescents were very similar. For example, all participants in the Verkuyten and Slooter study rejected freedom of speech when it involved psychological or physical harm. The results also show that adolescents apply a variety of considerations to their moral judgements including the social implications of a particular behaviour and the likely harm.

As we saw in the Verkuyten and Slooter study, the views that young people have of moral dilemmas is very much affected by their socio-cultural background. Both Piaget's and Kohlberg's theories of moral development (see 14.2) were developed in a Western cultural context, as has much of the research that followed. More recently researchers have become interested in how moral reasoning is affected by growing up in a society with very different values. Within Western culture, children and young people have fairly consistent views about what kinds of issue should be determined by personal choice and what issues fall within the legitimate authority of adults and other authorities. They consider that friends, recreational pursuits and appearance are matters of personal choice and cite concepts such as individual rights and personal autonomy in support of this view (Turiel, 2006). Helwig and colleagues (Helwig, Arnold, Tan, & Boyd, 2003) have studied the views of adolescents growing up in China to see whether these differ from those of peers growing up with Western-style democracy.

There are a number of reasons why a comparison with adolescents in China is pertinent to understanding the impact of the socio-cultural context on the development of moral reasoning. China has a communist political system in which individual rights and autonomy are often subordinated to group goals and centralised planning. China's general cultural orientation has been described as collectivist in contrast to the individualistic culture that predominates in Western society. As Helwig *et al.* point out, collectivism permeates both the way that children in China are educated and family life. In terms of education, there is a national, uniform curriculum, an emphasis on rote learning and respect for the authority of teachers. Chinese family life places great emphasis on respect for and obedience to elders, especially fathers and other male adults, and there is a strong sense of hierarchy.

In spite of these differences it appears that adolescents tend to experience the same kinds of conflicts with their parents in China as in North America (Yau & Smetana, 2003). Chinese adolescents reported disagreeing with their parents over such everyday issues as choice of activities, schoolwork, interpersonal relationships and helping around the house. Conflicts were more intense in early adolescence than in late adolescence. Adolescents primarily justified conflicts by appealing to personal autonomy but most conflicts were resolved by acceding to parents' wishes. It is perhaps not surprising in light of this pattern that Chinese adolescents in the Yau and Smetana study expressed a wish to have more autonomy from their parents than they actually had.

The focus of the Helwig *et al.* (2003) study was the view of Chinese adolescents (aged 13–18 years) on who should make decisions in three different social settings – peer group, family and school. A range of different scenarios were presented that included deciding, among a group of friends, which movie to go and see at the cinema, deciding where a family should go for a weekend outing, deciding where a class should go on a school field trip and deciding what the class should learn. Across the three settings there was general support for 'majority rule' as the most democratic way of reaching a decision. However, there were some differences across settings with majority decisions being most highly favoured among peers and for decisions about the family outing and class field trip, and an adult decision begin favoured for the school curriculum. In the case of majority decisions, the Chinese adolescents did not distinguish between adults and children, considering that they should all have a say in decisions about the family.

Overall the findings of the Helwig *et al.* (2003) study of Chinese adolescents support the picture emerging from the comparison of Muslim and non-Muslim adolescents. During adolescence there is increasing sensitivity to social context in the formation of social and moral judgements. Older adolescents are able to take a number of different factors into account before reaching a decision about appropriate behaviour and, to this extent, the development of moral reasoning should be seen as considerably more subtle than the six-stage model of Kohlberg suggests.

Gender differences

Another area where a suitably nuanced account of moral development in adolescence is appropriate is that of gender differences. Gilligan (1982) has been an influential exponent of the view that there are systematic differences between males and females. She has argued for gender differences in moral development that become more apparent in adolescence, claiming that males tend to focus on justice while women focus on caring and responsibility. Gilligan claims that these differences of emphasis reflect an underlying difference in the way that men and women see relationships among people. Thinking of people as separate beings, who are in continual conflict with one another, requires an ethic of justice in which there are rules and contracts. An ethic of caring and responsibility – which Gilligan sees as characteristically female – stems from a view of the inter-connectedness of people.

There is good evidence that there are some gender-linked differences in moral orientation. For example, when asked to recall a recent real-life moral dilemma from their own experience (Walker, de Vries, & Trevethen, 1987), women were more likely than men to report moral dilemmas that concerned relationships with other people while men were more likely to report impersonal dilemmas. Personal dilemmas were ones that involved a specific person or group of people with whom the person being interviewed had a significant relationship, such as a family member or close friend. Impersonal dilemmas, by contrast, involved people with whom the interviewee did not have a personal relationship. Examples of personal moral dilemmas included whether or not to put an elderly parent into a nursing home against his wishes or whether or not to tell someone that their partner was having an affair. Impersonal dilemmas often revolved around work and included whether or not to correct an employee's error or whether to reduce an employee's wages or, alternatively, take a cut in profits. However, across a range of tasks, both males and females in the Walker *et al.* study used both a justice and a responsibility/caring orientation indicating that, while there are some gender differences in moral orientation, these differences are not as clear cut as Gilligan argued.

17.2 RELATIONSHIPS

Within Western society there are significant changes in relationships over the lifespan (van Lieshout & Doise, 1998). Mothers and fathers are seen as the most frequent providers of emotional support in middle childhood. As children enter adolescence, same-sex friends are perceived to be just as supportive as parents and, by middle adolescence, they provide the main sources of support. In late adolescence romantic partners become a very important source of emotional support along with friends and mothers but there is an interesting sex difference. Males experience romantic relationships as most supportive while females receive equal support from a wider range of people – mothers, friends and siblings as well as romantic partners (Furman & Buhrmester, 1992). There are also age-related changes in perceived conflict, punishment and power. Tension in parent–child relationships tends to peak in early and middle adolescence as we saw in the study of Chinese adolescents (Yau & Smetana, 2003) and to lessen in late adolescence.

One way of illustrating these developmental changes in the relative importance of friends and family members is to look at patterns of self-disclosure. As we saw in our discussion of friendships, intimate relationships are characterised by self-disclosure (i.e. telling someone else the most important and personal information about yourself such as who you like and don't like and what you are planning for the future). Studies of intimate self-disclosure (Buhrmester, 1996) show that American second graders (age seven) and fifth graders (age ten) are most likely to tell their parents intimate personal information. However, by tenth grade (age 15) there is a marked change with intimate self-disclosure being highest to a friend and lowest to a parent. Disclosure to a romantic partner is greater than to parents. By college age romantic partners and friends are of equal importance but, interestingly, the importance of parents has begun to increase again. Of course, these are general indications of the pattern of self-disclosure over time

and there are large individual differences. On balance, girls tend to engage in higher levels of self-disclosure than boys and mother–daughter relationships may remain close across adolescence. Other members of the family such as siblings and grandparents may also be important for sharing personal information.

From early adolescence onwards, same-sex friends become increasingly important sources of support.

Furman and Buhrmester (1992) suggest that a number of factors may contribute to developmental shifts in perceived support from different members of a personal network. Adolescents typically distance themselves from their families and invest more time in peer relationships. Initially these relationships are friendships with same-sex peers but, in adolescence, romantic relationships become increasingly important. Advances in cognitive and social abilities in adolescence can facilitate self-exploration and validation of the adolescent's self-concept; and the adolescent's search for independence will lead to an increasing interest in issues and relationships outside the home.

Similarities between friends are the norm throughout development, as we have seen in preceding chapters, although there are interesting variations among groups in the way that friends are selected during adolescence. Hartup (1998), summarising research on adolescent friendships, notes that friends are more similar to one another than nonfriends in two main areas. These are attitudes to school and levels of achievement and normative behaviours such as smoking, drinking, drug use and antisocial behaviour. Friends also tend to like the same kinds of activities. There is an interesting difference between girls and boys in the similarity of sexual behaviour. Adolescent girls of similar age in the United States – both white and African-American – have been shown to have very similar attitudes towards sexual activity and to have similar sexual behaviour. However there was less similarity among boys especially in the level of sexual activity (Hartup, 1988).

Friendship throughout life can provide a context for social and emotional growth. Between 80 per cent and 90 per cent of people have a mutual friendship although the nature of the friendship will depend on such factors as age, gender, location and working pattern. Friends provide security and emotional support in the face of stress. For children this might be the stress of parental divorce, parental maltreatment or pressure of school. For adolescents and adults, friendship also provides emotional support for work-related problems and difficulties in relationships. Friends also provide security and support when young children first go to school and older

Families vary greatly in form across time and cultures. Multi-generational extended families like this are now quite rare, largely replaced by the nuclear family.

children change schools. Troubled children or those referred to clinics are more likely to have no friends than non-troubled children.

While people can choose their friends, they cannot choose their families. Each family member has a unique role within the family as mother, father, son, daughter, brother, sister, grandfather or grandmother or as a step-parent or step-child. Among the children within a family each occupies a unique position by virtue of birth order so, for example, the youngest child and the oldest child have a different role within the family. Each family member's behaviour depends, in part, on the behaviour of other family members and it involves a unique set of relationships with a known history.

Families take a wide variety of forms both across time and across cultures. Since the Second World War the multigenerational extended family – consisting of parents, children and older family members such as grandparents – has largely been replaced by a nuclear family consisting of two biological parents and their children. In more recent years the family unit has become even more diverse with single-parent families becoming increasingly common and more adults living alone. The number of unmarried teenage mothers has rapidly increased in the United States and their incidence is far higher than in Europe.

The quality of relationships between family members can affect other members of the same family. A meta-analysis of 68 previous studies (Erel & Burman, 1995) focused on the inter-relatedness of the parents' relationship with each other and the quality of parent–child relationships. The inter-parental relationship was measured according to global quality, marital satisfaction and absence of overt conflicts. The parent–child relationship was measured in terms of global quality but measures were also taken of between and within consistency of parental behaviour, satisfaction and absence of negative control and harsh punishments. Erel and Burman found strong support for a 'spillover hypothesis' in which the quality of marital relationships and the quality of parent–child relationships were strongly linked. Parents who had a strong and supportive relationship with each other responded more sensitively to their children; parents who had a negative or conflict-filled relationship with each other appeared to be less attentive and sensitive to their children – perhaps because they were emotionally drained by the negative relationship with their partner.

Attachment

The quality of relationships in adolescence is influenced by the quality of attachment relations in infancy (see 6.4). In a longitudinal study that spanned 20 years (Waters, Merrick, Trebous, Crowell, & Albaersheim, 2000), 50 young adults (aged 20–21 years), who had originally been observed at the age of 12 months, were given the Adult Attachment Interview (George, Kaplan, & Main, 1985). At the time of the follow up, 45 per cent were living at college, 24 per cent were still living at home and another 24 per cent were living independently. The remaining small group had other living arrangements such as being in the military.

BOX 17.1: INTERGENERATIONAL EFFECTS IN MENTAL DISORDERS

There are links between mental disorders in parents and children not only as a result of shared genes but also as a result of parenting. In one study (Andrews, Brown, & Creasey, 1990) mothers and daughters were interviewed to determine whether they had experienced psychiatric symptoms in the previous 12 months and, in the case of mothers, over the period of their daughter's childhood. Daughters were also interviewed about their early family experiences and asked about the quality of care they had received, their attitude to their mother, and physical and sexual abuse.

Mothers who had significant psychiatric symptoms fell into two categories – those who had had only one depressive episode of less than one year in their daughter's lifetime and those who had a chronic or recurrent disorder. Mothers in the former group were not more likely to have a daughter with a disorder than those who had not experienced an episode of depression – the incidence in the daughters was 5 per cent. However, where mothers had experienced a chronic or recurrent disorder, there was a 25 per cent chance that their daughter also suffered from a disorder. Andrews *et al.* found that early family experience was also an important as a predictor of the daughters' mental health. Eighty-nine per cent of the daughters with a mental disorder reported adverse early family experiences compared to only 27 per cent of those with no disorder. Some of this difference may have arisen because the daughters who were depressed gave a more negative report of their childhood experiences but even a more stringent interpretation of the reports showed clear differences between the clinical and non-clinical groups.

The precise pattern of cause and effect in this study is difficult to determine since both mothers and fathers contributed to adverse early effects. It is possible, for example, that the mother's depression had a negative influence on the marriage and so an indirect effect on the father's behaviour or that the father, as well as the mother, was subject to a psychiatric disorder. However, it is clear from the study that the relationship between persistent maternal disorders and disorders in the daughters was mediated by the daughter's early experience within the family.

One final point of interest about this study lies in the nature of the psychiatric disorders of the daughters. Daughters were less likely to have been clinically depressed in the year preceding the interview than their mothers but the overall incidence of psychiatric disorder was very similar in the two groups. This was because, among the daughters, there were cases of eating disorders and alcohol abuse as well as anxiety. Anxiety in the mothers – and adverse family experiences – thus gave rise not only to depression in the daughters but also to other mental disorders.

At the original one-year assessment, using the strange situation paradigm (see 6.4), infants had been classified as secure, insecure-avoidant and insecure resistant. The insecure-disorganised classification was not developed by Main and Solomon until 1986 and so was not in use in 1976 at the time of the original assessment. In order to examine the relationship between the infant classification of attachment and adult attachment, account was taken of intervening life events since the assumption is that attachment in childhood may be disrupted by negative life events such as loss of a parent, parental divorce, serious illness of either child or parent, parental mental illness (see Box 17.1) and physical or sexual abuse. Information about such events was gathered from the Adult Attachment Interview (AAI) but only events occurring before the age of 18 were considered since it was assumed that more recent events may not yet have had their full impact on attachment.

Early attachment security to the mother turned out to be very closely related to AAI security. Thirty-six out of 50 participants had the same secure-insecure classification at 12 months and 20 years later and only around one third showed a change in classification. Stressful life events had a significant effect on the likelihood of a securely-attached infant being insecurely attached in early adulthood. However, stressful life events did not inevitably lead to low attachment security in young adulthood. Eight participants, who experienced negative life events, did not change their secure attachment while nine others, who did not report such events, changed to less secure attachment. In one case, where parents responded with sensitive care to the childhood onset of a lifelong illness in childhood, attachment security increased from infancy to adulthood.

It is clear from these results that secure attachment to the mother in infancy is, in the majority of cases, the base from which other attachment relations are formed. However, positive and negative life events also have an important part to play in adult attachments and, of course, secure attachments to other member of the family, that were not assessed in the Waters *et al.* (2000) study. What is perhaps surprising is how powerful the effects of early attachment on later attachment seem to be given the huge range of experience that intervenes between 12 months and 21 years and the enormous cognitive changes that have occurred over this period.

17.3 GENDER DIFFERENCES IN ADOLESCENT FRIENDSHIPS

We have already hinted that there are some notable differences in the friendship patterns of male and female adolescents. This is an issue that has been explored in a number of recent studies, arguing for the existence of different 'cultures' in the peer relationships of girls and boys.

Maccoby was one of the first authors to argue that female–female interactions typically focus on the building of interpersonal connections whereas male–male interactions are more directed towards the development of individual status (Maccoby, 1990). In one study, carried out by Buhrmester and colleagues (Buhrmester, 1996), young adolescents were interviewed about their social interactions during the previous day. Females reported a higher number of interactions with same-sex friends than males and they also reported substantially higher levels of self-disclosure and emotional support than males did in their daily interactions. This pattern is consistent with the image of female–female friendships as 'face to face' and having an emphasis on talking in contrast to the image of male–male friendships as being 'side by side' with a focus on doing things together, notably sports and competitive games.

Buhrmester (1996) notes that, when male friends talk, their discussions often focus on what are described as 'agentically oriented' issues such as the achievements of sporting teams and individuals and the evaluation of the academic and sporting prowess of peers. These gender differences in the patterns of friendship support Maccoby's argument that there are different processes of socialisation at work for boys and girls, particularly in adolescence. The typical pattern of male friendships will often put adolescent boys into situations that reinforce the need for achievement, recognition and power.

Differences in the patterns of typical male and female friendships are also evident in the specific norms that they encourage. The norms for girls' friendships seem to actively reward intimate self-disclosure and the provision of emotional support and also actively discourage open competition and the discussion of status differences (Brown & Gilligan, 1992). This pattern is well illustrated in a study of adolescents' attitudes to being seen as better than their friends (Benenson & Schinazi, 2004).

The Benenson and Schinazi study focused on adolescents aged between 13 and 15 years, attending school in Canada. They were asked to complete a questionnaire that asked about their desire to be successful in four areas that are typically of concern in adolescence – romantic relationships, close friendships, academic achievement and sporting achievement. For example, to assess concern about academic success, participants were asked to rate (on a 6-point scale), 'How much do you care about getting good marks?' and 'How do you feel when you don't get good marks?' Then, in a second part of the questionnaire, they were asked to nominate two good friends of the same sex and to consider how they would feel if they performed better than each of their nominated friends and also how their friend would feel. Finally participants were asked about their current level of achievement in each of the four domains.

There were no differences in how much girls and boys wanted to succeed in each of the four domains and there were no age differences. However, girls reported that they would feel more negative about doing better than their friends than boys and also reported that they would care more. These differences were not related to actual levels of achievement. A similar pattern was found in a second study with 18-year-olds where participants rated their reactions to both doing better than their friends and achieving at the same level. Females preferred an outcome in which they and their friends performed at the same level to one in which they outperformed their friends whereas males rated the two outcomes similarly.

Friendships and relationships within the family change as young people move through various phases of life but some gender differences remain. This was evident in a study of young people aged between 20 and 35 years (Carbery & Buhrmester, 1998). Participants were identified as being in one of three family-role-defined phases of young adulthood: the single phase (i.e. romantically uncommitted), the married-without-children phase and the parenthood phase (i.e. married with young children). Participants rated the extent to which they received social support from friends and family members. In general, reliance on friends to satisfy social needs was greatest during the single phase and was reduced significantly during the marital and parenthood phases. Across all three phases, women report gaining higher levels of social support – especially emotional support – from friends than men did.

Many discussions of the socialising effects of peers (notably Maccoby, 1990) have tended to emphasise the negative aspects of boys' friendships. However, it is probably too simple to argue that male–male friendships have a negative influence in contrast to the values of mutual support that are characteristic of female–female friendships. Learning to work as a team and to succeed can also be seen in a positive light and, arguably, both male and female friendships can be seen as developing skills that are important for successful functioning in adulthood.

17.4 CONFLICT AND AGGRESSION

Most longitudinal studies show a general decrease in physical aggression as children enter adolescence. However, adolescence is also the period in which serious violent behaviour increases among a small section of the population (Dodge, Coie, & Lynam, 2006). Such behaviour is most common in encounters between males. Data from a large longitudinal survey of adolescent behaviour in the United States (Elliott, 1994) has shown that patterns of violent offending almost invariably begin during adolescence. Self-reports of serious violent offences (aggravated assault, robbery or rape) rise sharply from the ages of 12 to 20, and fewer than 1 per cent of first offences occur after the age of 20. Nearly 75 per cent of juvenile offenders (i.e. aged between 10 and 16 years) were convicted again between the ages of 17 and 24 years. The incidence of offending peaked at 17 years (Dodge *et al.*, 2006).

Gender differences in aggression are evident early on and remain throughout development. A longitudinal study of aggressive behaviour using data from six sites and three countries – United States, Canada and new Zealand – (Broidy *et al.*, 2003) found that boys showed a clear continuity in problem behavior from childhood to adolescence, with the strongest links occurring in relation to early physical aggression. Recurrent physical aggression during middle childhood increased the risk of continued physical violence as well as other nonviolent forms of delinquency during adolescence. However, for girls, there was no clear relationship between childhood physical aggression and adolescent offending. Overall levels of physical aggression were consistently lower in girls than boys across the age span.

Levels of aggression and delinquency are consistently higher in males than females. One study (Crijnen, Achenbach, & Verhulst, 1997) used the Child Behaviour Checklist to compare the patterns of internalising and externalising behaviours among 6- to 17-year-olds in 12 different counties with varying cultural settings (Australia, Belgium, China, Germany, Greece, Israel, Jamaica, the Netherlands, Puerto Rico, Sweden, Thailand and the United States). The Child Behaviour Checklist asks parents about a number of different aspects of their children's behaviour. The Checklist is used to derive a number of scales including internalising and externalising. Internalising behaviours refer to a broad class of behaviors in which children direct feelings and emotions inward whereas externalising behaviour is the expression of feelings and emotional responses that are directed outward into delinquent or aggressive behaviour.

The patterns of internalising and externalising were very consistent from one country to another. Externalising scores declined with age, while internalising scores increased; and boys obtained higher externalising scores but lower internalising scores than girls. Sex differences in patterns of violent behaviour are very striking. In the United States eight times as many adolescent boys as girls are arrested for violent crime although, to some extent, this is a changing picture. Dodge *et al.* (2006) note that there has been a slight trend for this ratio to decrease over time as more girls are involved in serious violence. In the National Youth Survey data reported by Elliott (1994), 42 per cent of males reported committing a serious violent offence at some time in their youth compared to 16 per cent for females. There was also a notable difference in the peak age of first offences for boys (16 years) and girls (14 years).

The National Youth Survey data paint a depressing picture of the developmental precursors of violent crime. Children begin with minor aggressive acts and delinquent behaviour in the early school years and progress to serious and frequent offending by the age of 17. The beginning of substance use and sexual activity add incrementally to the risk of aggressive behaviour during adolescence. Minor forms of delinquent behaviour and alcohol use typically precede more serious forms of violence; aggravated assault precedes robbery in 85 per cent of cases and robbery precedes rape in 72 per cent of cases. Thus, as Dodge *et al.* (2006) note, there is a chilling inevitability about the developmental path taken by a small proportion of the population in which behaviours become more serious and more violent with age. Fortunately, however, the picture changes after adolescence with self-reported aggressive behaviour declining between the ages of 18 and 25; and, as the National Youth Survey data suggest, there are virtually no new cases of antisocial behaviour that begin in adulthood.

KEY TERMS

Cyber-bullying
Repeated acts of aggression that are directed towards particular peers through the internet or mobile technologies.

Cyber-bullying

Aggression and bullying take many forms. A recent phenomenon has been the emergence of cyber-bullying. Bullying, in general, refers to repeated acts of physical and verbal aggression that are directed towards particular peers (i.e. victims). In the case of **cyber-bullying**, the aggression is channelled through the internet (e.g. email, text or video messaging, websites, etc.). Opportunities for cyber-bullying have increased with the wide ownership of mobile phones and computers. A recent report (YouGov, 2006) found that just over half of ten-year-olds in the UK owned a mobile phone with figure rising to 91 per cent for 12-year-olds. In addition, almost all children have access to a computer either at home or school.

Psychologists have recently begun to study cyber-bullying and they have found that it shares many of the characteristics of more traditional forms of bullying. In surveys of over 600 11–16-year-olds (Smith *et al.*, 2008), children reported on their recent experiences of both bullying and cyber-bullying. Nearly half (46 per cent) reported that they had been bullied in the last two months and almost one quarter (22 per cent) reported instances of cyber-bullying. Cyber-bullying most often took place outside school and the most frequent forms were phone calls and text messaging. Bullying that involved the use of videoclips was less common but perceived to have the greater effect on the victim. Most cyber-bullying was carried out by one student or a small group of students and lasted for a week or longer.

Victims of cyber-bullying often did not tell anyone else about their experiences – a pattern that is common among victims of bullying. Given that friends provide children with social support and a sense of self worth, it is not surprising to discover that the victims of persistent bullying tend to be anxious, insecure and isolated from the remainder of their peer group. They are also lacking in self-esteem and self-confidence and prosocial skills (see 10.2).

Unlike the pattern for physical aggression we discussed earlier, perpetrators of cyber-bullying were just as likely to be female as male. This is consistent with the more general finding that, although physical violence is less common among girls than boys, non-physical aggression is equally common in both sexes (Dodge *et al.*, 2006). Non-physical aggression is psychologically damaging and it is directed towards damaging self-esteem and social status. Cyber-bullying can be so devastating for victims precisely because it inflicts psychological harm.

17.5 GENDER ROLES IN THE FAMILY

The culture in which children are growing up has changed significantly in the last few decades. Notably, there have also been significant changes in family roles and working patterns. Many more women – including those with children – now work full or part time, and the number of 'stay at home dads' has tripled over a ten-year period to just under 3 per cent (Sinno & Killen, 2011). In the majority of cases, however, women still retain responsibility for childcare when children are young.

A recent study (Fulcher & Coyle, 2011) investigated the attitudes to family roles, and expectations of their own family roles, in children, 16–17-year-old adolescents and university students. The study was carried out in the United States where, as in many Western countries, the majority of women within a heterosexual household are employed but men still tend to have a greater responsibility for supporting the family financially while women tend to be more responsible for maintaining the home and looking after the children. The social-cognitive theory of gender development (Bussey & Bandura, 1999) argues that children look to adult models in the environment for information about gender appropriate behaviour (see 14.4). Fulcher and Coyle predicted that parents who modelled traditionally-gendered family roles of the male breadwinner and female caretaker, would impart these same values and expectations to their children while families with less gendered roles would impart different values and expectations. They were also interested in differences in the attitudes of males and females, predicting that males would report greater endorsement of traditional breadwinner-caregiver roles than girls.

As predicted, male adolescents and university students more strongly endorsed the traditional family roles than females of this age but this gender difference was not evident among the middle childhood group. Male participants across the age range were also more likely than females to assume that they would be working even if they had young children. There was also a clear gender difference in the way that children and young people reflected the values of their own family. Mothers' working patterns predicted their daughters' plans to work or stay at home with young children. Where mothers had a non-traditional work pattern their daughters' plans were also likely to be similarly non-traditional, whereas mothers with a more traditional work pattern were likely to have daughters who envisaged a similar working pattern for themselves. For sons, however, there was no clear relationship between their expectations and the working pattern in the family and, in general, males saw their future role as providing financially for their family rather than staying at home to look after children.

A somewhat similar picture emerged from another recent study, also carried out in the United States (Sinno & Killen, 2011). This study also focused on attitudes to the caretaking roles, this time using scenarios in which either working mothers or fathers took responsibility for looking after children outside of day care – so-called, 'second-shift parenting'. Children (aged 10 years) and young adolescents (aged 13 years) were asked their opinion about a hypothetical family in which either the mother or father was a second-shift parent. The second-shift father scenario was as follows:

> In the Smith family, there is a mother, a father, and their seven-year-old child. Both Mr and Mrs Smith work full time at a computer company. Mr Smith takes care of making dinner for the family, picking the child up from school and getting their child ready for bed. On Saturdays, Mrs Smith takes their child to the park.

According to the social-cognitive theory of gender development children look to adult models in the environment for information about gender-appropriate behaviour.

The roles of the two parents were reversed in the second-shift mother scenario. All children were presented with both scenarios in a counterbalanced design.

Participants were asked what they thought of the family arrangement, how good it was for the parents and the child, and to choose from among a set of statements as justifications for their view. They were also asked about the working patterns of their own parents.

Overall there were no differences in judgements about the suitability of a mother or father in the second-shift parenting role, for the family as a whole, but there were differences in the chosen justifications. Participants chose a social-conventional justification more often in relation to mothers than fathers. Socio-conventional justification included such items as, 'It works well for the family' and 'Parents decided together that this was the best arrangement for the family'. Judgements about the father in a second-shift parenting role focused more on unfairness with a view that it was generally 'unfair' for fathers to take on extra caretaking duties.

There was a difference in the responses of the two groups of children. Ten-year-olds were more likely to focus on fairness while 13-year-olds were more likely to focus on social-conventional justifications, especially in relation to mothers. Judgements were also affected by the working patterns of the participants' own parents. Those with parents who both worked full-time or with a mother who worked more than a father were more likely to appeal to issues of fairness whereas participants from families where only the father worked full time were more likely to select social-conventional justifications.

Judgements about how good the arrangements would be for the child in the hypothetical family tended to favour the mother as second-shift parent but female participants were generally more negative than males about second-shift parenting by either parent. Some participants used gender stereotypes to argue in favour of the mother as the second-shift parent, reflecting a view that mothers are more nurturing and are better at taking care of children. The greater use of social-conventional justifications among adolescents, especially in relation to mothers, can be seen as reflecting an increasing awareness of and reliance on gender norms at the point when adolescents are developing their own identity.

Children's experiences within their own families have a strong effect on their own expectations about family roles.

17.6 SUMMARY

As we saw in Chapter 14, views about the development of moral reasoning have developed very considerably since the pioneering theories of Piaget and Kohlberg. In this chapter we saw that reasoning about such topics as human rights is strongly affected by being a member of a particular religious or ethnic group. This suggests that the development of moral reasoning has to be seen within a particular socio-cultural context rather then being seen as universal. Moral concerns also need to be seen as slightly different for males and females.

Differences in friendship patterns of males and females become more marked in adolescence but, for both genders, romantic relationships tend to become increasingly important and time spent with peers and romantic partners increases as adolescents establish their increasing independence from their families. Relationships within the family do, however, continue to have a major effect on the quality of adolescents' relationships outside the family and the long-term consequences of the quality of early attachment are evident.

Differences in the pattern of male–male and female–female relationships become more marked in adolescence. Females tend to experience higher levels of social support from female friends and to have high levels of self-disclosure with these friends. Males tend to have more of a focus on doing things with their friends, notably sports and competitive games.

Physical aggression typically decreases in adolescence but, among a small sector of the population, serious violent behaviour increases. Where they occur, patterns of violent offending most commonly begin in adolescence and are considerably more common in males than females. However perpetrators of cyber-bullying, which is relatively common in adolescence, are just as likely to be female.

Adolescents' experiences of family roles within their own families have a strong effect on their own expectations about family roles. Mothers' working patterns tend to predict their daughters' plan to go out to work or stay at home when they have children.

FURTHER READING

Broidy, L. M., Nagin, D. S., Tremblay, R. E., Brame, B., Dodge, K. A., Fergusson, D., . . . Laird, R. (2003). Developmental trajectories of childhood disruptive behaviors and adolescent delinquency. *Developmental Psychology, 39*(2), 222–245.

Fulcher, M., & Coyle, E. F. (2011). Breadwinner and caregiver: A cross-sectional analysis of children's and emerging adults' visions of their future family roles. *British Journal of Developmental Psychology, 29*(2), 330–346.

Verkuyten, M., & Slooter, L. (2008). Muslim and non-Muslim adolescents' reasoning about freedom of speech and minority rights. *Child Development, 79*(3), 514–528.

Waters, E., Merrick, S., Trebous, D., Crowell, J., & Albaersheim, L. (2000). Attachment security in infancy and early adulthood: A twenty-year longitudinal study. *Child Development, 71*(3), 684–689.

ESSAY QUESTIONS

1. Give examples of ways in which the moral reasoning of adolescents is influenced by socio-cultural context.
2. Discuss the role of family and friends in providing social support during adolescence.
3. To what extent do the friendship patterns of male and female adolescents differ?
4. Discuss the potential effects of cyber-bullying and explain why some adolescents are more vulnerable to its effects than others.

References

Ahrens, R. (1954). Beitrage zur Entwicklung des Physiognomie – und Mimerkennes. *Zeitschrift für Experimentelle und Angewandte Psychologie, 2*, 599–633.

Ainsworth, M. D. S. (1969). Object relations, dependency, and attachment: A theoretical review. *Child Development, 40*, 969–1025.

Ainsworth, M. D. S., & Bell, S. (1970). Attachment, exploration and separation: Illustrated by the behaviour of one-year-olds in a strange situation. *Child Development, 41*, 49–67.

Ainsworth, M. D. S., & Marvin, R. S. (1994). On the shaping of attachment theory and research: An interview with Mary D. S. Ainsworth. *Monographs of the Society for Research in Child Development, 60*(2/3), 3–21.

Ainsworth, M. D. S., & Wittig, B. A. (1969). Attachment and exploratory behavior of one-year-olds in a strange situation. In B. M. Foss (Ed.), *Determinants of infant behaviour* (Vol. IV). London: Methuen.

Alexander, A. L., Lee, J. E., Lazar, M., Boudos, R., DuBray, M. B., Oakes, T. R., . . . Lainhart, J. E. (2007). Diffusion tensor imaging of the corpus callosum in autism. *Neuroimage, 34*(1), 61–73.

Amiel-Tison, C., & Grenier, A. (1985). *La surveillance neurologique au cours de la premiere annee de la vie*. Paris: Masson.

Andrews, B., Brown, G. W., & Creasey, L. (1990). Intergenerational links between psychiatric disorder in mothers and daughters: The role of parenting experiences. *Journal of Child Psychology & Psychiatry & Allied Disciplines, 31*, 1115–1129.

Arnett, J. J. (1999). Adolescent storm and stress, reconsidered. *American Psychologist, 54*, 317–326.

Baddeley, A. D. (2000). The episodic buffer: A new component of working memory. *Trends in Cognitive Science, 4*(11), 417–423.

Baddeley, A. D., & Hitch, G. J. (1974). Working memory. In G. A. Bower (Ed.), *The psychology of learning and motivation, Vol. 8* (pp. 47–89). New York: Academic Press.

Baillargeon, R. (1987). Object permanence in three and a half- and four and a half-month-old infants. *Developmental Psychology, 23*, 655–664.

Baillargeon, R., Spelke, E. S., & Wasserman, S. (1985). Object permanence in five-month-old infants. *Cognition, 20*(3), 191–208.

Baines, E., & Blatchford, P. (2009). Sex differences in the structure and stability of children's playground social networks and their overlap with friendship relations. *British Journal of Developmental Psychology, 27*, 743–760.

Bakeman, R., & Adamson, L. B. (1984). Coordinating attention to people and objects in mother–infant and peer–infant interaction. *Child Development, 55*(4), 1278–1289.

Baldwin, D. A., & Markman, E. M. (1989). Establishing word–object relations: A first step. *Child Development, 60*, 381–398.

Barnett, A. L. (2008). Motor assessment in developmental coordination disorder: From identification to intervention. *International Journal of Disability, Development & Education, 55*(2), 113–129.

Baron-Cohen, S. (1989). The autistic child's theory of mind: A case of specific developmental delay. *Journal of Child Psychology and Psychiatry, 30*(2), 285–297.

Baron-Cohen, S., Allen, J., & Gillberg, C. (1992). Can autism be detected at 18 months? The needle, the haystack, and the CHAT. *The British Journal of Psychiatry, 161*(6), 839–843.

Baron-Cohen, S., Leslie, A. M., & Frith, U. (1985). Does the autistic child have a theory of mind? *Cognition, 21*, 37–46.

Barry, C. (1994). Spelling routes (or Roots or Rutes). In G. D. A. Brown & N. C. Ellis (Eds), *Handbook of spelling* (pp. 27–50). Chichester: Wiley.

Bates, E. & MacWhinney, B. (1989). Functionalism and the competition model. In B. MacWhinney & E. Bates (Eds.) *The cross-linguistic study of sentence processing* (pp. 3–73). Cambridge: Cambridge University Press.

Beauchamp, G. K., Cowart, B. J., Mennella, J. A., & Marsh, R. R. (1994). Infant salt taste: Developmental, methodological, and contextual factors. *Developmental Psychobiology, 27*(6), 353–365.

Belsky, J. (2001). Emanuel Miller Lecture: Developmental risks (still) associated with early child care. *Journal of Child Psychology and Psychiatry, 42*(7), 845–859.

Benenson, J. F., & Schinazi, J. (2004). Sex differences in reactions to outperforming same-sex friends. *British Journal of Developmental Psychology, 22*, 317–333.

Bennett, M., & Sani, F. (2008). Children's subjective identification with social categories: A self-stereotyping approach. *Developmental Science, 11*, 69–65.

Berko, J. (1958). The child's learning of English morphology. *Word*, 14, 150–177.

Berninger, V., Vaughan, K., Abbott, R., Begay, K., Byrd, K., Curtin, G., . . . Graham, S. (2002). Teaching spelling and composition alone and together: Implications for the simple view of writing. *Journal of Educational Psychology, 94*, 291–304.

Bertenthal, B. I., & Fischer, K. W. (1978). Development of self-recognition in the infant. *Developmental Psychology, 14*, 44–50.

Best, C. T., McRoberts, G. W., & Sithole, N. M. (1988). Examination of perceptual reorganization for nonnative speech contrasts: Zulu click discrimination by English-speaking adults and infants. *Journal of Experimental Psychology: Human Perception & Performance, 14*, 345–360.

Bigelow, B. J. (1977). Children's friendship expectations: A cognitive-developmental study. *Child Development, 48*(1), 246–253.

Birch, S. A. J., & Bloom, P. (2004). Understanding children's and adults' limitations in mental state reasoning. *Trends in Cognitive Sciences, 8*(6), 255–260.

Birnholtz, J. C., & Benacerraf, B. R. (1983). The development of human fetal hearing. *Science, 222*, 516–518.

Bishop, D. V. M., & Adams, C. (1990). A prospective study of the relationship between specific language impairment, phonological disorders and reading retardation. *Journal of Child Psychology and Psychiatry, 31*, 1027–1050.

Bishop, D. V. M., & Edmundson, A. (1987). Language-impaired 4-year-olds: Distinguishing transient from persistent symptoms. *Journal of Speech and Hearing Disorders, 52*, 156–173.

Blasi, A., Mercure, E., Lloyd-Fox, S., Thomson, A., Brammer, M., Sauter, D., . . . Murphy, D. G. M. (2011). Early specialization for voice and emotion processing in the infant brain. *Current Biology: CB, 21*(14), 1220–1224.

Bogartz, R. S., Shinskey, J. L., & Schilling, T. H. (2000). Object permanence in five-and-a-half-month-old infants? *Infancy, 1*(4), 403–428.

Botting, N. (2005). Non-verbal cognitive development and language impairment. *Journal of Child Psychology and Psychiatry* (46), 317–326.

Bowlby, J. (1958). The nature of the child's tie to his mother. *International Journal of Psychoanalysis.* XLI, 1–25.

Bowlby, J. (1969). *Attachment and loss* (Vol. 1). Harmondsworth: Pelican Books.

Bradley, L., & Bryant, P. E. (1983). Categorising sounds and learning to read: A causal connection. *Nature, 301*, 419–521.

Braine, M. (1976). Children's first word combinations. *Monographs of the Society for Research in Child Development, 41*(1), 1–104.

Bremner, J. G. (1988). *Infancy*. Oxford: Blackwell.

Bremner, J. G., & Knowles, L. S. (1984). Piagetian stage IV search errors with an object that is directly accessible both visually and manually. *Perception, 13*(3), 307–314.

Broidy, L. M., Nagin, D. S., Tremblay, R. E., Brame, B., Dodge, K. A., Fergusson, D., . . . Laird, R. (2003). Developmental trajectories of childhood disruptive behaviors and adolescent delinquency. *Developmental Psychology, 39*(2), 222–245.

Brown, A. L., Kane, M. J., & Long, C. (1989). Analogical transfer in young children: Analogies as tools for communication and exposition. *Applied Cognitive Psychology, 3*(4), 275–293.

Brown, G., & Harris, T. (1980). *The social origins of depression*. London: Tavistock.

Brown, J. S., & Burton, R. R. (1978). Diagnostic models for procedural bugs in basic mathematical skills. *Cognitive Science, 2*, 155–192.

Brown, K. & Hanlon, C. (1970). Derivational complexity and order of acquisition in child speech. In J. Hayes (Ed.), *Cognition and the development of language*. New York: Wiley.

Brown, L., & Gilligan, C. (1992). *Meeting at the crossroads: Women's psychology and girls' development*. Cambridge, MA: Harvard University Press.

Bruner, J. S. (1975). The ontogenesis of speech acts. *Journal of Child Language, 2*(1), 1–19.

Bruner, J. S. (1983). The acquisition of pragmatic commitments In R. M. Golinkoff (Ed.), *The transition from prelinguistic to linguistic communication* (pp. 27–42). Hillsdale, NJ: Erlbaum.

Bryant, P. E., & Nunes, T. (2011). Children's understanding of mathematics. In U. Goswami (Ed.), *Childhood cognitive development, 2nd edition* (pp. 549–573). Chichester: Wiley-Blackwell.

Bryant, P. E., & Trabasso, T. (1971). Transitive inferences and memory in young children. *Nature, 232*, 456–458.

Buhrmester, D. (1996). Need fulfilment, interpersonal competence, and the developmental contexts of early adolescent friendship. In W. M. Bukowski, A. F. Newcomb & W. W. Hartup (Eds), *The company they keep: Friendship in childhood and adolescence*. Cambridge: Cambridge University Press.

Bullock, M., & Lütkenhaus, P. (1988). The development of volitional behavior in the toddler years. *Child Development, 59*, 664–674.

Burnham, D., & Mattock, K. (2010). Auditory development. In J. G. Bremner & T. D. Wachs (Eds), *The Wiley-Blackwell handbook of infant development* (Vol. 1, pp. 81–119). Chichester: Wiley-Blackwell.

Bushnell, I. W. R. (2003). Newborn face recognition. In O. Pascalis & A. Slater (Eds), *The development of face processing in infancy and early childhood* (pp. 41–53). New York: Nova Science Publishers.

Bussey, K., & Bandura, A. (1999). Social cognitive theory of gender development and differentiation. *Psychological Review, 106*(4), 676–713.

Butler, S. C., Berthier, N. E., & Clifton, R. K. (2002). Two-year-olds' search strategies and visual tracking in a hidden displacement task. *Developmental Psychology, 38*(4), 581–590.

Butterworth, B., Varma, S., & Laurillard, D. (2011). Dyscalculia: From brain to education. *Science, 332*, 1049–1053.

Butterworth, G. E. (2001). Joint visual attention in infancy. In G. Bremner & A. Fogel (Eds), *Blackwell handbook of infant development* (pp. 213–240). Malden, MA: Blackwell.

Butterworth, G. E., & Itakura, S. (1998). Development of precision grips in chimpanzees. *Developmental Science, 11*(1), 39–44.

Calkins, S. D. (2002). Does aversive behaviour during toddlerhood matter? The effects of difficult temperament on maternal perceptions and behavior. *Infant Mental Health Journal, 23*(4), 381–402.

Cameron, J. L. (2004). Interrelationships between hormones, behavior, and affect during adolescence: Understanding hormonal, physical, and brain changes occurring in association with pubertal activation of the reproductive axis. *Annals of the New York Academy of Sciences: Adolescent Brain Development: Vulnerabilities and Opportunities, 1021*(June), 110–123.

Campos, J. J., Bertenthal, B. I., & Kermoian, R. (1981). Early experience and emotional development: The emergence of wariness of heights. *Psychological Science, 3*, 61–64.

Campos, J. J., & Stenberg, C. R. (1981). Perception, appraisal and emotion: The onset of social referencing. In M. E. Lamb & L. R. Sherrod (Eds), *Infant social cognition: Empirical and theoretical considerations* (pp. 274–313). Hillsdale, NJ: Erlbaum.

Camras, L. A., & Sachs, V. B. (1991). Social referencing and caretaker expressive behavior in a day care setting. *Infant Behavior & Development, 14*(1), 27–36.

Caravolas, M., Volín, J., & Hulme, C. (2005). Phoneme awareness is a key component of alphabetic literacy skills in consistent and inconsistent orthographies: Evidence from Czech and English children. *Journal of Experimental Child Psychology, 92*(2), 107–139.

Carbery, J., & Buhrmester, D. (1998). Friendship and need fulfillment during three phases of young adulthood. *Journal of Social and Personal Relationships, 15*(3), 393–409.

Carey, N. (2012). *The epigenetics revolution: How modern biology is rewriting our understanding of genetics, disease, and inheritance.* New York: Columbia University Press.

Carpenter, M. (2006). Instrumental, social, and shared goals and intentions in imitation. In S. J. Rogers & J. H. G. Williams (Eds), *Imitation and the social mind: Autism and typical development* (pp. 48–70). New York: Guilford.

Catherine, A. (1994). Quantitative morphology of the corpus callosum in attention deficit hyperactivity disorder. *American Journal of Psychiatry, 151*(5), 665–669.

Chase, M. A., & Dummer, G. M. (1992). The role of sports as a social status determinant for children. *Research Quarterly for Exercise and Sport, 63*(4), 418–424.

Chliounaki, K., & Bryant, P. E. (2002). Construction and learning to spell. *Cognitive Development, 17*, 1489–1499.

Chomsky, N. (1965). *Aspects of the theory of syntax.* Cambridge, MA: MIT Press.

Chomsky, N. (1986). *Knowledge of language: Its nature, origins and use.* Westport, CT: Praeger.

Christophe, A., & Morton, J. (1998). Is Dutch native English? Linguistic analysis by 2-month-olds. *Developmental Science, 1*, 215–219.

Clark, E. (1995). *The Lexicon in acquisition.* Cambridge: Cambridge University Press.

Clearfield, M. W., & Mix, K. S. (2001). Amount versus number: Infants' use of area and contour length to discriminate small sets. *Journal of Cognition and Development, 2*(3), 243–260.

Cohen, L. B. (2001) An Information-Processing Approach to Infant Perception and Cognition. In T. Simone & G. Butterworth (Eds.), *Development of sensory, motor, and cognitive capacities in early infancy* (pp. 277–300). Hove: Elsevier.

Cole, M., & Cole, S. R. (1993). *The development of children (2nd edition).* New York: Freeman.

Cole, P. (1986). Children's spontaneous control of facial expressions. *Child Development, 57*, 1309–1321.

Connelly, V., Dockrell, J. E., & Barnett, J. (2005). The slow handwriting of undergraduate students constrains overall performance in exam essays. *Educational Psychology, 25*(1), 97–105.

Connelly, V., Johnston, R., & Thompson, G. B. (2001). The effect of phonics instruction on the reading comprehension of beginning readers. *Reading and Writing, 14*(5–6), 423–457.

Cornish, K., & Wilding, J. (2010). *Attention, genes, and developmental disorders.* New York: Oxford University Press.

Corriveau, K., Fusaro, M., & Harris, P. L. (2009). Going with the flow: Preschoolers prefer nondissenters as informants. *Psychological Science, 20*(3), 372–377.

Corriveau, K., & Harris, P. L. (2009). Choosing your informant: weighing familiarity and recent accuracy. *Developmental Science, 12*(3), 426–437.

Cossu, G. (1999). The acquisition of Italian orthography. In M. Harris & G. Hatano (Eds), *Learning to read and write: A cross-linguistic perspective* (pp. 10–33). Cambridge: Cambridge University Press.

Crain, W. (2005). *Theories of development: Concepts and applications* (5th ed.). London: Pearson Education.

Crijnen, A. A., Achenbach, T. M., & Verhulst, F. C. (1997). Comparisons of problems reported by parents of children in 12 countires: Total problems, externalizing and internalizing. *Journal of the American Academy of Child and Adolescent Psychiatry, 36*, 1269–1277.

Crook, C. K. (1978). Taste perception in the newborn infant. *Infant Behavior and Development, 1*, 52–69.

Cunningham, A. E., & Stanovich, K. E. (1997). Early reading acquisition and its relation to reading experience and ability 10 years later. *Developmental Psychology, 33*(6), 934–945.

Dahl, R. E. (2004). Adolescent brain development: A period of vulnerabilities and opportunities. *Annals of the New York Academy of Sciences, 1021*(1), 1–22.

Damon, W. (1977). *The social world of the child*. San Francisco: Jossey-Bass.

Damon, W. (1980). Patterns of change in children's social reasoning: A two-year longitudinal study. *Child Development, 51*, 1010–1017.

Dasen, P. (1972). Cross-cultural Piagetian research: A summary. *Journal of Cross Cultural Psychology, 3*, 29–39.

Davis, B. E., Moon, R. Y., Sachs, H. C., & Ottolini, M. C. (1998). Effects of sleep position on infant motor development. *Paediatrics, 102*(5), 1135–1140.

Davis, T. (1995). Gender differences in masking negative emotions: Ability or motivation? *Developmental Psychology, 31*, 660–667.

de Wolff, M. S., & van Ijzendoorn, M. H. (1997). Sensitivity and attachment: A meta-analysis on parental antecedents of infant attachment. *Child Development, 68*, 571–591.

DeCasper, A. J., & Fifer, W. (1980). Of human bonding: Newborns prefer their mothers' voices. *Science, 208*, 1174–1176.

DeCasper, A. J., Lecanuet, J.-P., Busnel, M.-C., Granier-Deferre, C., & Maugeais, R. (1994). Fetal reactions to recurrent maternal speech. *Infant Behavior and Development, 17*, 159–164.

DeCasper, A. J., & Spence, M. J. (1986). Prenatal maternal speech influences newborns' perception of speech sounds. *Infant Behavior and Development, 9*, 133–150.

DeLoache, J. S., Miller, K. F., & Pierroutsakos, S. L. (1998). Reasoning and problem solving. In D. Kuhn & R. S. Siegler (Eds), *Handbook of child psychology: Cognition, perception, and language* (pp. 801–850). Hoboken, NJ: Wiley.

Dennis, W., & Dennis, M. G. (1940). The effect of cradling practice upon the onset of walking in Hopi Indians. *Journal of Genetic Psychology, 56*, 77–86.

Dennis, W., & Najarian, P. (1957). Infant development under environmental handicap. *Psychological Monographs, 7*, 1–7.

deRegnier, R.-A., & Desai, S. (2010). Fetal development. In J. G. Bremner & T. D. Wachs (Eds), *The Wiley-Blackwell handbook of infant development* (Vol. 2, pp. 9–32). Chicester: Wiley-Blackwell.

Diamond, A. (1988). Abilities and neural mechanisms underlying AB performance. *Child Development, 59*, 523–527.

Dockrell, J. E., & McShane, J. (1992). *Children's learning difficulties: A cognitive approach*. Oxford: Blackwell.

Dodge, K. A., Coie, J. D., & Lynam, D. (2006). Aggression and antisocial behavior in youth In N. Eisenberg (Ed.), *Handbook of child psychology Vol. 3: Social, emotional, and personality development* (pp. 779–862). New York: Wiley.

Donaldson, M. C. (1978). *Children's minds*. London: Croom Helm.

Dunn, J., Cutting, A., & Fischer, N. (2002). Old friends, new friends: Predictors of children's perspectives on their friends at school. *Child Development, 73*(2), 621–635.

Dunn, J., & Kendrick, D. (1982). *Siblings: Love, envy, and understanding*. Cambridge, MA: Harvard University Press.

Ehri, L. C., & Robbins, C. (1992). Beginners need some decoding skills to read words by analogy. *Reading Research Quarterly, 27*(1), 12–26.

Eimas, P., & Quinn, P. (1994). Studies on the formation of perceptually based basic-level categories in young infants. *Child Development, 65*, 903–917.

Eimas, P. D., Siqueland, E., Jusczyk, P. W., & Vogorito, J. (1971). Speech perception in infants. *Science, 171*, 303–306.

Einav, S., & Robinson, E. J. (2012). When being right is not enough: Four-year-olds distinguish knowledgeable informants from merely accurate informants. *Psychological Science, 22*(10), 1250–1253.

Eisenberg, N., Fabes, R. A., & Spinrad, T. L. (2006). Prosocial development. In N. Eisenberg (Ed.), *Handbook of child development* (pp. 646–718). Hoboken, NJ: Wiley.

Eisenberg, N., Miller, P. A., Shell, R., McNalley, S., & Shea, C. (1991). Prosocial development in adolescence: A longitudinal study. *Developmental Psychology, 27*(5), 849–857.

Elliott, C. D., Smith, P., & McCulloch, K. (1996). *British Ability Scales II (BASII)*. Windsor: NFER-Nelson.

Elliott, D. S. (1994). Serious violent offenders: Onset, developmental course and termination: The American Society of Criminology 1993 Presidential Address. *Criminology, 32*, 1–21.

Ellis, R., & Wells, G. (1980). Enabling factors in adult–child discourse. *First Language, 1*, 46–62.

Ellis, S. (1997). Strategy choice in sociocultural context. *Developmental Review, 17*(4), 490–524.

Ellman, J. L., Bates, E. A., Johnson, M. H., Kamiloff-Smith, A., Parisi D., & Plunkett, K. (1996). *Rethinking innateness. A connectionist perspective on development.* Cambridge, MA: MIT Press.

Erel, O., & Burman, B. (1995). Interrelatedness of marital relations and parent–child relations: A meta-analytic review. *Psychological Bulletin, 118*(1), 108–132.

Evans, A. C. (2006). The NIH MRI study of normal brain development. *NeuroImage, 30*(1), 184–202.

Fabricus, W. (1988). The development of forward search planning in preschoolers. *Child Development, 59*(6), 1473–1488.

Falck-Ytter, T., Gredebäck, G., & Von Hofsten, C. (2006). Infants predict other people's action goals. *Nature Neuroscience, 9*(7), 878–879.

Fantz, R. L. (1965). Visual perception from birth as shown by pattern selectivity. *Annals of the New York Academy of Sciences, 118*, 793–814.

Feigenson, L., Carey, S., & Spelke, E. (2002). Infants' discrimination of number vs. continuous extent. *Cognitive Psychology, 44*(1), 33–66.

Fenson, L., Dale, P., Resnick, S., Bates, E., Thal, D., & Pethick, S. J. (1994). Variability in early communicative development. *Monographs of the Society for Research in Child Development, 59*(5), 1–73.

Fenson, L., Dale, P., Resnick, S., Bates, E., Thal, D., Reilly, J., & Hartung, J. (1990). *MacArthur communicative development inventories: Technical manual.* San Diego: San Diego State University.

Field, T. M., Hernandez-Rief, M., Diego, M., Figueiredo, B., Schanberg, S., & Kuhn, C. (2006). Prenatal cortisol, prematurity and low birthweight. *Infant Behavior and Development, 29*, 268–275.

Field, T. M., Woodson, R. W., Greenberg, R., & Cohen, C. (1982). Discrimination and imitation of facial expressions by neonates. *Science, 218*, 179–181.

Fisher, S. E. (2006). Tangled webs: Tracing the connections between genes and cognition. *Cognition, 101*(2), 270–297.

Flavell, J. H., Beech, D. R., & Chinsky, J. M. (1966). Spontaneous verbal rehearsal in a momery task as a function of age. *Child Development, 37*, 283–299.

Flavell, J. H., Miller, P. H., & Miller, S. A. (1993). *Cognitive development.* New Jersey: Prentice Hall.

Fogel, A. (1993). *Developing through relationships: Origins of communication, self and culture.* Hemel Hempstead: Harvester Press.

Fox, S. E., Levitt, P., & Nelson, C. A. (2010). How the timing and quality of early experiences influence the development of brain architecture. *Child Development, 81*, 28–40.

Fraiberg, S. (1974). *Insights from the blind.* New York: Basic Books.

Freeman, N. (1980). *Strategies of representation in young children: Analysis of spatial skills and drawing processes.* London: Academic Press.

Freeman, N. (1987). Current problems in the development of representational picture-production. *Archives de Psychologie, 55*, 127–152.

Freese, J., & Powell, B. (2003). Tilting at windmills: Rethinking sociological responses to behavioral genetics. *Journal of Health and Social Behavior*, 130–135.

Freud, S. (1927). Some psychological consequences of the anatomical distinctions beween the sexes. *International Journal of Psychoanalysis, 8*, 133–142.

Frith, U. (1985). Beneath the surface of surface dyslexia. In K. E. Patterson, J. C. Marshall & M. Coltheart (Eds), *Surface dyslexia* (pp. 301–330). London: Erlbaum.

Fulcher, M., & Coyle, E. F. (2011). Breadwinner and caregiver: A cross-sectional analysis of children's and emerging adults' visions of their future family roles. *British Journal of Developmental Psychology, 29*(2), 330–346.

Fulkerson, A. L., & Waxman, S. R. (2007). Words (but not tones) facilitate object categorization: Evidence from 6- and 12-month-olds. *Cognition, 105*(1), 218–228.

Furman, W., & Buhrmester, D. (1992). Age and sex differences in perceptions of networks of personal relationships. *Child Development, 63*, 103–115.

Gallistel, R., & Gelman, R. (1991). Preverbal and verbal counting and computation. In S. Dehaene (Ed.), *Numerical cognition.* Oxford: Blackwell.

Galton, F. (1869). *Hereditary genius.* London: Macmillan.

Gathercole, S. E. (2006). Nonword repetition and word learning: The nature of the relationship. *Applied Psycholinguistics, 27*, 513–543.

Gathercole, S. E., Willis, C. S., Baddeley, A. D., & Emslie, H. (1994). The children's test of nonword repetition: A test of phonological working memory. *Memory, 2*, 103–127.

Gauvain, M. (1995). Thinking in niches: Sociocultural influences on development. *Human Development, 38*, 25–45.

Gelman, R., & Gallistel, C. R. (1978). *The child's understanding of number.* Cambridge, MA: Harvard University Press.

Gelman, S. A., & Coley, J. D. (1990). The importance of knowing a dodo is a bird: Categories and inferences in 2-year-old children. *Developmental Psychology, 26*(5), 796–804.

Gentry, J. R. (1982). An analysis of developmental spelling in 'GNYS AT WRK'. *The Reading Teacher, 36*(2), 192–200.

George, C., Kaplan, N., & Main, M. (1985). *The adult attachment interview.* Berkeley: University of California.

Gervain, J., Mehler, J., Werker, J. F., Nelson, C. A., Csibra, G., Lloyd-Fox, S., . . . Aslin, R. N. (2011). Near-infrared spectroscopy: A report from the McDonnell infant methodology consortium. *Accident Analysis and Prevention, 1*(1), 22–46.

Gibson, E. J. (1988). Exploratory behavior in the development of perceiving, acting, and the acquiring of knowledge. *Annual Review of Psychology, 39*, 1–41.

Giedd, J. N. (2004). Structural magnetic resonance imaging of the adolescent brain. *Annals of the New York Academy of Sciences, 1021*(1), 77–85.

Gilligan, C. (1982). *In a different voice.* Cambridge, MA: Harvard University Press.

Gopnik, A., & Choi, S. (1995). Names, relational words and cognitive development in English and Korean speakers: Nouns are not always learned before verbs. In M. Tomasello & W. E. Merriman (Eds), *Beyond names for things: Young children's acquisition of verbs* (pp. 83–90). Hillsdale, NJ: Erlbaum.

Goswami, U. (2008). *Cognitive development: The learning brain.* Hove: Psychology Press.

Goswami, U. (2011). Inductive and deductive reasoning. In U. Goswami (Ed.), *Childhood cognitive development, 2nd edition* (pp. 399–419). Chichester: Wiley-Blackwell.

Goswami, U., & Brown, A. L. (1990). Melting chocolate and melting snowmen: Analogical reasoning and causal relations. *Cognition, 35*(1), 69–95.

Gottlieb, G. (1998). Normally occurring environmental and behavioral influences on gene activity: From central dogma to probabilistic epigenesis. *Psychological Review, 105*(4), 792–802.

Gough, P. B., Hoover, W. A., & Peterson, C. L. (1996). Some observations on a simple view of reading. In C. Cornoldi & J. Oakhill (Eds), *Reading comprehension difficulties: Processes and interventions* (pp. 1–13). Mahwah, NJ: Erlbaum.

Groen, G. J., & Parkman, J. M. (1972). A chronometric analysis of simple addition. *Psychological Review, 79*, 329–343.

Grolnick, W. S., Gurland, S. T., Jacob, K. F., & Decourcey, W. (2002). The development of self-determination in middle childhood and adolsecence. In A. Wigfield & J. S. Eccles (Eds), *Development of achievement motivation* (pp. 147–171). San Diego, CA: Academic Press.

Grossman, K., Grossman, K.E., Spangler, G., Suess, G. & Unzner, L. (1985). Maternal sensitivity and newborns' orientation responses as related to quality of attachment in Northern Germany. *Monographs of the Society for Research in Child Development, 50*(1/2), 233–256.

Haith, M. M. (1998). Who put the cog in infant cognition? Is rich interpretation too costly? *Infant Behavior and Development, 21*(2), 167–179.

Halit, H., de Haan, M., & Johnson, M. H. (2003). Cortical specialisation for face processing: Face-sensitive event-related potential components in 3- and 12-month-old infants. *NeuroImage, 19*(3), 1180–1193.

Hall, G. S. (1904). *Adolescence: Its psychology and its relations to physiology, anthropology, sociology, sex, crime, religion and education, Vol. 2.* New York: Appleton.

Happé, F. G. (1993). Communicative competence and theory of mind in autism: A test of relevance theory. *Cognition, 48*(2), 101–119.

Harlow, H., McGaugh, J. L., & Thompson, R. F. (1971). *Psychology.* San Francisco: Albion Publication Co.

Harris, M. (1992). *Language experience and early language development: From input to uptake.* Hove: Lawrence Erlbaum Associates.

Harris, M. (1996). *Language development (An Open University Study Guide).* Milton Keynes: Open University Press.

Harris, M., & Giannouli, V. (1999). Learning to read and spell Greek: The importance of letter knowledge and morphological awareness. In M. Harris & G. Hatano (Eds), *Learning to read and write: A cross-linguistic perspective* (pp. 51–70). Cambridge: Cambridge University Press.

Harris, M., Barlow-Brown, F., & Chasin, J. (1995). The emergence of referential understanding: pointing and the comprehension of object names. *First Language, 15*, 19–34.

Harris, M., Barrett, M., Jones, D., & Brookes, S. (1988). Linguistic input and early word meaning. *Journal of Child Language, 15*, 77–94.

Harris, M., Jones, D., Brookes, S., & Grant, J. (1986). Relations between the non-verbal context of maternal speech and rate of language development. *British Journal of Developmental Psychology, 4*, 261–268.

Harris, M., Yeeles, C., Chasin, J., & Oakley, Y. (1995). Symmetries and asymmetries in early lexical comprehension and production. *Journal of Child Language, 22*, 1–18.

Harris, P. L. (1989). *Children and emotion.* Oxford: Blackwell.

Harris, P. L. (2000). *The work of the imagination.* Oxford: Blackwell.

Harris, P. L. (2006). Social cognition. In D. Kuhn & R. S. Siegler (Eds), *Handbook of child development* (Vol. 2) (pp. 811–858). Hoboken, NJ: Wiley.

Harris, P. L., Brown, E., & Marriott, C. (1991). Monsters, ghosts and witches: Testing the limits of the fantasy-reality distinction in young children. *British Journal of Developmental Psychology, 9*, 105–123.

Harrison, L., & Ungerer, J. A. (2002). Maternal employment and infant–mother attachment security at 12 months postpartum. *Developmental Psychology, 38*(5), 758–773.

Hartup, W. W. (1998). The company they keep: Friendships and their developmental significance. In A. Campbell & S. Muncer (Eds), *The social child* (pp. 143–164). Hove: Psychology Press.

Hartup, W. W., & Laursen, B. (1992). Conflict and context in peer relations. In C. H. Hart (Ed.), *Children on playgrounds: Research perspectives and applications* (pp. 44–84). Albany, NY: State University of New York Press.

Hatano, G. (1990). Towards the cultural psychology of mathematical cognition. *Monographs of the Society for Research in Child Development, 55*(1–2), 108–115.

Hatcher, P. J., Hulme, C., & Snowling, M. J. (2004). Explicit phoneme training combined with phonic reading instruction helps young children at risk of reading failure. *Journal of Child Psychology & Psychiatry, 45*(2), 338–358.

Hay, D. F., Pedersen, J., & Nash, A. (1982). Dyadic interaction in the first year of life. In K. H. Rubin & H. S. Ross (Eds), *Peer relationships and social skills in childhood* (pp. 11–40). New York: Springer-Verlag

Hay, D. F., & Ross, H. S. (1982). The social nature of early conflict. *Child Development, 53*, 105–113.

Hayiou-Thomas, M. E., Bishop, D. V. M., & Plomin, R. (2005). Genetic influences on specific versus non-specific language impairment in 4-year-old twins. *Journal of Learning Disabilities, 38*, 222–232.

Heijmans, B. T., Tobi, E. W., Stein, A. D., Putter, H., Blauw, G. J., Susser, E. S., . . . Lumey, L. H. (2008). Persistent epigenetic differences associated with prenatal exposure to famine in humans. *Proceedings of the National Academy of Sciences of the United States of America, 105*(44), 17046–17049.

Helwig, C. C. (1995). Adolescents' and young adults' conceptions of civil liberties: Freedom of speech and religion. *Child Development 66*(1), 152–166.

Helwig, C. C., Arnold, M. L., Tan, D., & Boyd, D. (2003). Chinese adolescents' reasoning about democratic and authority-based decision making in peer, family, and school contexts. *Child Development, 74*(3), 783–800.

Henderson, S. A., Sugden, D., & Barnett, A. L. (2007). *The movement assessment battery for children: 2*. London: Harcourt Assessment.

Henry, L. (2012). *The development of working memory in children*. London: Sage.

Hepach, R., & Westermann, G. (2013). Infants' sensitivity to the congruence of others' emotions and actions. *Journal of Experimental Child Psychology 115*(1), 16–29.

Heyes, C. & Galef, B.G. (1996). *Social learning in animals*. US: Academic Press.

Hirsh-Pasek, K., & Golinkoff, R. M. (1996). *The origins of grammar*. Cambridge, MA: MIT Press.

Hitch, G., Halliday, M. S., & Littler, J. E. (1989). Item identification time and rehearsal rates as predictors of memeory span in children. *Quarterly Journal of Experimental Psychology, 41A*, 321–337.

Holmes, J. (1993). *John Bowlby and attachment theory*. London: Routledge.

Holyoak, K. J. K., Junn, E. N. E., & Billman, D. O. D. (1984). Development of analogical problem-solving skill. *Child Development, 55*, 2042–2055.

Hoover, W. A., & Gough, P. B. (1990). The simple view of reading. *Reading and Writing, 2*(2), 127–160.

Hornik, R., Risenhoover, N., & Gunnar, M. (1987). The effects of maternal positive, neutral, and negative affective communications on infants' responses to new toys. *Child Development, 58*, 937–944.

Horwitz, A. V., Videon, T. M., Schmitz, M. F., & Davis, D. (2003a). Double vision: reply to Freese and Powell. *Journal of Health and Social Behavior*, 136–141.

Horwitz, A. V., Videon, T. M., Schmitz, M. F., & Davis, D. (2003b). Rethinking twins and environments: Possible social sources for assumed genetic influences in twin research. *Journal of Health and Social Behavior*, 111–129.

Howe, N., & Ross, H. S. (1990). Socialization, perspective-taking, and the sibling relationship. *Developmental Psychology, 26*, 160–165.

Hsu, F.-H. (2002). *Behind deep blue: Building the computer that defeated the world chess champion*: New Jersey: Princeton University Press.

Hughes, M. & Donaldson, N. (1979). The use of hiding games for studying the coordination of viewpoints. *Educational Review*, 31(2), 133–140.

Hulme, C., & Snowling, M. J. (2009). *Developmental disorders of language learning and cogntion*. Chichester: Wiley-Blackwell.

Hulme, C., Thomson, N., Muir, C., & Lawrence, A. (1984). Speech rate and the development of short-term memory span. *Journal of Experimental Child Psychology, 38*, 241–253.

Hyams, N. (1986). *Language acquisition and the theory of parameters*. Dordrecht: Reidel.

Ifrah, G. (1985). *From one to zero: A universal history of numbers*. New York: Wiley.

Inagaki, K. (1990). The effects of raising animals on children's biological knowledge. *British Journal of Developmental Psychology, 8*(2), 119–129.

Inagaki, K., Morita, E., & Hatano, G. (1999). Teaching–learning of evaluative criteria for mathematical arguments through classroom discourse: A cross-national study. *Mathematical Thinking and Learning, 1*(2), 93–111.

Inhelder, B., & Piaget, J. (1958). *The growth of logical thinking from childhood to adolescence*. New York: Wiley.

Inhelder, B., & Piaget, J. (1964). *The early growth of logic in the child: Classification and seriation*. London: Routledge & Kegan Paul.

Isaacs, E. B., Edmonds, C. J., Lucas, A., & Gadian, D. G. (2001). Calculation difficulties in children of very low birthweight: A neural correlate. *Brain, 124*, 1701.

Ivry, R. (2013). Big data has left the station. *APS Observer, 26*. Retrieved from http://www.psychologicalscience.org/index.php/publications/observer/2013/january-13/big-data-has-left-the-station.html

James, W. (1890). *The principles of psychology*. New York: Dover.

Jansen, B. R. J., & van der Maas, H. L. J. (2002). The development of children's rule use on the balance scale task. *Journal of Experimental Child Psychology, 81*(4), 383–416.

Johnson, E. K., & Jusczyk, P. W. (2001). Word segmentation by 8-month-olds: When speech cues count for more than statistics. *Journal of Memory and Language, 44*, 548–567.

Johnson, M. H., & de Haan, M. (2011). *Developmental cognitive neuroscience* (3rd edition). Chichester: Wiley-Blackwell.

Johnson, M. H., & Morton, J. (1991). *Biology and cognitive development: The case of face recognition*. Oxford: Blackwell.

Joshi, M. S., & MacLean, M. (1994). Indian and English children's understanding of the distinction between real and apparent emotions. *Child Development, 65*, 1372–1384.

Jusczyk, P. W., & Aslin, R. N. (1995). Infants' detection of the sound patterns of words in fluent speech. *Cognitive Psychology, 29*, 1–23.

Jusczyk, P. W., Cutler, A., & Redanz, N. J. (1993). Infants' preference for the predominant stress patterns of English words. *Child Development, 64*, 675–687.

Kaitz, M., & Eidelman, A. I. (1992). Smell-recognition of newborns by women who are not mothers. *Chemical Senses, 17*(2), 225–229.

Karmiloff-Smith, A. (1979). *A functional approach to child language*: Cambridge: Cambridge University Press.

Karmiloff-Smith, A., Thomas, M., Annaz, D., Humphreys, K., Ewing, S., Brace, N., . . . Campbell, R. (2004). Exploring the Williams syndrome face-processing debate: The importance of building developmental trajectories. *Journal of Child Psychology and Psychiatry, 45*(7), 1258–1274.

Karp, R. J. (2010). Health. In J. G. Bremner & T. D. Wachs (Eds), *The Wiley-Blackwell handbook of infant development* (Vol. 2, pp. 62–86). Chichester: Wiley-Blackwell.

Kaufman, J., Csibra, G., & Johnson, M. H. (2003). Representing occluded objects in the human infant brain. *Proceedings of the Royal Society of London Series B-Biological Sciences, 270*, S140–S143.

Kelly, D. J., Quinn, P. C., Slater, A. M., Lee, K., Ge, L., & Pascalis, O. (2007). The other-race effect during infancy: Evidence of perceptual narrowing. *Psychological Science, 18*, 1084–1089.

Kirjavainen, M., & Theakston, A. (2012). Naturalistic data. *The encyclopedia of applied linguistics*. Chichester: Wiley-Blackwell.

Klahr, D. (1985). Solving problems with ambiguous subgoal ordering: Preschoolers' performance. *Child Development, 56*, 940–952.

Klahr, D., & Robinson, M. (1981). Formal assessment of problem-solving and planning processes in preschool children. *Cognitive Psychology, 13*, 113–128.

Koenig, M. A., & Harris, P. L. (2005). Preschoolers mistrust ignorant and inaccurate speakers. *Child Development, 76*, 1261–1277.

Kohlberg, L. (1963). The development of children's orientations toward a moral order. I: Sequence in the development of moral thought. *Human Development, 51*, 8–20.

Kreitler, S., & Kreitler, H. (1987). Conceptions and processes of planning: The developmental perspective. In S. L. Friedman, E. K. Scholnick, & R. R. Cockings (Eds), *Blueprints for thinking: The role of planning in cognitive development*. New York: Cambridge University Press.

Kuhl, P. K., & Meltzoff, A. N. (1982). The bimodal perception of speech in infancy. *Science, 218*, 1138–1141.

Kurtz-Costes, B., DeFreitas, S. C., Halle, T. G., & Kinlaw, C. R. (2011). Gender and racial favouritism in Black and White preschool girls. *British Journal of Developmental Psychology, 29*(2), 270–287.

Ladd, G. W., Kochenderfer-Ladd, B., & Rydell, A.-R. (2011). Children's interpersonal skills and school-based relationships. In P. K. Smith & C. H. Hart (Eds), *The Wiley-Blackwell handbook of social development, 2nd edition* (pp. 181–206). Chichester: Wiley-Blackwell.

Laeng, B., Sirois, S., & Gredeback, G. (2012). Pupillometry: A window to the preconscious? *Perspectives on Psychological Science, 7*(1), 18–27.

Lai, C. S., Fisher, S. E., Hurst, J. A., Vargha-Khadem, F., & Monaco, A. P. (2001). A forkhead-domain gene is mutated in severe speech and language disorder. *Nature, 413*, 519–523.

Landau, B. & Gleitman, L. (1985). *Language and experience: Evidence from the blind child*. Cambridge, MA: Harvard University Press.

Laplante, D. P., Brunet, A., Schmitz, N., Ciampi, A., & King, S. (2008). Project Ice Storm: Prenatal maternal stress affects cognitive and linguistic functioning in 5 1/2-year-old children. *Journal of the American Academy of Child and Adolescent Psychiatry, 47*, 1063–1072.

Leaper, C. (2011). Research in developmental psychology on gender and relationships: Reflections on the past and looking into the future. *British Journal of Developmental Psychology, 29*(2), 347–356.

Leman, P. J., Ahmed, S., & Ozarow, L. (2005). Gender, gender relations, and the social dynamics of children's conversations. *Developmental Psychology, 41*(1), 64–74.

Leslie, A. M. (1991). The theory of mind impairment in autism: Evidence for a modular mechanism of development? In A. Whiten (Ed.), *Natural theories of mind* (pp. 63–78). Oxford: Blackwell.

Leslie, A. M. (1992). Pretense, autism, and the Theory-of-Mind module. *Current Directions in Psychological Science, 1*(1), 18–21.

Leslie, A. M. (1995). A theory of agency. In D. Sperber, D. Premack & A. J. Premack (Eds), *Causal cognition: A multidisciplinary debate* (pp. 121–149). Oxford: Clarendon Press.

Levin, H. S., Culhane, K. A., Hartmann, J., Evankovich, K., Mattson, A. J., Harward, H., . . . Fletcher, J. M. (1991). Developmental changes in performance on tests of purported frontal lobe functioning. *Developmental Neuropsychology, 7*(3), 377–395.

Levy, S., Sutton, G., Ng, P. C., Feuk, L., Halpern, A. L., Walenz, B. P., . . . Denisov, G. (2007). The diploid genome sequence of an individual human. *Plos Biology, 5*(10), e254.

Lewis, M. (1999). Social cognition and the self. In P. Rochat (Ed.), *Early social cognition: Understanding others in the first months of life* (pp. 81–100). Mahwah, NJ: Erlbaum.

Liebermann, P. (1992). Human speech and language. In S. Jones, R. Martin, & D. Pilbeam (Eds), *The Cambridge encyclopaedia of human evolution*. Cambridge, UK: Cambridge University Press.

Linnell, M., & Fluck, M. (2001). The effect of maternal support for counting and cardinal understanding in preschool children. *Social Development, 10*(2), 202–220.

Locke, J. (1690). *An essay concerning human understanding*. London.

Lundberg, I., Olofsson, A., & Wall, S. (1980). Reading and spelling skills in the first school years predicted from phonemic awareness skills in kindergarten. *Scandinavian Journal of Psychology, 21*, 159–173.

Lytton, H., & Romney, D. M. (1991). Parents' differential socialization of boys and girls: A meta-analysis. *Psychological Bulletin, 109*, 267–296.

Maccoby, E. E. (1990). Gender and relationships: A developmental account. *American Psychologist, 45*, 513–520.

Maccoby, E. E., & Jacklin, C. N. (1974). *The psychology of sex differences*. Stanford, CA: Stanford University Press.

Maccoby, E. E., & Jacklin, C. N. (1987). Gender segregation in children. In H. W. Reese (Ed.), *Advances in child development and behavior* (pp. 239–287). New York: Academic Press.

MacFarlane, A. (1975). Olfaction in the development of social preferences in the human neonate. *CIBA Foundation Symposium, 33,* 103–117.

MacLeod, C. (1991). Half a century of research on the Stroop effect. *Psychological Bulletin, 109*, 163–203.

Main, M., & Solomon, J. (1986). Discovery of a new, insecure disorganized/disoriented attachment pattern. In M. Yogman & T. B. Brazelton (Eds), *Affective development in infancy* (pp. 95–124). Norwood, NJ: Ablex.

Mandler, J. M. (2000). Perceptual and conceptual processes in infancy. *Journal of Cognition and Development, 1*(1), 3–36.

Mans, L., Cicchetti, D., & Sroufe, L. A. (1978). Mirror reactions of Down's syndrome infants and toddlers: Cognitive underpinnings of self-recognition. *Child Development, 49*(4), 1247–1250.

Marcus, G. F., Pinker, S., Ullman, M., Hollander, M., Rosen, T. J., & Xu, F. (1992). Overregularization in child language. *Monographs of the Society for Research in Child Development, 57*(4).

Mareschal, D., Johnson, M. H., Sirois, S., Spratling, M. W., Thomas, M. & Westermann, G. (2007). *Neuroconstructivism: How the brain constructs cognition*. Oxford, UK: Oxford University Press.

Mareschal, D., & Kaufman, J. (2012). Object permanence in infancy: Revisiting Baillargeon's drawbridge study. In A. M. Slater & P. C. Quinn (Eds), *Developmental psychology: Revisiting the classic studies* (pp. 86–100). London: Sage.

Martin, C. A., Kelly, T. H., Rayens, M. K., Brogli, B. R., Brenzel, A., Smith, W. J., & Omar, H. A. (2002). Sensation seeking, puberty, and nicotine, alcohol, and marijuana use in adolescence. *Journal of the American Academy of Child and Adolescent Psychiatry, 41*, 1495–1502.

Marzke, M. W. (1992). Evolution of the hand and bipedality. In A. Lock & A. Peters (Eds), *Handbook of human symbolic evolution* (pp. 126–154). Oxford: Oxford University Press.

Maslen, R. J. C., Theakston, A. L., Lieven, E. V. M., & Tomasello, M. (2004). A dense corpus study of past tense and plural overregularization in English. *Journal of Speech, Language and Hearing Research, 47*(6), 1319–1333.

Masten, C. L., Guyer, A. E., Hodgdon, H. B., McClure, E. B., Charney, D. S., Ernst, M., . . . Monkg, C. S. (2008). Recognition of facial emotions among maltreated children with high rates of post-traumatic stress disorder. *Child Abuse & Neglect, 32*(1), 139–153.

Mayer, R. E. (1992). *Thinking, problem solving, cognition (2nd edition)*. New York, NY: W H Freeman.

Mayer, R. E., Sims, V., & Tajika, H. (1995). A comparison of how textbooks teach mathematical problem solving in Japan and the United States. *American Educational Research Journal, 32*(2), 443–460.

McGarrigle, J., & Donaldson, M. (1975). Conservation accidents. *Cognition, 3*(4), 341–350.

McGraw, M. B. (1943). *The neuromuscular maturation of the human infant*. New York: Hofner.

McKone, E., Kanwisher, N., & Duchaine, B. C. (2007). Can generic expertise explain special processing for faces? *Trends in Cognitive Sciences, 11*(1), 8–15.

McNeill, D. (1966) Developmental psycholinguistics. In I. Smith and G. A. Miller (Eds.), *The genesis of language: A psycholinguistic approach*. New York: Harper and Row.

Mehler, J., & Dupoux, E. (1994). *What infants know*. Oxford: Blackwell.

Mehler, J., Jusczyk, P. W., Dehaene-Lambertz, G., Dupoux, E., & Nazzi, T. (1994). Coping with linguistic diversity: The infant's viewpoint In J. L. Morgan & K. Demuth (Eds), *Signal to syntax: Bootstrapping from speech to grammar in early acquisition* (pp. 101–116). Mahwah, NJ: Erlbaum.

Meins, E., Fernyhough, C., Wainwright, R., Das Gupta, M., Fradley, E., & Tuckey, M. (2002). Maternal mind-mindedness and attachment security as predictors of theory of mind understanding. *Child Development, 73*(6), 1715–1726.

Meltzoff, A. N., & Decety, J. (2003). What imitation tells us about social cognition: A rapprochement between developmental psychology and cogntive neuroscience. *Philosophical Transactions of the Royal Society B, 358*, 491–500.

Meltzoff, A. N., & Moore, M. K. (1977). Imitation of facial and manual gestures by human neonates. *Science, 198*, 75–78.

Meltzoff, A. N., & Moore, M. K. (1989). Imitation in newborn infants: Exploring the range of gestures imitated and the underlying mechanisms. *Developmental Psychology, 25*, 954–962.

Meltzoff, A. N., & Moore, M. K. (1992). Early imitation within a functional framework: The importance of person identity, movement, and development. *Infant Behavior and Development, 15*, 479–505.

Meltzoff, A. N., & Williamson, R. A. (2010). The importance of imitation for theories of social-cognitive development. In J. G. Bremner & T. D. Wachs (Eds), *Infant development* (Vol. 1) (pp. 345–364). Chichester: Wiley-Blackwell.

Meltzoff, A. N., Kuhl, P. K., Movellan, J., & Sejnowski, T. J. (2009). Foundations for a new science of learning. *Science, 325*, 284–288.

Millar, S. (1975). Visual experience or translation rules? Drawing the human figure by blind and sighted children. *Perception, 4*(4), 363–371.

Miller, E. K., & Cohen, J. D. (2001). An integrative theory of prefrontal cortex function. *Annual Review of Neuroscience, 24*, 167–202.

Mischel, W. (1966). A social learning view of sex diffferences in behavior. In E. E. Maccoby (Ed.), *The development of sex differences* (pp. 56–81). Stanford, CA: Stanford University Press.

Miura, I. T., Okamoto, Y., Kim, C. C., Change, C.-M., Steere, M., & Fayol, M. (1994). Comparisons of children's cognitive representations of number: China, France, Japan, Korea, Sweden and the United States. *International Journal of Behavioral Development, 17*, 401–411.

Miyake, K., Chen, S.-J., & Campos, J. J. (1985). Infant temperament, mother's mode of interaction, and attachment in Japan: An interim report. *Monographs of the Society for Research in Child Development 50*(1–2), 276–297.

Moll, H., & Tomasello, M. (2007). How 14-and 18-month-olds know what others have experienced. *Developmental Psychology, 43*(2), 309–317.

Moll, H., & Tomasello, M. (2012). Three-year-olds understand appearance and reality—just not about the same object at the same time. *Developmental Psychology, 48*(4), 1124–1132.

Moore, C., & Frye, D. (1986). The effect of experimenter's intention on the child's understanding of conservation. *Cognition, 22*(3), 283–298.

Moshman, D. (1998). Cognitive development beyond childhood. In D. Kuhn & R. S. Siegler (Eds), *Handbook of child psychology Vol. 2: Cognition, perception and language* (pp. 947–978). New York: Wiley.

Murray-Close, D., Ostrov, J. M., & Crock, N. R. (2007). A short-term longitudinal study of growth of relational aggression during middle childhood: Associations with gender, friendship intimacy, and internalizing problems. *Development and Psychopathology, 19*(1), 187–203.

Muter, V., Hulme, C., Snowling, M. J., & Stevenson, J. (2004). Phonemes, rimes, and language skills as foundations of early reading development: Evidence from a longitudinal study. *Developmental Psychology, 40*, 663–681.

Neel, R. S., Jenkins, Z. N., & Meadows, N. (1990). Social problem-solving behaviors and aggression in young children: A descriptive observational study. *Behavioral Disorders, 16*, 39–51.

Nelson, C. A., Thomas, K. M., & de Haan, M. (2006). Neural basis of cogntive development. In D. Kuhn & R. S. Siegler (Eds), *Handbook of child psychology* (Vol. 2) (pp. 3–57). Hoboken, NJ: Wiley.

Nelson, K. (1977) First steps in language acquisition. *Journal of the American Academy of Child Pyschiatry*, 16(4), 563–583.

Newcombe, N. S. (2002). The nativist–empiricist controversy in the context of recent research on spatial and quantitative development. *Psychological Science, 13*(5), 395–401.

Newcombe, N. S. (2011). What is neoconstructivism? *Child Development Perspectives*, doi: 10.1111/j.1750–8606. 2011.00180.x

Nikolopoulos, D., Goulandris, N., Hulme, C., & Snowling, M. J. (2006). The cognitive bases of learning to read and spell in Greek: Evidence from a longitudinal study. *Journal of Experimental Child Psychology*, 94, 1–17.

Nucci, L. P., & Gingo, M. (2011). The development of moral reasoning. In U. Goswami (Ed.), *Wiley-Blackwell handbook of childhood cognitive development, 2nd edition* (pp. 420–445). Chichester: Wiley-Blackwell.

Nunes, T., & Bryant, P. E. (1996). *Children doing mathematics*. Oxford: Blackwell.

Nunes, T., Bryant, P. E., & Bindman, M. (1997). Morphological spelling strategies: Developmental stages and processes. *Developmental Psychology, 33*(4), 637–649.

Oakhill, J., & Yuill, N. (1996). Higher order factors in comprehension disability: Processes and remediation. In C. Cornoldi & J. Oakhill (Eds), *Reading comprehension difficulties: Processes and intervention*. Hillsdale, NJ: Erlbaum.

Oller, D. K. (1980). The emergence of speech sounds in infancy. In G. H. Yeni-Komshian, J. F. Kavanagh & C. A. Ferguson (Eds), *Child phonology, Volume 1: Production* (pp. 93–112). New York: Academic Press.

Oller, D. K., & Eilers, R. E. (1988). The role of audition in infant babbling. *Child Development, 59*, 441–449.

Oller, D. K., Niyogi, P., Gray, S., Richards, J. A., Gilkerson, J., Xu, D., . . . Warren, S. F. (2010). Automated vocal analysis of naturalistic recordings from children with autism, language delay, and typical development. *Proceedings of the National Academy of Sciences of the United States of America, 107*(30), 13354–13359.

Pacton, S., Fayol, M., & Perruchet, P. (2002). The acquisition of untaught orthographic regularities in French. In L. Verhoeven, C. Elbro & P. Reitsma (Eds), *Precursors of functional literacy* (pp. 121–137). Dordrecht, the Netherlands: Kluwer.

Pan, Y., Gauvain, M., Liu, Z., & Cheng, L. (2006). American and Chinese parental involvement in young children's mathematics learning. *Cognitive Development, 21*, 17–35.

Papousek, H., & Papousek, M. (1989). Forms and functions of vocal matching in interactions between mothers and their precanonical infants. *First Language, 9*, 137–158.

Pascalis, O., de Haan, M., & Nelson, C. A. (2002). Is face processing species-specific during the first year of life? *Science, 296*, 1321–1323.

Pasterski, V., Golombok, S., & Hines, M. (2011). Sex differences in social behaviour. In P. K. Smith & C. H. Hart (Eds), *The Wiley-Blackwell handbook of social development, 2nd edition* (pp. 281–298). Chichester: Wiley-Blackwell.

Pena, M., Maki, A., Kovacz, D., Dehaene-Lambertz, G., Koizumi, H., Bouquet, F., & Mehler, J. (2003). Sounds and silence: An optical topography study of language recognition at birth. *Proceedings of the National Academy of Sciences, 100*(20), 11702–11705.

Perner, J. (1991). *Understanding the representational mind*. Cambridge, MA: MIT Press.

Piaget, J. (1932). *The moral judgment of the child*. New York: Free Press.

Piaget, J. (1951). *Play, dreams and imitation in childhood*. London: Routledge.

Piaget, J. (1955). *The construction of reality in the child*. London: Routledge & Kegan Paul.

Piaget, J. (1962). *Play dreams and imitation in the child*. New York: Norton.

Piaget, J. (1976). *The grasp of consciousness: Action and concept in the young child*. Cambridge, MA: Harvard University Press.

Piaget, J., & Inhelder, B. (1956). *The child's conception of space*. London: Routledge.

Piattelli-Palmarini, M. (2001). Speaking of learning. *Nature, 411*(21 June 2001), 887–888.

Pine, D. S., Mogg, K., Bradley, B. P., Montgomery, L.-A., Monk, C. S., McClure, E., . . . Kaufman, J. (2005). Attention bias to threat in maltreated children: Implications for vulnerability to stress-related psychopathology. *American Journal of Psychiatry, 162*, 291–296.

Pinker, S. (1999). *Words and rules*. New York: Morrow Press.

Pinker, S., Lebeaux, D. S., & Frost, L. A. (1987). Productivity and constraints in the acquisition of the passive. *Cognition, 26*, 195–267.

Plunkett, K. (1997). Theories of early language acquisition. *Trends in Cognitive Sciences, 1*(4), 146–153.

Popper, K. (1999). *All life is problem solving*. Abingdon: Routledge.

Posada, G., & Kaloustian, G. (2010). Attachment in infancy. In J. G. Bremner & T. D. Wachs (Eds), *The Wiley-Blackwell handbook of infant development* (pp. 483–509). Chichester: Wiley-Blackwell.

Povinelli, D. J. (1995). The unduplicated self. In P. Rochat (Ed.), *The self in infancy: Theory and research* (pp. 161–192). Amsterdam: North-Holland/Elsevier Science Publishers.

Povinelli, D. J., & Simon, B. B. (1998). Young children's understanding of briefly versus extremely delayed images of the self: Emergence of the autobiographical stance. *Developmental Psychology, 34*(1), 188–194.

Premack, D., & Woodruff, G. (1978). Does the chimpanzee have a theory of mind? *Behavioral and Brain Sciences, 1*, 515–526.

Quartz, S. R., & Sejnowski, T. J. (1997). The neural basis of cognitive development: A constructivist manifesto. *Behavioral and Brain Sciences, 20*(4), 537–596.

Quine, W. V. (1960). *Word and object*. Cambridge, MA: MIT Press.

Quinn, P. C., & Eimas, P. D. (1996). Perceptual cues that permit categorical differentiation of animal species by infants. *Journal of Experimental Child Psychology, 63*(1), 189–211.

Quinn, P. C., & Eimas, P. D. (2000). The emergence of category representations during infancy: Are separate perceptual and conceptual processes required? *Journal of Cognition and Development, 1*(1), 5561.

Quinn, P. C., Eimas, P. D., & Rosenkrantz, S. L. (1993). Evidence for representations of perceptually similar natural categories by 3-month-old and 4-month-old infants. *Perception, 22*(4), 463–475.

Quinn, P. C., Westerlund, A., & Nelson, C. A. (2006). Neural markers of categorization in 6-month-old infants. *Psychological Science, 17*(1), 59–66.

Quinn, P. C., Doran, M. M., Reiss, J. E., & Hoffman, J. E. (2010). Neural markers of subordinate-level categorization in 6- to 7-month-old infants. *Developmental Science, 13*(3), 499–507.

Reddy, V. (2003). On being the object of attention: Implications for self–other consciousness. *TRENDS in Cognitive Sciences 7*(9), 397–402.

Riley, M., Greeno, J. G., & Heller , J. I. (1983). Development of children's problem solving ability in arithmetic. In H. Ginsburg (Ed.), *The development of mathematical thinking* (pp. 153–196). New York: Academic Press.

Rivera, S. M., Wakeley, A., & Langer, J. (1999). The drawbridge phenomenon: Representational reasoning or perceptual preference? *Developmental Psychology, 35*(2), 427–435.

Rochat, P. (2010). Emerging self-concept. In J. G. Bremner & T. D. Wachs (Eds), *The Wiley-Blackwell handbook of infant development* (Vol. 1) (pp. 320–344). Chichester: Wiley-Blackwell.

Ronqvist, L. & Van Hoften, C. (1994). Neonatal finger and arm movement as determined by a social and an object context. *Early Develoment and Parenting, 3*, 81–94.

Rose-Krasnor, L., & Denham, S. (2009). Social-emotional competence in early childhood. In K. H. Rubin, W. M. Bukowski & B. Laursen (Eds), *Handbook of peer interactions, relationships and groups* (pp. 162–179). New York: Guilford Press.

Roseboom, T., de Rooij, S., & Painter, R. (2006). The Dutch famine and its long-term consequences for adult health. *Early Human Development, 82*(8), 485–491.

Rosenblum, S., & Livneh-Zirinski, M. (2008). Handwriting process and product characteristics of children diagnosed with developmental coordination disorder. *Human Movement Science, 27*, 200–214.

Rotzer, S., Kucian, K., Martin, E., Aster, N. V., Klaver, P., & Loennexer, T. (2008). Optimized voxel-based morphometry in children with developmental dyscalculia. *Neuroimage, 39*, 417.

Roy, D. (2009). *New horizons in the study of child language acquisition*. Paper presented at the Proceedings of Interspeech 2009, Brighton. http://dspace.mit.edu/handle/1721.1/65900

Roy, D., Patel, R., DeCamp, P., Kubat, R., Fleischman, M., Roy, B., . . . Guinness, J. (2006). *The human speechome project*. Paper presented at the Proceedings of the Twenty-Eighth Annual Meeting of the Cognitive Science Society. Mahwah, NJ: Lawrence Erlbaum Associates. http://link.springer.com/chapter/10.1007/11880172_15

Roy, P., & Chiat, S. (2012). Teasing apart disadvantage from disorder: The case of poor language. In C. R. Marshall (Ed.), *Current issues in developmental disorders* (pp. 125–150). Hove: Psychology Press.

Rubin, K. H., Chen, X., McDougall, P., Bowker, A., & McKinnon, J. (1995). The Waterloo Longitudinal Project: Predicting internalizing and externalizing problems in adolescence. *Development and Psychopathology, 7*, 751–764.

Russell, J. (1978). *The acquisition of knowledge*. London: Macmillan.

Russell, J., Mauthner, N., & Sharpe, S. (1991). The 'windows task' as a measure of strategic deception in preschoolers and autistic subjects. *British Journal of Developmental Psychology, 9*(2), 331–349.

Rvachew, S., Abdulsalam, A., Mattock, K., & Polka, L. (2008). Emergence of the corner vowels in the babble produced by infants exposed to Canadian English or Canadian French. *Journal of Phonetics, 36*, 564–577.

Rykhlevskaia, E., Uddin, L. Q., Kondos, L., & Menon, V. (2009). Neuroanatomical correlates of developmental dyscalculia: Combined evidence from morphometry and tractography. *Frontiers in Human Neuroscience, 3*(1).

Saarni, C. (1984). An observational study of children's attempts to monitor their expressive behavior. *Child Development, 55*, 1504–1513.

Saarni, C., Mumme, D. L., & Campos, J. L. (1988). Emotional development: Action, communication and understanding. In N. Eisenberg (Ed.), *Handbook of child psychology Vol. 3: Social, emotional, and personality development*. (Editor in chief W. Damon). (pp. 237–309). New York: Wiley.

Sadato, N., Pascual-Leone, A., Grafman, J., Ibañez, V., Deiber, M.-P., Dold, G., & Hallett, M. (1996). Activation of the primary visual cortex by braille reading in blind subjects. *Nature, 380*, 526–528.

Sagi, A., Koren-Karie, N., Gini, M., Ziv, Y., & Joels, T. (2002). Shedding further light on the effects of various types and quality of early child care on infant–mother attachment relationship: The Haifa Study of Early Child Care. *Child Development, 73*(4), 1166–1186.

Sapp, F., Lee, K., & Muir, D. (2000). Three-year-olds' difficulty with the appearance–reality distinction: Is it real or is it apparent? *Developmental Psychology, 36*(5), 547–560.

Saxe, G. B. (1981). Body parts as numerals: A developmental analysis of numeration among the Oksapmin in Papua New Guinea. *Child Development, 52*, 306–316.

Saxton, M. (2000). Negative evidence and negative feedback: Immediate effcts on the grammaticality of child speech. *First Language*, 20(3), 221–252.

Saxton, M., Kulcsar, B., Marshall, G., & Rupra, M. (1998). The longer-term effects of corrective input: an experimental approach. *Journal of Child Language*, 25, 701–721.

Scholfield, P. J. (1994). Writing and spelling: the view from linguistics. In G. D. A. Brown & N. C. Ellis (Eds), *Handbook of spelling* (pp. 51–71). Chichester: Wiley.

Seymour, P. H. K., Aro, M., & Erskine, J. M. (2003). Foundation literacy acquisition in European orthographies. *British Journal of Psychology, 94*(2), 143–174.

Seymour, P. H. K., & Elder, L. (1986). Beginning reading without phonology. *Cognitive Neuropsychology, 3*, 1–36.

Shafer, G. (2005). Infants can learn decontextualised words before their first birthday. *Child Development, 76*, 87–96.

Shaklee, H., Holt, P., Elek, S., & Hall, L. (1988). Covariation judgment: Improving rule use among children, adolescents, and adults. *Child Development, 59*, 755–768.

Shalinsky, M. H., Kovelman, I., Berens, M. S., & Petitto, L.-A. (2009). Exploring cognitive functions in babies, children and adults with near infrared spectroscopy. *Journal of Visualized Experiments,* (29). Retrieved from http://www.jove.com/index/Details.stp?ID=1268

Siegal, M. (1988). Children's knowledge of contagion and contamination as causes of illness. *Child Development, 59*(5), 1353–1359.

Siegal, M. (1997). *Knowing children: Experiments in conversation and cognition.* Hove: Psychology Press.

Siegler, R. S. (1976). Three aspects of cognitive development. *Cognitive Psychology, 8*, 481–520.

Siegler, R. S. (1995). How does change occur: A microgenetic study of number conservation. *Cognitive Psychology, 28*(3), 225–273.

Siegler, R. S. (1996). *Emerging minds: The process of change in children's thinking.* New York: Oxford University Press.

Siegler, R. S., & Chen, Z. (2002). Development of rules and strategies: Balancing the old and new. *Journal of Experimental Child Psychology, 81*, 446–457.

Siegler, R. S., & Mu, Y. (2008). Chinese children excel on novel mathematics problems even before elementary school. *Psychological Science, 19*(8), 759–763.

Silk, A. M. J., & Thomas, G. V. (1986). Development and differentiation in children's figure drawings. *British Journal of Psychology, 77*, 399–410.

Simion, F., Valenza, E., Macchi Cassia, V., Turati, C., & Umiltà, C. (2002). Newborns' preferences for up-down symmetrical configurations. *Developmental Science, 5*, 427–434.

Sinclair, A. (1988). La notation numerique chez l'enfant. In H. Sinclair (Ed.), *La production de notations chez le jeune enfant: langage, nombre, rhymes et melodies.* Paris: Presses Universitaires de France.

Sinclair, D. (1978). Factors influencing growth and maturation. In D. Sinclair & P. Dangerfield (Eds.), *Human growth after birth, 3rd edition* (pp. 140–160). London: Oxford University Press.

Sinno, S. M., & Killen, M. (2011). Social reasoning about 'second-shift' parenting. *British Journal of Developmental Psychology, 29*, 313–329.

Slater, A. M. (1989). Visual memory and perception in early infancy. In A. M. Slater & G. Bremner (Eds), *Infant development* (pp. 43–71). Hove: Lawrence Erlbaum.

Slegel, L. S., & Ryan, E. B. (1989). The development of working memory in normally achieving and subtypes of learning disabled children. *Child Development, 60*, 973–980.

Smith, L., & Yu, C. (2008). Infants rapidly learn word-referent mappings via cross-situational statistics. *Cognition, 106*(3), 1558–1568.

Smith, L. B. (2005). Cognition as a dynamic system: Principles from embodiment. *Developmental Review, 25*(3–4), 278–298.

Smith, L. B., & Sheya, A. (2010). Is cognition enough to explain cognitive development? *Topics in Cognitive Science, 2*(4), 725–735.

Smith, L. B., & Thelen, E. (2003). Development as a dynamic system. *Trends in Cognitive Sciences, 7*(8), 343–348.

Smith, L. B., Thelen, E., Titzer, R., & McLin, D. (1999). Knowing in the context of acting: The task dynamics of the A-not-B error. *Psychological Review, 106*(2), 235–260.

Smith, P. K., Mahdavi, J., Carvalho, M., Fisher, S., Russell, S., & Tippett, N. (2008). Cyberbullying: Its nature and impact in seconday school pupils. *Journal of Child Psychology and Psychiatry, 49*(4), 376–385.

Snow, C.E. (1989). Social perspectives on the emergence of language. In B. MacWhinney (Ed.), *The emergence of language* (pp. 257–276). Mahwah, NJ: Erlbarum.

Snowling, M. J. (1981). Phonemic deficits in developmental dyslexia. *Psychological Research, 43*(2), 219–234.

Snowling, M. J., Gallagher, A., & Frith, U. (2003). Family risk of dyslexia is continuous: Individual differences in the precursors of reading skill. *Child Development, 74*, 358–373.

Sodian, B., & Frith, U. (1992). Deception and sabotage in autistic, retarded and normal children. *Journal of Child Psychology and Psychiatry, 33*, 591–605.

Spelke, E. S. (1998). Nativism, empiricism, and the origins of knowledge. *Infant Behavior and Development, 21*, 181–200.

Spelke, E. S. (2003). What makes us smart? Core knowledge and natural language. In D. Gentner & S. Goldin-Meadow (Eds), *Language in mind: Advances in the study of language and thought* (pp. 277–311). Cambridge, MA: MIT Press.

Spelke, E. S., & Kinzler, K. D. (2007). Core knowledge. *Developmental Science, 10*(1), 89–96.

Stack, D. M. (2010). Touch and physical contact during infancy: Discovering the richness of the forgotten sense. In J. G. Bremner & T. D. Wachs (Eds), *The Wiley-Blackwell handbook of infant development* (Vol. 1, pp. 352–567). Chichester: Wiley-Blackwell.

Stack, D. M., & Muir, D. W. (1990). Tactile stimulation as a component of of social interchange: New interpretations for the still-face effect. *British Journal of Developmental Psychology, 8*, 131–145.

Stanovich, K. E. (1986). Matthew effects in reading: Some consequences of individual differences in the acquisition of literacy. *Reading Research Quarterly, 21*(4), 360–407.

Steiner, J. (1979). Human facial expression in response to taste and smell stimulation In H. Reese & L. P. Lipsitt (Eds), *Advances in child development and behaviour* (pp. 257–295). New York: Academic Press.

Stern, D. (1985). *The interpersonal world of the infant.* New York: Basic Books.

Stevenson, H. W., Lee, S.-Y., Chen, C., Stigler, J. W., Hsu, C.-C., Kitamura, S., & Hatano, G. (1990). Contexts of achievement: A study of American, Chinese, and Japanese children. *Monographs of the Society for Research in Child Development, 55*(1–2), 1–107.

Striano, T., & Reid, V. M. (2006). Social cognition in the first year. *Trends in Cognitive Sciences, 10*(10), 471–476.

Suarez, S. D., & Gallup, G. G. (1981). Self-recognition in chimpanzees and orangutans, but not gorillas. *Journal of Human Evolution, 10*(2), 175–188.

Sugden, D., & Wade, M. (2013). *Typical and atypical motor development.* London: Mac Keith Press.

Tam, H., Jarrold, C., Baddeley, A. D., & Sabatos-DeVito, M. (2010). The development of memeory maintenance: Children's use of phonological rehearsal and attentional refreshment in working memory tasks. *Journal of Experimental Child Psychology, 107*, 306–324.

Tanner, J. M. (1978). *Fetus Into Man.* Cambridge, MA: Harvard University Press. In Gottlieb, G. (1998) Normally occurring environmental and behavioural influences on gene activity: From central Dogma to probabilistic epigenesis. *Psychological Review, 105*(4), 792–802.

Tanner, J. M. (1990). *Fetus into man: Physical growth from conception to maturity, Revised edition.* Cambridge, MA: Harvard University Press.

Tardif, T. (1996). Nouns are not always learned before verbs: Evidence from Mandarin speakers' early vocabularies. *Developmental Psychology, 32*, 492–504.

Thomas, G. V. (1995). The role of drawing strategies and skills. In C. Lange-Kuttner & G. V. Thomas (Eds), *Drawing and looking* (pp. 107–122). Hemel Hempstead: Harvester.

Thomas, G. V., & Tsalimi, A. (1988). Effects of order of drawing head and trunk on their relative sizes in children's human figure drawings. *British Journal of Developmental Psychology, 6*(2), 191–203.

Thomas, J. R., & French, K. E. (1985). Gender differences across age in motor performance: A meta-analysis. *Psychological Bulletin, 98*(2), 260–282.

Thomas, M. S. C., & Johnson, M. H. (2008). New advances in understanding sensitive periods in brain development. *Current Directions in Psychological Science, 17*(1), 1–5.

Thompson, P. M., Giedd, J. N., Woods, R. P., MacDonald, D., Evans, A. C., & Toga, A. W. (2000). Growth patterns in the developing brain detected by using continuum mechanical tensor maps. *Nature, 404*(9 March 2000), 190–193.

Thorkildsen, T. A. (1989). Justice in the classroom: The student's view. *Child Development, 60*, 323–334.

Thorstad, G. (1991). The effect of orthography on the acquisition of literacy skills. *British Journal of Psychology, 82*, 527–537.

Tizard, B., & Hughes, M. (1984). *Young children learning: Talking and thinking at home and at school.* London: Fontana.

Tomasello, M. (1992). *First verbs: A case study of early grammatical development.* Cambridge: Cambridge University Press.

Tomasello, M. (2006). Acquiring linguistic constructions. In D. Kuhn & R. S. Siegler (Eds), *Handbook of child psychology* (pp. 255–298). Hoboken, NJ: Wiley.

Tomasello, M., Akhtar, N., Dodson, K., & Rekau, L. (1997). Differential productivity in young children's use of nouns and verbs. *Journal of Child Language, 24*, 373–387.

Tomblin, J. B., Records, N. L., Buckwalter, Z. X., Smith, E., & O'Brien, M. (1997). Prevalence of specific language impairment in kindergarten children. *Journal of Speech and Hearing Research, 40*, 1245–1260.

Towse, J. N., & Hitch, G. J. (2007). Variations in working memory due to normal development. In A. R. A. Conway, C. Jarrold, M. J. Kane, A. Miyake & J. N. Towse (Eds), *Variations in working memory* (pp. 109–133). Oxford: Oxford University Press.

Towse, J. N., & Saxton, M. (1998). Mathematics across national boundaries: Cultural and linguistic perspectives on numerical competence. In C. Donlan (Ed.), *The development of mathematical skills* (pp. 129–150). Hove: Psychology Press

Tronick, E. Z., Als, H., Adamson, L., Wise, S., & Brazelton, T. B. (1978). The infant's response to entrapment between contradictory messages in face-to-face interactions. *Journal of the American Academy of Child Psychiatry, 17*, 1–13.

Turati, C. (2004). Why faces are not special to newborns: An alternative account of the face preference. *Current Directions in Psychological Science, 13*, 5–8.

Turiel, E. (1983). *The development of social knowledge: Morality and convention.* Cambridge: Cambridge University Press.

Turiel, E. (2006). The development of morality. In N. Eisenberg (Ed.), *Handbook of child psychology: Volume 3, Social, emotional and personality development* (pp. 789–857). Hoboken, NJ: Wiley.

Valenza, E., Simion, F., Macchi Cassia, V., & Umiltà, C. (2002). Face preferences at birth. *Journal of Experimental Psychology: Human Perception and Performance, 22,* 892–903.

Van Geert, P. (1991). A dynamic systems model of cognitive and language growth. *Psychological Review, 98*(1), 3.

van Lieshout, C. F. M., & Doise, W. (1998). Social development. In A. Demetriou, W. Doise & C. F. M. van Lieshout (Eds), *Life-span developmental psychology* (271–316). New York: Wiley.

Vaughn, B. E., Deane, K. E., & Waters, E. (1985). The impact of out-of-home care on child–mother attachment quality: Another look at some enduring questions. *Monographs of the Society for Research in Child Development, 50*(1/2), 110–135.

Verkuyten, M., & Slooter, L. (2008). Muslim and non-Muslim adolescents' reasoning about freedom of speech and minority rights. *Child Development, 79,* 514–528.

Vihman, M. M. (1992). Early syllables and the construction of phonology In C. A. Ferguson, L. Menn & C. Stoel-Gammon (Eds), *Phonological development: Models, research, implications* (pp. 393–422). Timonium, MD: New York Press.

Vygotsky, L. S. (1934/1962). *Thought and language.* Cambridge, MA: MIT Press.

Vygotsky, L. S. (1980). *Mind in society.* Cambridge, MA: Harvard University Press.

Waddington, C. H. (1957). *The strategy of the genes.* London: Allen & Unwin.

Wagner, L., Swensen, L. D., & Naigles, L. (2009). Children's early productivity with verb morphology. *Cognitive Development, 24*(3), 223–239.

Wakeley, A., Rivera, S., & Langer, J. (2000). Can young infants add and subtract? *Child Development, 71*(6), 1525–1534.

Walker, L. J., de Vries, B., & Trevethen, S. D. (1987). Moral stages and moral orientations in real-life and hypothetical dilemmas. *Child Development, 58,* 842–858.

Wang, L., Huettel, S., & De Bellis, M. D. (2008). Neural substrates for processing task-irrelevant sad images in adolescents. *Developmental Science, 11*(1), 23–32.

Wang, L., McCarthy, G., Song, A. W., & LaBar, K. S. (2005). Amygdala activation to sad pictures during high-field (4 tesla) functional magnetic resonance imaging. *Emotion, 5*(1), 14.

Waters, E., Merrick, S., Trebous, D., Crowell, J., & Albaersheim, L. (2000). Attachment security in infancy and early adulthood: A twenty-year longitudinal study. *Child Development, 71*(3), 684–689.

Wellman, H. M., Lopez-Duran, S., & LaBounty, J. (2008). Infant attention to intentional action predicts preschool theory of mind. *Developmental Psychology, 44*(2), 618–623.

Wellman, H. M., Cross, D., Bartsch, K., & Harris, P. L. (1986). Infant search and object permanence: A meta-analysis of the A-not-B error. *Monographs of the Society for Research in Child Development, 51*(3), 1–51.

Werker, J. F., Gilbert, J. H. V., Humphreys, G. W., & Tees, R. C. (1981). Developmental aspects of cross-language speech perception. *Child Development, 52,* 349–355.

Werker, J. F., & Tees, R. C. (1984). Cross-language speech perception: Evidence for perceptual reorganization during the first year of life. *Infant Behavior and Development, 7,* 49–63.

Westermann, G., & Ruh, N. (2012). A neuroconstructivist model of past tense development and processing. *Psychological Review, 119,* 649–667.

Westermann, G., Mareschal, D., Johnson, M. H., Sirois, S., Spratling, M. W., & Thomas, M. S. C. (2007). Neuroconstructivism. *Developmental Science, 10*(1), 75–83.

White, B. L., Castle, P., & Held, R. (1964). Observations on the development of visually-directed reaching. *Child Development, 35,* 349–364.

WHO Motor Development Study: Windows of achievement for six gross motor development milestones, 2006. *Acta Paediatrica Supplement, 450,* 86–95.

Wigfield, A., Eccles, J. S., Schiefele, U., Roeser, R. W., & Davis-Kean, P. (2006). Development of achievement motivation. In N. Eisenberg (Ed.), *Handbook of child psychology* (pp. 933–1002). Hoboken, NJ: Wiley.

Willatts, P. (1990). Development of problem-solving strategies in infancy. In D. F. Bjorklund (Ed.), *Children's strategies: Contemporary views of cognitive development* (pp. 23–66). Hillsdale, NJ: Lawrence Erlbaum Associates.

Willatts, P. (1997). Beyond the 'couch potato' infant: How infants use their knowledge to regulate action, solve problems, and achieve goals. In J. G. Bremner, A. Slater & G. Butterworth (Eds), *Infant development: Recent advances* (pp. 109–135). Hove: Psychology Press/Erlbaum.

Williams, D. M., & Lind, S. E. (2013). Comorbidity and diagnosis of developmental disorders. In C. R. Marshall (Ed.), *Current issues in developmental disorders* (pp. 19–45). London: Psychology Press.

Wilmut, K., & Wann, J. (2008). The use of predictive information is impaired in the actions of children and young adults with Developmental Coordination Disorder. *Experimental Brain Research, 191*(4 December), 403–418.

Wimmer, H., & Perner, J. (1983). Beliefs about beliefs: Representation and constraining function of wrong beliefs in young children's understanding of deception. *Cognition, 13*(1), 103–128.

Wojslawowicz Bowker, J. C., Rubin, K. H., Burgess, K. B., Rose-Krasnor, L., & Booth-La-Force, C. (2006). Behavioral characteristics associated with stable and fluid best friendship patterns in middle childhood. *Merrill-Palmer Quarterly, 52*, 671–693.

Wolke, D., & Meyer, R. (1999). Cognitive status, language attainment, and pre-reading skills of 6-year-old very pre-term children and their peers: The Bavarian longitudinal study. *Developmental Medicine and Child Neurology, 41*, 94–109.

Wonjung, O., Rubin, K. H., Bowker, J. C., Booth-LaForce, C., Rose-Krasnor, L., & Laursen, B. (2008). Trajectories of social withdrawal from middle childhood to early adolescence. *Journal of Abnormal Child Psychology, 36*(4), 553–566.

Woodhead, M. (1989). 'School starts at five . . . or four years old?': The rationale for changing admission policies in England and Wales. *Journal of Education Policy, 4*(1), 1–21.

Woods, S. S., Resnick, L. B., & Groen, G. J. (1975). An experimental test of five process models for subtraction. *Journal of Educational Psychology, 67*, 17–21.

Woolley, J. D., & Van Reet, J. (2006). Effects of context on judgments concerning the reality status of novel entities. *Child Development, 77*, 1778–1793.

Woolley, J. D., & Wellman, H. M. (1993). Origin and truth: Young children's understanding of imaginary mental representations. *Child Development, 64*, 1–17.

Wynn, K. (1992). Addition and subtraction by human infants. *Nature, 358*(6389), 749–750.

Xu, F., & Spelke, E. S. (2000). Large number discrimination in 6-month-old infants. *Cognition, 74*(1), B1–B11.

Xu, F., Spelke, E. S., & Goddard, S. (2005). Number sense in human infants. *Developmental Science, 8*(1), 88–101.

Yau, J., & Smetana, J. (2003). Adolescent–parent conflict in Hong Kong and Shenzhen: A comparison of youth in two cultural contexts. *International Journal of Behavioral Development, 27*(3), 201–211.

YouGov. (2006). The Mobile Life Youth Report: The impact of the mobile phone on the lives of young people. Retrieved from http://cdn.yougov.com/today_uk_import/YG-Archives-lif-mobileLife-YouthReport-060919.pdf

Younger, B. A., & Cohen, L. B. (1986). Developmental change in infants' perception of correlations among attributes. *Child Development, 57*, 803–815.

Zelaso, N. A., Zelaso, P. R., Cohen, K., & Zelaso, P. D. (1993). Specificity of practice effects on elementary neuro-motor patterns. *Developmental Psychology, 29*, 686–691.

Zimmerman, F. J., Gilkerson, J., Richards, J. A., Christakis, D. A., Xu, D., Gray, S., & Yapanel, U. (2009). Teaching by listening: The importance of adult–child conversations to language development. *Pediatrics, 124*(1), 342–349.

Zoia, S., Barnett, A. L., Wilson, P., & Hill, E. (2006). Developmental coordination disorder: Current issues. *Child: Care, Health and Development, 32*(6), 613–618.

Zosuls, K. M., Martin, C. L., Ruble, D. N., Miller, C. F., Gaertner, B. M., England, D. E., & Hill, A. P. (2011). 'It's not that we hate you': Understanding children's gender attitudes and expectancies about peer relationships. *British Journal of Developmental Psychology, 29*(2), 288–304.

Key terms

Accommodation: When a new experience is inconsistent with existing schemas the system must be adapted to accommodate the new information.

Alphabetic strategy: Reading by recognition of individual letters.

Assimiliation: When dealing with new information that is consistent with an existing schema the information is assimilated into this schema.

Attachment: The forming of a close emotional bond, particularly between mother and baby.

Attention Deficit/Hyperactivity Disorder: This is one of the most common developmental disorders. It is characterised by a triad of difficulties: chronic and pervasive inattention, impulsive behaviour and hyperactivity.

Autism: Childhood autism is a rare developmental disorder, often manifest before the second year of life, which involves a profound failure in social, linguistic and imaginative development.

Backpropagation algorithm: An algorithm for learning in connectionist networks.

Balance beam task: A balance beam is pivoted in the middle and it has a number of pegs spaced at equal intervals on either side of the fulcrum. Weights are placed at different peg positions and children are asked to predict which side of the balance will go down.

Big data: A research approach that involves collecting large amounts of data and using automated, computer-based methods to analyse it.

Canonical babbling: Babbling that begins at around six months, and consists of recognisable syllables composed of a consonant sound and a vowel.

Cardinality: When counting, the final number reached is the total.

Central executive: A component of Baddeley and Hitch's working memory model. It is a mechanism for controlling attention – its main function is to ensure that the limited resources of working memory are used as effectively as possible in a given task.

Chronological age: The child's actual age in years and months.

Clinical interviews: An interview in which the researcher asks questions but keeps the conversation as open as possible.

Cochlea: A spiral-shaped organ in the inner ear, crucial for hearing.

Communicative Development Inventory: A tool for measuring the size and growth of children's vocabulary.

Comorbidity: When two or more disorders are present in the same individual e.g. specific language impairment often co-occurs with other developmental disorders.

Concrete operational stage: Piaget's third developmental stage in which children begin to use logical rules to solve problems. They can deal with more than one salient feature of a problem at a time and are no longer dominated by appearance. However, they are not yet able to deal with abstract problems. This stage lasts from the ages of 6 or 7 to 11 or 12.

Connectionist models: Models of learning implemented on a computer in which there are many interconnected nodes.

Conservation tasks: Tests designed to see whether the child understands that some properties of an object or substance remain fundamentally the same even when there are external changes in shape or arrangement.

Core knowledge: The idea that certain aspects of knowledge are innate.

Corpus callosum: A thick bundle of nerve fibres in the centre of the brain that acts as the major connection between the left and right hemispheres, transferring information between them.

Cortisol: A hormone released in response to stress.

Critical period: The period of time during which a particular ability can be learned.

Cross-sectional: A research design in which children of various ages are studied at the same time.

Cyber-bullying: Repeated acts of aggression that are directed towards particular peers through the internet or mobile technologies.

Developmental co-ordination disorder (DCD): Developmental co-ordination disorder is diagnosed in children who, for no medical reason, fail to acquire adequate motor skills.

Developmental dyscalculia: A disorder of mathematical understanding. The core feature is a severe disability in learning arithmetic.

Developmental dyslexia: A syndrome causing problems with learning to read and spell, despite normal intelligence. Also known as word blindness.

Dizygotic: Non-identical twins, genetically only as closely related as regular siblings.

Egocentrism: To consider the world entirely from one's own point of view.

Electroencephalography (EEG): A technique that uses sensors placed on the head to measure changes in electrical activity generated by neural activity in the brain.

Embodiment: The idea that cognition is shaped by the body.

Emerge: The way in which complex behaviour can arise out of more simple behaviour, such as in connectionist models where many interconnected simple processing units can learn high-level complex tasks.

Epigenetics: The study of how genes can be turned on and off by experiences.

Equilibration: Using the processes of accommodation and assimilation to produce a state of equilibrium between existing schemas and new experiences.

Event-related potentials (ERP): Specific waveforms of neural electrical activity that are derived from the EEG.

Executive functions: The system that controls cognitive functions such as planning and executing actions. It is linked to the prefrontal areas of the brain.

False belief task: A test to see whether a child will act on a knowingly incorrect belief, or be aware that a second person who is not in possession of a certain piece of information may act 'incorrectly'.

Familiarisation-novelty preference method: A way of using infants' looking times to infer their knowledge.

Feral children: Children who have grown up with little or no human contact.

Foetal Alcohol Syndrome: A pattern of physical and mental abnormalities found in babies whose mothers were heavy drinkers during pregnancy.

Formal operational stage: The final stage in Piaget's theory from 11 or 12 years onwards, in which the child becomes able to consider all possible combinations in relation to the whole problem and to reason about an entirely hypothetical situation.

FOXP2 gene: Mutation of this gene, among others, in humans causes speech and language impairments.

functional Magnetic Resonance Imaging (fMRI): A technique that measures regional blood flow in the brain that correlates with neural activity.

Goal-directed reaching: The ability to successfully attain a desired object. This ability emerges at around three or four months and gradually becomes more precise over the first year of life.

Habituation: Method used to assess abilities of infants in which a stimulus is presented repeatedly until the infant's attention decreases significantly. Then a novel stimulus is presented and the increase in attention is measured.

Hill climbing: A method for solving problems – at each point of the solution you would choose an action that takes you closer to the goal.

Imprinting: A biological predisposition for a behaviour that is triggered by, and linked to, a specific environmental stimulus.

IQ: The ratio of mental age, defined by an intelligence test, to chronological age, with a score of 100 representing 'average IQ'.

Joint attention: An aspect of early communication – a mother and her child both looking at the same object.

Larynx: Part of the vocal tract, it is involved in breathing and sound production. Commonly known as the 'voice box'.

Learning disability: Children who have a low IQ score are considered to have a learning disability. This can be profound, severe, moderate or mild, depending on the IQ score.

Linguistic nativism: The view that children's capacity for language is largely driven by internal factors.

Logographic strategy: Reading by recognition of whole words.

Longitudinal: A research design in which data are gathered from the same individuals over a period of time.

Mean Length of Utterance: This is a measurement in morphemes of the average length of utterance.

Means-ends analysis: A method for solving problems based on performing sub-goals to achieve the final goal.

Memory span: The number of items that can be accurately recalled in the correct order.

Mental age: This gives an indication of a child's level of cognitive function in years and months. This may or may not be the same as chronological age, which is the child's actual age in years and months.

Mind mindedness: Describes the way in which parents appropriately interpret their infants' desires and intentions.

Monozygotic: Twins that developed from one zygote, so are genetically identical.

Morpheme: The smallest unit of meaning in language.

Morphology: The form and structure of words in a language, especially the consistent patterns that may be observed and classified.

Myelination: The production of the myelin sheath that surrounds axons, forming insulation and improving conductivity.

'Naughty Teddy' study: McGarrigle and Donaldson's (1975) study where the experimenter sets out two rows of coins which are are adjusted until children agree that both contain the same number. Then, under the control of the experimenter, a glove puppet known as 'Naughty Teddy' moves the coins in one row so that it is longer than the other row. Children are then asked whether the two rows contain the same or a different number of coins.

Near Infra Red Spectroscopy (NIRS): A technique for assessing brain activation based on the observation that increased neural activity is associated with changes in the oxygenation of blood.

Noble savage: A character unspoilt by society, in contrast to being 'corrupted' by education.

Object permanence: The understanding that objects have substance, maintain their identities when they change location, and ordinarily continue to exist when out of sight.

One-to-one correspondence: Counting each object only once.

Orthographic strategy: Reading by recognition of groups of letters, or orthographic units.

Orthographic transparency: A consistent relationship between the sounds of a language and the spelling so that a particular sound always has the same spelling.

Overregularisation errors: The tendency to apply grammatical rules in situations that should be exceptions to those rules.

Phonemes: The smallest sound categories in speech in any given language that serve to distinguish one word from another.

Phonological loop: A component of Baddeley and Hitch's working memory model. It is used for holding speech-based information.

Place holder: The use of zero to mark the column value, even though the column is empty.

Place value: The convention of each column in numbers representing certain values, i.e. units, tens, hundreds, etc.

Positron Emission Tomography (PET): A brain scanning method that shows activity in the brain by measuring blood flow to different brain areas.

Power grip: A grip in which the fingers wrap around the objects.

Precision grip: A grip in which there is full opposition of the fingers and thumb. This is only found in humans.

Preferential looking paradigm: In a preferential looking experiment, an infant is familiarised, over a series of training trials to a novel stimulus. The infant is then presented with a second, different, stimulus. If the infant looks longer at the second stimulus, this suggests that the infant can discriminate between the stimuli.

Preformationist theories: These are based on the idea that the essential characteristics of an individual are fully specified at the outset of development.

Prefrontal cortex: Part of the frontal cortex, its primary function is to co-ordinate a wide range of neural processes. The PFC serves a key function in cognitive control in maintaining information about the current goal of a task and the means to achieve that goal.

Prematurity: Babies born before 37 weeks of weeks of pregnancy are classed as premature.

Pre-operational stage: Piaget's second stage of cognitive development involving internalisation of forms of actions that the infant has already mastered. The key feature of this stage, which lasts from two to six or seven years, is that the child is able to focus only on one salient feature of a problem at a time and is dominated by the immediate appearance of things.

Pre-reaching: Movements of the arm and hand made by newborns towards an attractive object.

Prosocial behaviour: Altruistic behaviours such as sharing, helping, caregiving and showing compassion.

Prosodic pattern: The rhythmical properties of a language.

Reading comprehension impairment: A disorder in which children have significant difficulty in understanding text even though they can read individual words.

Reduplicated babbling: Babbling that begins at around eight months, and consists of repetitions of the same sound.

Reversibility: The child has an understanding that actions can be reversed.

Rouge removal task: A small amount of rouge is surreptitiously placed on a child's face. Then the child is allowed to look in a mirror. This task tests mirror recognition.

Sally-Ann task: A test of theory of mind in which a girl doll (Sally) hides a marble and then goes for a walk. A second doll (Ann) then moves the marble while Sally is still away and so cannot see what has happened. The children are asked where Sally will look for the marble.

Schemas: Structured organisation of knowledge and actions.

Self-organisation: An important concept in dynamic systems – it means that a system can arrange itself in an orderly state without an external agent or plan.

Self-regulation: The ability to actively control levels of arousal and emotional responses.

Semantic bootstrapping: The linking of certain semantic categories such as 'person' or 'thing' to their corresponding grammatical word class and syntactic categories by a series of 'linking rules'.

Sensitive period: A time of heightened ability to learn.

Sensorimotor period: Piaget's first stage in the process of adaption, from birth to about two years, in which infants co-ordinate sensory perceptions and motor abilities to acquire knowledge of the world.

Smarties task: A false-belief task in which children are shown a Smarties tube that contains pencils rather than Smarties. Children are asked what another child, who has not seen inside the Smarties tube, will think is inside.

Social referencing: The gauging of others' emotional reactions before deciding one's own reaction.

Specific language impairment: This term is used to describe cases in which children's language skills are much worse than would be expected from their level of nonverbal intelligence and where the difficulties with language cannot be explained by other known causes such as deafness or a pervasive developmental disorder such as autism.

Stages: Piaget's theory says that development proceeds along a series of stages that are characterised by qualitatively different systems of thinking and action.

Statistical learning: The ability to detect regularly occurring patterns in the environment.

Stepping reflex: A reflex elicited when a baby is supported in a standing position and the feet are brought into contact with a surface, such as a table or the floor. The baby responds by making stepping movements, as though walking.

Still-face procedure: This involves mothers and their infants and it is divided into three periods of interaction. 1. Mothers are instructed to interact normally with their infant. 2. They are instructed not to respond as normal and to adopt a still face with a neutral expression. 3. Mothers resume their normal pattern of responsive interaction.

Strange situation: Used in attachment studies. The child is observed first with the mother, next with a stranger, then alone, and finally when reunited with stranger and mother.

Symbolic play: Piaget believed that symbolic play, where one object stands for another, serves as a rehearsal for real life in the imagination; he developed a three-stage theory of symbolic play.

Synaptogenesis: The forming of new connections between neurons.

Syntactic bootstrapping: This involves inferring information about the syntactic properties of words from their position in the sentence and extending these inferences to new cases that occur in similar syntactic positions.

Tabula rasa: A blank slate.

Theory of mind: The ability to think about other people's mental states and form theories of how they think.

Tower of Hanoi: A puzzle often used to study means-ends problem solving. It consists of three pegs; on the first peg there is a series of disks of increasing size, placed with the largest disk at the bottom. The child's task is to move the blocks to the last peg one by one so that they end up in the original order.

Transitive inference: Understanding the relation between objects.

U-shaped development: A type of non-linear development where performance is initially high but then temporarily decreases before recovering again.

Violation-of-expectation method: A way of using infants' looking times to infer their knowledge. The assumption is that infants look longer at something unexpected. So, for example, if they look longer at a physically impossible than at a possible event one can infer that they understand the physical impossibility.

Visuospatial scratchpad: A component of Baddeley and Hitch's working memory model. It is used for holding visual and spatial information.

Vocabulary spurt: The sudden increase in vocabulary size that occurs at about 12 months.

Wisconsin Card Sorting Task: A task to test mental flexibility in which cards are sorted first by one rule and then the sorting rule is switched.

Working memory: The system for attending to, processing and remembering information over short periods of time in a temporary store.

Zone of Proximal Development: The gap between what a learner can do without help and what she cannot do even with help. Therefore, it describes the problems that the learner can solve with someone's help.

Author Index

Subject Index

Locators in *italic* refer to figures and tables